OPPORTUNITIES

in

W9-BVE-483

Adult Education Careers

OPPORTUNITIES

in

Adult Education Careers

REVISED EDITION

BLYTHE CAMENSON

McGraw Hill

New York Chicago San Francisco Lisbon London Madrid Mexico City
Milan New Delhi San Juan Seoul Singapore Sydney Toronto

Library of Congress Cataloging-in-Publication Data

Camenson, Blythe.
    Opportunities in adult education careers / by Blythe Camenson.
        p.   cm.
    includes bibliographical references.
    Prev. ed.: Opportunities in adult education careers. Lincolnwood, Ill. :
VGM Career Horizons, c2000
      ISBN 0-07-149306-9 (alk. paper)
        1. Adult education—Vocational guidance—United States.   2. Continuing
education—Vocational guidance—United States.   I. Camenson, Blythe.
Opportunities in adult education careers.   II. Title.

    LC5219.C24   2008
    375.0023—dc22   2007047029

1 2 3 4 5 6 7 8 9 10 11 12 13 14 15 16 17 18 19 20   DOC/DOC   0 9 8

ISBN   978-0-07-149306-2
MHID   0-07-149306-9

Interior design by Rattray Design

McGraw-Hill books are available at special quantity discounts to use as premiums and sales promotions or for use in corporate training programs. To contact a representative, please visit the Contact Us pages at www.mhprofessional.com.

This book is printed on acid-free paper.

I would like to dedicate this book to Ellen Raphaeli, adult educator, lifelong friend, and big sister.

Contents

Acknowledgments

I would like to thank the following professionals for sharing information about their work and providing insights into the world of adult education careers:

Claire Best, ESL Instructor
Cheryl-Lani Branson, Social Worker/Student Advocate
Judy Burns, Continuing Education Online Instructor
Jean Campbell, GED Counselor
Pat Carroll, Educational Medical Consultant
Karen Carver, Computer Lab Instructor
Marshall J. Cook, Writing Professor
Joy Davis, Basic Skills Instructor
Rosemary Day, English Instructor
Adele Fuller, Career Counselor
Lynn Goodwin, Tutor/Student Literacy Coordinator
Phyllis Hanlon, Business Writing Instructor
Barbara Hogue, Cosmetology Instructor

Sheila Levitt, GED Instructor
Bernard LoPinto, Correctional Facility Education
    Supervisor
Geraldine Mosher, Computer Instructor
Ellen Raphaeli, Associate Professor, English
Gail Rubin, Aerobics Instructor
Louise Tenbrook Whiting, Continuing Education Court-
    Mandated Courses
Terry Thompson, Computer Learning Center Coordinator
Debi Violante, Assistant to the Supervisor of Adult
    Education

I would also like to thank Josephine Scanlon for her assistance in preparing this revision.

1

ADULT EDUCATION FIELD

MANY ADULTS REALIZE the importance of continued learning as a means to achieving greater success in their careers and overall satisfaction with life in general. The world seems to change rapidly, as we are introduced to more advances in technology that lead to new and different career options.

Nearly half of all adults participate in some form of adult education every year in an effort to keep up with changes in their fields and technological advances that may affect their lives in various ways. This thirst for knowledge creates many career opportunities for adult education teachers who can lead courses for career advancement, skills upgrading, and personal enrichment. The demand for qualified instructors is expected to increase as more adults seek additional training and education. Employment in adult education is expected to grow faster than the average of other fields over the next ten years.

In addition to teachers, adult education programs offer opportunities for career and vocational counselors, program directors, and other administrators.

Main Areas of Adult Education

Adult education teachers instruct in three main areas: adult continuing education; adult remedial education, also known as adult basic education; and adult vocational-technical education, which also includes prebaccalaureate training and training for college credit.

Adult Continuing Education

Adult continuing education instructors teach courses that students take for their own personal enrichment or enjoyment. Subject areas might include cooking, swimming, exercise and physical fitness, gardening, writing for publication, a foreign language, and finance, to name just a few.

Other instructors help people update their job skills, maintain licenses, or adapt to technological advances. For example, an adult education teacher may teach courses that will help keep a radiology technician's skills current, or train students in the use of computer software programs such as Quicken or Photoshop.

Some courses are mandated by courts or other bodies of law or are offered by community service organizations. These typically cover such topics as drunk driving, domestic violence, suicide prevention, crisis intervention, AIDS prevention, teen pregnancy prevention, gambling and other addictions, and financial management to help offenders stop writing bad checks.

Adult Remedial Education

Adult basic education teachers provide instruction for students who need to improve their literacy skills, who did not complete high school and are studying to take the General Educational Development (GED) examination, or who need to upgrade their skills to find a job. This category also includes teachers of English to speakers of other languages (TESOL) and those who provide instruction for citizenship classes.

Adult Vocational-Technical Education and Prebaccalaureate Training

Adult vocational-technical education teachers, also called career-technology teachers, provide instruction for occupations that do not require a college degree, such as plumber, dental hygienist, paramedic, x-ray technician, auto mechanic, and cosmetologist. They also work in junior or community colleges, where they provide students with prebaccalaureate training and training for college credit.

Other adult education teachers help students upgrade their skills so they can reach the level necessary to enroll in an academic program. These courses are often a prerequisite for admission and do not offer college credits.

In addition, some four-year colleges and universities offer extension programs with credit-bearing courses that are taught by adult education instructors.

Career and Vocational Counseling

Students working to achieve high school equivalency, acquire new job skills, or upgrade existing skills often use the services of their program's career or vocational counselors. These counselors help students identify their skills and interest areas and then use this information to select possible career paths. Counselors can also help job candidates improve their résumé-writing and interviewing skills.

Adult Education Administration

Just as in any work setting, the adult education field requires administrators to plan programs, supervise instructors and other staff members, schedule classes, oversee staff meetings, and manage finances and budgeting.

Some administrators may interact with other community agencies to identify needed services and the different populations they will serve. They might also write grant proposals or participate in fund-raising events to finance their programs.

Employment Settings

Adult education teachers work in a variety of settings, making this field appealing to those who might prefer a less traditional working environment. Many are employed by public school systems, community and junior colleges, and four-year colleges and universities. But opportunities also exist with businesses that provide formal education and training for their employees and with schools and institutes that offer training in areas such as automotive repair, bartending, business, computers, electronics, and medical technology. Instructors can also find positions with language centers, jails and prisons, the military, dance studios, health clubs, job training centers, community organizations, parks and recreation centers, labor unions, computer online services, and religious organizations.

Choosing Your Area of Specialization

Many adult educators come to this field having already mastered a particular skill area or specialization. If, for example, you are an experienced landscaper, you might decide to share your knowledge with others who may want a similar career or who just want to beautify their homes. Once you have reached that decision, you'll have to determine the most appropriate job setting. Would you prefer to teach in an adult continuing education program held at a community college or perhaps offer classes through a local nursery or gardening center? In another example, a professional cosmetologist with several years of experience might decide to change gears and teach others the profession in a vocational-technical institution.

If you are just starting your own university training and would like to teach adults, your choices of specialization are much wider and are not limited to your current skills. Would you prefer working with students who require basic education skills such as reading and math, or would you prefer working with students from overseas, helping them upgrade the language skills they will need to enter college?

The adult education field is also an option for students who are pursuing a master's degree in counseling. Although administrative positions in adult education programs are often filled from within, there are also advanced-degree programs that prepare candidates specifically for roles within adult education administration.

If you are interested in a career as an adult educator, counselor, or administrator, you should choose your path based on your own interests and skills, the amount of training necessary to reach your goals, and the job availability predicted in the various areas. Whether you are entering this field from another profession or choosing adult education as the end goal, you have numerous choices that can be professionally and personally rewarding in each area.

Working Conditions

Of the approximately 560,000 adult education teachers employed nationwide, most work part-time, teaching one or two courses in the evenings or on the weekends.

The majority of those who work full-time are employed in the vocational-technical end of adult education. Some are also employed by community colleges. Although most adult education teachers work in a classroom setting, some are consultants to businesses and teach classes at the job site.

Some adult education teachers have several part-time teaching assignments or work a full-time job in addition to their part-time teaching job, leading to long hours and a hectic schedule.

To accommodate students who may have job or family responsibilities, many adult education courses are offered at night or on weekends and range from two- to four-hour workshops and one-day mini-sessions to semester-long courses.

Because adult education teachers work with adult students, they generally don't encounter some of the behavioral or social problems sometimes faced by those who teach younger students. Unless court mandated, the adults are there by choice and usually are highly motivated, which are attributes that can make teaching these students rewarding and satisfying.

However, teachers in adult remedial education deal with students at different levels of development who may lack effective study skills and self-confidence and who may require more attention and patience than other students.

Education and Training

Training requirements vary widely by subject and by state and provincial regulations. In general, teachers need work experience or other experience in their field and a license or certificate in fields where these usually are required for full professional status. In some cases, particularly at educational institutions, a bachelor's, master's, or doctoral degree is required, especially to teach courses that can be applied toward a four-year degree program. In other situations, an acceptable portfolio of work is required. For example, an applicant for a job teaching a photography course would need to show examples of previous work.

Most states, provinces, and the District of Columbia require adult remedial education teachers to have a bachelor's degree from an approved teacher-training program, and some require teacher certification. Some school boards, such as those that provide GED training or counseling, require their instructors to have a master's degree.

Adult education teachers update their own skills through continuing education to maintain certification requirements, which vary among institutions. They may take part in seminars, conferences, or graduate courses in adult education, training and development, or human resources development, or may return to work in business or industry for a limited time.

Businesses are playing a growing role in adult education, as they form consortiums with training institutions and community colleges and provide input to curriculum development. Adult education teachers maintain an ongoing dialogue with businesses to determine the most current skills required in the workplace.

Teaching adults requires a wide variety of skills and aptitudes, including good communications skills; the power to influence, motivate, and train others; organizational, administrative, and communication skills; and creativity.

Adult remedial education instructors in particular must be patient, understanding, and supportive to make students comfortable and to develop trust.

Some teachers advance to administrative positions for school boards, in departments of education, for colleges and universities, for government-funded community agencies, and in corporate training departments within private business. Such positions may require advanced degrees, such as a doctorate in adult and continuing education.

Job Outlook

Rising demand for adult education courses for career advancement, skills upgrading, or personal enrichment and enjoyment is expected to spur faster-than-average employment growth through 2014. Many job openings will come from the need to replace people who leave the occupation, whether to take other jobs, because of family responsibilities, or to retire. The need for teachers in adult literacy, basic education, and secondary-education classes is expected to grow, with significant employment growth anticipated for teachers of English to speakers of other languages. In addition, the need for self-enrichment teachers is expected to grow as more people embrace lifelong learning and as course offerings expand.

Opportunities should be best in fields such as computer technology, automotive mechanics, and medical technology, which offer very attractive—and often higher-paying—job opportunities outside of teaching.

Salaries

Although few teachers have huge salaries, you can earn a respectable living in adult education. Many choose to work part-time in adult education to supplement their salary from a primary career.

Salaried adult education teachers who usually work full-time have median earnings around $39,000 a year, with the majority earning from $29,200 to $53,000.

Earnings vary widely by subject taught, academic credentials, experience, region of the country, and budget of the institution.

Part-time instructors generally are paid hourly wages—usually from about $15 to $50 an hour or more—and do not receive benefits or pay for preparation time outside of class.

Full-time adult education personnel generally receive benefits such as health insurance, paid vacations, and sick leave.

Job Hunt

If you have an employer in mind for whom you'd like to work, a phone call or an introductory letter sent with your résumé is a good way to start. Some organizations such as adult education centers or community colleges have telephone job hotlines that are updated regularly with current openings.

If you would like some more ideas on possible job settings and how to approach them, you can explore the professional associations listed in the Additional Resources section at the end of the book. Many of these associations produce monthly or quarterly newsletters with job listings and publish openings on their websites.

Don't overlook the obvious. Many positions are listed weekly in the classified sections of newspapers. The Internet is also a great resource. You can search for adult education jobs at career sites such as www.Monster.com and www.CareerBuilder.com, searching by location or area of interest.

In addition, adult education positions at universities and colleges are often announced in the *Chronicle of Higher Education*, a weekly periodical with a large employment section. It is available through libraries or by contacting:

Chronicle of Higher Education
1255 Twenty-Third Street NW, 7th Floor
Washington, DC 20037
www.chronicle.com

2

Adult Continuing Education

Adult continuing education can be divided into two major sectors: personal enrichment and skills upgrading.

Personal Enrichment

Personal enrichment teachers provide instruction in a wide variety of subjects that students take for interest, fun, or self-improvement. Some teach a series of classes that provide students with useful life skills, such as cooking, personal finance, and time management classes. Others provide group instruction intended solely for recreation, such as photography, pottery, and painting courses. Many others provide one-on-one instruction in a variety of subjects, including dance, singing, or playing a musical instrument.

The instruction self-enrichment teachers provide seldom leads to a particular degree and attendance is voluntary, but dedicated and talented students sometimes go on to careers in the arts. This occupation also includes teachers who conduct courses on academic subjects in a nonacademic setting, such as literature, foreign language, and history courses.

Although personal enrichment instructors don't necessarily have to have any particular degree, they are, of course, usually proficient in their field. A pottery instructor, for example, must be an accomplished potter and also must have the ability to teach others. A writing instructor should have a portfolio of published work. In other words, those who can, do, and those who can, also teach.

Some areas, though, do require certain licensing or certificates. For example, a SCUBA instructor should be trained and authorized by a certifying body such as the Professional Association of Diving Instructors (PADI) or the National Association of Underwater Instructors (NAUI).

Employment Settings for Personal Enrichment Courses

You can find enrichment courses in a variety of settings, including universities and colleges offering evening adult education programs; vocational-technical schools with adult evening programs; adult education and community centers; health centers, hospitals, and rehabilitation centers; recreation organizations such as the YMCA; libraries; Internet services such as AOL; and even some prisons.

Skills Upgrading

Some professionals must stay current in their fields by completing a certain number of continuing education units each year. These courses are usually taught by trained professionals who are licensed in their field. For example, someone providing continuing education to nurses should also be a trained nurse.

In addition, some students take courses on their own to upgrade their skills so they can be promoted in their current job or land a better job elsewhere. Courses could range from how to use a particular computer program to improving business-writing skills. These courses are taught by instructors who have expertise in the particular areas.

Employment Settings for Skills-Upgrading Courses

Skills-upgrading courses can be found in most of the same settings as personal enrichment courses, as well as in corporate offices, where businesses might directly employ instructors to work with their personnel.

Trainers employed in a corporate setting teach communications skills between staff and management, conduct seminars and workshops, run motivational sessions, teach new skills, and upgrade existing ones.

A corporate trainer could work with employees on a new computer system or provide orientation to new employees. The opportunities can be as varied as the company's enterprises.

In addition, there are several centers throughout North America that provide computer-training services for people with disabilities. Learners at these centers are either people who have been disabled from birth or who face dealing with a new disability that, in many cases, forces them to switch careers or learn new skills in order to do their current job. Disabilities range from mild back injuries, for example, which might force a wallpaper hanger to change jobs, to very severe disabilities, in which someone has use of only one finger or is so paralyzed that she or he needs to blow through a puff stick to be able to type.

Salaries

Salaries in this field vary widely, depending on the employer and the area of the country in which you might be employed. Some personal enrichment instructors are paid hourly wages, generally anywhere from $15 to $75 an hour. Others are paid a percentage of the registration fee per student, which could range from $30 to $80 or more, depending on the type of course or the organization offering it. The more students you attract, the better your salary. However, some employers might require a minimum number of students before a class is even offered.

Some corporations employ full-time instructors or trainers who are paid an annual salary. In general, salaries in private corporations are higher than those in educational institutions, and a corporate trainer with a few years' experience could expect to earn $60,000 a year or more.

Profiles

What better way is there to learn about a profession than from specialists working directly in the field? The profiles that follow in this chapter cover adult continuing education classes conducted by a self-employed health professional, classes held in a four-year university, classes sponsored by a state district attorney's office, classes offered by an online campus, classes offered through the YMCA, classes held in a vocational-technical high school, and classes offered through a computer-training center.

Pat Carroll—Educational Medical Consultant

Pat Carroll teaches continuing education programs for the health profession through her Connecticut-based company, Educational

Medical Consultants. Her work takes her all over the United States and Canada. She is also a clinical practitioner, medical writer, and business consultant.

Pat has earned a number of degrees, including an A.A.S. in respiratory therapy, an A.S. and B.S. in nursing, a B.S. in health sciences, and an M.S. in education. She has been working in this field for more than twenty years.

Getting Started

Pat's love of teaching began with using her stuffed animals as students when she was a child. Her love of learning has never abated, and today she subscribes to more than thirty professional journals so she can keep current on the latest developments in health care. Sharing this love of learning with others seemed like a natural step.

She began her career as a respiratory therapist, although her primary interest was nursing. She subscribed to a nursing journal while studying for her respiratory therapist license, and when she realized that it didn't have many good articles about respiratory patients, she wrote one. It was well received, so she wrote more and then went to nursing school.

While working as a respiratory therapist and nurse, Pat was contacted by a company that sponsors nursing seminars and asked if she would be interested in traveling around the country to lead seminars. She enjoyed working on the seminars but found it difficult to maintain her regular hospital schedule and travel at the same time. So she took a job at a business school teaching in a program for medical assistants. Since her schedule was only twenty hours a week, she was able to start building her own business while still working.

Pat's articles attracted the attention of medical manufacturers, who asked if she did consulting work. Although she didn't have any experience in that area, she said yes and was hired to design educational programs. Her work involves helping to train the nurses and other health professionals who will use a new product or device designed by a medical manufacturer. She doesn't market or sell the product but provides education about the condition for which it was designed and how the product is used for that condition.

After two years, her business had gotten busy enough that Pat was able to stop teaching and build the business full-time. She has gained a national reputation through her writing and teaching, mainly through the speeches and lectures she delivers at conventions for nurses and health professionals throughout North America.

What the Work Is Like

In addition to medical manufacturers, Pat also works as a consultant for pharmaceutical companies and colleges to provide continuing education to people who work in the health professions. Her students are people working as nurses or in other health fields such as respiratory therapy, radiological technology, and physical therapy, who take her courses to keep up with new advances in medicine. Some are fulfilling continuing education requirements based on state or provincial requirements for licensure; others want to learn new information and stay current in their field.

When approached to develop an educational program, Pat asks the client what the people who will use the product (nurses, for example) need to know to understand the product or drug and use it safely. Then she begins her research, which includes Internet searches for articles that have been published on the same topic, since she needs to be an expert in the area before she can give an educational program.

The Internet provides the author, title, and name of the journal where the pertinent articles are published. With this information in hand, Pat then goes to the library to locate the articles. She reads and studies every one of them to understand all of the information.

After she's completed her research, Pat writes an outline of what she wants to teach. When she has reviewed the outline with the client to make sure nothing is missing, she designs slides that she'll use during the presentation. The final step of the planning process is to put together a handout that each person who attends the seminar can take home. The handout summarizes all of the information and a complete list of the articles Pat reviewed on the topic.

When she has to travel to give a presentation, Pat likes to arrive the day before the seminar. She checks the room where she will be speaking to see what it looks like and if it is set up properly. On the day of the presentation, she gets to the room early to double-check everything to make sure there are no problems and to greet the people who come for the seminar. After the presentation, she meets with people who have questions or want more information. Audiences can be as small as fifty and as large as one thousand.

When she isn't preparing a seminar or traveling, Pat takes care of office work. She spends a lot of time with e-mail and on the Internet, which is the way she keeps up with new advances. She also has a lot of paperwork, which clients need to make sure the educational programs she designs are of high quality and not sales pitches for products or services.

Pat works on average about sixty hours a week over six days. About fifty hours are spent on her consulting business, whether in her home office or traveling, and she also tries to work as an emergency room (ER) nurse one evening a week.

Upsides

Pat says that her work is never boring, and she enjoys being on the cutting edge of new advances in health care. "I can't imagine a better job," she says. "I love the fact that I am there when brand new drugs and devices are being developed. I get excited about these interesting new things, and I love sharing that excitement with the people who come to hear me speak."

Downsides

For Pat, the downside is the travel. After nearly twenty years, she finds herself visiting the same cities over and over, and like many business travelers, she says that it isn't at all glamorous. As much as she loves her work, she would like to work fewer hours.

Advice from a Professional

Pat advises that one of the most important things to understand is that the learning process of adults is very different from that of children. It's essential to remember that adults need to know why they are learning something, and they often do better when they are actively involved in what they are learning.

"If you want to teach adults, you need to know your subject matter well," Pat says. "It is most helpful if you have life experience that you can bring to your teaching. Adults learn best if you can help them solve problems, and many times you can do that best by relating your own experiences. That's why I maintain a clinical practice as an ER nurse myself."

Marshall J. Cook—Professor, University of Wisconsin–Madison

Marshall J. Cook is a full professor in the department of communication programs within the Division of Continuing Studies at the University of Wisconsin–Madison. He is also a writer with hundreds of articles to his credit, a couple of dozen short stories, and numerous books, including *How to Be a Great Coach: 24 Lessons for Turning on the Productivity of Every Employee, Writing for the Joy of It, Freeing Your Creativity, How to Write with the Skill of a Master and the Genius of a Child, Slow Down and Get More Done, Leads and Conclusions, Hometown Wisconsin,* and *Your Novel Proposal: From Creation to Contract,* which he co-wrote with this author, Blythe Camenson.

Getting Started

Marshall has a B.A. in creative writing and an M.A. in communications/print journalism, both from Stanford University. He attended law school for about four months and was teaching a class at the University of Santa Clara in California, when he realized that he liked studying the law more than the actual work of being a lawyer.

Around the same time that he made this decision, a teacher at Santa Clara died, and Marshall was hired to replace him. He worked there for four years in the English department. He describes this period as the rebirth of an old dream. "Ever since I was a kid, the only two things I really wanted to do were to teach and write," he says. "And I found something that let me do both—which is really nice. I got the class at Santa Clara basically just to make a few bucks to put myself through law school, and I discovered I really liked it. I don't think I was really that good at it at first, but it really appealed to me."

Marshall started at the University of Wisconsin in 1979 as a program coordinator on the academic staff. Although it rarely happens this way any longer, he was able to move from the academic staff track to a tenure track. He became an assistant professor, which is a professor without tenure. After working for the requisite five to six years, he applied for tenure at the associate professor level, and three years later he became a full professor.

What the Work Is Like

Only two of the courses Marshall teaches are credit bearing; all others are continuing education units, which makes his work different from that of a traditional campus teacher. The Division of Continuing Studies is a separate division within the university with the primary mission of adult education. He teaches a lot of workshops and also does some consulting and on-site training of newspaper people, corporate communicators, and a variety of others. For example, he runs media workshops for police officers called Preparing to Be Interviewed by the Press, and another on publishing newsletters. A third workshop, which focuses on stress management, follows the title of his book *Slow Down and Get More Done.*

Marshall explains the wide variety of programs that he teaches. "Basically, I offer anything we can sell to the public. We're an income-generating unit, unlike campus teaching, and we're responsible for paying our own way."

He develops and publicizes the workshops and personally teaches sixty to seventy of them a year, in addition to guest speaking and helping at other conferences.

Although Marshall teaches much more than the average university professor, his job doesn't include a research component. His research is all practical, and his publications are all mass media, because that's what he teaches.

Upsides

The greatest upside for Marshall is the diversity of his job. He describes it as a rare opportunity to combine writing with another career that enhances the writing rather than detracts from it. He says, "The writing helps me teach, and the teaching helps me write."

Downsides

Although Marshall finds his work very stimulating, it can be quite tiring. He travels a great deal, bringing the workshops to where the people are. Christmas and the summer are slower times, but he also has very busy seasons. There are times when he conducts three workshops in a week, and he has to be careful not to overschedule himself.

Advice from a Professional

"These days to become a full professor on a tenure track, you'd need to get your Ph.D., and it should be in a field you have some passion for," says Marshall.

"It's a wonderful thing if you get the chance to do it, because you not only deal in ideas, but you get to share them and watch them grow as you interact with young minds that aren't nearly as trained as yours but are flexible and hungry for the knowledge you have."

Louise Tenbrook Whiting—Adult Educator

Louise Tenbrook Whiting is a certified online therapist, life coach, and clinical hypnotherapist who specializes in communication skills, assertiveness, sexual abuse, domestic violence, chemical dependency, and crisis intervention.

She has a B.A. in psychology and an M.A. in counseling psychology and has been in the field for more than thirty years. She has participated in numerous other training programs covering such topics as suicide prevention/intervention, child abuse, rape crisis counseling, elder abuse, spousal abuse, assertiveness training, communication training, hotline training, grief counseling, and courses in teaching adult education.

Here Louise talks about teaching a class called Checks and Balances, which is designed for the first-time offender and is sponsored by the Orange County District Attorney's office in Southern California as part of its bad-check restitution program.

Getting Started

Louise found her first job in her field by answering a classified ad in the newspaper that read, "Help wanted—office manager to work with volunteer employees." When she called about the job, she was told only that she would learn more at her first interview at the home of a well-known community leader, not in an office.

During the interview, she learned that she would be managing a crisis intervention/suicide prevention hotline and that her duties would include hiring, firing, and supervising volunteer help. When she questioned the location of the hotline office, she was told that she would be given that information only if she was hired for the position. Louise was hired after a second interview, but she was still not given the office location until the evening before she was to report for work. She was intrigued by the cloak-and-dagger secrecy surrounding the job and was very excited about her new "mystery" management position.

Working on the hotline brought Louise into contact with people that until then she had only seen on the evening news. Due to the nature of some of the calls, there were occasions when the FBI and the local police conferred in her office. This was during the time when the serial killer Ted Bundy was on the loose. Although he was from Seattle, not California, he had been a hotline volunteer. Louise read all she could about him and carefully scrutinized all volunteers working under her supervision.

Always interested in a new challenge, Louise frequently perused the classified ads for something that looked interesting and just a bit different from what she'd done in the past that would allow her to further use her license or skills. The job teaching the bad-check class sounded different, and the ad stated "will train."

She was hired after two telephone interviews and one personal interview. She was given a training manual and worked closely with experienced teachers, observing their teaching and training techniques. Finally, she did some co-teaching before going out on her own.

What the Work Is Like

Checks and Balances is an eight-hour class that Louise teaches to groups of students who are legally required to attend after a merchant (most commonly places such as a Target, Kmart, Wal-Mart, and supermarkets) files a formal complaint that the district attorney is obligated to follow up.

People come into the class one of two ways, although both are court mandated. In the first scenario, a first-time offender has the option of taking the class in lieu of facing a misdemeanor charge in court. In the second scenario, a person goes to court and is still ordered to attend the class. Many of these people have written more than one bad check; others have written only one but are caught in a domino effect when that one check bounces and sets off a chain reaction of insufficient funds for any subsequent checks written. Often they are required to pay $350 to $400 per check, plus complete community service hours and a one-year summary probation. When the class is offered in lieu of these penalties, many people take this option. An arrest warrant is issued for anyone who fails to attend.

Louise emphasizes that the people who attend the class are regular everyday folks, not necessarily people who habitually write bad checks. Many get into trouble because they live paycheck to paycheck, juggling their bills and trying to survive, which can sometimes lead to difficulties. The Checks and Balances class teaches life skills that, when followed, will help in preventing this from happening again.

Students come to this class with mixed emotions. Some are angry, irritated, or hostile; others feel embarrassed or humiliated. One thing they all have in common is that none of them wants to be there. They have preconceived ideas about what the class will be like and the kind of people who will attend. None of them expect it to be the way it is, and for the most part they are pleasantly surprised. As the class begins, though, Louise is definitely not the most popular person in the world, and she has to work around this for the next eight hours.

Her initial goal is to get the students to relax and not expect eight hours of being berated for having bounced a check. She opens with a humorous story or anecdote, and fortunately her storytelling skills usually ensure that she gets a laugh. She uses the story to illustrate some of the feelings the students may be experiencing and tries to keep the class moving until she feels that they are becoming responsive.

Once she reaches that point, the students introduce themselves and describe what happened that brought them to class. This helps the students to realize that they all have a lot in common and, more important, that none of them is "bad."

Louise uses humor throughout the day to help keep the atmosphere friendly and supportive. She covers a variety of topics, from basic bookkeeping and check-balancing skills to taking control and making positive life changes. She emphasizes appropriate values, attitudes, and behaviors.

One of the things that keeps the work interesting is that each time she teaches the class, it is to an entirely new group of people. Even though some reactions and responses are the same, she still hears and learns something new in every session. There are a variety of reasons that checks bounce, from direct deposits being made late to a simple miscalculation; some reasons are laughable, some are sad, but they are seldom boring.

Louise works hard to make the class an informative, interesting, and rewarding learning experience while keeping it as enjoyable as possible. Based on the positive student evaluations she receives, she is pleased to see that she is succeeding.

Given the nature of the course, her relationship with each student is short-term, and she doesn't get to see the results of her work. Often, she can see where further training or intervention is warranted, but her job is done and she must hope that the students will succeed on their own.

Although the class is eight hours, Louise works much longer than that. She has each student fill out a registration form and sign into the class. At the end of the class, the students complete evaluation forms and receive certificates of completion that Louise has made out and signed. This certificate can be presented to the court when needed. At the end of the day, she completes a report and returns all paperwork to the office for its records. She also reviews course materials during the week and conducts online research into areas covered in the class, such as finances, investing, money management, wealth, and prosperity.

Because of her background with crisis intervention, suicide prevention, domestic violence, and counseling, Louise also teaches a domestic violence/spousal abuse class. This class is court mandated as well, and it is geared toward offenders who have been charged with a felony. This is a different population from the bad-check class, and students come from all socioeconomic levels, from corporate executives to unemployed laborers. The common denominator is violence, and most of the students are angry, hostile, and resentful of having to attend the class. Louise teaches this group in a hospital setting because most of those who attend are also drug abusers and/or alcoholics, whose charges may be lessened by opting for treatment.

This class is more difficult to teach because the attendees may try to sleep through the meetings or become angry and leave. Louise can make progress if she is able to break through their defenses, but she's found that the prognosis is typically not good. In her experience, it is usually better to deal with the spouse or significant other and encourage him or her to make necessary life changes.

In describing this class Louise says, "What I teach is something that should have been learned in childhood. Because the violent behavior is so ingrained, by the time a person ends up in a program, he or she may have no desire to change. It is challenging and definitely needed, yet it is also stressful and potentially dangerous."

Advice from a Professional

Louise advocates education as the best preparation for this type of work. Although a degree might not be required to teach in some areas, it can certainly lend credibility to an instructor's qualifications. She recommends taking classes in your own areas of interest, doing research, and reading everything currently available on the subject.

She also suggests doing volunteer work that will give you training and hands-on experience and will allow you exposure to both the best and worst aspects of this type of work. The more education you have, the more doors it will open.

Volunteering to speak or to run training for groups in your community will help you to become known for your expertise. Since you may also be asked to write and teach programs, Louise recommends honing your skills in speaking, training, and writing.

Judy Burns—AOL Online Instructor, Screenwriting

Judy Burns teaches Introduction to Screenwriting on AOL through its Online Campus. She is a writer, producer, and story consultant with extensive prime-time credits to her name. Judy also teaches screenwriting at UCLA Extension, Ithaca College, University of California–Riverside, and other universities around the country.

Getting Started

Online education generally occurs in two settings: through a university or an online service. Judy explains that the university courses generally are more like correspondence courses, and instructors are paid an established rate for the course. Online services generally pay per student.

Judy was interested in online teaching, and, knowing that traditional universities sponsor online classes, she decided to investigate the online services and found the AOL Online Campus. She and another teacher wrote a proposal that was accepted by AOL's program coordinator.

She began by offering a free class, which is an AOL requirement for new instructors. In this way, the program coordinator can evaluate the teacher to ensure that he or she is suited to working in the online environment.

What the Work Is Like

The course Judy teaches on AOL is divided into three parts. Part one consists of learning how to create or find a story, pitch the idea, develop the story spine to introduce essential information, introduce and develop new characters, use mythological archetypes, and write a story outline.

Part two looks more closely at story structure, character motivation, subplots, setups and payoffs, development of tension and conflict, and writing the beat outline—the blueprint for a feature film screenplay.

Part three consists of formatting the script, writing professional dialogue and narrative, constructing the scene and sequence line, getting the script into a marketable form, and presenting it to agents and the industry.

Judy finds teaching online to be very energizing. The same dynamics exist in an online classroom as in a standard classroom, but in a more controlled way. Although an online teacher can't look students in the eye, she can get their attention and keep them interested. Judy can tell she's got her students' interest when they begin to really chatter. When this happens, she stops lecturing and asks them to count off and let her know what they're thinking. They usually respond resoundingly.

One disadvantage to teaching screenwriting online is that the students have to see the films outside the classroom. Normally she would show a film in a standard class and talk about it at the same time the students watch it.

Confidentiality is another issue that can be extremely difficult to maintain in an online setting. In a standard classroom, Judy tells the students that what is said in the classroom stays in the classroom. For everyone's protection, she maintains a policy that no one's ideas may be stolen; if students don't agree with this policy, Judy asks them to leave the class. She has found that students in her online classes are generally reluctant to put their material out until the class has been together for about ten or fifteen weeks. It takes longer to build trust online than it does in person, but by the tenth week, they all feel they know each other and begin to post their material.

Advice from a Professional

Based on her experience, Judy advises that it's easier to teach an online class if you design your course so that you're teaching in lecture mode rather than in workshop mode. With a workshop, you spend more time dealing with students' work than lecturing and teaching, so the lecture format allows teachers to deliver more information to the students.

To find a program, search the Web for educational institutions and see whether they offer online courses. When you find what you are looking for, send an e-mail to the program director with your résumé and a course proposal.

An alternative is to set up a home page and offer classes on your own. To do this, you'll need some knowledge of computers, any necessary software, and the appropriate equipment to be able to work effectively.

Gail Rubin—Aerobics Instructor

Gail Rubin is a full-time public relations professional who also teaches aerobics part-time at the YMCA of Greater Albuquerque.

Getting Started

Gail has a B.A. in communications from the University of Maryland–College Park. Although she doesn't need the degree to work as an aerobics instructor, she does have to be able to communicate well with the class.

She enjoys keeping fit and had attended step-aerobics classes for about three years when she decided she wanted to teach aerobics. Years before, she had attended water aerobics classes and had an opportunity to fill in for the teacher a couple of times. Since she'd always liked working up a sweat and leaping around to music, teaching aerobics seemed like a fun way to do that and get paid for it.

When she noticed a steady turnover of aerobics instructors at the YMCA where she took classes, Gail asked her instructor about the possibility of becoming a teacher. She learned that the aerobics coordinator was just starting a training class to prepare for an expected wave of turnovers, and Gail decided to take the training and certification classes and start teaching.

The YMCA provides instructor certification for its teachers. Gail took two weekend training classes and trained for three months to learn cuing, choreography, stretching, and building a routine.

Most health clubs require additional certification from other organizations, and additional classes are required to maintain certification for both YMCA and health club teaching. All aerobics instructors are required to have current certification in CPR and first aid, which Gail earned through Red Cross classes.

What the Work Is Like

Most of the classes that Gail teaches are held during weekday mid-mornings, and the majority of the students are older women, although a few older men regularly show up. Their goals include getting or staying fit, losing weight, and improving flexibility, blood pressure, and heart rate.

Gail has several responsibilities as a low-impact instructor at the YMCA. She prepares the room for class, which involves bringing in music and setting up the stereo, making sure the room is safe for aerobic activities (clean floor, comfortable temperature), and having students sign an attendance logbook. Once class begins, she leads the students through warm-up, stretching, aerobic conditioning, muscle conditioning, cool down, and stretching. During class, she observes the students for any health problems and responds appropriately with assistance as needed. She must also keep the aerobics program coordinator informed of any planned absences and arrange for a substitute teacher.

The management of aerobics instructors at the YMCA is minimal. Instructors are required to show up on time, provide an upbeat class, keep the attendance log, and clock in and out. Aside from a meeting every month or so, they are solely responsible for their classes.

Gail says that because aerobics instructors have a reputation for being constantly chirpy and cheerful, she needs to maintain a certain degree of that kind of sunny personality to charm the class, cheer them on to work their hardest, and keep them wanting to come back. She offers the example of a very shy and quiet classmate in her step class who took the instructor training course. Once this classmate began teaching the early morning step class, attendance dwindled and the class was ultimately canceled because the instructor just didn't have the personality to pull people in so early in the morning.

Gail teaches three regular aerobics classes on Monday, Wednesday, and Friday, which last an hour and fifteen minutes each. She occasionally fills in for other aerobics instructors in the evening or substitutes in the muscle-toning class. She really enjoys being in front of her class, chatting with them during stretches and making some occasional "goofy" comments to relax them and get them into the workout. Her routine doesn't change much, but she does gradually work in different physical moves to keep both herself and the students from getting into a rut.

Because the same people come week after week, the instructor can learn a little bit about their lives outside the gym. Some ask for information about exercise or diet, and Gail provides them with the best answers possible.

Teaching aerobics is not Gail's main source of income, but it is a part-time endeavor with some great benefits. For her main occupation, she works out of her home as a public relations professional/writer. Gail takes a midmorning break to teach her class, returns home to shower, and then gets back to the better-paying PR work.

One of the benefits of being an instructor at the YMCA is automatic membership. Because her public relations work takes her to Washington, DC, for extended periods at a time, she has applied to be a substitute aerobics instructor at the YMCA in that area. As a part-time employee, she has free access to the YMCA's facilities, including the indoor swimming pool, fitness equipment, many aerobics and exercise classes, sauna, and free towel service. In addition, she can write off all her costs for aerobic shoes, music, clothes, and equipment.

Upsides

"I get paid to work out!" Gail enthuses. "I feel great after work. I like to know that my students have had a good workout. I enjoy saying to people, 'Why, yes, I am an aerobics instructor.'"

Downsides

As much as she enjoys working out, the need to do so on a regular schedule can be difficult. She doesn't have the option of not showing up if she isn't in the mood to exercise because the class depends on her to be there. In addition, it can be hard on her body to teach more than one class a day.

Advice from a Professional

Gail's first piece of advice is about disposition. She says, "If you want to be an aerobics instructor, you've got to have an almost cheerleader-like personality. If you're not motivating your students, they will not show up for class."

She also emphasizes that you must be in pretty good shape to begin with, you must enjoy music and movement and people, and you must not be afraid to look foolish every now and then. Of course, you have to learn the basics of teaching aerobics, which you can investigate through a local YMCA or health club; either should be able to refer you to training classes.

In summary, Gail recommends learning to teach a range of aerobics, such as low/high impact, step, and spinning. This will make you much more marketable than if you just know one type.

Phyllis Hanlon—Business Writing Instructor

Phyllis Hanlon teaches business writing in an adult evening program held at Bay Path Vocational-Technical High School in Charlton, Massachusetts. She began freelance writing more than ten years ago and started teaching soon after that.

Getting Started

Phyllis graduated from the Salter School/New England School of Accounting with a medical secretarial diploma. She eventually moved from the medical world to a nonprofit art organization.

She began her own continuing education three years later as an adult evening student at Assumption College in Worcester, Massachusetts, where she received an associate degree in liberal studies (summa cum laude) in two years. After another six months, she completed requirements for a communications certificate on a business track and the following year received a communications certificate on a creative track. Two years after that, she earned her bachelor's degree.

Prior to all of her continuing education, Phyllis became a certified aerobics instructor and taught a variety of fitness classes for two years. She also taught religious education classes to first and third graders as well as junior high school students for several years. In addition, she taught members of her church (both children and adults) liturgical dance.

Phyllis has not only written for magazines and newspapers, she has also edited newsletters and other written communications as part of her own business. Phyllis is a board member and secretary of the Society of Professional Communicators, through which she has been exposed to many experts in the field of communications. She has attended workshops and seminars that have strengthened her skills and introduced her to new ones.

Phyllis says that she has been happier than ever since she returned to school years ago, describing herself as someone who could be a perpetual student. Her academic background prepared her well for the corporate world, where she worked as an administrative assistant for various managers. In this job, she had the opportunity to compose and edit numerous letters that dealt with vendors, other businesspeople, and organizations. She also wrote solicitation and late-payment reminder letters. When upper management asked her to create the letters without their assistance, she realized that she had a knack for writing.

Once she'd left the corporate world and began her own freelance writing career, Phyllis saw an opportunity to help others by teaching one of her own strengths. She had no formal training, but her confidence in the subject and willingness to share the information with others gave her the impetus to teach. The other teaching experience she'd received from her church and the exercise classes gave her some preparation for her current job.

When a local vocational-technical high school advertised for teachers for their evening adult education classes, Phyllis jumped at the chance. Since she had been mulling over the possibility of teaching a business-writing class, she wrote a proposal outlining the areas of business writing that she would cover in the class and submitted it to the director. After speaking with the director, her proposal was accepted.

Although she has considered pursuing a teaching certificate, it is not required for teaching adult personal enrichment courses, and Phyllis enjoys the work she is now doing.

What the Work Is Like

At the vocational-technical high school where Phyllis works, adult night classes range from computer topics to dancing. The class that she teaches runs for seven weeks. The students don't get college credit but can receive a certificate of completion if necessary for tuition reimbursement by their employers or for their own personal use.

Phyllis developed the curriculum for her business-writing class, which has only five students. Although she's had experience teaching aerobics, she admits to having been nervous before her first business-writing class. In the three months before classes began, she created an outline for the class, typed up lessons and handouts, and organized a curriculum. Since this was a noncredit, evening class, she didn't want the students to have to buy a book and believed that the handouts would provide enough hands-on activities to learn the skills she was trying to teach.

She still puts a lot of time into each class, reviewing the agenda each week and usually adding comments, worksheets, or extra lessons. She worries about running out of topics or areas to discuss and would rather have work left over.

Prior to beginning any of the preparations for the classes, Phyllis spoke with a writing teacher she had in college. The teacher proved to be a wonderful resource, providing a workbook designed for teachers and giving Phyllis some hints that she has found very useful. Using that book and two others, she has been able to compile in-depth worksheets that reinforce each lesson.

Her particular teaching style is to stand or walk around as she speaks so that she can make eye contact with the students and make them feel comfortable. She emphasizes the joy-of-learning aspect of the course and tries to avoid making any students feel pressured or uncomfortable. Since the students are at different levels of grammar and punctuation skills, Phyllis tries to work on all the issues that concern them.

At the beginning of the first class, she distributes a questionnaire with demographic questions and asks the students to indicate the areas they would like her to address. Since she likes to work with real-life examples, she also asks them to keep their eyes open for any business communications—letters, memos, e-mail—that are noteworthy for their clear, concise message or, conversely, for their jumbled confusion.

Phyllis uses one of her courses as an example to illustrate her students' needs. In this particular class, the students were all women who held full-time jobs with various companies. During the first class, she asked them why they were taking the course. Two said their bosses had seen the catalog, circled the business-writing class, and placed it on their desks with the "strong suggestion" that they take it. One woman wanted to improve her grammar and punctuation skills. Another had difficulty expressing herself concisely and was looking for a way to streamline her writing. The fifth wanted to write memos and letters for her boss without getting them back "all covered with red-pen marks."

Phyllis teaches a two-hour class one night a week and is considering applying to other area night-school programs in the future. Since she has the curriculum developed, the bulk of the work has been done. A seasoned teacher told her that the first time teaching the course she would be nervous; the second time she would be a little more comfortable; and the third time out she would feel secure. Phyllis thinks she was right.

During the day she still pursues her own marketing communications business, meeting with clients, writing brochures and articles, and working on other assignments. Her involvement with a professional organization also keeps her busy and current with industry trends. In her day-to-day activities, she keeps her eyes open for material she can use in her classes.

Upsides

Phyllis enjoys every aspect of her job as a part-time business-writing teacher. Because she considers herself basically a student at heart, she enjoys the preparation, which feels like her own home-work. She finds it very gratifying to develop her own class activi-ties and feels that she is giving something to her students.

She also finds the students themselves to be interesting and fun to work with. Being adults, they are concerned with job advance-ment and top performance in their present positions, and Phyllis is happy to think she can influence them and their accomplishments in the workplace. Fortunately for her, she can't see any downsides to the job.

Advice from a Professional

For those who are considering teaching adults, Phyllis advises think-ing about your favorite types of activities. If you have been involved in an academic area or some other activity for a long time, believe your skills are strong, and can talk authoritatively about the sub-ject, that is a good starting point.

She also recommends carefully considering your own personal-ity type. Would you be able to explain this activity or subject to a group of strangers? Do you have a fear of speaking in public? You must consider your own comfort level because having the knowl-edge and being able to impart it are two different things.

If you don't have a teaching certificate and have not been involved in a teaching role before, the easiest way to begin is in an adult education program at a local high school or community college. Typically the classes are noncredit, which relaxes the restrictions on teachers.

Phyllis says, "As long as you are sure you can communicate a subject you know well and love to your students, I would encourage you to try. The experience can be very uplifting and exciting. When you provide information that will strengthen an existing skill or introduce a new one, the satisfaction you receive is tremendous."

Karen Carver—Computer Lab Instructor

Karen Carver is a computer lab instructor who worked for Independence, Inc., in Lawrence, Kansas, an independent living center that provides computer training to people with disabilities. She functioned as a lab instructor and the center's webmaster for fifteen years.

Getting Started

Karen uses a wheelchair and found the idea of helping others to learn something that could aid them in their search for employment appealing. Her first experience with Independence, Inc., was as a student, and she became well-acquainted with the staff from taking their classes. When a position opened up, she applied and was hired and began to learn new software from additional classes and through her own studies.

What the Work Is Like

Karen's students were disabled adults who ranged in age from high schoolers to senior citizens and who had disabilities that ranged from mild to severe to terminal. For many students, the main goal was just trying to overcome the fear that they couldn't operate a computer. Once they learned that they could, they'd eagerly take the next step of learning the programs more in-depth. Students chose their courses themselves but did have to demonstrate that they'd learned the basics beforehand or could prove basic ability if they didn't want to take a beginning class.

Many students wanted to gain working skills; others wanted to learn only word processing, so they could type letters at home. Some came to learn spreadsheets, so they could do their own financial statements.

A number of students were sent to the program from the Vocational Rehabilitation Department. These are students who wanted to take computer science through college or vocational-technical schools. The Voc-Rehab sent them to Independence, Inc., to take at least one class, so that the agency knew the student could handle the computers, and it could then assist them with higher education.

Some of the students couldn't afford home computers, so they used the center to do work for school. This was fine, as long as they had some type of disability. Others wanted to keep up their computer skills while looking for a new job. In Karen's experience, there were also those who kept coming back for the opportunity to socialize with the other people there. Since the students came from all aspects of society, they were a very interesting group. Some students wanted to learn computers merely so they could play games. Although the center does have a few games, instructors try to discourage people from spending hours on them in the lab, which takes away time from those who wish to learn software for work.

Karen began as a teacher but eventually spent most of her time working on the center's website. When she was teaching classes, she occasionally had an assistant, but more often she taught on her own. At times she had as many as thirteen students on a computer at once. Classes lasted one hour, and she usually only taught one class a day.

She worked from 8:00 A.M. to 12:30 P.M., four days a week, and 5:00 to 7:30 P.M. one night a week. When she wasn't teaching a class, Karen worked on material for the next day's class, while also assisting students who weren't in structured classes. These were users who came in during time when classes weren't scheduled and worked on anything they wished.

Karen taught Introduction to Computers, which was a basic class for people who had no computer experience. It covered everything from understanding the keyboard to explaining all the buttons and lights on the computer. It also covered how to hook up a computer and how disks store information. She would then move on to an introduction to word processing, databases, and spreadsheets, using such programs as WordPerfect, Microsoft Word, and Excel. Other courses covered the Internet, and two were on basic troubleshooting.

Karen had to be a good troubleshooter herself, so that she could quickly fix anything that went wrong with the computers. As an instructor, she was responsible for preparing her lessons, which might include making up hard-copy handouts or disks for certain classes. She was also responsible for grading her own classes and documenting students' progress.

Since Independence, Inc., is a nonprofit organization, the Computer Learning Center gets new computers only when funding is available, and even then it can only purchase whatever model can be found at the best price. As a result, the center has many models, although all are IBM compatible. The computers at the lab use different versions of Windows, and some have different features that might confuse new users. Karen found that most students seemed to have a considerable amount of trepidation when it came to touching or operating a computer.

Karen's schedule also included working one night a week to help students who weren't able to utilize the lab during the day. She was also required to be available for one-on-one training with students during hours when classes weren't in session. Even when she had an assistant, it was still difficult to keep up with the number of students needing help. Despite screening students in order to place those with equal ability in the same class, instructors usually wound up with one or two who had great difficulty keeping up and a few whose skills far surpassed the others.

Although the instructors also function as troubleshooters, there were still times when a problem arose that none of them could fix. When this happened, they appealed to the program coordinator for help. (See the profile of Terry Thompson, computer learning center coordinator, in Chapter 6.)

Karen's duties also included regularly updating software and fixing any computer or software problems, as well as reviewing and revising teaching plans as needed and making any necessary class changes. At the end of each course, the students are asked what they would like to see taught next, which enables the staff to keep up with what their users are interested in. The center also sends out yearly surveys to businesses to see what type of software they utilize; in this way they can be sure they are teaching what is used in the community.

When Karen began working on the lab's website, she was able to work from home. At first she just entered the lab's newsletter on the Internet, processed data to keep track of the number of people who used the lab, and reviewed lesson plans. Later, she was asked to design a trivia website. She didn't know HTML, and the center didn't want to use a page publisher because many servers don't accommodate them. After many frustrating months of learning through trial and error, she was able to design the site. Because it has to be accessible to people with different disabilities, Karen had to create two versions, one with graphics and one without.

Upsides

Karen enjoys the contact with different people and the various personalities she encounters. She also likes having access to all the different software offered at the lab.

She says, "The best part, though, is when, after a long period of frustration, that light finally goes on in someone's head, and they take off and figure out how to do things. It's also very rewarding finding out that someone who had only a GED landed a well-paying job because of his or her computer skills."

Downsides

The downside is the difficulty in keeping up with the work. The instructors rarely have enough help during classes, and limited funding makes it difficult to keep as current with the computer world as necessary.

Karen also feels frustrated when students quit a class because they believe they'll never learn. "Of course, it's impossible to have a 100 percent success rate, but that doesn't keep us from trying," she says. "It also doesn't keep us from feeling that we've personally failed the person who leaves, even though it really isn't our fault."

Advice from a Professional

Karen advises that you need a lot of patience to work in this field. She points out that many people with disabilities have self-esteem problems and can't succeed if they feel mistreated by someone who doesn't take time to help them without making them feel guilty. It's important for a teacher in this situation to remember that because a person is physically disabled doesn't mean that he or she has no knowledge or is mentally challenged just because he or she is computer illiterate.

And because much of the time is spent teaching alone, it's important to have a wide knowledge of the computers and software being used. If there is a problem with a program or the computer, you need to find the problem and, hopefully, save the project the student is working with.

A Final Thought

You have seen in this chapter that adult continuing education offers an extremely varied list of possibilities for teachers. The profiles presented here are just a sample of the many options available. If you would like to teach adults in a continuing education setting, consider your interests, talents, skills, and experience to determine whether you can turn them into a rewarding career.

3

Adult Basic Education

Adult literacy and remedial education teachers instruct adults and out-of-school youths in reading, writing, speaking English, and performing elementary mathematical calculations—basic skills that equip them to solve problems well enough to become active participants in society, to hold a job, and to further their education.

The instruction provided by these teachers can be divided into three principal categories: remedial or adult basic education (ABE) is geared toward adults whose skills are either at or below an eighth-grade level; adult secondary education (ASE) is geared toward students who wish to obtain their General Educational Development (GED) certificate or other high school equivalency credential; and English literacy instruction is for adults with limited proficiency in English.

Traditionally, the students in these adult education classes have been primarily those who did not graduate high school or who passed through school without acquiring the knowledge needed to meet their educational goals or to participate fully in today's high-skill society. Increasingly, however, students in these classes are immigrants or other people whose native language is not English. Educators who work with adult English-language learners are usually called teachers of English as a second language (ESL) or teachers of English to speakers of other languages (ESOL).

ABE programs also provide support to developmentally challenged students to help them live and work more independently by studying personal/home management, communication, computation, reading, writing, and life skills. These programs can also focus on teaching students citizenship skills.

Finally, some adult remedial education programs—also known by the preferred term of *developmental programs*—are provided at junior colleges, vocational-technical schools, and community colleges to bring students up to the standard required for admittance into credit-bearing courses toward a degree or certificate. This area of adult education is covered in Chapter 4.

Differences Between Adult Basic Education and Adult Remedial Education

Although adult basic education and adult remedial education sound the same, there are some distinct differences. The major difference between the two is the skill level of the student. Students whose skills fall below the sixth-grade level on a college entrance exam (all colleges and universities in all fields of education use the sixth-grade level as the independent level, especially in reading) are considered unable to function on an independent level in reading, math, or English. Those students are not admitted to a technical college without first enrolling and succeeding in ABE courses to bring up their skill levels.

Adult remediation courses, now mostly known as *developmental courses*, are designed for students who can function independently (seventh grade and above) but whose test scores on the college entrance exam indicate that their abilities in math, English, or reading need strengthening before they can take the courses required to complete their certificates, diplomas, or associate degrees.

As in all colleges, placement in math, English, or reading classes is determined by scores made on the ASSET entrance exam. This is a placement test developed by ACT (American College Testing Program), a nonprofit organization that provides assessment and research services in education. The exam measures basic writing, numerical, and reading skills, as well as advanced mathematical skills in algebra and geometry.

ABE centers are federally funded and located at many facilities in each state. They are separate from colleges and universities. Community colleges legally cannot teach ABE courses, since ABE courses are tuition-free and also offer no credit. (For more information on developmental courses taught at community colleges and technical schools, see Chapter 4.)

ABE and Literacy Programs

Literacy helps individuals continue to learn new information, read for pleasure, read newspapers to be informed about the world and their communities, handle everyday tasks, and function independently to manage their own needs. Literacy is also important to allow older people to remain in or rejoin the workforce or to contribute to society through volunteerism and civic participation.

A number of factors help explain why so many adults in the United States and Canada demonstrate literacy skills in the lowest proficiency level. Many are immigrants who have not yet learned to speak English. Others ended their formal education before completing high school, while still others have physical, mental, or health conditions that keep them from participating fully in activities at work, school, or at home. Studies indicate that low literacy affects many aspects of life, not least of which is employment. For example, a Statistics Canada study indicates that each additional year of education a person receives is worth 8.3 percent in a paycheck. Using an annual base salary of $30,000, this amounts to an additional $2,490 per year. In addition, the nine million Canadians who have low literacy are about twice as likely to be unemployed than those with full literacy skills.

Adult basic education teachers (sometimes called *remedial education teachers*), teach basic academic courses in mathematics, languages, history, reading, writing, science, and other areas using instructional methods geared toward adult learning. They teach these subjects to students sixteen years of age and older who demonstrate the need to increase their skills in one or more of the subject areas mentioned.

Classes are taught to appeal to a variety of learning styles and usually include large-group, small-group, and one-on-one instruction. Because the students often are at different proficiency levels for different subjects, adult basic education teachers must make individual assessments of each student's abilities beforehand. In many programs, the assessment is used to develop an individualized education plan for each student. Teachers are required to evaluate students periodically to determine their progress and potential for advancement to the next level.

For many students the classroom has been a place of disappointment and failure, so teachers in ABE programs may have to assist them in acquiring effective study skills and the self-confidence they need to reenter an academic environment. Teachers also may encounter students with a learning or physical disability that requires additional expertise to help these students achieve their goals.

All adult literacy and remedial teachers must prepare lessons, do any related paperwork, and stay current in their fields. Attendance for students is mostly voluntary, and course work is rarely graded. Many teachers also must learn the latest uses for computers in the classroom, as computers are increasingly being used to supplement instruction in basic skills and in teaching ESOL. ABE teachers may refer students for counseling or job placement. (For more information on adult education counseling, see Chapter 5.) Here is a sample literacy job listing:

> A county library is seeking an experienced adult literacy specialist to work at the library's Second Chance Program. This is a part-time, 15 to 20 hours a week, temporary position.
>
> The successful candidate will primarily be responsible for student support activities that will include: providing workshops and experiences for the students to promote the development of personal advocacy and leadership skills; offering computer-assisted learning and instruction in the use of the Internet; tracking and recording student achievements, including the development and implementation of an "exit interview" questionnaire; assisting with student recruitment and volunteer training; and supervising part-time student advocates. Must be available some nights and weekends.
>
> Minimum Requirements: B.A. or B.S. degree with a major in education, psychology, communications, humanities, social science, or a closely related behavioral science field.
>
> Experience: One year of full-time or its equivalent experience in adult literacy programs or as a certified teacher of educationally or economically disadvantaged groups. Additional qualifying experience of the type noted above may be substituted for the

required education on a year-for-year basis up to a maximum of four years. The selection process includes an application and an interview.

ESL Programs

Millions of people around the world speak or are studying how to speak English. They choose to learn English for a number of reasons: to attend colleges and universities in English-speaking countries, to ensure better business communications, to enhance employability, to facilitate government relations, to create a more rewarding travel experience, or, for many, to be able to communicate day-to-day in the English-speaking country in which they live.

English as a second language (ESL) teachers help adults to speak, listen, read, and write in English, often in the context of real-life situations to promote learning. More advanced students may concentrate on writing and conversational skills or focus on learning more academic or job-related communication skills. These teachers instruct adults from a wide range of cultures who possess varied abilities and who speak a variety of languages. Some students have college degrees, and many advance quickly through the program owing to a variety of factors, such as their age, previous language experience, educational background, and native language. Others may need additional time due to these same factors. Because the teacher and students often do not share a common language, creativity is an important part of fostering communication in the classroom and achieving learning goals.

It is safe to assume that the demand for English instruction around the world also will continue to rise. This means many opportunities for instructors who are interested in living and working outside of North America.

Sample ESL Job Listings

Following are just a few examples of some job listings for ESL instructors.

Position: ESL, one (1) 2-year term renewable instructorship. Duties: teach ESL for academic purposes; assist in ESL curriculum development/research. Required: M.A. in TESOL or equivalent; 2 years' teaching experience overseas or in intensive English program. Summer employment is possible. Send letter of interest, CV, 3 letters of reference.

Position: ESL high school teacher. Duties: classroom instruction. Requirements: valid state secondary credential authorizing ESL or bilingual instruction. Qualifications: appropriate student teaching or equivalent.

Position: international language education center has full-time and part-time openings for ESL teachers. Duties: preparing lesson plans and instructing adults in ESL courses, monitoring student performance, advising students on progress, administering written and oral exams, grading student exams, other duties as directed. Requirements: B.A. in education, communication, or any related field. One year of ESL adult teaching experience in a classroom setting (excluding tutoring and volunteer work) or certificate in Teaching English to Speakers of Other Languages (TESOL certificate).

Position: community organization seeks part-time ESL instructors to teach English to Spanish-speaking adults in evening classes. Qualifications: minimum B.A. and at least 2 years of teaching experience.

Position: private learning company is now seeking full-time and part-time ESL teachers. Qualified candidates must be energetic, goal oriented, and enjoy working with people. College students are encouraged to apply. Requirements: high school diploma required; associate degree preferred. Intensive training will be provided.

Position: teaching English in Korea. Energetic individuals from native English-speaking countries are needed to teach English to students in Korea. Requirements: bachelor's degree from an accredited university in the United States, Canada, Australia, New Zealand, South Africa, Great Britain, or Ireland; must be a citizen of one of the above-mentioned countries; must be a native English speaker; must be in good physical and mental health; no criminal record.

GED Programs

The General Educational Development (GED) tests give adults sixteen and older who did not graduate from high school the opportunity to earn a high school equivalency diploma. The GED diploma is recognized by employers and educators and has increased education and employment opportunities for millions of adults since 1942.

The GED was developed and is administered by the General Educational Development Testing Service and is taken by more than 750,000 adults each year. About one out of every seven high school diplomas awarded each year are earned by people who have passed the GED tests.

For students who wish to earn a GED credential to get a job or qualify for postsecondary education or adult secondary education, teachers provide help in acquiring the necessary knowledge and skills to pass the test. The GED tests students in subject areas such as reading, writing, mathematics, science, and social studies while at the same time measuring students' communication, information-processing, problem-solving, and critical-thinking skills. The emphasis in class is on acquiring the knowledge needed to pass the GED test, as well as preparing students for success in further educational endeavors.

The GED Testing Service contracts with nearly thirty-five hundred official GED testing centers in the United States, Canada, and overseas to provide test materials and to monitor services to examinees. The GED testing program is jointly administered by the GED Testing Service of the American Council on Education and each participating state, provincial, or territorial department or ministry of education.

About 65 percent of GED test takers plan to enter a college, university, or trade, technical, or business school during the year following the test. The average age of people taking the GED exam is 24.7. More than 95 percent of employers nationwide employ GED graduates on the same basis as high school graduates in terms of hiring, salary, and opportunity for advancement.

The adult education programs of most school boards provide classes to help students prepare for the GED battery of tests. Instructors work with a curriculum found in most secondary schools—English, math, science, social studies, and history.

School boards with GED programs hire qualified people to administer the tests. In addition, many counselors opt to work with GED test takers to help determine career goals upon completion. (For more information on GED counseling opportunities, see Chapter 5.)

Sample GED Job Listings

Read the following GED job listings to see what is required for this type of work.

> Position: county school board seeks qualified GED instructors for adult education classes held at satellite community centers. Qualifications: bachelor's degree and state high school teaching certificate. Hours: 25 to 30 a week; half day on Saturdays. Duties:

prepare adults from the age of 16 for the GED exam. Must be able to work with a wide range of subjects: language usage, reading comprehension, math, science, and social studies.

Position: career training institute seeks full-time GED instructor. Requirements: bachelor's degree. Prior teaching experience with an adult population is desired; preference will be given to those with GED teaching experience.

Position: GED instructor to provide applied academic instruction to students, teaching from approved basic education curriculum. Plan, prepare, and implement instructional units. Provide individual student case management and work as part of the Career Education Team in developing the employability of students. Work closely with vocational instructors to ensure that curriculum meets needs of students. Academic instructor will be able to make recommendations for curriculum revisions. Administer and grade tests. Requirements: bachelor's degree in education with valid teaching certificate required.

Citizenship Programs

Although there are exceptions, applicants for naturalization must be able to read, write, speak, and understand words in ordinary usage in the English language. Applicants for U.S. or Canadian citizenship must also have knowledge of the appropriate national history and government.

Sample Job Listing for Citizenship Classes

Read the following listing to get an idea of what this position entails.

Position: adult educator for citizenship preparation classes offered by a university continuing education program. Must possess a bachelor's degree and be certified to teach high school or adults.

Hours: 12 hours per week, Monday through Thursday, 7:00 to 10:00 P.M. Benefits: discounted tuition for university courses.

Employment Settings

Teachers of adult literacy and remedial education held about ninety-eight thousand jobs in 2004. About one in three was self-employed, and many additional teachers worked as unpaid volunteers. Many of the jobs are federally funded, and additional funds come from state, provincial, and local governments, which employ the majority of these teachers in adult learning centers, libraries, community colleges, juvenile detention centers, and corrections institutions, among other places. Others work for private educational institutions and for social service organizations, such as job-training or residential-care facilities.

Teaching English as a second language (TESL) often falls into the category of ABE but with more varied job settings. In addition to evening ABE programs through public schools, you can find ESL classes on the campuses of community colleges and four-year colleges and universities, in private language schools, and also as part of the regular curriculum in the primary and secondary grades.

Education and Training

Requirements for teaching adult literacy and basic and secondary education vary by state or province and by program. Programs that are run by state, provincial, and local governments require high accountability to student achievement standards. Most jurisdictions require teachers to have some form of credential; the most common are a public school teacher license, an adult education credential, or both. However, programs in states or provinces that do not have these requirements still generally require that ABE teachers have at least a bachelor's degree and, preferably, a master's degree.

Teaching experience, especially with adults, also is preferred or required. Although programs run by private religious, community, or volunteer organizations generally develop standards based on their own needs and organizational goals, most also require paid teachers to have at least a bachelor's degree. Volunteers usually do not need a bachelor's degree but often must attend a training program before they are allowed to work with students.

Most programs recommend that adult literacy and basic and secondary education teachers take classes or workshops on teaching adults, using technology to teach, working with learners from a variety of cultures, and teaching adults with learning disabilities. ESOL teachers also should have courses or training in second-language acquisition theory and linguistics. In addition, knowledge of the citizenship and naturalization process may be useful.

While knowledge of a second language is not necessary to teach ESL students, it can be very helpful for instructors in understanding their students' perspectives. GED teachers should know what is required to pass the exam, and they should be able to instruct students in the subject matter. Training for literacy volunteers usually consists of instruction in effective teaching practices, needs assessment, lesson planning, the selection of appropriate instructional materials, characteristics of adult learners, and cross-cultural awareness.

Adult education and literacy teachers must have the ability to work with students who come from a variety of cultural, educational, and economic backgrounds. They must be understanding and respectful of their students' circumstances and be familiar with their concerns. All teachers, both paid and volunteer, should be able to communicate well and motivate their students.

Professional development among adult education and literacy teachers varies widely. Both part-time and full-time teachers are expected to participate in ongoing professional development activities to keep current on new developments in the field and to enhance skills already acquired. Each jurisdiction's professional development system reflects its unique needs and organizational structure, and attendance by teachers at professional development workshops and other activities is often outlined in its policy. Some teachers are able to complete professional development activities through alternative delivery systems such as the Internet or distance learning.

Opportunities for advancement again vary by area and program. Some part-time teachers are able to move into full-time teaching positions or program administrator positions, such as coordinator or director, when such vacancies occur. Others may decide to use their classroom experience to move into policy work at a nonprofit organization or with the local, state, provincial, or federal government or to perform research.

Job Outlook

Opportunities for jobs as adult literacy and remedial education teachers are expected to be favorable over the next several years, as employers' increasing demands for a more literate workforce will lead more workers to seek courses in adult literacy, basic education, and secondary education.

Significant employment growth is anticipated especially for ESOL teachers, who will be needed by the increasing number of immigrants and other residents living in North America who need to learn or improve their English skills. Demand for ESOL teachers will be greatest in areas that have large populations of residents who have limited English skills, such as California, Florida, Texas, and New York. However, many other regions have begun to attract large numbers of immigrants, making good opportunities in this field widely available.

Changes in immigration policy and citizenship requirements also mandate a basic competency in English and civics. A survey by the U.S. Department of Education's National Center for Education Statistics estimated that nearly 30 percent of the adult population had only rudimentary reading and writing skills. Most adults at this level could pick out key facts in a brief newspaper article, for example, but could not draft a letter explaining an error on their credit card bill. A subgroup in this category, representing roughly 6 percent of the total adult population, was unable to perform even the simplest literacy tasks.

What does this all mean? The number of people in the United States and Canada who desire ABE, GED, and ESL instruction is on the rise. As public school systems, government agencies, and private enterprises continue to work toward filling the demand, opportunities for ABE and ESL teachers will continue to grow.

The demand for adult literacy and basic and secondary education often fluctuates with the economy. When the economy is good and workers are hard to find, employers relax their standards and hire workers without a degree or GED or good proficiency in English. As the economy softens, employers can be more selective, and more students may find that they need additional education to get a job.

In addition, adult education classes often are subject to changes in funding levels, which can cause the number of teaching jobs to fluctuate from year to year. In particular, budget pressures may limit federal funding of adult education, which may cause programs to rely more on volunteers if other organizations and governments do not make up the difference.

Salaries

According to the most recent statistics available, in 2004, adult literacy and remedial education teachers had median hourly earnings of $18.74. The majority earned between $14.07 and $25.49, while the lowest 10 percent earned less than $10.57, and the highest 10 percent earned more than $34.94.

Those who work part-time are usually paid by the hour or for each class that they teach and receive few or no benefits. Full-time teachers are generally paid a salary and receive health insurance and other benefits if they work for a school system or government.

Profiles

The profiles that follow in this chapter include a student literacy coordinator and tutor, an ESL instructor, and a GED instructor.

Lynn Goodwin—Tutor and Student Literacy Coordinator

Lynn Goodwin works as a student literacy coordinator for Project Second Chance, a program offered through Contra Costa County in California. She is also a volunteer tutor not only at Project Second Chance but at the Sylvan Learning Center and in America Online's Academic Assistance Center (AAC) as well. She has more than twenty-five years' experience in high school and college education as well as several years running a private acting class.

Lynn earned a B.A. in drama and theater at Vassar College in Poughkeepsie, New York, and an M.A. from San Francisco State University, also in drama and theater, with a minor in community college teaching.

Getting Started

Lynn came by her interest in education naturally, following the example of her mother, who taught English. Lynn learned a lot about teaching by comparing her mother's methods to those of other teachers. Education and academic success were also important to her father, a business owner who often helped with math homework.

She was attracted to teaching adults because they, unlike adolescents, choose to learn. She felt that she had ideas to offer, and Project Second Chance supplied her with techniques to communicate them effectively.

"In the information age, people who cannot read signs, fill out a form, read to their children, read a note from a child's teacher, or read labels operate with a frustrating disability that also can cause great embarrassment," Lynn says. "Often nonreaders become masters of deception. As I got older and more frustrated with the public school system, I felt a greater need to help those who fell through the cracks."

She began by simultaneously volunteering at Project Second Chance and tutoring for AOL's Academic Assistance Center. With a recommendation from AAC, she was hired as a tutor with the

Sylvan Learning Center. Lynn volunteers at all three places but has had to cut back her volunteering hours since she was hired at Project Second Chance as a paid staff member working twenty hours a week. She specializes in working with students in the computer rooms and functions as a student advocate. Lynn points out that volunteering to work with adult learners can often lead to paid employment in the field.

What the Work Is Like

The students at Project Second Chance are adults who read below a fifth-grade level. Many have learning disabilities such as dyslexia. About a third are not native English speakers; although they speak English, they have trouble reading and writing the language. Many come to the program for personal improvement, hoping to give more to their children than they had for themselves.

Within this setting, Lynn's job has two focuses: improving learner recruitment and communication, and making the computer rooms accessible to learners. To accomplish her goals, she has designed assessment interviews that are conducted with the learner at six weeks, six months, and upon exit from the program. The interviews help her to assess learner progress and address concerns. Those who are leaving the program are asked questions to find out why they are leaving and what they learned.

Lynn is also involved with student recruitment and put out Learn to Read cards at the local convenience stores and county day-care centers. She contacts school secretaries and adult school administrators to help spread the word and is also placing ads on the county bus system. She invites learners to help recruit others who need the program's services and at the same time offers them use of the computer room.

To keep the computer room up to date, Lynn assesses the existing software by inviting tutors to bring their students in to use the systems. She also asks the tutors to recommend any software that would enhance their students' learning. The center offers programs in phonics, reading, writing, math, typing, Quicken, and GED preparation as well as games that tap into a variety of skills.

Lynn's job certainly keeps her busy. In addition to tutoring, the paid staff at Project Second Chance also works at recruitment, textbook maintenance, ordering, training, and other program tasks. She is becoming involved in designing new methods of recruitment and retention as well as looking for new approaches to make the computer rooms work more effectively.

As a tutor, Lynn is dedicated to helping a learner in any way possible. She works on skills, such as getting facts, finding the main idea, and recognizing supporting details. She also works on writing skills and creates spelling lists based on what the learner wants to know.

Since most of the tutoring is done in the library, it can often become crowded, but tutors work in separate cubicles so students do have privacy. Lynn works with students on an individual basis, which she enjoys. "Because I work with one person at a time, it is seldom boring," she says. "Besides, if I show signs of boredom, it demeans the self-confidence of my learner. Instead, I am upbeat, finding what is positive or correct and building from there whenever possible. The growth makes the job worthwhile."

Upsides

Lynn gets great satisfaction when she sees comprehension in a learner's eyes. She also enjoys the receptive attitude of the staff and the computer programs she uses.

In addition, she appreciates the people she's contacted who want to help spread the word about adult education and the energy that is generated by both tutors and learners. Overall, Lynn likes the feeling that the program is making a difference in the lives of both learners and tutors.

Downsides

"I hate the early morning calls from learners canceling our sessions. Another downside is the frustration that occurs when a learner becomes impatient with herself or himself or is easily defeated."

Advice from a Professional

Lynn advises that to succeed as a literacy instructor, it's important to care about people and to learn to listen and be creative, particularly when it comes to solving problems. It is also helpful to be open to the job requirements and willing to venture in new directions with your work.

A large part of the work of tutors and student coordinators is to match learners with tutors, to provide the necessary materials, and to be available to solve problems. They also train tutors to work with the variety of students they will encounter.

Lynn points out that because many adult learners failed in the public school system, it is up to the instructor to provide a positive, trusting environment that will foster individual success. The traditional classroom often does not work for these learners, who may have negative impressions of the classroom setting.

Lynn enthusiastically praises volunteers and stresses the need for tutors and program coordinators to value them highly. Based on her experience, she advises that even when working with a small group of students, you will need trained volunteers to assist you.

She also suggests volunteering and interning as excellent ways to explore this career—you can check with your local library for opportunities. If you want to earn the credentials for a paid career, contact the education department of your local university for information about requirements.

In summary, Lynn advises that since funding for adult literacy programs is limited, grant writing is a desirable additional skill.

Claire Best—ESL Instructor

Claire Best taught English as a second language to adults through an adult education program affiliated with her local school board as well as in a private language center. She also worked overseas for many years teaching English as a foreign language to first-year university students.

Getting Started

Claire says that she started in TESOL the same way many others do—she "just fell into it." She had a B.A. in English and, although she wasn't sure how she wanted to use it, she didn't think that she was going to teach. She also earned an M.Ed. with a concentration in counseling.

She had been working part-time with an adult education program counseling GED students on career choices after they passed their high school equivalency but needed to put in more hours to make a decent living. A friend who was the director of the ESL evening program at one of the satellite schools offered Claire a job. This was her start in the field, and all of her training was learned on the job.

The experience she gained through working in adult education led to a job in a private language program and then to her first job overseas.

What the Work Is Like

Claire says that there's a big difference between teaching in the United States and teaching overseas. While the classes she taught in this country were filled with a variety of students from around the world, the overseas classes are filled with students from the host country.

On a larger level, she says that in the United States, when your class is finished, your workday is basically done. Overseas, however, your workday might be over, but the experience of living in another country is constantly with you. Claire prefers teaching overseas and being immersed in another culture. She finds this far more exciting and one of the main benefits to the profession, since she can work almost anywhere.

Despite the cultural differences, though, the work of teaching is basically the same regardless of the location. Claire instructs students in the basic English language skills of reading, writing, listening, and conversation. Like any teacher, she is responsible for designing lesson plans and for administering and grading tests. She also helped to develop the teaching program and materials used in the classroom.

Her jobs in the United States required many more teaching hours than her university jobs overseas, where she preferred the administrative aspects of the work to the actual teaching. In her last job overseas, she was the director of a program.

Advice from a Professional

Claire feels that many people think that if they can speak English, they can teach it. This may be true in some places, and travelers wanting to earn extra money to help pay for their trip may be able to find work tutoring or providing practice in conversation skills. But as the number of professionally trained teachers increases, opportunities for unqualified teachers decreases.

She points out that teaching English as a second or foreign language is not the same as teaching it as a first language. There is a foundation of knowledge and methodology for this field of study that includes linguistics, second-language acquisition, education practices, sociology, anthropology, psychology, testing and measurement, and other related subjects.

Claire's advice is first to volunteer to see if this profession is right for you. If it is, then you should plan for your career and get specialized training, which will open up many more jobs to you. She recommends that the best way to find a job, especially a job overseas, is to attend the annual TESOL conference. Recruiters come in from all around the world to staff their programs.

Sheila Levitt—GED Instructor

Sheila Levitt worked with the adult education program through the school board in Dade County, Florida, for ten years, providing GED preparation to students in a variety of settings. She earned a B.A. in English and an M.Ed. from the University of Florida–Gainesville.

Getting Started

Sheila didn't set out to be an adult education teacher. Without a career plan when she completed her master's degree, she took the advice of a friend who suggested that she contact the school board about employment opportunities. The short-term position she accepted ended up lasting for ten years.

What the Work Is Like

For most of her time with the adult education program, Sheila worked in a room in a community church that was donated to the school board. Members of the community could sign up for the free classes offered.

The students came from different backgrounds. Some were high school age and working toward a GED. Others were older and were being encouraged to go back to school by their family members or employers. And some took classes for their own satisfaction and sense of achievement. Some students attended classes for a week or two for a refresher course; others spent months preparing to take the GED exam.

Sheila worked thirty hours a week, Monday through Friday, with an hour break for lunch. She and the two other teachers alternated between working with students individually and in groups. Teaching materials provided by the school board covered all the areas required for the GED. New students were tested to determine their reading levels and were then started at the appropriate level of learning materials. As the students progressed, they were advanced to more difficult materials.

Upsides

Although helping students to increase their reading, writing, and math skills is a very challenging endeavor, Sheila enjoyed the work and found it extremely rewarding and exciting to witness students' improvement. She says, "When we all felt it was time for them to sign up for the test, everyone rooted for them. The best part was when a student came back to the center to let us know that he or she had passed the GED. That smile and the thanks were worth everything."

Another advantage was that, at least in her particular setting, teachers didn't have to deal regularly with administration. Instead, they were provided with the classroom and the materials and given the freedom to develop their own class structure and teaching methods.

Downsides

Sheila only found one downside to the job, but it is an important one. Since teachers are paid on an hourly basis, there are no benefits, health insurance, sick leave, or vacation. And if attendance at the center dropped, hours could be reduced. Several times her hours were cut to twenty-five per week for months at a time, making it difficult to budget finances and pay bills.

Advice from a Professional

Sheila recommends that to provide GED instruction, you need the same qualities that you would for any teaching job: knowledge of the subject matter, a lot of patience, a lot of enthusiasm, and a love of teaching.

She believes that the benefits to teaching adults is that you don't have the discipline problems you'd find in a high school, and your students, for the most part, are much more motivated. If you want to teach secondary-level material but don't want to deal with the problems found in schools, adult education is a good alternative to consider.

A Final Thought

You have just read the accounts of professionals working in three different areas of adult basic education and have seen the combination of training and personal attributes that are necessary to work in this challenging field. You may be just the right person to help others learn English as a second language or prepare for the GED exam. What a rewarding and challenging career this can be for the right individual.

4

ADULT VOCATIONAL-
TECHNICAL EDUCATION AND
PREBACCALAUREATE TRAINING

VOCATIONAL-TECHNICAL EDUCATION prepares students for careers by teaching a combination of academic and specific occupational skills. It covers a wide range of occupations, including such positions as welder, dental hygienist, emergency medical technician, automotive mechanic, plumber, electrician, automated systems manager, radiology technician, farmer, and cosmetologist.

Adult education teachers working in the vocational-technical (voc-tech) sector have traditionally offered instruction in these and other occupations that do not require a college degree. Their students could be high school graduates or GED holders, or they might have left high school without finishing.

But vocational-technical education is changing and now incorporates both school-based and work-based learning to prepare students for postsecondary education as well as employment. In fact, vocational-technical education prepares students for the bulk of North America's jobs. Although the majority of jobs don't require a four-year college degree, many do require some education beyond high school, often at the community college level. Some postsecondary education is essential for most of today's occupations.

The current vocational-technical education field encompasses postsecondary institutions up to and including universities providing prebaccalaureate training for courses offering college credit. It is also offered in secondary schools. Whatever the setting may be, vocational-technical education allows students to explore career options and develop the skills they will need both in school and in the workplace.

Vocational-Technical Education and the Law

The Carl D. Perkins Vocational and Applied Technology Education Act, Public Law 101–392, defines vocational-technical education as organized educational programs offering sequences of courses directly related to preparing individuals for paid or unpaid employment in current or emerging occupations requiring other than a baccalaureate or advanced degree. Programs include competency-based applied learning, which contributes to an individual's academic knowledge, higher-order reasoning, problem-solving skills, and the occupation-specific skills necessary for economic independence as a productive and contributing member of society.

According to the National Assessment of Vocational Education study, the most frequent uses of funds include: occupationally relevant equipment, vocational curriculum materials, materials for learning labs, curriculum development or modification, hiring vocational staff, staff development, career counseling and guidance activities, efforts for academic-vocational integration, supplemental services for special populations, remedial classes, and expansion of tech-prep programs.

The United States competes in a global economy. The purpose of the Perkins Act is to prepare a workforce with the academic and vocational skills needed to compete successfully in a world market.

Employment Settings

Career and technical education is a massive enterprise. Thousands of comprehensive high schools, vocational and technical high schools, area vocational centers, and community colleges offer vocational and technical education programs. Virtually every high school student takes at least one career and technical education course, and one in four students takes three or more courses in a single program area. One-third of college students are involved in career and technical programs, and as many as forty million adults engage in short-term postsecondary occupational training.

Given these facts, you can see that there are many possible job settings for vocational-technical teachers. Settings can be as varied as the different occupations the voc-tech and prebaccalaureate training sectors cover.

Vocational-technical education is very popular in public secondary schools. There are also many vocational-technical institutes that offer training specifically geared toward preparing students to enter the workforce immediately upon completion of the program. In addition, there are many private schools, such as cosmetology and computer schools, that provide vocational-technical training in one specific subject area.

The hundreds of community colleges throughout the United States and Canada offer a variety of job-training programs, courses for college credit, preparatory and adult education courses, as well as customized workforce training. Programs are usually two years and cover arts and sciences, business occupations, health occupations, technical fields, trades, and service occupations.

Two programs at the secondary level are also of interest to instructors considering a career in adult voc-tech education: career academy programs and tech-prep education.

Career Academy Programs

Career academies are high school programs that are usually schools-within-schools—smaller administrative units operating within larger schools—that are occupationally focused. These educational structures bring together groups of students and teachers who work together over a two- to three-year period.

There are more than eleven hundred career academies in operation throughout the United States and Canada, some established as long ago as the early 1960s. Their students are typically high school juniors and seniors who study such areas as environmental technology, applied electrical science, horticulture, sports education, business education, travel and tourism, aviation technology, computer engineering, avionics, building trades, and health care careers.

Career academy programs are very effective, most notably in preparing members of special populations and students seeking to enter nontraditional occupations. The career academy concept has been so successful that it is now recommended for all students who want education and training leading to existing jobs in the public and private sectors.

Although career academies have several distinct elements that distinguish them from traditional education and training programs, their graduates are academically and technically proficient and qualified to continue with postsecondary education or enter the labor market.

Some of the characteristics of a career academy program are:

- Block scheduling
- Reduced class size
- Integrated academic and vocational content
- Thematic learning partnerships with business mentoring
- Structured, out-of-school learning experiences

Tech-Prep Education

Tech-prep education was introduced in 1990 as a significant innovation in the American education reform movement. It is designed as a 4 + 2 or a 2 + 2 planned sequence of study in a technical field beginning as early as the ninth year of school. This means that the sequence includes either four or two years of regular study plus two years of postsecondary occupational education or an apprenticeship program of at least two years following secondary instruction, and it culminates in an associate degree or certificate.

Tech prep is an important school-to-work transition strategy, helping all students make the connection between school and employment.

The Perkins Law requires that tech-prep programs have seven elements:

1. An articulation agreement between secondary and postsecondary consortium participants

2. A 2 + 2 or 4 + 2 design with a common core of proficiency in math, science, communication, and technology
3. A specifically developed tech-prep curriculum
4. Joint in-service training of secondary and postsecondary teachers to implement the tech-prep curriculum effectively
5. Training of counselors to recruit students and to ensure program completion and appropriate employment
6. Equal access of special populations to the full range of tech prep programs
7. Preparatory services such as recruitment, career and personal counseling, and occupational assessment

States are required to give priority consideration to tech-prep programs that offer effective employment placement; transfer to four-year baccalaureate programs; are developed in consultation with business, industry, labor unions, and institutions of higher education that award baccalaureate degrees; and address dropout prevention and reentry and the needs of special populations.

Students earn an associate degree or a two-year certificate. In addition to competence in math, science, and communication, graduates are prepared for work in at least one field of engineering technology; applied science; mechanical, industrial, or practical art or trade; or agriculture, health, or business.

Duties of the Voc-Tech and Prebaccalaureate Instructor

Adult education instructors prepare and grade lessons and assignments, complete all required paperwork, attend faculty and professional meetings, and keep current in their field. They use a combination of classroom instruction, hands-on laboratory work, and on-the-job training to address students' different learning styles and enhance their success.

Increasingly, adult voc-tech teachers integrate academic and vocational curricula so that students obtain a variety of skills. For example, an electronics student may be required to take courses in principles of mathematics and science in conjunction with hands-on electronics skills.

Generally, teachers demonstrate techniques that the students then apply and critique the students' work so they can learn from their mistakes. A carpentry instructor, for example, will teach various carpentry techniques, including the use of tools and equipment, watch students perform the same functions, and have them repeat procedures until they meet specific standards required by the trade.

As minimum standards of proficiency are established or revised for students in various vocational-technical fields, teachers must be aware of new standards and develop lesson plans to ensure that students meet basic criteria. Also, adult education teachers and community colleges are assuming a greater role in students' transitions from school to work by helping to establish internships and providing information about prospective employers.

Education and Training

Public school teachers must be licensed to work in all states and provinces and in the District of Columbia; licensure is not required for teachers in private schools. Usually licensure is granted by the state or provincial board of education or a licensure advisory committee. Teachers may be licensed to teach the early grades (usually nursery school through grade three); the elementary grades (one through six or eight); the middle grades (five through eight); a secondary education subject area (usually grades seven through twelve); a special subject, such as reading or music (usually grades K through twelve); or guidance counseling and, in some areas, adult education.

Although requirements for regular licenses vary by jurisdiction, all localities require a bachelor's degree and completion of an approved teacher-training program with a prescribed number of subject and education credits and supervised practice teaching. Some also require a master's degree in education, which involves at least one year of additional course work beyond the bachelor's degree with a specialization in a particular subject.

A master's degree is more often than not the minimum requirement for teaching academic subjects in junior or community colleges, but more and more instructors are going on to earn doctorate degrees.

In many locations, vocational teachers have many of the same requirements for teaching as their academic counterparts. However, because knowledge and experience in a particular field are important criteria for the job, some jurisdictions will license vocational education teachers without a bachelor's degree, provided they can demonstrate expertise in their field. A minimum number of hours in education courses may also be required.

Job Outlook

The future looks bright for adult vocational-technical education teachers over the next several years. Employment growth will result from the need to train not only young adults for entry-level jobs but also experienced workers who want to switch fields or whose jobs have been eliminated because of changing technology or business reorganization.

Adults returning to college to enhance their career prospects or to update their skills also will continue to create new opportunities for postsecondary teachers, particularly at community colleges and for-profit institutions that cater to working adults. Increased cooperation between businesses and educational institutions to ensure that students are taught the skills desired by employers should also add to growth at this level. However, since many adult education programs receive state, provincial, and federal funding, employment growth may be affected by government budgets.

The job market for secondary school teachers varies widely by geographic area and subject specialty. Many inner cities and rural areas have difficulty attracting enough teachers, so job prospects should continue to be better in these areas than in suburban districts, which are less affected by high crime and poverty rates, overcrowding, or remote locations and relatively low salaries.

Teachers who are willing to relocate and who obtain licensure in more than one subject should have a distinct advantage in finding a job. With enrollments of minorities increasing, coupled with a shortage of minority teachers, efforts to recruit minority teachers should intensify.

Salaries

Salaries for vocational-technical teachers can vary widely based on work setting and subject taught. Those who work in public schools are generally paid on the same scale as other teachers in the same school system. According to the American Federation of Teachers, beginning teachers with a bachelor's degree earned an average of $31,704 in the 2003–2004 school year. The estimated average salary of all public elementary and secondary school teachers in the same year was $46,597. Private school teachers generally earn less than public school teachers, but they may be given other benefits, such as free or subsidized housing.

Earnings for vocational and technical education teachers in community colleges, voc-tech centers, and career academies vary widely by subject, academic credentials, experience, and region of the country. Part-time instructors usually receive few benefits.

Profiles

The firsthand accounts that follow in this chapter include a cosmetology instructor, an associate professor of English at a community college, an English instructor at a voc-tech institute, a basic skills instructor at a technical college, and a computer instructor at a voc-tech institute.

Barbara Hogue–Cosmetology Instructor

Barbara Hogue is a cosmetology instructor at the Arizona Academy of Beauty in Tucson, Arizona. She has been teaching for more than twenty years.

After earning a GED, Barbara completed eighteen hundred hours of cosmetology training to become a hairdresser. Once she became licensed by the state board of cosmetology, she worked for several years in licensed salons in Tucson. She later completed another six hundred hours of instructor's training and then was tested and licensed again by the state board of cosmetology as an instructor.

In addition, to maintain her accredited teacher status, she attends yearly seminars and upgrade classes on teaching techniques and the latest hair trends.

Getting Started

Barbara recalls wanting to be a hairdresser since childhood. But once she got to cosmetology school, she realized that her real desire was to teach, in addition to providing hair, skin, and nail care.

She found cosmetology training different from any other schooling she'd ever had and admired her teachers' patience and their willingness to make learning fun. Each day brought the opportunity to learn a new skill, with encouragement by the instructors along the way. It was this combination of active learning and strong teacher involvement that led Barbara to decide she wanted to teach.

In general, a student enrolls in cosmetology school as a student instructor and studies the teaching techniques established by the state and the federal governments, if that school offers student loans or grants. A student instructor learns how to give lectures, use visual aids, demonstrate techniques, give detailed step-by-step instruction, create tests, keep records, perform evaluations, and provide counseling.

Barbara was hired by the school as a full-time instructor after she passed the instructor's exam and received her license. She has worked for the school on and off for twenty years. Generally, a school will train instructors with the expectation of hiring them upon completion of their training and licensing.

What the Work Is Like

The Arizona Academy of Beauty operates year-round, with an ongoing enrollment. New classes start every week or two, with a rotating curriculum. The exception is the nail program, which starts every four weeks. This program does not rotate but is timed so new students will be "on the floor" by the time the senior students leave. This means that students acquire actual hands-on experience with the public by performing salon services for a reduced price. This is a common practice among cosmetology schools, most of which offer reduced prices on hair, skin, and nail care so that students can gain practical experience.

The two phases of the school are the freshman curriculum and the clinic floor. The first is a basic teaching and hands-on application (on mannequin heads for hair students or on plastic fingers for nail students). Once students understand the basic techniques, they are encouraged to bring in willing patrons (friends and relatives) so they can practice on live models.

After they have practiced and mastered the basic techniques, students advance to the clinic floor, where they work on paying customers. They take appointments, establish a regular clientele, learn customer service, and deal with challenging situations as they prepare to enter a salon atmosphere. This phase of the training takes many hours of time and is based on local requirements.

In addition to learning the mechanics of the trade, students must maintain an appropriate work ethic and understanding of procedures, all under the constant supervision of an instructor.

It is the instructor's responsibility to provide students with the skills, both manual and emotional, to handle a wide variety of services and people. The instructor is always fully responsible for each student and his or her performance and is obligated to the customer to provide him or her with satisfactory service.

This can prove challenging for an instructor. For example, occasionally a personality clash arises between student and client, or a client is unhappy with the service provided. Dealing with an angry or unhappy customer can be very defeating for some students, who lose confidence after such an encounter. It is up to the instructor to maintain a student's level of confidence and try to intervene in any situation where a client may be unhappy or impatient, while still smiling and offering the best solution for client and student.

Instructors must also be able to teach students who have learning disabilities. This requires the ability to work with those specific problems to evaluate the students and prepare them for state testing that will not offer much leeway for the disability.

The varied ages of the students, their life experiences, their attitudes, and the creative curve also present challenges. In some instances, the age difference between student and teacher can lead to miscommunication and frustration. Older students sometimes have difficulty accepting instruction from younger teachers, and some young students resist learning from their elders.

Fortunately, Barbara finds that after spending months together in the school environment, the students learn about each other and become very caring and helpful to each other. Many close friendships are formed among the students.

She feels that the teacher's job is to remain neutral, to try to reach all the students in a class, and to move easily among the students. For example, an instructor is responsible for twenty students plus the customers they are working on, at all different levels and phases of ability and instruction. It makes for a full day.

Barbara works full-time, from 8:00 A.M. to 5:00 P.M. Tuesday through Saturday, with an hour for lunch. Her typical day begins with a morning lecture, followed by the demonstration of a technique that students then practice while Barbara monitors their progress. Her job is to constantly teach, monitor, apply, and execute one technique after another, until the student is proficient and graduated from the program.

Barbara submits grades to the main office once a month and presents each student with an evaluation (report card). She is responsible for keeping a detailed file on each student and making sure they all have all the tools necessary to learn the basic applications. The school and state cosmetology board keep track of students' hours.

Upsides

Barbara most enjoys the opportunity to interact with different people and to help students and clients feel better about themselves. She feels it is an honor to be asked to do someone's hair for a special occasion, such as a wedding, graduation, prom night, or anniversary. Many hairdressers do the hair of the deceased, especially if the deceased was a client or relative of a client. "Students become close to you over time, and I have even had the privilege to teach a second generation," she says. "To be asked to share in other people's lives is a very special honor and one that hairdressers probably get to enjoy more often than any other profession."

Another reward for Barbara is meeting students who still remember her years after graduation and thank her for making a difference in their lives. She also genuinely enjoys watching self-confidence grow in students who face personal challenges.

She says, "I love watching how the young woman with several children, recently divorced and feeling as if she had no future, can blossom and start to feel confident in herself. If you get to be a part of this successful change, that is a reward. Or to watch a grandmother, who has always wanted to do this but has put it off all these many years because of her family and other responsibilities, to finally recognize her goal, and you helped to make it possible, that's a reward."

She appreciates getting to make a difference by giving someone a chance to recognize her own potential for success and by watching students turn negative life experiences into positive ones. In addition, the pay and benefits are generally good, and the ongoing variety of people and keeping abreast of new styling trends and teaching techniques prevents professional burnout.

Downsides

The negative part of the job, according to Barbara, is that it requires a high amount of energy on a daily basis. The job requires walking and standing and being on your feet for most of the shift. It's not uncommon for hairdressers to suffer from back trouble or leg and feet problems after years in the profession. Much of the stress can be avoided by the use of support hose, comfortable shoes, proper diet and proper rest, and not straining the body in odd positions when doing a service.

"There is a lot of paperwork for those schools that are accredited. And to keep a perky personality and a smile going can sometimes get hard to do at times as well. But the rewards far outweigh a long, tiring day."

Advice from a Professional

Barbara recommends becoming an instructor as an ideal job for someone who still enjoys the profession but is tired of working behind a chair. You will still be able to enjoy meeting clients, express your creativity, and make a difference in the lives of a lot of people. If you enjoy being busy and like variety in your daily activity, this career is a good choice because it is never boring.

She says, "Patience, the desire to help, the desire to give, and a fairly easygoing personality seem to be a plus as a teacher. It is a people profession, and enjoying people is a must. A desire to want a student to succeed is a plus as well."

Ellen Raphaeli—Associate Professor of English

Ellen Raphaeli recently retired as an associate professor of English at Northern Virginia Community College–Alexandria, where she taught for twenty-five years. In addition to this position, she volunteered her time tutoring in a women's prison, taught high school English, and taught English as a foreign language overseas.

She earned her A.B. in English with a secondary teacher's certification and her M.A. in English language and literature from the University of Michigan–Ann Arbor. She has also completed graduate work toward a doctorate.

Getting Started

Ellen says that she became a teacher by accident rather than intention. Her initial goal was to become a psychiatric social worker, which required a two-year graduate school program. She planned to teach for a year to save money for graduate school but found that she loved the work. As soon as she taught her first lesson as a student teacher, she knew this was what she wanted to do. Her first job after graduation was as a high school English teacher.

When she began her graduate program after teaching for a year, it was not in social work but in English language and literature. Since there was a strong possibility that her husband would get a job overseas, she also did some cognate work in teaching English as a foreign language.

The move abroad did happen, and Ellen taught an English reading class at a university and an English conversation class at an adult education center. She was anxious to get back to high school teaching when her family returned to the United States. However, by this time she was the mother of two toddlers, and she didn't want to work full-time.

The public school systems were not hiring part-time teachers, but they suggested that she try one of the area community colleges instead. She applied to two local community colleges and was offered a job at Northern Virginia Community College. She started with a composition course and then was offered a second course at the school's other campus. At the beginning of the next term, she was offered a third course to replace a teacher who had quit. By the spring quarter, she'd taught six courses as an adjunct faculty member, but she wasn't happy with the uncertainty of her part-time position. Adjunct faculty are subject to classes being offered or taken away at the last moment, so their positions are tenuous at best. In addition, the number of classes available to adjunct faculty at the community college had begun to dwindle.

By the end of that year, Ellen was ready for a full-time job, but she had difficulty finding one. Four-year schools, including extension facilities, would not hire her because she didn't have a Ph.D. The public schools had tight budgets and would rather hire a beginning teacher for less money than they would have to pay someone with a master's degree and experience.

Her luck suddenly changed just before the beginning of the fall semester when she was offered a full-time position at Northern Virginia Community College (NVCC) to replace a teacher who had resigned unexpectedly.

What the Work Is Like

Most full-time English faculty members teach fifteen hours a week, which is divided into five three-hour classes. At NVCC, all faculty members teach at least some composition classes and may additionally teach classes in literature, technical writing, business writing, creative writing, or other special electives approved by the State of Virginia for teaching at the freshman or sophomore level.

In addition to her fifteen hours of teaching, Ellen had ten office hours a week, five that followed a fixed schedule and five that were flexible. By her own choice, all of her classes were in the morning, so she would arrive on campus five days a week by about 7:45 for her 8:00 class and leave by about 12:30. Some of her colleagues prefer an afternoon or evening schedule; others like to squeeze all their teaching into four days a week. She returned to campus some afternoons for meetings or workshops or special projects. Overall, however, most of her working time was spent off campus preparing for classes or grading papers.

Early in her career at NVCC, Ellen kept track for several months of the time she was spending on the job, including teaching, keeping office hours, attending meetings, preparing for classes, and grading papers. She found that, on average, she spent seventy hours a week on work. Although she spends fewer hours on work now, she still doesn't have a forty-hour-a-week job.

Upsides

Ellen enjoyed the people she worked with, both students and colleagues. She says that this is fortunate, since the organization of the campus is a bit unusual. Unlike most colleges, there are no individual faculty offices. Instead, there are large office areas in which individual work spaces containing a desk, a bookcase or two, and a file cabinet are defined by five-foot-high dividers. The humanities division where Ellen worked houses about forty people, including faculty, administrative staff, and a division chair. She says, "We have no privacy, but we're never lonely."

One of the things Ellen liked most about her work is the potential to do good. While she acknowledges that she is not quite as fervently idealistic as she was when she started out, she always believed in what she was doing, helping students think more critically and communicate more effectively and, hopefully, exciting them about literature.

She also liked the flexibility of college teaching and the freedom to determine her own teaching schedule. A lot of this freedom came from her particular working environment; for example, she might not have had as much leeway working on a smaller campus or in a department where a larger group coveted the same schedule.

Downsides

The aspect of the job that Ellen liked least is grading. She says that grading is different from marking, which is the most tedious part of the work. But marking is, at least ideally, of profit to the students, who can learn something from the marks and comments on their papers.

Grading, on the other hand, involves evaluating whether work is competent (whether it merits a C), whether its quality exceeds what the average competent student produces (and merits a B or an A), or whether it is less than competent, average, college-level work (D or F). Ellen found putting that mark on the paper and, worse than that, assigning a grade for the semester, to be very stressful.

Students' perceptions of grades can add to the stress. Ellen points out that many students equate a C with failure, while others think of a grade as a fairly arbitrary measure that can be adjusted through persistent negotiation. Ellen says, "Students have told me that they "need a B"; otherwise, they will lose their scholarship, their student visa, their chance to transfer, their permission to continue to attend college, their family's respect. And some of what they tell me is probably true. I do not like hurting a student's feelings. When a student has put forth extraordinary effort during an academic term but has produced less-than-competent work, I have wished I could reward intentions. Of course, I cannot."

Advice from a Professional

Ellen recommends such adult education areas as distance learning or teaching the learning disabled or teaching English as a second language as excellent ways to supplement a career teaching a traditional subject at the community college level.

She advises you to remember that there are strong social dimensions to teaching, and she believes that you must really like other people and be marginally comfortable with yourself to be happy in the work. A teacher has to be able to talk to an angry student, for example, without becoming personally angry or defensive.

"Having a sense of humor is helpful, too. It is good to be able to laugh with a class, to lighten things up a bit when material is heavy, and it is good to be able to laugh at yourself rather than being absolutely mortified when you say or do something really foolish in front of twenty-five people from whom you wish respect. Finally, it's probably good not to say or do really foolish things very often."

Rosemary Day—English Instructor

Rosemary Day is an English instructor at Central New Mexico Community College (formerly Albuquerque Technical-Vocational

Institute), a community college/voc-tech institute. She earned her B.A. in English and M.A. in humanities at State University of New York (SUNY) at Buffalo and her Ph.D. in English at the University of New Mexico.

Getting Started

Rosemary's interest in teaching began in childhood, when her dolls played the role of her students. As she progressed through her own education, her goals changed—from wanting to teach kindergarten to fifth grade to junior high to senior high—until she got to college and realized that she wanted to have adult interaction with her students.

Her love of literature also began in childhood, so the question of her major was basically predetermined by the time she started college. When she began her doctoral studies, Rosemary was motivated by the need to communicate with people in a learning environment about the material she was reading, because reading in isolation left her desiring connection. She finds that teaching English fulfills both the love for written material and the need for human connection.

She got her first teaching job when she was living in a small town in northern New Mexico. She submitted a résumé at a university extension center and was hired on the spot to teach three evening college courses at the local high school. She taught there part-time for three years and then returned to school for her doctorate.

For her current job, she submitted her résumé and application at the community college and all area secondary schools, public and private. She taught two courses a semester at the university and was hired part-time at the voc-tech community college. The following summer she was hired for a full-time position.

What the Work Is Like

Rosemary's students have varied backgrounds. They come from different cultures and range from adolescents to senior citizens, single and married, many with children. Some are liberal arts college freshman and sophomores and vocational-technical students in a range of programs, such as computer programming and networking, accounting and business, design-drafting tech, health occupations, electronics-engineering tech, culinary arts, and legal assistance.

Rosemary teaches several courses, including required courses in composition, grammar, and technical communication, and elective literature courses. She teaches six courses in the fall and spring semesters and three during the summer term, for a total of fifteen a year. She needs to maintain this workload to meet her salary and benefits coverage but is able to teach more classes in the fall and spring terms so that her summer schedule is lighter.

She meets with students in eighteen hours of class time and six office hours, plus six official duty hours. Although this adds up to thirty hours, the additional preparation and grading work, plus technical communication assignments, add at least another twenty hours to each week. During the summer, she teaches twelve class-hours a week for twelve weeks and usually does some preparation for the fall term as well.

Rosemary is also required to attend meetings that cover departmental and disciplinary issues and those relevant to other activities. For example, she is involved with distance education, teaching a course on the Internet, various committees, and satellite televised conferences.

On a typical day, she usually runs into former and current students in hallways and likes to catch up and find out how they are doing. Her classes are quite active, since she moves around the room, trying to create interaction and discussion and helping students work in groups or individually. "I love the way the world drops away while I am in class; nothing else seems to exist," Rosemary says. "I am totally in the moment, which I find quite fulfilling. I often barely manage to eat or take a break on my long days, usually two a week. I visit with faculty in all disciplines in hallways, in my or their offices, by the microwave or the copy machine. That helps all of us stay current and not isolated in our disciplines. I really do like how full these days are, even though they can be tiring."

On her two shorter days, she teaches one or two classes and attends to grading and preparation work. Staff meetings are held on Friday.

Upsides

One of the things Rosemary likes most about her work is the fulfillment that comes with seeing students learning to believe in themselves. Some students at the community college level are unsure of their ability to handle college work, and their realization that they can do it is very rewarding.

Downsides

The only downside for Rosemary is that her teaching load requires her to spend half of every weekend grading papers, assignments, and exams. Teaching an online course adds to this situation, because online discussion rooms and e-mail interaction with students takes the time of two to three classes. Nevertheless, she does find distance education exciting and considers it an area of professional growth and learning for her as well as for her students.

Advice from a Professional

Rosemary suggests getting an M.A. or Ph.D. in English and being prepared to teach part-time in a tight job market. She also recommends keeping other options open, such as editing and technical writing. Although you may be required to take some courses in education, she feels that the most valuable how-to-teach learning occurs while you're actually teaching.

She advises keeping your résumé uncluttered and your cover letter to one page. Having been part of the review process, she knows that long accounts of your experience are not seen as relevant to the needs of voc-tech junior college students. Be sure that your résumé and letter are meticulously accurate because they will serve as examples of your own care and intelligence and as models of what you will teach and require of students.

Once you are hired, Rosemary advises that you remain open to feedback from students and ideas from other teachers. Embrace technological advances that can be used for classroom presentations, and be able to help students use the Internet wisely, particularly when conducting research.

Joy Davis—Basic Skills Instructor

Joy Davis is an instructor at Bessemer State Technical College, a community/technical college located in Bessemer, Alabama. She has a B.A. in English from the University of Montevallo in Alabama as well as an M.A. in higher education from the University of Alabama–Tuscaloosa.

Getting Started

When she graduated from college, Joy learned of an immediate opening at a small private school near her home. She applied for the job and was hired to teach English and Spanish. Although she gained teaching experience in this position, she found that teaching high school wasn't fulfilling.

A friend who was president of the local community college told her about an opening in the school's ABE center. Since she was interested in a change, Joy applied for the position and was subsequently hired.

What the Work Is Like

Joy teaches students from all majors. She explains that all Bessemer State students are required to take the ASSET placement test, and those who do not meet the designated score for their chosen major must enroll in developmental courses to try to improve their skills. For example, the designated reading score for a major area such as accounting might be 42. Any student who scores below 42 is enrolled in the basic reading course to try to improve reading skills. When skills improve, the student moves into the appropriate classes to complete the requirements for the degree. Students are allowed three semesters of remediation; those whose skills do not improve cannot move forward in the program.

Some students want a refresher course in reading or English. Others are returning to school after many years on a job. Sometimes these students feel they aren't ready for the required courses, so they enroll themselves in the developmental courses first.

Along with the basic skills courses in reading and English, Joy teaches voc-tech English to college students who want a certificate or diploma in a certain program such as welding, automotive, and nursing. And since Alabama state law requires that all students who complete a program in a community college have basic English and math courses, she teaches everything from basic reading to advanced English composition.

Teachers in the Alabama college system are required to work forty hours a week and must post office hours for student conferences. Joy typically reports at 7:30 A.M. for an 8:00 class. The 8:00 hour is set aside for developmental courses, such as basic writing.

Although developmental courses are counted as noncredit toward a degree, students are given institutional credit. An advantage is that students receive grades of S (satisfactory) or IP (in progress). These grades cannot impact their overall GPA scores, so students are never penalized for taking developmental courses. This is particularly important to Joy because the purpose of developmental courses is to allow students to acquire the skills they need without fear of failing. In addition, taking developmental course work entitles students to free tutoring services, mentoring, and, in some cases, additional financial aid.

Joy teaches three to four classes a day, grades an endless number of compositions, and tries to be available for conferences. When classes are over, she prepares for the next day's classes, making sure that she has the proper handouts, that she has graded all papers, and that she knows the material.

She describes most of her days as being fairly hectic, with students who need to see her, papers to grade, and additional paperwork to be completed. Since the school is federally funded, accurate rolls must be kept. Teachers call roll at every class meeting, drop students who miss a certain number of days, refer students for personal counseling, and then must keep up with all of the corresponding paperwork.

Upsides

Joy genuinely likes her working environment. Since she has been at the college for a long time, she has many friends there and enjoys the company of her colleagues.

She says, "The most rewarding part of my job is something that all teachers anticipate. It is the student who, almost in an instant, expresses understanding. When I am lecturing, I look at my students. I watch their expressions, hoping that I will see that one look that says, 'Oh, yes, I understand now.' When I see it, I breathe a sigh of relief.

"Many times, when I'm ready to give up, it's that look that keeps me going. So, more than anything else, the students keep me wanting to teach."

She also appreciates when a former student returns to express gratitude for the demands Joy imposes on her students. She expects a great deal from them, but she also gives a great deal in return, which she tells all of her classes at the beginning of each semester.

Joy describes the best part of her job as convincing students that they can succeed. Many of her students have started in developmental courses, finished them successfully, gone on to the required course work, and then achieved academic degrees with honors. Seeing these students accept their diplomas at the graduation ceremony is a source of tremendous gratitude to a dedicated teacher.

Downsides

Joy finds the worst part of her job to be the grading. Bessemer has fairly high standards, which sometimes make it difficult for her to help a student. She feels badly when a student fails, especially when the student has worked hard.

Another downside is the seemingly endless stream of paperwork, which includes forms for nearly every aspect of her job.

Advice from a Professional

"Teaching, at its easiest, is difficult," Joy says. "Teaching adults is even harder. Many of them must unlearn things they've been doing for years. To enjoy teaching, a person must be patient, compassionate, and willing to struggle to show students how a certain task is done correctly. Teaching is emotionally draining and physically demanding, but it is well worth the effort."

She feels that getting a master's degree is essential for anyone who wants to teach and recommends that prospective teachers should begin by teaching some part-time courses at local community or technical colleges. Teaching just one course can give you experience in being in command of a classroom full of adult learners. Tutoring and mentoring can also be vehicles for teaching experience.

Geraldine Mosher—Computer Instructor

Geraldine Mosher is a computer instructor with Central New Mexico Community College (formerly the Albuquerque Technical-Vocational Institute). She started her work there as a math and English tutor in the adult learning center and moved to the continuing education division a year and a half later. She is currently employed in the school's workforce training center.

She earned her B.A. from the University of Michigan–Ann Arbor, with a major in English and minors in chemistry and Spanish, and received her M.A. in education from Century University in Albuquerque, New Mexico, with a specialization in adult education. She has also taken numerous computer programming and training courses.

Getting Started

Although Geraldine always knew that she wanted to teach, she was disappointed with the discipline problems in the public school system and, therefore, did not go into the field of teaching. After finishing a career with the Foreign Service at embassies and consulates overseas, she realized that by teaching adults she would be much less likely to be working with people who didn't want to learn. While studying for her B.A., she took all of the required education courses to obtain a teaching certificate but lacked one semester of student teaching to qualify. She never did get it because she decided not to go into teaching at that time. Later, she got knowledge of computers from many continuing education courses and received her master's degree in adult education.

For her first job in this field, Geraldine applied to be an English and math tutor at Albuquerque Technical-Vocational Institute (TVI) and passed both the qualifying tests and the interview. While she was working there, a memo was circulated to all offices asking if any employees were interested in teaching continuing education classes. She responded that she was qualified to teach computer classes and was hired.

During the years that she worked for TVI's Continuing Education Division, Geraldine taught various classes including Computer Literacy, DOS, Quicken, Windows, and WordPerfect. When the continuing education division was discontinued, its duties were assumed by either the workforce training center (training for businesses) or the emeritus classes (training for senior citizens). In the workforce training center, she still teaches basically the same subjects: Introduction to Computers, Windows, Quicken, and WordPerfect.

What the Work Is Like

Geraldine finds that teaching adults through the continuing education division and workforce training center is a relatively easy and rewarding way to teach. First of all, she teaches only subjects she has agreed to and with which she is most comfortable. Second, she has relatively free rein as to how she teaches her classes, as long as the appropriate subject matter is covered in the allotted time.

The continuing education classes were usually twelve hours in length and were broken up into two Saturdays of six hours each (three in the morning and three in the afternoon). For weekday courses, the twelve hours were broken up into three sessions of four hours each on different days—for example, on three consecutive Monday afternoons.

Some continuing education students were sent to the classes by their employers; others were private individuals who wanted to learn and paid for the classes themselves.

The training sessions taught through the workforce training center might be a one-time full-day class (six to seven hours) or two-hour classes once a week for six to eight weeks. Since the workforce training center contracts with businesses to train their employees, most students are not there wholly voluntarily; raises or promotions may depend on their taking the classes.

Upsides

Geraldine finds that the greatest reward about teaching is the thrill when "the light bulb goes on"; when a student has struggled with some concept or exercise and then finally understands what you have been teaching.

Downsides

The part of the work that she dislikes the most are the administrative details, such as checking that the people attending match the names on the roster and also having the students fill out evaluation forms after every class.

Advice from a Professional

Geraldine feels that teaching in an adult education setting requires excellent knowledge of the subject matter more than a particular degree. She suggests being willing to start teaching at a low salary to prove yourself and be willing to go beyond the requirements of the job.

She recommends sitting in on other teachers' classes as a good way of learning because this will allow you to observe what works and what doesn't and what you like and dislike about the teaching methods.

"Most important," she concludes, "I believe that anyone who enters the teaching profession, whether teaching adults or children, should love to teach beyond all else."

A Final Thought

You can see that the vocational-technical and prebaccalaureate environments can accommodate teachers with many different skills and interests. Whether you have proven experience in a vocation that you would love to share with others or are a teacher who wishes to help students improve their skills to continue their education and better themselves, you may find a place in this field for your own rewarding career.

5

CAREER AND VOCATIONAL COUNSELING

THE PRIMARY GOAL of career and vocational counselors is to help people make informed choices about their education and career options. They explore and evaluate a client's education, training, work history, interests, skills, and personality traits, and arrange for aptitude and achievement tests to assist the client in making career decisions. They also help people to develop their job-search skills and assist clients in locating and applying for jobs. In addition, career counselors provide support to people who have lost jobs, are experiencing job-related stress, or have other career transition issues.

Career and vocational counseling is an integral part of adult education and key to its effective delivery. Good counseling programs help people to acquire the knowledge, skills, and experience necessary for them to identify options, explore alternatives, and succeed in society.

These counseling programs help to prepare workers for the changing workplace by teaching labor market changes and complexity of the workplace, improving decision-making skills, increasing self-esteem and motivation, building interpersonal effectiveness, maximizing career opportunities, improving employment marketability and opportunities, promoting effective job placement, and strengthening employer relations.

Areas of Specialization

Counseling is a wide-ranging field, with many options for those who are interested in helping others to make good choices in different areas of their lives.

High school counselors advise students in such areas as college majors, admission requirements, entrance exams, and financial aid, and on trade, technical school, and apprenticeship programs. They help students develop job finding skills such as résumé writing and interviewing techniques.

College career planning and placement counselors assist students and alumni with career development and job hunting techniques.

Elementary school counselors observe younger children during classroom and play activities and confer with their teachers and parents to evaluate the children's strengths, problems, or special needs. They also help students develop good study habits. They do less vocational and academic counseling than do secondary school counselors.

School counselors at all levels help students to understand and deal with their social, behavioral, and personal problems. They emphasize preventive and developmental counseling to provide students with the life skills needed to deal with problems before they occur and to enhance personal, social, and academic growth.

School counselors work with students individually, in small groups, or with entire classes. They consult and work with parents, teachers, school administrators, school psychologists, school nurses, and social workers.

Rehabilitation counselors help people deal with the personal, social, and vocational effects of their disabilities. They may counsel people with disabilities resulting from birth defects, illness or disease, accidents, or the stress of daily life. They evaluate the strengths and limitations of individuals, provide personal and vocational counseling, and may arrange for medical care, vocational training, and job placement.

Rehabilitation counselors interview individuals with disabilities and their families, evaluate school and medical reports, and confer and plan with physicians, psychologists, occupational therapists, and employers to determine the capabilities and skills of the individual. Conferring with the client, they develop a rehabilitation program, which may include training to help the person develop job skills. They also work toward increasing the client's capacity to live independently.

Career and employment counselors help individuals make wise career decisions. They explore and evaluate the client's education, training, work history, interests, skills, and personal traits, and may arrange for aptitude and achievement tests. They also work with individuals to develop job-seeking skills and assist clients in locating and applying for jobs.

Mental health counselors emphasize prevention and work with individuals and groups to promote optimum mental health. They help individuals deal with addictions and substance abuse, suicide, stress management, problems with self-esteem, issues associated with aging, job and career concerns, educational decisions, issues of mental and emotional health, and family, parenting, and marital problems. Mental health counselors work closely with other mental health specialists, including psychiatrists, psychologists, clinical social workers, psychiatric nurses, and school counselors.

Other counseling specialties include marriage and family, multicultural, or gerontological counseling. A *gerontological counselor* provides services to elderly persons who face changing lifestyles due to health problems and helps families cope with these changes. A *multicultural counselor* helps employers adjust to an increasingly diverse workforce.

Counselors provide special services, including alcohol and drug prevention programs and classes that teach students to handle conflicts without resorting to violence. They also try to identify cases of domestic abuse and other family problems that can affect a student's development. The tools they employ to evaluate and advise students include interviews, counseling sessions, and tests.

They may operate career information centers and career education programs.

Features of a Successful Counseling Program

The following have been identified by the U.S. Department of Education, Office of Vocational and Adult Education, as key components in successful career guidance and counseling programs:

- A planned sequence of activities and experiences to achieve specific competencies such as self-appraisal, decision making, goal setting, and career planning

- Accountability (outcome oriented) and program improvement (based on results of process/outcome evaluations)
- Qualified leadership
- Effective management needed to support comprehensive career guidance programs
- A team approach in which certified counselors are central to the program
- Adequate facilities, materials, and resources
- Strong professional development activities so counselors can regularly update their professional knowledge and skills
- Different approaches to deliver the program such as outreach, assessment, counseling, curriculum, program and job placement, follow-up, consultation, referral

Clients and Employment Settings

Anyone can benefit from career and vocational counseling. Career exploration can begin as early as the primary grades and continue through the secondary years. Career counselors also work with adults who fall into a variety of categories, including disabled, disadvantaged, minorities, non-native English speakers, the incarcerated, school dropouts, single parents, displaced homemakers, teachers, administrators, parents, and employers.

Vocational and educational counselors hold more than three hundred thousand jobs throughout Canada and the United States. Although they work primarily in school settings, additional opportunities exist in a wide variety of public and private establishments, including healthcare facilities; job training, career development, and vocational rehabilitation centers; social agencies; correctional institutions; and residential-care facilities, such as halfway houses for criminal offenders and group homes for children, the elderly, and the disabled.

Counselors also work in organizations engaged in community improvement and social change, drug and alcohol rehabilitation programs, and government agencies. A growing number of counselors are self-employed and work in group practices or private practice, due in part to new laws allowing counselors to be paid for their services by insurance companies and to the growing recognition that counselors are well-trained, effective professionals.

Opportunities for Career and Vocational Counselors

Through a variety of adult education programs and settings, counselors have many opportunities to participate in an education and training system that integrates academic and vocational education, that encourages individuals' participation in further education, and that allows counselors to renew their commitment to serving the most at-risk or disadvantaged of our society and to respond to business and economic development.

Counseling services are offered to adult students in a variety of programs such as ABE and GED prep programs, in welfare-to-work programs and school-to-work programs, and in all the settings mentioned earlier in this chapter.

Described here is just one example of an effective education program that utilizes career counselors to the fullest.

School-to-Work Opportunities

The School-to-Work Opportunities Act provides federal funds to the states to create comprehensive, coherent, statewide school-to-work opportunities systems that will prepare all individuals pursuing these opportunities for high-wage, high-skill jobs in today's competitive global marketplace. These systems contain three core elements:

1. Work-based learning experiences provide a structured environment in which students can learn transferable skills. Employers provide hands-on workplace opportunities for students to study more complex subject matter and workplace skills.

2. School-based learning opportunities include teachers working with students to simulate actual workplace activities and relationships through the use of team-oriented assignments and project development. In addition, educators work with business and industry to enhance the potential for their students' success in future workplace experiences.

3. Community-based and connecting activities help students use the knowledge and skills learned through other School-to-Work activities in settings that are connected to community service organizations. Volunteerism, citizenship, personal traits, as well as job-specific skills are reinforced through these activities; they also promote opportunities for minorities, women, and people who have disabilities.

Graduates of these systems receive a high school diploma or its equivalent in addition to a recognized skills certificate. Others receive a certificate or diploma indicating completion of one or two years of postsecondary education, while others enter a registered apprenticeship program or enroll in a college or university. The act emphasizes the importance of counselors in building successful school-to-work systems.

School-to-work opportunities are an exciting and dynamic way of learning geared toward preparing all youth for career employment, further education, and lifelong learning. Individuals are prepared for first jobs in high-skill, high-wage careers, achieve high academic and occupational standards, and are prepared for further postsecondary education and training.

School-to-Work Counselors

For career guidance and counseling to be effective, all counselors must become proactive in their efforts to help students and adults maximize their career opportunities. To accomplish this, counselors must:

• Help individuals acquire the knowledge, skill, and experience necessary to discover their interests, identify career options, explore alternatives, make choices, and succeed in society
• Work together with teachers, other school staff, students, parents, employers, and the community to influence students' learning and career development
• Help individuals make the connection between what they are learning and the broad range of career possibilities
• Form broad-based partnerships with all of those involved in helping individuals join the worlds of school and work
• Help students to master workplace basics
• Help students find appropriate employment, continue their education and/or training, and find other community services necessary for a successful transition from school to work
• Coordinate individuals' career plans and portfolios to position them to reach their career goals

Working Conditions

Most school counselors work the traditional nine- to ten-month school year with a two- to three-month vacation, although an increasing number are employed on ten-and-a-half-month or eleven-month contracts. They generally have the same hours as teachers. College career planning and placement counselors may work long and irregular hours during recruiting periods.

Rehabilitation and employment counselors generally work a standard forty-hour week.

Self-employed counselors and those working in mental health and community agencies often work evenings to counsel clients who work during the day.

Counselors must possess a lot of physical and emotional energy to handle the array of problems they address. Dealing with these day-to-day problems can cause stress and emotional burnout.

Because privacy is essential for confidential and frank discussions with clients, counselors usually have private offices.

Education and Training

Approximately eight out of ten counselors have master's degrees, with areas of study in such fields as college student affairs, elementary or secondary school counseling, education, gerontological counseling, marriage and family counseling, substance abuse counseling, rehabilitation counseling, agency or community counseling, clinical mental health counseling, counseling psychology, career counseling, or a related field.

All states and provinces require school counselors to hold a state school counseling certification and to have completed at least some graduate course work; most require the completion of a master's degree. Some states require public school counselors to have both counseling and teaching certificates and to have had some teaching experience before receiving certification.

For counselors based outside of schools, most states and provinces and the District of Columbia have some form of counselor licensure that governs their practice of counseling. Requirements typically include the completion of a master's degree in counseling, the accumulation of two years or three thousand hours of supervised clinical experience beyond the master's degree level, the passage of a state-recognized exam, adherence to ethical codes and standards, and the completion of annual continuing education requirements.

Counselors must be aware of educational and training requirements that are often very detailed and that vary by area and by counseling specialty. Prospective counselors should check with state and local governments, employers, and national voluntary certification organizations to determine which requirements apply.

As mentioned, you will typically need a master's degree to be licensed as a counselor; a bachelor's degree may qualify you to work as a counseling aide, rehabilitation aide, or social service worker. To work as a counselor in public employment, some states require you to have a master's degree; others accept a bachelor's degree with appropriate counseling courses.

You can usually find counselor education programs in colleges and universities in departments of education or psychology. Fields of study include college student affairs, elementary or secondary school counseling, education, gerontological counseling, marriage and family counseling, substance abuse counseling, rehabilitation counseling, agency or community counseling, clinical mental health counseling, psychological counseling, career counseling, and related fields.

Courses are grouped into eight core areas: human growth and development, social and cultural diversity, relationships, group work, career development, assessment, research and program evaluation, and professional identity. In an accredited master's degree program, you will be required to complete forty-eight to sixty semester hours of graduate study, including a period of supervised clinical experience in counseling.

Graduate programs in the United States and Canada in career, community, gerontological, mental health, school, student affairs, and marriage and family counseling are accredited by the Council for Accreditation of Counseling and Related Educational Programs (CACREP). While completion of a CACREP-accredited program is not necessary to become a counselor, it makes it easier to fulfill the requirements for state and provincial licensing. Another organization, the Council on Rehabilitation Education (CORE), accredits graduate programs in rehabilitation counseling. Accredited master's degree programs include a minimum of two years of full-time study, including six hundred hours of supervised clinical internship experience.

You may also elect to be nationally certified by the National Board for Certified Counselors, Inc. (NBCC) or the Canadian Counselling Association. To earn the NBCC general practice credential "National Certified Counselor," you must hold a master's degree with a concentration in counseling from a regionally accredited college or university; you must have at least two years of supervised field experience in a counseling setting (graduates from counselor education programs accredited by CACREP are exempted); you must provide two professional endorsements, with one being from a recent supervisor; and you must have a passing score on the NBCC's National Counselor Examination for Licensure and Certification (NCE). While this national certification is voluntary and is distinct from state licensing, in some states those who pass the national exam are exempted from taking a state certification exam. NBCC also offers specialty certifications in school, clinical mental health, and addiction counseling, which supplement the national certified counselor designation. These specialty certifications require passage of a supplemental exam. To maintain their certification, counselors retake and pass the NCE or complete one hundred credit hours of acceptable continuing education every five years.

To earn certification from the Canadian Counselling Association, you must be a member in good standing and possess a graduate degree in counseling or a related professional field from an educational institution that is recognized by the Association of Universities and Colleges of Canada. Requirements include graduate course work in counseling theory, a supervised counseling practicum with at least 120 hours of direct client contact, and course work in six additional areas. You must also provide two professional references and a valid criminal police-check report conducted within the last twelve months, and pay any appropriate administration fees.

Another organization, the Commission on Rehabilitation Counselor Certification, offers voluntary national certification for rehabilitation counselors in the United States and Canada. Some employers may require rehabilitation counselors to be nationally certified. To become certified, you usually must graduate from an accredited educational program, complete an internship, and pass a written examination. (Certification requirements vary according to an applicant's educational history. For example, employment experience will be required if you have a counseling degree in a specialty other than rehabilitation.) After meeting these requirements, you are designated "Certified Rehabilitation Counselor." To maintain certification, you must successfully retake the certification exam or complete one hundred credit hours of acceptable continuing education every five years.

Other counseling organizations also offer certification in particular counseling specialties. Usually, becoming certified is voluntary, but having certification may enhance your job prospects.

Some employers provide training for newly hired counselors; others may offer time off or provide help with tuition if it is needed to complete a graduate degree. You will be required to participate in graduate studies, workshops, and personal studies to maintain your certificates and licenses.

To work as a counselor, you should have a strong desire to help others and should possess the ability to inspire respect, trust, and confidence. You should be able to work independently or as part of a team and follow the code of ethics associated with your respective certifications and licenses.

Advancement Opportunities

Prospects for advancement vary by counseling field. School counselors can move to a larger school; become directors or supervisors of counseling, guidance, or pupil personnel services; or, usually with further graduate education, become counselor educators, counseling psychologists, or school administrators.

Some counselors choose to work for a state's or province's department of education. For marriage and family therapists, doctoral education in family therapy emphasizes the training of supervisors, teachers, researchers, and clinicians in the discipline.

Counselors can become supervisors or administrators in their agencies. Some move into research, consulting, or college teaching or go into private or group practice.

Job Outlook

The outlook for counselors is extremely good because overall employment of counselors is expected to grow between 18 and 26 percent through 2014. Although, as in any field, job prospects will vary with location and specialization, opportunities in general should also be very good because the number of job openings that arise should exceed the number of graduates coming out of counseling programs.

Employment of school counselors is expected to grow with increases in student enrollments at postsecondary schools and colleges and as more states require elementary schools to employ counselors. Expansion of the responsibilities of these counselors should also lead to increased opportunities. For example, counselors are becoming more involved in crisis and preventive counseling, helping students deal with issues ranging from drug and alcohol abuse to death and suicide.

Although schools and governments realize the value of counselors in helping their students to achieve academic success, budget constraints at every school level will dampen job growth of school counselors. However, federal grants and subsidies may help to offset tight budgets and allow the reduction in student-to-counselor ratios to continue. Job prospects should be more favorable in rural and inner-city schools.

Demand for vocational or career counselors is expected to grow as multiple job and career changes become common and as workers become increasingly aware of the counselors' services. In addition, state and local governments will employ growing numbers of counselors to assist beneficiaries of welfare programs who exhaust their eligibility and must find jobs. Other opportunities will arise in private job-training centers that provide training and other services to laid-off workers and others seeking to acquire new skills or new careers.

Salaries

Median annual earnings of educational, vocational, and school counselors in 2004 were $45,570. The majority earned between $34,530 and $58,400, while the lowest 10 percent earned less than $26,260, and the highest 10 percent earned more than $72,390. School counselors can earn additional income working summers in the school system or in other jobs.

Median annual earnings in the industries that employed the largest numbers of educational, vocational, and school counselors were as follows:

Elementary and secondary schools	$51,160
Junior colleges	$45,730
Colleges, universities, and professional schools	$39,110
Individual and family services	$30,240
Vocational rehabilitation services	$27,800

Self-employed counselors who have well-established practices, as well as counselors employed in group practices, generally have the highest earnings, as do some counselors working for private firms, such as insurance companies, corporations, and private rehabilitation companies.

Profiles

The profiles that follow here include a career counselor, a social worker/student advocate, and a GED counselor/test administrator.

Adele Fuller—Career Counselor

Adele Fuller works as a freelance career counselor for The Phoenix Project, a welfare-to-work program sponsored by the City of Albuquerque. She also works as an adult educator with corporate clients for Central New Mexico Community College (formerly Albuquerque TVI) in the workforce training division. In addition, she teaches writing seminars to small business owners through South-West Writers Workshop and gives career facilitation skills workshops to agency personnel working with the welfare population through the New Mexico Career Development Association.

She earned her B.A. in English literature from Gettysburg College in Pennsylvania and her M.A. in counseling from Montclair University in Montclair, New Jersey.

Getting Started

Adele says that she found her profession after many years of uncertainty and some frustration from being a stay-at-home mom. After years of volunteering for her church, children's schools, and community, she realized that she was drawn to groups—forming them, helping them grow, and watching how they worked. Deciding to focus on her interest in group dynamics, Adele returned to graduate school at the age of forty-one to pursue an M.A. in counseling, taking as many group dynamics courses as she could. When she got her degree at age forty-four, she still didn't have a specific career in mind. She knew she didn't want to work as a therapist with the mentally retarded, addicted, or developmentally handicapped populations, but she had no idea what she did want to do.

During this time Adele's marriage ended in divorce, and the difficult years of personal despair and fear made it clear who her population was—women in transition! She decided to look for a job at a community college that had some kind of outreach program for women and found one after six months of networking. She was hired not only to run the women's outreach program but to help with unemployed men and women referred to the program by the Job Training Partnership Act. Without quite realizing that it was happening, Adele found herself becoming a career counselor.

She counseled thousands of adults during her years at the college, working both with individuals and in group seminars that she designed and taught. The workshops showed Adele that in addition to good counseling skills, she also needed strong training and presentation skills, so she returned to the local community college and earned a Train-the-Trainer certificate within a year's time. This gave her the additional tools and confidence she needed to conceive, plan, design, and present a program to any population with professional competence. This combination of skills allowed Adele to teach not only career development issues, but other life issues, or "soft skills," as well.

This experience led to an interest in trying to gain corporate training experience, and over the next few years Adele worked for outplacement agencies and put together customized training programs for local corporations in need of skills training for their employees. She covered topics including communication skills, assertiveness training, networking skills, career development, and dealing with depression during the job search, among others.

Adele also became a member of the speaker's bureau for the college and joined Toastmasters International to develop her speaking skills. She found that public speaking is a natural offshoot of training and group facilitation and can be used as another way of educating an adult audience. Although she feels that public speaking is not essential to this field for those who are less extroverted, Adele sees it as a good way to enhance presentation skills and the ability to think on one's feet, which is what adult training is all about.

After six years, she relocated from New Jersey to Albuquerque, New Mexico. When she found that full-time jobs in her field were scarce, Adele decided to see if she could survive as a freelancer. Though she moved to Albuquerque as a complete stranger, she found that her networking skills got her fairly steady employment within a ten-month period. Believing that career counselors get to practice what they teach, Adele sees this as a chance to use all the tools she has acquired for her many clients.

What the Work Is Like

Adele teaches life skills to welfare clients, communications and basic reading to corporate employees, and career facilitation skills to agency personnel who work with the welfare population. She is also helping to design and implement a writing course intended to help small business owners market their businesses more successfully.

On a typical day, she presents life-skills material to a group of eight or nine clients from 8:00 A.M. to 1:00 P.M. The material includes discussion, written exercises, activities, and feedback sessions. After class, she may have a one-hour session with a member of the class and then a brief meeting with other instructors and staff members; teamwork is an essential part of her working environment. She spends about an hour in the evening preparing and reviewing notes for the next day's class.

Adele points out that adult educators work in two environments—the private arena, in which they design their curriculum, map out their lesson plans, and prepare for class; and the social arena, in which they perform as trainer/educator/entertainer. Because of the wide range of life experience they bring to class, adults are not taught like children. Rather, they are invited into an interactive dialogue in which their experience is affirmed as new information is added. They must be respected, encouraged, and engaged as well as taught, and the patronizing or inept trainer will not be tolerated very long. Adults vote with their feet—they simply walk out.

Adele says that while most trainer/educators enjoy the delivery more than the planning, they soon learn that thorough planning is essential to a good delivery, so equal energy must be given to both. She compares a trainer to a writer or an entertainer who is always collecting anecdotes, toys, and gimmicks to use as educational devices in the classroom. The best trainers have a spontaneous, down-to-earth style; an excellent sense of humor; and an ability to roll with the punches that their group delivers. Like most other things in life, this takes lots of practice.

As a freelancer, Adele typically spends about ten to fifteen hours a week in the classroom actually training. Another five hours are spent on preparation, along with five to ten hours for background meetings, networking with potential clients, phone calls, and wool-gathering for new ideas and materials. She says that no two days are alike, and she has great flexibility with her time. She finds the work well suited to a person who likes change, freedom, independence, and creativity.

Upsides

Adele enjoys working with a highly diverse population that includes all economic, ethnic, and educational levels. She loves the interaction with her students and believes that she learns as much as she teaches. As her classes progress, students share their lives, dreams, and struggles, and it is extremely rewarding to see adults not only absorb the material but make substantial changes and improvements in their lives as well. For Adele, this is the reward that goes beyond any paycheck. At the end of the day she feels that her work has mattered, and that makes everything else bearable.

Downsides

As a freelancer, work can be unpredictable and income often unsteady. In addition, Adele is responsible for carrying her own health insurance and retirement plan. Freedom versus security is a daily reality, and for those who find this uncomfortable, finding a steady job within an academic or corporate environment is another alternative. However, Adele points out that in addition to training and educating, in most cases you will also be responsible for administrative duties and other tasks that will inevitably comprise part of the job description.

Advice from a Professional

Adele says that if you love working in a group adult environment, enjoy motivating others toward knowledge and full living, and don't mind being in front of people facilitating the learning experience, then adult education/training might be for you.

Whether you enter the field through career counseling, as Adele did, or as an Adult Basic Education (ABE) teacher, you will find certain fundamental themes—a passion for learning as well as teaching, an ability to communicate orally, an interest in preparing and/or designing class materials, and a humility that accompanies every experience in front of an audience.

She stresses that adult educators must be part motivational personalities, part teachers, part clowns, and totally passionate about their work to be truly effective. The learning curve never stops but then neither do the rewards.

Adele recommends formal education that includes writing, presentation, and counseling/training skills. In fact, anything to do with human communication, from literature to psychology, is helpful, along with specific programs in counseling, education, and/or adult training. If you are teaching a technical subject, such as computers or mechanical skills, obviously expertise is needed in that field.

Although an M.A. in a related field, whether counseling, education, or business, is certainly helpful, it's not always necessary in certain areas. Additional activities that would help are studying public speaking skills, participating in and learning about group dynamics, improving writing skills, and networking diligently to find out what training subjects are needed in your community. People with extroverted personalities, an ability to communicate, a need for daily variety in the workplace, and a strong desire to help others may thrive in this field.

Cheryl-Lani Branson—Social Worker/Student Advocate

Cheryl-Lani Branson is a social worker/student advocate who has held several positions. Here she discusses her work in a welfare-to-work adult education program that is administered through Brooklyn College in Brooklyn, New York. Cheryl-Lani earned her B.A. in English literature from the University of Hartford in Connecticut, her M.A. in counselor education from Queens College of the City University of New York, and her master's in social work (M.S.W.) from Hunter College School of Social Work in New York City.

Getting Started

Cheryl-Lani decided to attend social work school to become an employee assistance counselor (EAP). Unfortunately, at the time she completed her degree, most companies using EAP were downsizing, as were most social work departments. Since counseling the unemployed is not that different from counseling the employed, Cheryl-Lani felt it was a natural transition from trying to find work in EAP to becoming a counselor in a welfare-to-work adult education program.

After her getting her M.A. in counseling, she interned at both a college and a vocational rehabilitation facility. When she returned to school for her master's in social work, she interned with displaced homemakers and at a psychiatric facility. These internships trained Cheryl-Lani in a broad range of skills that she could use with any client population. She also trained in group work while obtaining her M.S.W., which strengthened her abilities to teach coping skills to the adult education population.

For her job, she responded to an ad in the *New York Times* but didn't immediately get hired. The person who had been hired quit on the second day, and Cheryl-Lani was called. After being interviewed by five people, she was brought on board.

What the Work Is Like

The students Cheryl-Lani taught in this education-to-work program were mandated to attend by the Human Resources Department, the agency responsible for public assistance. The goal of the program is to help people get a job or to educate them toward getting a GED, or both.

The five-month program consists of in-class adult basic education or GED training and work-site experience. Students can extend the program beyond the five months if they are close to getting their GED.

When Cheryl-Lani joined the program, it had a multitude of long-standing problems and no one to solve them. The first thing she did was to spend several weeks assessing the client population and staff needs while counseling students in crisis right away. Within the first half hour of starting the job, she had a client who was suicidal. She also did some ongoing, longer-term counseling. For the most part, clients came on their own for counseling, but referrals also came from their adult ed teachers, from the public assistance staff, and from the support staff.

Often clients came to her after she had organized several workshops. Part of the job included locating speakers on a variety of topics that would educate the students, especially in the areas of physical and mental health. For instance, she arranged for speakers to address domestic violence, which is a huge problem with the program's client population. After the talks, several clients approached Cheryl-Lani to talk with her and get advice about handling their own domestic violence situations.

She also led a workshop during student orientation called Coping with Change, geared toward the many students who had spent years on public assistance. Coming into a full-time program was quite traumatic for them, so the workshop was an attempt to neutralize and normalize the stress they might be experiencing.

Advocacy was another component of Cheryl-Lani's work. This included trying to get clients to talk to legislators and register to vote so that they could have a voice in the public assistance laws. She was in a position to recommend policy and, more specifically, could recommend that a client be suspended from the program or be given an extension in order to work on their issues.

The bulk of her time was spent in assessment and referral of students. The vast majority of people who came to her needed a resource, or referral, for housing, legal, advocacy, health, learning disabilities, domestic violence, mental health, immigration, and substance abuse resources, to name a few.

Cheryl-Lani was able to arrange her own schedule and had a lot of freedom within the context of an eight-hour day. She never found the work boring, partly because much of her day was spent following up with resources and making arrangements, talking with staff, and looking at policy.

The job had many opportunities for both networking and leading. Cheryl-Lani relates an amusing story about the work atmosphere to demonstrate this point. When she was first hired, there was a refrigerator in her office. It turns out that part of the reason her predecessor left on her second day on the job was this very refrigerator, which she felt would lead to distractions. Cheryl-Lani, on the other hand, recognized that staff would need to come in for their food, which would be a great way to get to know people. She was right and got to meet her colleagues while demonstrating her flexibility.

Upsides

Cheryl-Lani enjoyed counseling the students, especially when she was able to show them how to be advocates for themselves. She also liked having the ability to structure her day, to assess which needs were the most important, and to work as part of a team with the student services staff.

She also enjoyed the opportunities to negotiate. These included negotiating with government employees to get clients exempt from the program to handle personal matters such as substance abuse or mental health issues; negotiating with Medicaid to get client services; negotiating with outside agencies to get speakers for the classes; and, in one case, negotiating with five different agencies to get a domestic violence victim the appropriate follow-up and care. Although negotiating usually took a lot of follow-up, she utilized one resource well and found that she could count on it in the future.

Downside

The only downside for Cheryl-Lani was the salary, which would have been higher if she worked in the private sector.

Advice from a Professional

Cheryl-Lani advises that the minimum preparation one should have for this type of work is a master's degree in some area of counseling and, preferably, a master's in social work.

She has found that specific training in case management and group work is also a great help. An excellent way to start is to volunteer, as Cheryl-Lani did, to see whether you enjoy the work, and then get formal training in counseling. Many organizations train their volunteers in specific techniques for working with clients.

She feels that a successful social worker/student advocate should be able to multitask and follow through with projects and ideas. A strong sense of compassion and connection to others as well as solid counseling skills are also vitally important.

Jean Campbell—GED Counselor/ GED Exam Administrator

Jean Campbell worked as a GED counselor with the school board of Broward County, Florida, for five years. She earned her B.A. in psychology at the University of Massachusetts, Boston, and her master's in education (M.Ed.) from Boston University.

Getting Started

While she was studying for her master's degree, Jean's goal was to practice mental health counseling and eventually get her doctorate in psychology. After she graduated, however, she moved from Boston to Florida, where she had no luck finding a mental health counseling job. An acquaintance told her about the GED program, and after an initial inquiry, Jean was interviewed and immediately hired.

The director was impressed with her education and had an immediate opening for a GED test administrator. Jean did the job for about six months and then was given more hours and moved into a GED counselor position. She worked for the school board for about five years and then moved into a mental health counseling position at a private agency.

What the Work Is Like

When Jean worked as a test administrator, the GED exam was given over a four-day period for several hours each morning. Working with another administrator, she seated the students, took their entrance tickets, and checked them against the roll they'd been given. She read them the directions, handed out the tests, timed the various sections of the tests, then collected the exams and turned them into the GED office. This was done each week with a new group of test takers.

Jean says that this job was "more than boring." Of the four or so hours she worked each morning, three and a half were spent quietly waiting for the time to pass. She spent the time reading the test questions to see if she remembered all the math and science she'd learned in high school. "I never understood why the job required you to have a master's degree," she says.

Her work got more interesting when she was given a counseling position. The county had three GED counselors, and Jean worked in the southern and central part of the county. The GED preparation centers were spread out all over the county and used a variety of facilities, such as a storefront in a strip mall, a room in a church, and the cafeteria of an old school. There were also centers in a prison and a half-way house.

Jean worked between twenty-five to thirty hours and set her own schedule. She tried to visit each center at least once a month, meeting with students at each location to discuss their progress and their goals for after completing the GED exam. Some planned to enroll in the community college, some planned to go into technical schools, and others had no real idea what they were going to do once they finished. It was Jean's job to help them define their interests and let them know what options were available to them.

Sometimes she worked with the students individually and sometimes in groups. Since they were all anxious about taking the GED exam, she tried to encourage them and focus on what they wanted to do after the exam. She always maintained the attitude that students would succeed. She feels that they appreciated her optimism and confidence in their abilities.

Upsides

The job allowed Jean a lot of freedom to determine her priorities and schedule. She feels that the students were all appreciative of the attention, and she enjoyed interacting with them.

Downsides

Unfortunately, there were too many centers to cover for Jean to be able to follow up with as many students as she would have liked. By the time the month rotation had come around, many had left the prep program, taken the exam, and moved on. In many cases, she never heard if they passed or went on to enroll in a community college or technical program, although some did come back to the center to let their instructor know how things had gone for them.

Another downside for Jean was the amount of driving the job required. She was always on the road and didn't have a regular office space. She worked out of her car, without a desk, which made it hard to keep papers and files and supplies.

Advice from a Professional

Jean finds that working with adults can be very rewarding, especially seeing how happy they are when they've accomplished something and have goals they can continue to work toward. However, she advises finding a full-time job that provides benefits, because taking a part-time job with an agency doesn't guarantee that you will be given a full-time position. "It often does happen in some settings," she says, "but check out first, before you commit yourself to a long wait, that it can happen in the setting you're thinking of working for."

A Final Thought

Counseling is a vast field that offers opportunities for a wide range of interests and skills. Helping adults to cope with important changes in their lives and careers and to make wise choices that will affect them and their families can be very rewarding work. Perhaps this valuable and important career is the right choice for you.

6

ADULT EDUCATION ADMINISTRATION

EVERY SCHOOL AND adult education program needs skilled administrators to provide direction and to oversee the day-to-day management of educational activities. Adult education administrators can work in any of the settings mentioned in earlier chapters, including schools, colleges and universities, technical institutes, businesses, correctional institutions, museums, and job-training and community service organizations.

Administrators are responsible for establishing a program's educational standards and goals and for ensuring that the staff upholds the policies and procedures needed to fulfill them. To this end, they develop academic programs, train and motivate teachers and other staff, and manage guidance and other student services. In addition, they administer record keeping, prepare budgets, and handle relations with parents, prospective students, employers, or others outside of education. They are ultimately responsible for the supervision of subordinate managers, management support staff, teachers, counselors, librarians, coaches, and others.

A small organization such as a community center may hire one administrator to handle all functions. In a university or large school system, responsibilities are divided among many administrators, each with a specific function.

Job Titles and Responsibilities

It takes a number of administration professionals to effectively run a school or adult education program.

Principals manage the secondary schools where many adult education and vocational-technical teachers are employed. They set the academic tone of the school, evaluating teachers and helping them to improve their skills. Visiting classrooms, reviewing instructional objectives, and evaluating learning materials are a large part of their day-to-day work. Principals meet with other administrators, students, parents, and representatives of community organizations. An important component of their work involves preparing budgets and reports on various subjects, including finances, health, and attendance, and overseeing the requisitioning and allocation of supplies. As school budgets become tighter, many principals are trying to encourage financial support for their schools from local businesses.

In response to a growing need for more involvement in students' emotional welfare, principals face the added responsibilities of providing additional services to students in need. With the help of adult education teachers and community organizations, principals may establish programs to combat the increase in crime, drug and alcohol abuse, and sexually transmitted disease among students.

Some schools address the increase in teenage pregnancies by offering parenting classes for students, and many have family resource centers and social service referrals.

Assistant principals aid in the overall administration of a school by programming student classes and coordinating transportation, custodial, cafeteria, and other support services. They usually handle discipline, social and recreational programs, and health and safety. They also may counsel students on personal, educational, or vocational matters.

Central office administrators manage public schools in school district central offices. This group includes those who direct subject area programs such as English, music, vocational education, special education, and mathematics. They plan and evaluate curriculums and teaching techniques and help teachers improve their skills and learn about new methods and materials. They oversee career counseling programs and testing, which measures students' abilities and helps place them in appropriate classes. Central office administrators also include directors of programs in adult education areas such as guidance and school psychology.

Academic deans working in colleges and universities develop budgets and academic policies and programs. They direct and coordinate activities of deans of individual colleges and chairpersons of academic departments.

Dean of continuing education is a position increasingly found at four-year and community colleges. This job may be classified under a variety of titles, such as *dean of career and technical education, dean of liberal studies and adult education,* or *dean of workforce development,* depending on the policies of the school. In addition to the regular duties of the dean's position, responsibilities focus on supervising vocational and technical divisions of the school, which may include training for business and government, adult basic education and ESL, and continuing education programs.

In response to the changing needs of adult students, the dean may also be responsible for designing and implementing new education options, such as online courses and flexible scheduling. Responsibilities also include collaborating with local businesses and industry to establish partnerships aimed at enhancing student opportunities.

Program coordinators who are responsible for the overall administration of adult education programs are generally employed by community colleges, technical schools, or community centers. They provide leadership, coordination, and assistance to teachers of adult education courses. Responsibilities include scheduling classes, hiring and evaluating instructors, and preparing budgets and reports. Depending on their employment setting, program coordinators may be involved in consultations with other administrators and community representatives and may work to develop programs in partnership with local and/or community businesses and other schools to enhance educational opportunities for their students.

College or university department heads or *chairpersons* are in charge of departments such as English, mathematics, or vocational training. They coordinate schedules of classes and teaching assignments; propose budgets; recruit, interview, and hire applicants for teaching positions; evaluate faculty members; and perform other administrative duties in addition to teaching.

Deans of students, or *directors of student services*, direct and coordinate admissions, foreign student services, and health and counseling services, as well as social, recreation, and related programs. In a small college, they may counsel students.

Registrars are custodians of students' education records. They register students, prepare student transcripts, evaluate academic records, oversee the preparation of college catalogs and schedules of classes, and analyze registration statistics.

Directors of admissions manage the process of recruiting and admitting students and work closely with financial aid directors, who oversee scholarship, fellowship, and loan programs.

Directors of student activities plan and arrange social, cultural, and recreational activities, assist student-run organizations, and may orient new students. Athletic directors plan and direct intramural and intercollegiate athletic activities, including publicity for athletic events, preparation of budgets, and supervision of coaches.

Working Conditions

Education administrators hold management positions with significant responsibility. Coordinating and interacting with faculty, parents, and students can be fast-paced and stimulating but can also be stressful and demanding. Some jobs include travel.

Principals and assistant principals whose main duty is discipline may find working with difficult students frustrating, but it is also challenging.

Most education administrators work more than forty hours a week, including many nights and weekends when school activities take place. Unlike teachers, they usually work year-round.

Employment Figures

Education administrators held about 442,000 jobs in 2004. More than half worked in elementary and secondary schools; the rest worked as preschool or child care administrators and postsecondary administrators. About two in ten worked for private education institutions, and six in ten worked for state and local governments, mainly in schools, colleges, and universities and departments of education. Fewer than 4 percent were self-employed. The rest worked in child day-care centers, religious organizations, job training centers, and businesses and other organizations that provided training for their employees.

Education and Training

Education administrator is not usually an entry-level job. Many administrators begin their careers as teachers or in related occupations and complete a master's or doctoral degree in administration or adult education. Because of the diversity of duties and levels of responsibility for administrators, their educational backgrounds and experience vary considerably.

Principals, assistant principals, central office administrators, academic deans, and program coordinators usually have taught or held another related job before moving into administration.

Advancement Opportunities

You may be able to move up to a senior administrator position from related staff jobs such as recruiter, program director, career placement counselor, or financial aid or admissions counselor. Earning a higher degree will generally improve your advancement opportunities, too.

To be considered for a position as education administrator, you must first prove yourself in your previous jobs. In evaluating candidates, supervisors look for determination, confidence, innovation, motivation, and managerial attributes, such as the ability to make sound decisions and to organize and coordinate work efficiently. Since much of an administrator's job involves interacting with others—from students to parents to teachers to the community at large—you must have strong interpersonal skills and be an effective communicator and motivator. Knowledge of management principles and practices, gained through work experience and formal education, is important.

To work in a public school as principal, assistant principal, or school administrator in a central office, you will generally need a master's degree in education administration or educational supervision and a state teaching certificate. Some principals and central office administrators have a doctorate in education administration.

You may be able to work as a program coordinator with a bachelor's degree and related experience. Many community centers and small schools weigh experience more heavily than education. A proven track record in teaching the subjects you will be responsible for supervising can go a long way.

Most private schools require a master's or doctoral degree, but a bachelor's degree may suffice because these schools are not subject to state certification requirements.

Academic deans usually have a doctorate in their specialty. Admissions, student affairs, and financial aid directors and registrars often start in related staff jobs with bachelor's degrees (any field usually is acceptable) and get advanced degrees in college student affairs or higher education administration. A Ph.D. or Ed.D. usually is necessary for top student affairs positions.

Computer literacy and a background in mathematics or statistics may be assets in admissions, records, and financial work.

Many colleges and universities offer advanced degrees in higher education administration, educational supervision, and college student affairs. Education administration degree programs include courses in school management, school law, school finance and budgeting, curriculum development and evaluation, research design and data analysis, community relations, politics in education, counseling, and leadership. The National Council for Accreditation of Teacher Education accredits programs.

Educational supervision degree programs include courses in supervision of instruction and curriculum, human relations, curriculum development, research, and advanced pedagogy courses.

Education administrators advance by moving up an administrative ladder or transferring to larger schools or systems. They also may become superintendent of a school system or president of an educational institution.

Job Outlook

The need for professionals to administer education programs will continue to grow as education and training take on greater importance in everyone's lives. Job opportunities for administrators in adult education should be excellent because of the ever-increasing number of adults who decide to pursue additional training for personal or career enhancement.

Since enrollments of students in secondary schools is expected to grow slowly over the next decade, the opportunities for administrators in these schools will be limited. However, the number of postsecondary school students is projected to grow more rapidly, creating significant demand for administrators at that level. Opportunities may vary by geographical area, as enrollments are expected to increase the fastest in the West and South, where the population is growing, and to decline or remain stable in the Northeast and the Midwest. School administrators also are in greater demand in rural and urban areas, where pay is generally lower than in the suburbs. Principals and assistant principals should have very favorable job prospects. A sharp increase in responsibilities in recent years has made the job more stressful, discouraging some teachers from taking positions in administration. Principals are held more accountable for the performance of students and teachers, while at the same time they are required to adhere to a growing number of government regulations. In addition, overcrowded classrooms, safety issues, budgetary concerns, and teacher shortages in some areas all create additional stress for administrators. Many teachers feel the higher pay of administrators is not high enough to compensate for the greater responsibilities.

Job prospects also are expected to be favorable for college and university administrators, particularly those seeking nonacademic positions. Public colleges and universities may be subject to funding shortfalls during economic downturns, but increasing enrollments will require that institutions replace the large numbers of administrators who retire and even hire additional administrators.

Of particular interest to those working in adult education, a significant portion of growth will stem from an increase in the private and for-profit segments of higher education, in schools that cater to working adults who might not ordinarily enroll in postsecondary education. These schools allow students to earn a degree, receive job-specific training, or update their skills in a convenient manner, such as through part-time programs or distance learning. As the number of these schools continues to grow, more administrators will be needed to oversee them.

Salaries

Salaries of education administrators depend on several factors, including the location and enrollment level in the school or school district. In 2004, secondary school administrators had median annual earnings of $74,190; postsecondary school administrators had median annual earnings of $68,340.

According to a survey of public schools conducted by the Educational Research Service, in the 2004–2005 school year high school principals had average salaries of $82,225, and assistant principals earned an average of $68,945.

The College and University Professional Association for Human Resources reports that median annual salaries for selected administrators in higher education in 2004–2005 were as follows:

Chief academic officer	$127,066

Academic Deans

Business	$120,460
Arts and sciences	$110,412
Graduate programs	$109,309
Education	$107,660
Nursing	$100,314
Health-related professions	$100,185
Continuing education	$91,800
Occupational or vocational education	$79,845

Other Administrators

Chief development officer	$114,400
Dean of students	$75,245
Director, student financial aid	$63,130

| Registrar | $61,953 |
| Director, student activities | $45,636 |

Benefits for education administrators are generally very good. Many get four or five weeks vacation every year and have generous health and pension packages. Many colleges and universities offer free tuition to employees and their families.

Profiles

The profiles that follow in this chapter include an education supervisor in a correctional facility, a computer learning center coordinator, and an assistant to the supervisor of adult education in a career and technology center.

Bernard LoPinto—Education Supervisor

Bernard LoPinto is an education supervisor at Mid-Orange Correctional Facility in Warwick, New York. He worked as a correctional educator for twelve years until his promotion to supervisor.

He earned his B.A. in English from St. John's University in New York City and his M.A. in reading from Hofstra University, Hempstead, New York. He also received a Certificate of Advanced Study in Education Administration from State University of New York at Cortland.

Getting Started

After teaching for seventeen years, Bernard was unemployed for a year, unable to find a job in a public school. As a last resort, he visited a New York State Employment Service office, determined to find a job in civil service. What he found was the listing for teachers in correctional facilities. He submitted his information and, within a few months, had a position at a nearby state facility.

He became interested in administration when he transferred to a newly opened facility. Having more experience than most of the other teachers did, Bernard became an unofficial trainer, particularly to those who seemed to be having problems with discipline and classroom management. When he saw how a teacher's life could significantly improve with a little instruction and how a better trained teacher could change an entire class, he decided that he wanted to teach teachers and started working toward administrative certification.

Aside from his experience as a public school teacher and graduate work, all of Bernard's training as a correctional educator has been on-the-job. He says, "I owe my knowledge to my colleagues who showed me the ropes, to the Department of Corrections training program, and to my students who broke me in without mercy."

While studying for his certificate in education administration at SUNY Cortland, he took the civil service test for education supervisor. After three years on the promotions list, he was hired as a supervisor by Mid-Hudson Correctional Facility.

What the Work Is Like

The students are adult male inmates who are enrolled by requirements of the New York State Department of Correctional Services. Inmates with reading and math levels below 5.0 on the Test of Adult Basic Education (TABE) are required to attend classes all day. Inmates scoring below 8.0 on the TABE are required to attend school half-days, and those scoring at 8.0 in reading and math are permitted to attend a voluntary GED class at night.

Bernard works a forty-hour week in an office that has been converted from an empty classroom. His day starts at 8:00 A.M., with inmates waiting to see him to help them find old GED records or to complain about their class or their teacher. He helps with education records but does not entertain complaints. Having learned that inmates can be quite manipulative, Bernard knows that the best way to deal with manipulation is to cut it off early.

On Monday mornings the staff runs the program committee, the body that makes sure every inmate in the facility is in a work or education program. At times there have been more than forty inmates on a waiting list for school; part of Bernard's job is to program as many as possible into some kind of class. As soon as an opening occurs in a class, he must fill it.

Upsides

Bernard appreciates having the authority to make changes necessary to running the school and feels that his presence has been a positive influence. Even small changes, such as forbidding wearing hats in the building and loitering in corridors, have improved the learning atmosphere.

Downsides

He regrets that the amount of time spent on management activities keeps him from devoting more time to being an instructional leader. For example, when a new GED exam was introduced, the New York State Education Department mandated new learning standards for adult education. Bernard implemented a staff development program to help his teachers meet these challenges within a few months.

Advice from a Professional

"More than anything else, education is what keeps people from returning to prison," Bernard says. "This knowledge is what motivates me most. We may be an individual's last chance to stay free and society's last chance to stay safe."

He advises that correctional educators need to be people managers who are able to recognize when someone is trying to manipulate them. At the same time, they must be sensitive to the educational and emotional needs of their students, many of whom are people to whom school has been the scene of many failures.

Bernard also recommends having some background in special education, since many of the students have undiagnosed learning disabilities, and there are few special education programs in correctional education.

Terry Thompson—Computer Learning Center Coordinator

Terry Thompson is the Computer Learning Center Coordinator at Independence, Inc., an independent living center in Lawrence, Kansas. He earned his B.A. in psychology from Purdue University in West Lafayette, Indiana.

Getting Started

Terry worked in psychology research after graduation, but the position was grant-funded and came to an end. He held a job in corporate computing for several years but continued to look for a more meaningful way to contribute to improving people's lives. He describes his present position as a perfect combination of his psychology training, computer knowledge, and desire to help others.

He applied for his job with a strong professional background and good communication skills but lacking some of the preferred, if not required, qualifications such as knowledge of computer-based assistive technologies for people with disabilities. He believes that his passion must have compensated for these deficits because he genuinely wanted the job and must have adequately conveyed this during his interview.

What the Work Is Like

Independence, Inc., receives funding to provide services to persons with physical, mental, and cognitive disabilities. The Computer Learning Center serves an average of fifty students per month. Most are adults of working age who state that improved job marketability is their primary reason for seeking computer training.

Independence, Inc., embodies the philosophy that governs all independent living centers—that people with disabilities are free to make their own choices. Each student declares a formal goal or goals upon entering a path of study and then receives whatever training may be appropriate for them to attain this goal. This allows for very individualized training. Some formal classes are provided, but much of the training is through students' working independently toward attaining the goals they've set. The only requirements are occasional prerequisites for certain intermediate or advanced lines of study.

Many students hope to find employment utilizing their new computer skills. Others may want to establish an e-mail account or to learn how to efficiently use the Internet.

As coordinator of the Computer Learning Center, Terry is responsible for all facets of program management, including student counseling, student goal planning and tracking, budget management, marketing, outreach, curriculum development, teaching, and staff hiring and supervision.

His days don't follow a particular routine. Instead, he makes a list of tasks that need to be done, prioritizes them, and outlines a proposed itinerary for the week. He has learned that it can be very difficult to adhere to a specific schedule, given problems that arise with students, the staff, and the computers. These problems often demand immediate attention, causing Terry to rearrange his priorities. The exceptions are scheduled tasks that involve other people, such as meetings with other agency staff members, meetings or presentations within the community, or previously scheduled appointments with students. He rarely cancels or reschedules appointments, preferring to delegate tasks to staff members so that he can keep his appointments.

The job descriptions of instructors in the computer lab are much more clearly defined. They assist students, either by teaching formal classes on particular topics or helping as needed with students who are studying independently. About 40 percent of Terry's job involves direct training similar to that provided by instructors; the remainder is spent on administrative duties.

Upsides

"I try not to dwell on what is satisfying or not satisfying about my work," Terry says. "When there is something to be done, I do it. Each moment brings new challenges, and each moment old challenges are met. If I take time to assess whether I like or dislike what I'm doing, then I'm not actually engaged in doing that task. So I don't think in this way."

If pressed to choose, however, he says that the entire job is satisfying because everything he does will directly benefit another person. Since he often knows and works closely with the recipients of these benefits, he is strengthened by watching them grow and by receiving their positive feedback. This is a level of satisfaction that he didn't experience in the corporate world.

Downsides

The distractions that interrupt his priorities can be frustrating if he doesn't keep in mind that they are part of the workday.

Some of Terry's co-workers express dissatisfaction with their salaries, since employees at not-for-profit social service agencies generally earn less than they would with the same skills in a for-profit environment. As someone who left the for-profit world for the nonprofit, Terry feels a greater appreciation for the intrinsic rewards associated with helping others.

Advice from a Professional

Terry feels that his line of work, computer training for persons with disabilities, is unique. Jobs are not always plentiful, but there are related positions that are more common, such as special education teachers or directors, occupational therapists, physical therapists, and jobs within disabled student services departments at colleges or universities.

He advises that most reasonable-paying jobs in this area will require administrative or managerial skills, and encourages getting as much supervisory and managerial experience as possible. He says, "If your knowledge base is diverse and if you are dedicated and hardworking, these qualities will be recognized, and if you are not promoted in your present position, you will at least be building your résumé. If a person hopes to earn a reasonable living in social services, he or she will have to develop these administrative qualities."

Debi Violante—Assistant to the Supervisor of Adult Education

Debi Violante is the assistant to the supervisor of adult education at the Lancaster County Career and Technology Center in Lancaster, Pennsylvania. She has gained her expertise through a variety of computer and continuing education courses.

Getting Started

Considering herself a lifelong learner, Debi first became interested in the Lancaster County Career and Technology Center as a prospective student. A phone call requesting more information about the courses offered led to a conversation about both how she was looking for a job and the supervisor was looking for an assistant.

Her training was 100 percent on the job. The adult education supervisor showed her the procedures for the tasks that must be completed each day and gave her an overview of the department's mission. She also spent a day training with someone who does the same job at one of the school's other campuses. She feels that her computer skills and previous customer service experience, combined with her ability to multitask, are her best qualifications.

What the Work Is Like

Many of the center's students have been downsized from long-held positions and want to develop new skills or update those they already have. Some are women working to update their skills in order to reenter the job market after raising children. Others are people interested in a career change or young adults without a college background who are interested in a career.

A typical day begins at 9:00 A.M., when Debi listens to voice-mail messages, gathers the necessary information, and returns the calls. Most of the calls are from people wanting more information about courses, and Debi spends a good amount of time describing the content, cost, hours, and benefits. The school has a printed catalog and a website that are available to anyone who is interested, but she has found that many people prefer to hear a friendly voice elaborate on the information. Calls of this nature come in throughout the day and can sometimes interrupt her other work, but since they are the lifeblood of the school, they take priority.

The ability to work on many different tasks at one time is essential because, in addition to contact with prospective students, there are currently enrolled students who will visit Debi for assistance. They may want to check the status of their student loan or other source of funding, or they might need the answer to a school scheduling question. Sometimes they stop by to ask her to donate blood for the school's health department or to buy a cake for a fund-raiser. She enjoys getting to know the students and being able to greet them by name.

As assistant to the supervisor of adult education, Debi must maintain a firm grasp of all school policies concerning classes, students, and payments. Any money that comes in or is paid out of the adult education budget must be accounted for promptly. She keeps complete records in a traditional filing system as well as in spreadsheet and database format on the computer.

The ability to prioritize is important, but it can be lost when the day takes on a different direction. As an assistant, Debi must be available to assist with whatever project her supervisor is working on (such as new classes starting or classes canceled due to under-enrollment, letters or grant proposals to be typed, brainstorming for new ways to handle the volumes of data needing to be stored, and so forth). She is sometimes frustrated by the inability to find enough quiet time to accomplish what was on her own "to do" list.

Due to budget restrictions, not every senior administrator has an assistant. For this reason, Debi is also responsible for helping the director of adult education, the director of curriculum for the school, and the tech-prep coordinator with various word processing assignments.

Upsides

The most rewarding part of the work for Debi is being able to help others. She says, "I once spoke to an older man who had lost a long-held job after his company downsized. He was interested in taking computer courses since he discovered how necessary they are in today's market.

"After talking for a few minutes, it was evident that this man was quite intelligent, and I learned that he had been quite successful in marketing before losing his job. Unfortunately, he had not been able to find a position comparable to the one he'd left; we speculated that his age may have had something to do with it. It broke my heart to learn that he was working in a department store and supplementing his income by drawing from his retirement money. He wasn't terribly excited about learning so many new skills to secure employment until I mentioned an organization that would pay for his education because he was a displaced worker. I could hear the hope in his voice, and by the way he thanked me, one would think that *I* had offered to pay for his schooling. Experiences such as this one are extremely gratifying and are not uncommon in adult education."

Downsides

Debi acknowledges that the downside of her job is the salary. As a widowed mother of three, she needs to earn enough money to support her family and has decided to look for other employment. She regrets having to make this decision because she appreciates the joys of helping adults improve their lives and enjoys interacting with her coworkers.

Also, all employees receive an annual cost of living raise, but there is no additional compensation for exemplary work.

Advice from a Professional

If you are interested in adult education administration work, Debi suggests that you examine your motives, financial needs, and personality. Patience is important, both with yourself and with the expectations of your superiors.

She advises that computer training is essential. In addition, you must be able to handle multiple priorities, pay attention to detail, and communicate effectively in person and on the phone.

A Final Thought

You have just read the accounts of three professionals who work in very different areas of adult education administration. You can see that this field has many opportunities for someone with the right combination of skills and interests. Perhaps you aspire to an administrative position that you can combine with your interest in helping adults make informed choices about their education alternatives. If so, you should be able to plan a career that can benefit you and all those you will help along the way.

ADDITIONAL RESOURCES

General

General information on adult education is available from the following sources.

American Association for Adult and Continuing Education
10111 Martin Luther King Jr. Hwy., Ste. 200C
Bowie, MD 20720
www.aaace.org

American Association for Vocational Instructional Materials
www.aavim.com

Association for Career and Technical Education
ACTE Headquarters
1410 King St.
Alexandria, VA 22314
www.acteonline.org

Canadian Association for the Study of Adult Education
260 Dalhousie St., Ste. 204
Ottawa, ON K1N 7E4
www.oise.utoronto.ca/CASAE

Council of Ministers of Education, Canada
www.cmec.ca

ERIC Clearinghouse on Adult, Career, and Vocational Education
www.eric.ed.gov

ERIC Clearinghouse on Rural Education and Small Schools
www.eric.ed.gov

U.S. Department of Education
Office of Vocational and Adult Education
www.ed.gov/about/offices/list/ovae

Continuing Education

For information on adult continuing education teaching positions, contact local government, state, and provincial adult education departments; schools, colleges, and universities; religious organizations; and the wide range of businesses that provide formal training for their employees.

Canadian Association for University Continuing Education
c/o Centre for Continuing and Distance Education
http://cauce-cpuc.ca

Council for Adult and Experiential Learning
55 E. Monroe St., Ste. 1930
Chicago, IL 60603
www.cael.org

Learning Resources Network
P.O. Box 9
River Falls, WI 54022
www.lern.org

University of Saskatchewan
464 Williams Bldg.
221 Cumberland Ave. North
Saskatoon, SK S7N 1M3
www.cauce-aepuc.ca

Adult Basic Education

Information on adult basic education programs and teacher certification requirements is available from state and provincial departments of education and local school districts as well as the following sources.

ABC CANADA Literacy Foundation
4211 Yonge St., Ste. 235
Toronto, ON M2P 2A9
www.abc-canada.org

Commission on Adult Basic Education
www.coabe.org

National Adult Literacy Database
Scovil House
703 Brunswick St.
Fredericton, NB E3B 1H8
www.nald.ca

National Center for Family Literacy
325 W. Main St., Ste. 300
Louisville, KY 40202-4237
www.familylit.org

National Center for the Study of Adult Learning and Literacy
NCSALL/World Education
44 Farnsworth St.
Boston, MA 02210
www.ncsall.net

National Institute for Literacy
1775 I St. NW, Ste. 730
Washington, DC 20006-2401
www.nifl.org

ProLiteracy Worldwide
1320 Jamesville Ave.
Syracuse, NY 13210
www.proliteracy.org

TESOL

For information on teaching English as a second language and job openings, contact:

Teachers of English to Speakers of Other Languages, Inc. (TESOL)
700 S. Washington St., Ste. 200
Alexandria, VA 22314
www.tesol.org

GED

For information on the GED, contact:

American Council on Education
1 Dupont Circle NW
Washington DC, 20036
www.acenet.edu

Vocational-Technical Education

For information about adult vocational-technical education teaching positions, you can contact state and provincial departments of vocational-technical education. Additional information is available from:

VTECS
1866 Southern La.
Decatur, GA 30033-4097
www.v-tecs.org

School Teaching

Information on licensure or certification requirements as well as approved teacher training institutions is available from local school systems and state and provincial departments of education.

For information on teachers' unions and education-related issues, contact:

American Federation of Teachers
555 New Jersey Ave. NW
Washington, DC 20001
www.aft.org

Canadian Education Association
317 Adelaide St. West, Ste. 300
Toronto, ON M5V 1P9
www.cea-ace.ca

Canadian Teachers' Federation
2490 Don Reid Dr.
Ottawa, ON K1H 1E1
www.ctf-fce.ca

National Education Association
1201 16th St. NW
Washington, DC 20036-3290
www.nea.org

For a list of institutions with accredited teacher education programs, contact:

National Council for Accreditation of Teacher Education
2010 Massachusetts Ave. NW, Ste. 500
Washington, DC 20036
www.ncate.org

For information on voluntary national teacher certification requirements, contact:

National Board for Professional Teaching Standards
1525 Wilson Blvd., Ste. 500
Arlington, VA 22209
www.nbpts.org

Counseling

For general information about counseling, as well as information on specialties such as school, college, mental health, rehabilitation, multicultural, career, marriage and family, and gerontological counseling, contact:

American Counseling Association
5999 Stevenson Ave.
Alexandria, VA 22304
www.counseling.org

Canadian Counselling Association
16 Concourse Gate, Ste. 600
Ottawa, ON K2E 7S8
www.ccacc.ca

For information on accredited counseling and related training programs, contact:

Council for Accreditation of Counseling and Related Educational
   Programs
American Counseling Association
5999 Stevenson Ave.
Alexandria, VA 22304
www.cacrep.org

For information on national certification requirements for counselors, contact:

National Board for Certified Counselors
3 Terrace Way, Ste. D
Greensboro, NC 27403
www.nbcc.org

For information on certification requirements for rehabilitation counselors and a list of accredited rehabilitation education programs, contact:

Council on Rehabilitation Counselor Certification
300 N. Martingale Rd., Ste. 460
Schaumburg, IL 60173
www.crcertification.com

State and provincial departments of education can supply information on colleges and universities that offer approved guidance and counseling training for state certification and licensure requirements. Employment service offices administered by states and provinces have information about job opportunities and entrance requirements for counselors.

Administration

For information on secondary school principals, assistant principals, and central office administrators, contact:

American Association of School Administrators
801 N. Quincy St., Ste. 700
Arlington, VA 22203-1730
www.aasa.org

American Federation of School Administrators
1101 17th St. NW Ste. 408
Washington, DC 20036
www.admin.org

Canadian Association of Principals
300 Earl Grey Dr., Ste. 220
Kanata, ON K2T 1C1
www.cdnprincipals.org

Canadian Association of School Administrators
1123 Glenashton Dr.
Oakville, ON L6H M51
www.casa-acas.ca

National Association of Secondary School Principals
1904 Association Dr.
Reston, VA 20191-1537
www.principals.org

For information on college student affairs administrators, contact:

National Association of Student Personnel Administrators
1875 Connecticut Ave. NW, Ste. 418
Washington, DC 20009
www.naspa.org

For information on collegiate registrars and admissions officers, contact:

American Association of Collegiate Registrars and Admissions
    Officers
1 Dupont Circle NW, Ste. 520
Washington, DC 20036
www.aacrao.org

Envisioning

the

New City

ENVISIONING THE NEW CITY

A Reader on Urban Ministry

Eleanor Scott Meyers, Editor

Westminster/John Knox Press

Louisville, Kentucky

Unless otherwise noted, scripture quotations are from the New Revised Standard Version of the Bible, copyright © 1989 by the Division of Christian Education of the National Council of the Churches of Christ in the U.S.A., and are used by permission.

Scripture quotations marked KJV are from the King James Version of the Bible.

Scripture quotations marked NEB are taken from *The New English Bible,* © The Delegates of the Oxford University Press and The Syndics of the Cambridge University Press, 1961, 1970. Used by permission.

Scripture quotations marked RSV are from the Revised Standard Version of the Bible and are copyrighted 1946, 1952, © 1971, 1973 by the Division of Christian Education of the National Council of the Churches of Christ in the U.S.A. and are used by permission.

Additional acknowledgments for previously published material may be found at the back of the book.

Book design by
Kristen Dietrich

First edition

Published by Westminster/John Knox Press
Louisville, Kentucky

This book is printed on acid-free paper that meets the American National Standards Institute Z39.48 standard. ∞

PRINTED IN THE UNITED STATES OF AMERICA

2 4 6 8 9 7 5 3 1

Library of Congress Cataloging-in-Publication Data

Envisioning the new city : a reader on urban ministry / Eleanor Scott
Meyers, editor. — 1st ed.
     p.   cm.
Includes bibliographical references.
ISBN 0-664-25315-6

   1. City churches.   2. City clergy.   I. Meyers, Eleanor Scott.
BV637.E58   1992
253'.09173'2—dc20   91-43041

This book is dedicated to all those who live and worship in faith communities in the cities of North America—especially those who choose to follow the vocation of ministry in these large metropolitan areas. My prayer is that their visions for our cities and for the churches might be emboldened and their spirits and labors renewed.

Where there is no vision, the people perish.

(Proverbs 29:18, KJV)

Contents

PART THREE:
PASTORAL DIMENSIONS OF MINISTRY IN CITIES

THE NEW SPIRITUALITY AND EMPOWERMENT

ETHICAL FOUNDATIONS FOR URBAN MINISTRY STRATEGIES

PART FOUR:
CASE STUDIES OF CONGREGATIONS
AND EDUCATION FOR MINISTRY

FOREWORD

The view of Los Angeles from a jet approaching the airport at dusk can be electrifying. Millions of lights blink and move, stretching out in every direction to create an urban icon whose sheer scope and scale can take the breath away. It is a sight no human being living in any previous century could have imagined, since neither air travel nor the megacity—two of the major artifacts of our time—had been invented yet. But once one is on the ground, the aesthetic thrill quickly dissipates. The icon dissolves into the hurry and confusion of big city edginess. Indeed, the German playwright Bertolt Brecht, who once lived briefly in the City of the Angels, remarked afterward that while he had heard that Shelley thought hell was a place rather like London, in his own opinion it was probably much more like Los Angeles.

The city as hell? Why then in America do so many of our cities bear names that suggest just the opposite? Providence and Philadelphia come to mind. Even those who founded the Big Apple wanted to start over with a "new" York that would presumably be an improvement on the old one. Some of the smaller communities in America go by names such as Unity (Maine), New Hope (Missouri), New Harmony (Florida), and Paradise (California). These places never became big cities. But they might have. The vision of a New Jerusalem has been a constant in the American imagination since the beginning.

Heaven and hell, dwelling place of angels and pesthole of fiends, aesthetic delight and eye-searing monstrosity: the contemporary city has had more contradictory things said about it than any other single feature of the modern world. It seems to attract our fondest hopes and our worst fears. It is both utopia and dystopia, the romantic object of songs about toddelin' towns and satin dolls, and the scene of our most terrifying fantasies. Is there anyone left who can look at the city unsentimentally, without using it as a projection screen for nostalgic

13

reveries or xenophobic terrors, and still love it? Is there anyone left who remembers that the city is its people, and that everything from its postcard skylines to its tunnels of electrical wiring should be there to help its people make it a *civitas*, a community of citizens?

I am thankful that the answer to all these questions is yes. The present book bears witness to my evidence. The writers assembled here are not content merely to observe the shining symmetry of the city from ten thousand feet. Nor do they trash it as a concrete jungle or a bonfire of vanities. Rather, they approach it as people who live and work in cities. They not only love the people with whom they share those cities, they have confidence in them, too. So let the reader be aware: This book is neither a dirge nor a paean. It neither wallows in the violence and discord of urban life nor passes by from a safe distance. It is an unblinking but affectionate book about cities and ministering in them. It conveys to the reader a spirit of both realism and hope.

It is *hope* that I want to underline most in these prefatory paragraphs. And it *is* hope, not optimism. Once familiar with the ominous statistics of out-of-control urban growth, especially in the poor world (as they are grimly catalogued in the essays by Clinton E. Stockwell and Valerie E. Russell), or who knows how desperate life in cities can be for people whose jobs are fleeing, whose schools are crumbling, and whose neighborhoods are reeling under the onslaught of crime and drugs (graphically etched by James P. Stobaugh, Elizabeth W. Markson, and Barbara Brown Taylor, among others), no one can possibly remain a mere optimist for very long. The writers of these fascinating and varied essays are not optimists. But they are hopeful, and their hopefulness springs from a resource that people without faith in God will find difficult to understand.

Whence comes this faith? It is not derived from some nifty new version of the teleological argument for God's existence. Rather it is based on their actual experience with the people of God in the cities of this world today. They know a Christ who walks the city streets again. And just as the streets of the city are concrete, so this book is blessedly lacking in generalizations. We don't just hear about "homeless people"; rather, we meet Jessie dragging along her Giant Eagle grocery bag. We see the faces and hear the voices of the people in several engaging case studies from various locales. We view the big town in the new light of Letty Russell's metaphor of the city as a battered woman. We hear about emerging new liturgies that strengthen and bind together the ordinary people who are the only real resource for building a new community in the urban wilderness. In short, what we get is a portrait suffused with a confidence both rightly modest and appropriately extravagant, both lyrical and matter-of-fact.

Maybe I was especially ripe for the message this collection brings. All my adult life, with the exception of a three-year exile in Ohio, I have lived in big cities. During my seminary years I worked one summer at a church in Stepney, which was then the Cockney dock section of London. The following year I was a chaplain at Temple University, a noisy commuter campus in north Philadelphia. For nearly a decade I lived with my family in Roxbury, a predominantly black section of Boston, working part-time in an inner-city ministry called the Blue Hill Christian Center. Just before that, we had lived for fifteen months in Berlin, almost within sight of the brick and barbed-wire Wall, at a time when that city seemed to be the stage on which the whole world was playing out its deadly war games. During the last decade I have lived for about a year in the largest megalopolis in the world, Mexico City. I've also visited Tokyo, Bombay, São Paulo and other non-Western cities. During these years I have been: mugged in Chicago, burglarized in Boston, nearly asphyxiated in Mexico City, interrogated by border guards in Berlin, and hopelessly lost in the Tokyo subway system. In retrospect, however, I do not regret a single day or night that I have spent in a city. It has been a lifelong love affair.

But it is precisely as a lover of cities that I have found myself so discouraged, so angry, and so in need of a hint of a new vision. I know exactly what Barbara Brown Taylor means when she says that "the city we love is also the city we sometimes hate." No one who lives, as I do, in the Boston area can fail to hear the truth in that statement. Bostonians live in a "city set upon a hill" which once liked to call itself "the Athens of America." But as racial animosity, ethnic divisions, fiscal parsimony, and class divisions have wreaked their havoc on the city I love, I admit that I have felt some hatred, and occasionally some fear. Consequently I drank this book in like a cool lemonade on a hot day. At last—brothers and sisters saying something sensible and credible about cities and about urban mission with none of the hand-wringing or crepe-hanging I'd gotten so tired of.

I also welcome this book because, frankly, as a teacher, I've been waiting for it. A year or two ago, in cooperation with a colleague who is a Puerto Rican Pentecostalist pastor, I offered a course on urban ministry that met at Twelfth Baptist Church, which the young Martin Luther King, Jr., had attended as a student. The class was made up of some thirty people who ranged from a Harvard Ph.D. candidate to an African American woman Pentecostal pastor who had never finished high school. There were Asian and Hispanic and African American and white students representing disparate denominations and ages, from storefront chapels, downtown churches, and teetering old inner-city white elephants. We all learned a lot from each other, and the class had a zestful, upbeat quality. But what book could we use? I looked, inquired, searched, but in vain. I could find nothing. Of course there were lots of books on urban mission that pictured the city as a great place to go fishing for souls. And there were piles of surveys and diagnoses. But where was the book we needed—one that combines sound biblical theology, careful social analysis, and concrete descriptions of what is actually going on? Where was that book?

Finally, I concluded that it just did not exist, at least not then. But it does now. Gentle reader, you now hold that book in your hands. As the voice said to Augustine in the garden, "Take up and read."

Harvey Cox

ACKNOWLEDGMENTS

It has been a privilege to edit this collection of writings by a group of wonderful, skilled, and committed folks. Their names appear in the table of contents. Others who have been importantly involved in the Urban Ministry Collective, but whose written work is not in this volume, include Wesley James, David Bos, Donna Bivens, Penny Mann, Katie Jeffress, and Gary Cuneen. I am indebted to each of these folk for their visions and for their work on this project.

A special word of appreciation goes to Susan Purdy. Susan has contributed much of the brains and the passion behind the editing tasks. Her careful and persistent work with the individual authors endeared her to us all. For me her clear questions, good advice, hard work, and new friendship provided many of the sustaining moments that made this book possible. In addition I want to thank Kathy Darrah and Margaret Kohl (in Kansas City) and Eileen Weston (in Berkeley) for their fine assistance with many aspects of this project and book.

I am grateful to the leadership of the Lilly Endowment and Saint Paul School of Theology, who together provided a grant that enabled the development of this working group of urban ministers and seminary professors. Those at the Endowment are to be commended for their understanding that the urban church and its ministry must be revitalized and for their courage to foster experimental programs to enable this important work. The administration and faculty of Saint Paul has always been committed to a vital ministry in the city. I am appreciative of their support for my work while I was in their midst.

I also want to thank my friend and colleague Bill McKinney, the dean of Hartford Seminary. When I first told him of my despair at trying to prepare students for ministry in urban churches without the necessary resources, Bill said, "Write and tell Lilly." That is where it all began.

17

Introduction:

Teaching Ourselves

the City

Eleanor Scott Meyers

Today the theory and practice of ministry is dramatically challenged by the conditions in our urban centers. The extent of homelessness alone represents a critical level of new political and economic realities that affect the church's development, maintenance, and mission. The need for new visions for our cities and our churches is the challenge addressed by this book.

New visions emerge out of urban ministry when worship and congregational life involves community-building, participation in the development of public policy, and a lively spirituality—one that builds on the already existing spirituality of the local people. The task of envisioning a new city through the ministry of city churches relies on a strategy of reconnecting with neighborhoods and people through networking and community organizing. New visions in our churches for cities and for ministry in turn rely on new educational programs for ministerial leadership. There are stories to tell in the cities; some are hard to hear, but others are filled with grace and hope!

National, regional, and local church leaders need to understand cities, and ministry in cities, in new ways. We have to understand what life is like in urban communities today. Within changing economic, political, and cultural situations, this is a difficult task. Soup kitchens and shelters for the homeless, which are major ministerial programs in many urban churches now, are important to the daily lives of thousands of individuals, but in the long run the ministry in the city calls for visions that move far beyond food pantries and temporary dormitories for a relative few of the vast sea of people in urgent need.

The mainline denominations built large churches and developed extensive ministries in the cities during the first half of the twentieth century. Today, due to population shifts among urban residents and the separation of races and classes within our churches, the traditionally white "old-line" urban congregations have lost most of their former members. Many churches have closed and the buildings have been sold to house restaurants or other businesses. Some mainline church buildings have been purchased by independent urban congregations that lack the economic base to build a church building. Many are merely boarded up and left to crumble for lack of anyone to pay the bills. Some remain open, serving a small, elite membership, by the philanthropy of a wealthy member. Others struggle on through a strategy of deferred building maintenance, low salaries, and financial support from the denomination. Today some of these struggling congregations are beginning to grow slightly again in numbers but not in financial stability.

In the spring of 1989, a group of urban missioners and seminary professors who were committed to the education of leadership for urban churches gathered to join in a dialogue about the dilemmas, challenges, and joys of urban ministry and to address the question of how to prepare future urban leaders for the church. Using a case-study method, we wrote and talked about our various settings for ministry: in urban neighborhoods, in churches, in seminary classrooms. Together we were seeking clearer perspectives on our work: We felt we needed a better definition for the church and ministry; we were looking for new visions for our cities.

Through this dialogue, across professional, class, racial, gender, geographical, educational, experiential, and disciplinary divisions, we came together to teach ourselves the city once again, to envision a new city in the midst of the current economic, political, and cultural breakdown in which we find ourselves in the United States today. Our work became a spiritual task, a soul-searching journey. Led by the story of the San Lucas congregation in Chicago, we committed ourselves to learn and work from the scriptural admonition that "where there is no vision, the people perish" (Proverbs 29:18, KJV).

Four issues rose to the top of our agenda.

There is a new context for urban ministry today. The existence of a "new poor" and of the many women and children (primarily people of color) and elderly living in poverty cannot be denied by the church. The increasingly poor and pluralistic city that must be home to the church is home to a multi-ethnic population frequently caught in the horizontal violence of cross-ethnic and interracial strife, poor-on-poor crime, and destruction of already poor and blighted neighborhoods. We see this horizontal violence as part of a result of increased vertical violence in the form of increasing institutionalized racism. Essays in this book document expanding structural racism and its effect on the lives of people in urban areas where the racial-ethnic poor are ghettoized.

In this new context, churches often become involved in direct services (homeless shelters, day-care centers, food kitchens, etc.) in an attempt to address the needs of those in the neighborhood victimized by the deteriorating social conditions. As a result of direct involvement with services, church members are able to gather an immense amount of data about their neighborhoods and those who live there, members as well as nonmembers. Relying on this access to information, congregations could develop ministries that affect public policy. However, this potential benefit of the service orientation of ministry in the city today is often left dormant because many in the church disagree or are unclear about the relationship of the church to the development and maintenance of public policy. New visions for the city, for ministry, and for spiritual well-being in urban neighborhoods are interwoven with public policy issues.

Another possible benefit of the new setting for urban ministry today is the increased opportunity for interdependent, cross-denominational work. At the grassroots level in our cities, many congregations and church leaders are involved in networks and coalitions to address the needs of the neighborhoods and their urban residents. Through such involvement, church leaders, both professional clergy and the laity, are learning new skills, including how to live in creative tension with indigenous community organizers. This development is having a key impact on the context, content, and form of ministry. These new alliances build on the fact that a goal of both the church's ministry and community-based organizing is empowerment of those who have been disenfranchised. Congregations that acknowledge, study, and act vigorously within this new context find themselves creating new visions and bringing healing ministries and new life to their neighbors, neighborhoods, and congregations.

New types of engagement are needed for ministry in the city. Urban ministry faces a spiritual problem at least as much as—and maybe more than—a material problem. Members of urban congregations need a lot of nourishment to be sustained in their environments. This calls for a new pastoral presence in the city, one quite different from the traditional clinical pastoral education (CPE) models. City churches need models for pastoral ministry built on new definitions of what pastors are and do.

Urban pastors must be *community* pastors, individuals trained in community-building, persons skilled in organizing, in neighborhood ritual leadership, and in cultural development. Pastors of city churches must understand leadership development and spiritual development for individuals and groups—and stay busy enabling the ministry of others in the congregation and in the neighborhood.

At the heart of the new community leadership work stand major life-or-death issues such as AIDS, drugs, unemployment, health care, violence, and loss. Through the ministry of the church, people are enabled to face their everyday world, their often pain-filled lives, in such a way that their lives today are made possible in light of new visions, current victories, and future hopes. Connections are created through worship and ritual as well as through programs of education and advocacy.

New hymns are written, new liturgies lived out—liturgies telling the story of life in the neighborhood and how it is like or not like the gospel story. New metaphors for God are discovered and invoked. The contemporary stories and definitions for God arise out of the deep spiritual soul of the city and its people. In today's cities we address a god who understands the feeling of powerlessness, a god fully acquainted with grief.

Today the urban minister's "believing foot" must be there! City pastors must retain a vision of what can be. Big-city congregations need to see their pastors walking in faith toward what should be while living in the not yet: "We've come this far by faith, Leaning on the Lord. . . . " A certain type of "urban" spirituality grows out of material poverty, a spirituality that often keeps folks keeping on. We in the church must challenge the notion that the theologies of poor people are always "false consciousness." Some are, but others are not; many are squarely facing the death-dealing reality of everyday life in the ghetto.

Our pastoral agendas must be action-filled. There is nothing new, really, about this imperative, for Christian faith has never touted the luxury of belief without putting one's faith to work. But it is time to act more boldly and in unison with others, including new partners in the city such as the homeless, the police, community organizers, residents of neighborhood projects, government leaders, prostitutes, social workers, former drug-abusers, the unemployed.

Evangelism, mission, church membership development, women's fellowship, and worship take on new faces, new strategies. Racism lies at the heart of these pastoral tasks and needs to be addressed. You cannot work in the city without working on racism. We need to be "saved" or liberated from our racism and learn to faithfully live out of newly found friendships across racial and ethnic lines if our congregations are to be places where people of all ethnic backgrounds in the neighborhood are full participants in ministry. This will be facilitated when white folk learn to follow the leadership of people of color and poor people in the neighborhood. These new structural relationships in leadership will help us all work on the tensions between race and class around which plans for ministry must be carefully articulated.

As one strategy for moving into mission, church-based community organizing can be a powerful pastoral tool. Careful organizing provides a basis for identifying the commonalities across racial, ethnic, gender, sexual preference, neighborhood, and faith groups. These pastoral models—organizing and ritual-building to promote the material and spiritual well-being of the neighborhood—address whole persons and whole communities. The integration of the spiritual and the material for ministry can come from the power of scripture, a scripture read by individuals and communities with their backs against the wall. Action developed in this way will give participants the power to endure because it is faithful to people in the full range of their lives.

As we develop public ministry rooted in faith, we must carefully analyze our goals: Whose language and values do they reflect? white, upper- and middle-class backgrounds? certain forms of education based in presuppositions that no longer pertain? As we begin, there is a need to be "pre-political" and "pre-strategic" and "pre-theological." That is, we must listen to the deep spirit moving within us and others and not assume that we know how to be the church in mission or how to worship or how to organize right now. It is a new day, and if we indeed seek a new city, we will have to watch, listen, pray, and think—in concert with others, including the poor—before we act. If we do this, we will develop a ministry that moves from the heart, not just out of the crisis.

Urban ministry requires new programs for ministerial education.   Seminaries, in order to prepare students for new ministries in the new context, need to develop closer ties between the classroom experience and the practice of ministry. Urban ministry in the new context requires a lay cadre of educated and educating "friends," second-career people, the retired, and underemployed youth, whose work is *blessed* and who are sent out on behalf of the church. Educational programs must move out beyond the seminary itself. The faculty and curriculum of seminaries need to address educational strategies concerning planned social change for laity as well as for students preparing for church employment. In educational programs that address ministry in context, those who teach and those who learn often switch roles, enabling new levels of education to occur.

Many issues that lie beyond the contextualization of educational processes need to be addressed. For instance, new recruitment of faculty and students to broaden the racial and gender mix of the community of learning and teaching is necessary, or attempts at curricular and programmatic reforms will fail.

Denominational leaders, seminary professors, and practitioners need to join together in an effort to develop new church school curricula addressing social issues and planned community change. In other words, professors and urban ministers together must contribute to the categories of discourse for the future generations of the church.

We now invite you to join our dialogue by reading and working with this book among the people with whom you share in ministry and teaching.

Part One

Cities and the Church:
Faith, the Bible, and Strategy

To carry out the work and wor- ship of the church in our cities of the 1990s, we face tough but surmountable challenges, and we need faithful passion, scrip- tural encouragement, and clear strategies. This is the word car- ried in the first set of essays in this reader. Donna Schaper's bold, inspirational writing about ministry illustrates how ur- ban dwellers, desperate for transformation, often find their ef- forts blocked by strategies and faith gone awry, or simply gone—captive to other interests. The work of the Sojourners Community reminds us that new cities may not be envisioned, that ministry may not be carried out, without being rooted deeply in the biblical tradition. Jim Wallis lays out the gospel imperative here: that the church must act in behalf of those ignored and oppressed by society. David Mann tells the story of one urban dweller and a congregation that fought city hall—and won—as part of a ministry to bring life to their marginalized community. In telling this story, he outlines how congregational leadership can be developed to exercise spiri- tual renewal of congregations. In Schaper's words, "God is alive in cities . . . liberation is on its way."

E.S.M.

BRICKS WITHOUT STRAW:

MINISTRY IN THE CITY

Donna Schaper

One of the most important rhythms of scripture is that of Jesus speaking to the disciples: "You have heard it said unto you . . . but I say instead . . . ." At this point everyone is surprised. Instead of full barns, full souls (Luke 12:14–21). Rather than dutiful fasts, the poor feasting (Luke 14:12–14). You know the pattern. You have heard the rhythm. It is all part of Jesus' begging that we open our eyes, cease denial, and understand the power of God come to earth to set the captives free. The rhythm is Christ against culture, proclaiming transforming vision even now available for those who will open their eyes.

Ministry in cities is desperate for these transformations. We are stuck in old, ordinary ways. Christ may be battling culture, but we are not. We are instead circling around in Egypt, obeying the slick Pharaohs, forgetting that God is calling us. We exhaust ourselves in these circles, forgetting the Jerusalems that might yet be, so weary are we of making bricks without straw.

Most of our typewriters don't work, our roofs are leaking, our neighbors hungry, our congregations aging poorly and believing only barely. We spend our days in private, circling in the Egypts of our own self-consciousness. The luxury of the future has disappeared. We spend our days often alone, and if not alone, bereft of the graces of communities to form words and use hands to hold each other up. God's glories do break through, even in Egypt, and a hymn or an action or a friend or a story or a memory touches us just frequently enough to allow us to go on. We still partially believe that we shall overcome, despite the unraised budgets that suggest otherwise. As Rosemary Ruether puts it, we are linguistically deprived and eucharistically starving.[1] There is little happiness in ministry in cities. We know how deeply stuck we are in the mud of Egypt, and we don't know our way out. Yet.

Here I examine six of the "stuck places" and wonder aloud about some of the escapes I dimly see. My experience has forced me to take the captivity, and my consent to the captivity, very seriously. That's why a problem-solution format is not honest or possible for me. Instead, I see layers of blindness and denials, some conscious and some not. Obviously, the solution is to open our eyes, to help each other see. But even the best of awakenings may not get us out of Egypt. We would still have to walk to the exits, step by heavy step, into the unknowns of the promises of God. We would have to trust each other. We'd have to act on what we saw; we'd have to agree on the escapes, because not one of us can make a way out of Egypt alone. The captivity is not private, even if most of the solutions proposed are. So my thoughts set down here are just words with all their limitations. I offer them as routes out of bondage, acknowledging that they may also be detours.

We are stuck. We believe that what we have heard said is true instead of knowing in our bellies that it is not. Culture becomes our Christ, and the scriptural rhythm passes us by. What are these common captivities? First, we apply private solutions to public problems. Second, we think in short-range rather than long-range terms. Third, we are too much the properties of our own awesome individualities; we too little belong to each other or to communities. Fourth, we have lost our biblical languages because of private, individual captivities and use instead the foreign languages of psychology and management. Fifth, we govern ourselves bureaucratically rather than democratically, and sixth, we think of the poor as our burden rather than our blessing.

These six snarls blossom into sin as we see their consequences on our own lives, on other people, and on the land. They wrap around each other in mutually reinforcing ways and become systematized by their incessant interaction, causing oppression and injustice to flourish. They become our value system. We consent to injustice by voting for these values; we vote for them because we see no other way. We make bricks without straw, seeking justice prior to transformation, seeking to worship both God and the mammon of cultural instruction.

Here I must be confessional. I know these mistaken attempts to build bricks without straw because I have snarled myself in each with some frequency. I pass too much of my existence in the short-term, individual, fearful prison cells of bricks without straw. I confess my frequent consent to Egypt in my values. I see that same sin in many of my colleagues. The process of leaving Egypt begins in confession and ends in liberation. Grace and forgiveness are the methods God uses to restore the ancient cities and us within them.

Private Solutions to Public Problems

There is a mythology of the private that informs our simplest behavior. If a whale gets stuck in the ice, donate money to the crusade to save it. Don't worry about the thousands of whales who are dying from eating the garbage that you put in their water. If you are stuck in a traffic jam on the expressway, "manage" your frustration with a new breathing "technique." Don't ask about automobiles and their power to deplete resources while keeping the interest in public transportation low. Consider the private over the public. This value is so widespread in this culture that I actually heard a renowned philosopher suggest to a group of architects whom he was trying to recruit for peace work that they give up two hours a week for peace—the rest of their time would still be theirs for selfish pursuits.

The primacy of privacy in the culture affects ministry in significant ways. It loads the minister[2] with self-importance, making him or her think that he or she is the only person considering the whole. This fatigues those who minister, because we see enemies instead of partners. Constantly we think we have to make the pitch to congregants or local officials be "what's in it for them." This pitch violates the rhythm of the gospel and cuts us off from our power. It also causes us to make false promises that somehow we will be able to give people what they want rather than engage them in the struggle of transformation which leads to Egypt-leaving.

In cities, ministries are even more plagued by privatism. The very term, "urban ministries" tells all. We immediately flag the otherness of our ministry by calling it by its location. People in cities—many or most of them racial-ethnic—don't call their ministry "urban." They live in cities; they make their home there. Why state the obvious? It is white denominations that use the term "urban ministry," and we use it because we want people to know that we don't belong there, in cities, with them, with the others.

The most common critique of white laypeople against their traveling ministers, those who leave "home" to relate to others, is that they are out of their place. That language has its ancestry in the old story about how the minister's proper place is in the stands with the women and children, watching the game on the field while the real men are playing. The image deserves a careful unpacking. The sexism is intriguing. But the line drawn between private and public, between domestic life and economic or political life, and between the minister's proper and improper place is quite telling. What the real men do on the field is not the proper province of the clergy. This complaint against religion knows no geography; ministers in cities, suburbs, and towns hear the same thing. "I don't come to church to hear about the world's problems. I come to church for comfort, for help in living my private life." In the way that Egypt is a mind-set, privacy is one of its oppressions. Until we break loose of the hold that privatism has on us and transcend ourselves, our ministries will resemble the story of those frustrated folk in Egypt, who kept trying to make bricks but, having no straw, failed to accomplish even this simple task.

Short-Term Versus Long-Term Solutions

A similar pattern emerges when we note how many ministries in cities spend their precious time taking care of victims. The short-term is mightily preferred over the long-term. We all give lip service to the misery of this pattern, but few find their way out of it. As a society, we seem to be intent on making more victims, whether through poorly conceived welfare policies or the number of social "workers" per square foot. Furthermore, pathos produces fuller pocketbooks than transformation. The more "clients" our kitchens can serve, the more our salaries are justified. The more transformation of victims into agents, trained and willing to work for long-term goals, the less likely the salary.

The story is told of a missionary who spent every day down on the banks of the river, bandaging the wounded who came to her. Finally one day she had had enough and walked to the headwaters. There she found out who was hurting her people and camped, determined to stop them.

Ministers in cities would do well to follow her example. We can be quite eloquent about the privatism that is hurting our people—about its formation into racism and sexism and classism, about its almost automatic consequences of poverty and humiliation and bad health and bad schools, each of which reproduces itself across the generations—incorporating these ideas into a memorable Sunday-morning sermon. Eloquent action is much harder to find. Upstream ministry, although rare, can be beautiful. Upstream, clients and victims turn into members of congregations and community organizations. Time is taken to nourish leadership, to feed it the good bread of scripture and community, of hope and promise, to educate it and ourselves to the real sources of oppression. In upstream ministry, soup kitchens become training centers, shelters become places of education and organization, mental health centers become sites of anger formation, welfare offices become places to protest. Communities don't need "workers"; they need work.

It is difficult to deny the hard truth that we are all in need of needy people, that the economic reality is systematized to need them to stay in need and that ministry is the tail that wags the dog by feeling good about its chance to "serve"—and sometimes keeps the needy *needy*. Again we are the captives of mammon, the fully-owned subsidiary of cultural values known as the quick, the doable, the pragmatic, the microwave.

Nobody really wants to come to a discussion group on racism at the church because everybody knows it would take more than six sessions. "You have heard it said" that goodness resides in the quick and the easy, but "I say unto you" that many seeds will be planted before any will grow. Scripture entices us to a developmental notion of the human being, to an understanding that conversion, turning toward God and away from culture, is a once-in-a-lifetime choice that takes a lifetime to do. There is nothing quick and easy about the spirit's development within us or our people.

Formation of Communities

One way out of stuck places is the joyous and arduous formation of communities. A white woman reported to the pastor of a nearby church that she was giving her infant son a shot of liquor in his bottle every night so he would go to sleep so she could go to sleep in order to stay awake at her factory job the next day. She was working to pay off medical bills for the premature birth of this child, born by caesarean section. The bill was eight thousand dollars. She had no insurance and no husband. She shared a hospital room with a sixteen-year-old African American woman who was delivering her third child at the expense of the state. The white woman was angry, not at the health care or insurance system, or even at the absent father of her child, but instead at her roommate. Both of these women are part of the public to whom we must minister. One woman was poor enough to qualify for assistance; the other was not. The pastor spent half an hour "counseling" the woman who had actually come to him because she was afraid of her own anger, having picked a fight with an African American woman in a bar the previous weekend. She wanted spiritual help, help in understanding the caughtness and stuckness of her life, which might prevent her from passing on to her child her sense of stuckness coupled with unbridled anger. Here was a candidate for a values transformation who got instead a quick, short-term bit of counseling.

The minister and his congregation missed an opportunity. They missed helping this woman see her way into a transformed and less hostile set of values, and worse, from the vantage point of community-building, they missed a chance to develop a new caretaker, to heal a wounded person so that she might join forces in healing others. If she had been invited to worship, to become a part of a community that, like her, was looking for freedom from the anger of living in Egypt, the community might have been enriched by her transformation. She could easily have become a leader and a care-giver in that congregation. Instead she was sent away empty, eating bread that does not satisfy, being starved of the only nourishment that could have saved her, the nourishment of a thriving community of Egypt-leavers.

The building of communities takes place when we engage in "upstream" ministries, ministries that address public issues and break down social barriers between groups, ministries that recognize the role of the church in community organizing and acknowledge that the most constructive relationship between the one who needs and the one who would serve is that of partnership.

Professional and Biblical Languages

If one word can embody the problem within the ministry model most prevalent in religious communities today, that word is *referral*. At least the woman whose story is described above got half an hour; more often she would be referred to someone else. Referral is the refusal of the stranger and the handing of him or her back to the "experts." Rather than acting within our healing capacities, we refer to the falsehoods of professional care. Seminaries train pastors in referral; denominations sponsor frequent workshops on the subject. Thus most parishioners will back off if asked to call on a troubled family or a drug addict or a suicidal person, insisting they don't know what to say. Is human suffering that much a mystery? Do we really assume that the experts know what to say? Here we see the cycle that disempowers communities. Like an unused muscle, communities that refuse to care for their own and for the stranger become flaccid. The power to care is given away, and when that happens, communities voluntarily consent to make-believe warmth and intimacy or poignant calls for prayers at the "concerns time" in the service.

Congregations that choose to identify with the suffering around them don't send the strangers away. They welcome them into their midst; if there is little suffering evident in their own congregation, they travel to Central America or else-where, and there they make friends with trouble. A number of congregations retain vitality precisely because they do enter the difficulties of their members and neighbors with hope, be-cause they do keep the experts in their proper, secondary place. There is nothing wrong with professional care-givers. It is their habit of substituting themselves for communities that is wrong. It is our abuse of their service that is wrong. The com-bination is lethal. The languages of psychology and the Bible are not opposed; they can coexist quite meaningfully. The problem is the abandonment of the biblical language and para-digm in favor of the victim-of-sickness paradigm. The conver-sation between the two is essential for public ministries these days.

A simple chart can show how congregations could be differ-ent were they to do their ministry at the gates of Egypt rather than from its centers. I refer to such congregations as sites of public rather than private ministries.

Public	Private
Upstream, developing community	Downstream, aiding victims
Focus on parish and beyond	Focus on members
Preventive community-building	Medical crisis methods
Communities of partners	Communities of clients
Conflict anticipated	Conflict minimized
Power in flux	Power bases solidified
Biblical, developmental language	Social scientific language
Democratically governed	Bureaucratically governed

The position of any person in a public congregation is that of learner and participant. Ministers and congregants are equally bound by Egypt, equally in need of the liberation the exits pro-vide, equally alert to the upstream nature of their work. Both the short-term and the private are understood as mammon, as addictions, if you will, as fixes from which we need freedom.

Public congregations resemble Alcoholics Anonymous more than any other American institution. (It is no accident that church basements fill on weekday evenings and sanctuaries do not on Sunday mornings.) Here we have confessed sinners, people aware of their captivity, lay authority grounded in the power of its own healing, an absolute dependence on the power of God. Possibly the *communidades de base* are like this in their respect for learning, their need to stay close to scripture, their understanding of transformation as crucial. Certainly women's consciousness-raising groups were, and are, like public ministry sites. There the rhythm has always been: "I thought this is what it meant to be a woman, and now I find. . . . " Again, scripture reminds us of the difference between stuckness and freedom: Once we were slaves in Egypt, and now we are together, on our way out.

Bureaucratic Versus Democratic Communities

Communities, it must be noted, are not anti-private. Rather, they are the defenders of the small against the large. One could actually argue that private congregations are anti-private because they load more on individual selves than those selves have any capacity to bear. To recommend public sites for ministries is to recommend protection for the private; it is to allow intimacy, to have room and space to be. Right now we are plagued by the privacies of Egypt, where it is assumed our welfare worker has the right to know more about us than even our family, where a therapist gets conversation we keep from our spouse or children, where bureaucrats don't bother to call us by name or even to listen to us.

The very word *community* needs to be scrutinized. Many cite it as their goal, but few are actually on their way toward it. Seminaries in many ways, and especially through the requirement of clinical pastoral education, have taught a whole generation of clergy to close the door to their office and counsel clients in that privacy. Few have been taught, officially, how to build communities that take care of themselves or how to bring people into positions of self-governance. Most clergy expect to find themselves in one-on-one situations; groups, where communal activity occurs, are somewhat threatening. The very diversity of groups means conflict, and conflict is something we have been taught to fear.

John McKnight of Northwestern University draws a picture of community that turns the typical organizational chart upside down.[3] He shows us that the picture of privacy the world has in mind for us is that famous sequence of boxes that make up a bottom-heavy organizational chart: one box on the top, all the rest pyramiding underneath. Here we get assignments to make bricks. The goal of the experience is to move up, to get on top of each other, to accept the "fact" that some of us deserve to have others telling us what to do. McKnight argues that a more wholesome picture of community is the reverse of the standard organizational chart, and thus he turns the chart upside down, showing what liberation might look like. You have heard it said unto you that community is a well-managed bureaucratic maze, but I say unto you that community is a place where everyone enjoys decision-making power about how we get to the gates and when and how we make a break for it. Community is not the achievement of better management. It is the achievement of itself.

We must also remember that communities are not perfect. It is the ideology of better-managed bureaucracies, not of democratically open communities, that strives toward perfection. Here we understand and make room for imperfection, including that of the "less abled" and of ourselves, remembering how long it was that we were content in Egypt. Right now the United States is a great community for the young and the strong and the smart; it is a less-than-comforting community for the old or the sick or the dull. Genuine community makes room for lots of difference and actually enjoys the knocking about of all that difference.

We have been stuck in our own isolation for a long time, most of us for most of our lives. These lives have been lived in the twentieth century, a time when individualism has been encouraged by everything from tracking in schools to competitive retirement positions on the job. We have been pitted against each other as individuals and as groups. To assume that we can create happy communities just by a transformation of values or directions is innocent in the extreme. Racism and sexism and classism—the systematized versions of individualism—now have neighborhoods and salary structures to back them up. Egypt is not just a mind-set. We will have to be gentle with our hopes for communities.

None of us is going anywhere alone. Certainly we will not get out of Egypt by ourselves. The promise has always been from God to *people*, not persons. When and as we slowly learn or relearn the skills of community-building, we will find the breach between public and private healed. We will restore streets to dwell in and there we will happily, if imperfectly, live.

The Blessing of the Poor

Ministry gets stuck when we forget the promise that the poor are blessed. We forget God's strategy, as Robert McAfee Brown puts it so well, in empowering the powerless rather than enlightening the powerful.[4] It is the poor who are to lead us and themselves out of trouble. The stuck place is our blindness to this capacity in the poor. We have come to see the poor as needy, as lazy, as different, as useless—the things we trick ourselves into thinking we are not. In fact, the poor have great capacities. They can find the way out of Egypt if we get out of their way. They can lead us out if we associate with them rather than handing them a can of beans and asking them to leave "our" space now.

You have heard it said, but I say unto you. This is the rhythm of the surprises of God. The oppressive news of mammon, blaring at us all the time, proves to be false, whereas the good news of God turns out to be true. Ask any of the thousands who have lived their life among the poor.

Ministry in cities is stuck. It is stuck without community in quick fixes and in the capacity for only short-term experience. It is stuck obeying the counsel of mammon toward bureaucratic structure and social-service language and the presumed uselessness of the poor. It wants to fix things, to help things, to care as long as the price is right. We have come to care like the bank cares and the hospital cares and the car mechanic cares: We care with our vulnerability not showing, with our need disguised. We care because it sounds like the right thing to do rather than because through caring we see our salvation. We advertise great caring; we promise we can give people what we think they need. Instead we might become partners with them.

Ministry in cities will transform as it becomes vulnerable in caring. As we confess our captivity to mammon's words and styles, we will find ourselves forgiven and pushed out of the stuck places we have been. A parachutist once said he had never jumped out of a plane but had been pushed 234 times to the ground. Maybe our own exhaustion will push us out of the old ways. In case anyone hasn't noticed, making bricks without straw is hard work. Religious institutions these days bump along from one crisis to another. I'm convinced that our denominations, in their suburban captivity and their redlining of ministries in cities, actually enjoy this crisis mentality. Their power peaks along with crisis. Allan Boesak[5] talks about the "overextended" nature of much ministry and says that it is all to keep up appearances, to make sure we *look* like we are doing something important without actually letting any power change hands. The gospel talks about rest; most ministers in cities haven't done that for years.

We will know that God is alive in cities and that liberation is on its way when power changes hands and we use our power to disbelieve mammon. In their book, *Poor People's Movements*,[6] Frances Fox Piven and Richard A. Cloward say that the only real power the poor have is that of unbelief. We are free to not believe what mammon is saying. This removal of faith from mammon to be turned toward God accentuates our already serious marginality. But it may turn out that the very shoestring on which most of us operate is our greatest resource. That we are not always financially viable may prove to be the path our marginality walks to the centers of power. On the other hand, those centers may be too solid for us even to touch them—which is even more reason to ignore what they have to say and how they do things quickly and in the short term and by themselves. Defeat may be our opening to build communities on the edges, in the cracks and margins. We do not need to make bricks without straw. We can open our eyes, examine our situation, and see and hear for ourselves. We can be forgiven our consent to captivity. We can begin to locate the exits. You have heard it said that you are stuck, but I say unto you, "Let my people go."

Donna Schaper is pastor of the First Congregational Church in Riverhead, New York. Formerly executive director of the Urban Academy in Chicago, she is also the author of several books, including Common Sense for Men and Women in Ministry *(The Alban Institute, 1990);* Narratives Against the Current *(Luramedia, 1989); and* Superwoman Turns Forty *(Luramedia, 1988).*

Notes

1. These phrases are from a lecture by Rosemary Ruether, delivered at Garrett-Evangelical Theological Seminary, Evanston, Ill., Spring 1986.

2. The use of the word *minister* here is intended to mean paid or professional minister; while it is used here in the specific, it is not meant to exclude the ministry of the whole people of God.

3. John McKnight, unpublished paper read as part of business ethics panel, Community Renewal Society, 1986.

4. Robert McAfee Brown, *Unexpected News: Reading the Bible with Third World Eyes* (Philadelphia: Westminster Press, 1984).

5. Allan Boesak is one of South Africa's leading antiapartheid activists.

6. Frances Fox Piven and Richard A. Cloward, *Poor People's Movements: Why They Succeed, How They Fail* (New York: Random House, 1979).

• 2 •

THE SECOND REFORMATION

HAS BEGUN

Jim Wallis

A Tale of Two Cities

My neighborhood of Columbia Heights runs along 14th Street, scene of Washington, D.C.'s much-publicized "riots" following the assassination of Martin Luther King, Jr., in the bitter spring of 1968. The now infamous "riot corridor," as the area is still called, even today bears the scars of the frustrated and angry violence that erupted when people's hopes were suddenly and brutally cut down. Burned-out buildings and vacant lots remain after more than twenty years.

Several years ago, my sister Barbara was walking through the neighborhood with her five-year-old son, Michael. They were on their way to the Sojourners day-care center. Michael surveyed the scene on the block and, looking up at his mother with puzzlement, asked, "Mommy, was there a war here?"

Indeed, the empty shells of buildings, piles of rubble, and general devastation all around could easily give that impression. Perhaps the eyes of a child can see what jaded adult vision quickly passes over or too easily accepts: there was and is a war here. It goes on every day, and the casualties are everywhere.

The people who inhabit this and similar neighborhoods are not only neglected and ignored by political decision-makers, they are war victims. They are the wounded and dying of a system that has ravaged their lives and their communities. It is no wonder that those who make it through refer to themselves

44

as "survivors." But many are not surviving. The forces that
have declared war on them are global and impersonal, but the
consequences for the people here are very personal indeed.

For most of the fourteen years the Sojourners Community
has lived in Washington, D.C., the inner-city neighborhoods of
the capital have been invisible to the nation. Everyone knows
the official Washington, with its marble, monuments, and
malls. But "the other Washington" has been off limits to the
blue-and-white tour buses and to the consciousness of the rest
of the country.

Here are substandard tenements instead of stately government offices. Here children play in back alleys strewn with
glass, trash, and syringes instead of running in beautiful parks.
Here the only monuments are to neglect, indifference, and the
stranglehold of entrenched racism on the city that proclaims
itself a beacon of freedom to the world. Here the homeless
huddle literally in the shadows of the great houses of state
power, trying to keep warm by sleeping on the grates that expel hot air from the heating systems of the State Department,
the Pentagon, and the halls of Congress.

Even the name of Washington, D.C., tells the tale of two
cities. The white residents and professionals who run the federal capital live in "Washington." The African American residents who are the city's vast majority are from "D.C."—the
District of Columbia. This capital of the so-called free world is
still virtually a segregated city, especially in housing, schools,
and social interchange.

A word heard often in D.C. is *colony*. The District of Columbia didn't obtain even partial home rule until 1974. But still,
District residents (700,000 people) have no voting representa-
tion in Congress, and all actions taken by the elected city government are subject to congressional veto.

The forces of housing gentrification and real estate specula-
tion are slowly pushing African American residents into more
overcrowded neighborhoods or out of the city altogether.
Once-poor ghetto neighborhoods are being transformed into
upscale yuppie enclaves with prices too high for any of their
former inhabitants.

Until recently, neither the District's extremes of wealth and poverty nor its racial polarization have been well known beyond the beltway, the highway encircling the metropolitan area. For most Americans—at least most white Americans—the nation's capital has been known as the site for great high school trips, or for the Cherry Blossom Festival, or as the home of the Redskins. Mostly, Washington, D.C., is known as the most powerful city in the world, and it's no wonder that its powerless underside has been so easily and so long overlooked.

But suddenly Washington, D.C., began making national and international headlines—not as the center of power but as the "murder capital" of the nation. Quickly the media cameras, so used to turning away from "the other Washington," focused their attention on neighborhoods overrun with drugs and guns. D.C. became famous. National magazines did cover stories that spoke of the "two Washingtons," while nervous local officials rushed to assure anxious tourists that the killing was limited to "certain parts of the city."

Columbia Heights has become the murder capital of the murder capital, according to the Metropolitan Police Department. The killings continue unabated on the streets where we live, and in recent months they have come very close to home. At a recent meeting in the Sojourners Neighborhood Center, one local resident asked, "What does it mean to live in the most murderous neighborhood in the most murderous city in the most murderous nation in the world?"

In 1983 I traveled to the war zones of Nicaragua on the first team of a project known as Witness for Peace. In a refugee resettlement camp, I met a thirteen-year-old boy named Agenor, who made a great impression on me. His baseball cap, tattered shirt, and beat-up tennis shoes reminded me of the kids who run up and down the streets of my own neighborhood. But this thin Nicaraguan boy carried a heavy automatic weapon on his back. He was a member of the citizen's militia, defending against contra attacks and a feared U.S. invasion. As I returned home, Agenor's face, with his searching brown eyes and shy smile, was etched in my memory.

I met Eddie on the street the day I got back. He also was thirteen. While telling Eddie about my trip, I had a terrible thought. If the U.S. government continued to escalate its war in Nicaragua and eventually sent troops, Eddie—a young African American man from a poor family with few other options—would be among the first to go. That had been the pattern in the Vietnam War.

In that moment, I imagined the awful possibility of Eddie and Agenor meeting on some Nicaraguan battlefield, raising their guns to aim at each other, and one or both being killed. The great ideological confrontation between East and West would come down to Eddie and Agenor shooting each other— two young men, one black and one brown, dying in the name of a global conflict between two white superpowers. Instead of that horrible picture, I tried to imagine Eddie and Agenor playing baseball together.

Eddie did not die on a Nicaraguan battlefield, as I had feared. He died instead in March 1989 of gunshot wounds on the streets of his own neighborhood. Eddie was seventeen. He became, for a short while, the latest victim and the newest statistic in the city's epidemic of violence.

One month later, we at Sojourners were all gathered at church on Sunday morning. During the intercessions, the news was announced that another young man, Anthony, had been killed a few nights earlier. I watched faces around the room grimace in pain and the tears begin to flow. Anthony had attended our community's day-care center many years earlier. We know the whole family. After the service, Martha, who had been Anthony's teacher, flushed with anger. "He was such a sweet and sensitive boy. It has to be the system!"

After church that day, I found myself in a funeral home, viewing the body of a handsome, once vital young man, now cold and dead. His grieving mother and brothers and sisters were all there. There wasn't much to say.

Vincent Harding, author and historian of the civil rights movement, recently made a trip to what was then West Germany, where he led retreats for African American soldiers. Many told Harding that they were reenlisting in the Army so

that they could keep from coming home to their own neighborhoods, where they were afraid of being killed. Young African
Americans were deciding to stay in the Army to save their lives.

We are losing a whole generation of young people in our
cities to poverty, drugs, and violence. Washington, D.C., is a
city out of control, reeling from the brutal consequences and
tremendous suffering of a global economic, social, and spiritual crisis that has yet to be named, understood, or addressed.
It is a crisis of the highest magnitude, and its points to a global
reality that we must recognize and squarely face.

Through these painful and senseless events, something has
become quite clear to me: Washington, D.C., stands now as a
parable to the world. The crisis in the capital of the wealthiest
and most powerful nation in the world tells the story of the
crisis the whole world now faces. In Washington, D.C., today,
we see a mirror of what the global system has become. The
brutal paradoxes of the capital of the world's one remaining
superpower have become a parable that can teach us what we
must learn to survive.

Washington, D.C., is literally the symbol of power. People
stream to the official city to exercise power, to influence power,
or just to be around power. The power holders and the power
groupies alike are intoxicated with the smell of it. The key
word here is *access*. Access to power—that's what everyone is
always fighting for in this town. Power, like money, becomes
its own justification. How you get it or what it is used for are
beside the point; having power is what's important.

As power defines official Washington, powerlessness defines
"the other Washington." Here are the people who clean the
hotel rooms, cook the food, and drive the cabs for the powerful—if they have work at all. The work force has been reduced
to an underemployed labor pool supplying the bottom rungs
of the service economy.

If Washington is the most powerful city in the nation, D.C. is
the most powerless, without control even over its own affairs
and destiny. As the "last colony," D.C.'s relationship to Washington symbolizes the relationship many other parts of the
world have with that powerful city.

The revealing paradoxes exist on almost every level of life in Washington, D.C. Housing costs are among the highest in the country, as are the rates of homelessness. Infant mortality is at Third World levels in the same city with more lawyers and real estate developers than any other in the nation. Unemployment of African American youth is upwards of 60 percent, while white professional couples with two incomes search for investments. Scholastic Aptitude Test scores for D.C.'s public school students are one hundred points below the national norm, while Washington's private school students score a hundred points above it.

Nineteen million tourists spend a total of $1.5 billion each year here, while the D.C. jail runs out of money for toilet paper. The downtown hotel business is booming, while more and more women and children move into the city's shelters or onto the streets.

Washington's affluent suburbs are rated among the most desirable places to live in the nation, while the death rate in African American D.C. increases due to a lack of good health care. Young white men pay some of the highest college tuition rates in the country at local universities, while their African American counterparts are nine times more likely than they to be the victims of homicide.

Washington, D.C., is a microcosm of the dynamics that now govern the world order. The current drug war brings all these contradictions into sharp relief.

No one knows the exact numbers, but an extraordinary percentage of D.C. youth is involved in the drug traffic. As in source countries such as Colombia, drug trafficking has become a livelihood for the poor. In the high-stakes atmosphere of drugs and money, life becomes cheap indeed. A journalist who worked there told me that in Colombia now, it costs only forty dollars to have someone murdered. In both Colombia and Washington, D.C., poverty sets the stage for tragedy, and the drama of drugs simply carries out the executions.

In the current economic and cultural environment, it becomes very difficult to tell young people, "Just say no to drugs." What we are in effect telling them is to be content working part-time at McDonald's (the eighth largest employer in Washington, D.C., according to local newspapers) and pursue the American Dream as best they can. In a changing economy, the better jobs and brighter future we want to promise inner-city children are just not there.

Meanwhile, the dominant images that assault them daily—through television, movies, and popular music—tell young people that their very worth and status as human beings come from how much they can possess and consume. Fancy clothes, new cars, a nice house, and lots of gold around their necks become the aspirations of inner-city youth. In that, they are no different from most Americans.

The crucial difference is that these inner-city youth are virtually denied legal access to the alluring attractions of American consumer culture. They are shut out by an economy that has no room for them.

Washington, D.C., like the rest of the global system, is now run by a two-tiered economy. At the top is a booming sector of highly paid managerial and professional elites; at the bottom is an increasingly impoverished population who serve the high-tech economy but whose labor and even consumption are less and less needed. Whole sectors of the global population are now simply defined outside of the economic mainstream. And to be shut out of the global economy means to be consigned to death. Like Jesus' parable of the rich man and the beggar Lazarus, millions and millions of God's children are now shut outside the gate of the global economy.

More and more children live in poverty in America. According to the Children's Defense Fund, one out of every five children—including about half of all African American children—are born poor. The gap between rich and poor has steadily grown as a changing economy leaves more and more people behind. The swelling ranks of the hungry and homeless, now including many families, points to a highly visible moral contradiction in a nation that prides itself on its standard of living.

The earth itself suffers along with the poor. Our politically neglected and continually poisoned environment faces real threats from global warming trends, ozone depletion, acid rain, and toxic and nuclear wastes, creating contaminated wa-

ter, unhealthy food, polluted air, and ravaged wildlife. We will
not escape the consequences of our behavior.

As Native American leader Chief Seattle said years ago,
"This we know. The earth does not belong to people. People
belong to the earth. This we know. All things are connected.
Whatever befalls the earth befalls the people of the earth. We
did not weave the web of life. We are but a mere strand in it.
Whatever we do to the web, we do to ourselves!"[1]

In the United States, public school education, health care,
low-cost housing, the family farm, and the industrial workplace are all in a state of crisis. Crime is out of control, and the
proposed solutions fail to deal adequately with either underlying causes or individual responsibility, neglecting both perpe-
trators and victims.

The fight against racism has been halted at the highest levels
of government, and its ugly resurgence is upon us. Hard-won
progress made by women for equal rights is now under attack
from many quarters. The nation's foreign policy continues to
violate its expressed values and causes untold human suffering, principally to poor people of color. Our collective conscience has been numbed, and the sanctity of life is diminished
with each passing year of moral accommodation to nuclear
weapons and "national security" systems based on mutual suicide pacts.

Things are especially hard on the minority youth that inhabit our inner cities. They are the ones whose dreams and
hopes for the future have been denied. There is no room for
them in this society, and they know it. With no place, no stake,
and no future available to them, they are finding their own
road to "success." And it is a very dangerous road indeed, with
many casualties strewn along the way.

In our neighborhood, children eight, nine, and ten years old
wear beepers on their belts. It is not because they are young
lawyers and doctors, but because drug dealers call the children
at play when a drug run has to be made. It is safer for the
dealers to use children for their drug runs, as detection and
punishment are less likely for the very young.

Young people can make more money in a day or a week

than they ever dreamed possible. Thousands of dollars are available to them in an economy that has never offered them more than uncertain part-time employment at minimum wage. And many are taking the option.

In a series of articles called "At the Roots of the Violence," *The Washington Post* described the unwritten code of conduct of the drug dealers in their own words: Never back down. . . . Be willing to kill or die to defend your honor. . . . Protect your reputation and manhood at all costs. The drug dealers who live by this code are known on the street as "soldiers." A reporter asked one of them why they are always so ready to shoot. His answer: greed for money.

The *Post* then commented on the code of the street, calling it a way of behaving that flies in the face of traditional American values.

Is that really true? What values are reflected in American foreign policy? What code of ethics governs the wars of Wall Street? Does not the enshrinement of greed and the glorification of violence every day on TV sets and movie screens reinforce cultural values?

What message does their society give young people every day about what is most important in life? Have they not been convinced, like most other Americans, that status and success come by way of material acquisition? Does the way people get rich even matter in America?

With great danger to themselves and others, are not these children of the poor pursuing the same glittering, materialistic dream as others, in the quickest and perhaps only way they see open to them? Ironically, highly paid entertainers and professional athletes become the role models encouraging young African American children to reject the big money they can make in the drug traffic and settle for minimum wage.

When George Bush launched his war on drugs, he took careful aim to avoid the causes of the problem, then launched volleys that fell short of addressing even the symptoms. His critics cry out for more money to be spent on the symptoms; even they ignore the underlying causes and corruptions of drugs.

However, on *Nightline*, after the president's speech, two incarcerated drug traffickers at Lorton, Virginia, prison spoke prophetically. One said it was the materialistic values—the cars, the clothes, the gold—that was killing them. The other said it was the economics, the injustice in the cities, that was the core of the problem. The combination of the two—a systemic economic injustice and an insatiable lust for possessions—is indeed the formula that is causing the death and destruction.

Perhaps our dominant cultural values now reflect the emptiness of our situation most of all. Television now rules the popular culture. Consumption has become our highest cultural value and social purpose. In fact, material consumption is the only universal form of social participation left for Americans. Everything else has been either marginalized or completely co-opted by the frenzied desire for things.

Consumption is what both the rich and the poor, and everyone in between, seem to care most about. Not only does consumption define the culture, materialism has *become* the culture in America. There is no longer any doubt that things are more valued than people and that people have, themselves, become commodities. We are faced with an almost totally economic definition of life. The result is a culture that has lost its meaning.

Drugs are not the only narcotic here. The money that comes from drugs is the addiction that is leading to violence. That addiction—addiction to materialism—is fed every hour of every day in this society. It is not only legal to feed that addiction, it is the whole purpose of the system. It is our reason for being as a people: to possess and consume.

The images dance before us every waking moment. The images attract, lure, create desire; they awaken the greed and covetousness of our worst selves. Our children are glued to the TV screen; the beat of incessant consumption pounds in our ears. Shopping malls have become the temples, shrines, and communal centers of modern America.

I read a magazine article recently that seriously suggested one of the reassurances we have of global community is that you can travel all over the world and see the golden arches of

McDonald's. One thing that we can all do is buy and eat hamburgers together—all over the world.

The issue here is deeper than greed and selfishness. Material consumption—buying and using things—has become the only means left of belonging in America. If we can't buy, if we can't consume, we simply don't belong.

In New Mexico last summer, I read a newspaper column about a new product. It is a simulated car phone. For five dollars, you can buy a piece of plastic that looks like a car phone. But it doesn't work. It's just a piece of plastic. That's not greed, that's belonging.

After creating such an over-powering, all-encompassing, all-defining addiction, we block the poor from satisfaction. It is an unspeakable cruelty to create an addiction and then deny its satisfaction, the whole time feeding the desire. Materialism is literally killing the poor, while at the same time it is destroying the nation's soul.

The violent underside of American society is not a social aberration that we can safely and morally distance from "traditional American values." Rather, the frightening carnage is a frustrated mirror image of the twisted values that now govern the wider society.

The crisis of our inner cities will not change until we change. Social transformation will not occur without a transformation of values. It is not only the country's physical infrastructure that is deteriorating; the moral structures and foundations of the nation are also crumbling.

We should know by now that we can't have an economic system that leaves masses of people behind without ensuring endless conflict. We should know by now that we can't have security based on weapons and technology that lead us to become participants in a mutual suicide pact. We should know by now that growth and progress that abuse, exploit, and destroy our natural environment will end up choking us to death. We should know by now that we cannot deny human dignity to our neighbor because of race or class or sex without destroying our own soul. The logic of the system is literally killing us.

New Vision

Any new vision will have to fundamentally challenge the system at its roots and offer genuine alternatives based on the critical moral values that we still possess. Since such a challenge and such an alternative are unlikely to come from the top of American society, the vision will necessarily have to originate from the bottom, the margins, and those middle sectors of society where dislocation and/or more independent social values offer the possibilities of new imagination.

Two crucial constituencies for such a task are the poor themselves and places within the religious community where fresh thinking and renewal are now taking place. The future will not be constructed from the mere shuffling of elite personnel at the top but rather will be a response to a transformation of values and action at the grass roots.

Despite the lack of recognition, we are indeed in a social crisis. It is a crisis that confronts us with choices—critical choices of national values and direction. Honest truth-telling and bold moral vision for the future are urgently needed. The combination of the two is in fact the essence of what political leadership must be in the days ahead.

A discernable hunger exists in the nation for just such leadership. The American people deserve to be offered such a choice. And, even more important, we have a religious responsibility to offer it. That has always been the prophetic vocation.

The biblical prophets challenged the ways things were while at the same time helping people imagine new possibilities. They were not afraid to confront the king, to defend the poor, or to say that what God had in mind was far different from what most people had settled for. Rankled by injustice, sickened by violence, and outraged by oppression, the prophets defined true religion as doing justice, loving kindness, and walking humbly with your God. (See Micah 6:8.)

Our political convictions must grow out of that kind of faith—a faith that does justice. We should be less interested in the ideology of left and right and more interested in whether justice is really being done—especially to the mar-

ginalized and downtrodden for whom the God of the Bible
seems to have such a special concern. That same biblical perspective sees the accumulation of wealth and weapons as the
wrong road to national security and instead offers the possibility of an economy that has room for everyone, an environment treated as a sacred trust, and a commitment to resolving
our conflicts in ways that do not threaten the very survival of
the planet.

That political vision directly confronts the barriers of race,
class, and sex which so violate God's creative purpose and still
wreak such violence among us. To enjoy a culture in which
human values and creativity can truly flourish will mean being
set free from our captivity to consumption and its totally economic definition of life. What is most human, rather than what
is most profitable, must become the critical question.

On a flight home recently, I found myself on an airport
shuttle bus with other travelers. Two attractive young white
couples were having a loud conversation about their favorite
restaurants around the world. Many of the rest of us would
have preferred not to listen, but the closeness of the quarters
left us no choice. Finally, one of them exclaimed in praise of
his favorite place, "It's just a wonderful restaurant—you can
spend three hundred dollars for dinner in your shorts!"

The next day was Saturday, and the food line formed early
outside the Sojourners Neighborhood Center, only one-and-a-
half miles from the White House. Each week three hundred
families receive a bag of groceries critical for getting them
through the next seven days. Just before the doors are opened,
all those who helped prepare and sort the food join hands to
pray.

The prayer is normally offered by Mary Glover, a sixty-year-
old African American woman who knows what it is to be poor
and knows how to pray. She prays like someone who knows to
whom she is talking. You can tell that Mary Glover has been
praying to her God for a long time.

She thanks God for the gift of another day. Then she
prays, "Lord, we know that you'll be coming through this
line today, so help us to treat you well." Mary Glover knows

very well who it is that waits in line with the hungry and huddles with the homeless to keep warm on the steam grates of Washington, D.C.

A few years ago at a press conference held by the Reagan White House, Edwin Meese, then attorney general, declared to the nation that there are no hungry people in America. Who is it that knows the heart of God better? One of the most powerful white men in this country? Or a poor, African American, sixty-year-old woman who in society's view doesn't really count for much?

In Matthew 25, Jesus says, "I was hungry and you gave me nothing to eat. I was thirsty and you gave nothing to drink. I was a stranger and you didn't take me in. I was naked and you didn't clothe me. I was sick and in prison and you didn't come to see me."

And the people said, "Lord, Lord. When did we see you hungry and thirsty and naked, a stranger, sick, and imprisoned? We didn't know it was you. Had we known it was you we would have done something. We would have responded. Had we just known it was you, we would have at least formed a Social Action Committee. But we didn't know it was you!"

Then Jesus says, "As you have not done it to the least of these, you have not done it to me" (*see* Matt. 25:42–45). To those who would name his name, Jesus asks, "How much do you love me? I'll know how much you love me by how you love them."

Mary Glover understands Matthew 25. Her prayer is the best commentary on the twenty-fifth chapter of the Gospel of Matthew I've ever heard. She helps me remember who and where Jesus is.

God is in this with us. God is not distant and far away and somehow in charge of making things turn out right. God is enmeshed with us in the human situation. "God with us"— Emmanuel—the heart of Christian faith is the incarnation.

In Jesus, God hits the streets. God is now walking in our streets, and in our shoes. God knows the pain of Anthony's mother when I held her hand in the funeral home as she wept at the loss of her twenty-year-old son.

Perhaps an image of God for us in our times is an African

American grandmother in the inner city weeping and mourning the loss of her grandchildren—a whole generation of young people who are simply being abandoned and destroyed. If we become angry—with all of our sin, complicity, and limited compassion—how angry must God be at what's happening?

At the founding of Sojourners Community and magazine in 1971, we were seminary students in Chicago. Something very exciting was happening among us. We were wrestling with the gospel that had captured our hearts, which we believed was the only hope we really had.

One of the things we did in those early days was to make a study of every biblical reference to the poor—every single verse in the Bible that talked about God's love for the poor, about God being the deliverer of the oppressed. We discovered that the Bible was full of poor people.

In the Old Testament, the suffering of the poor was the second most prominent theme. Idolatry was the first, and the two were often connected. In the New Testament we found that one out of every sixteen verses was about the poor. In the Gospels, it was one out of every ten; in Luke, one of every seven; and in James, one of every five verses.

One member of our group decided to try an experiment. He found an old Bible and a pair of scissors, and he cut out of that Bible every single reference to the poor. It took him a very long time. When he came to Amos and read, "Let justice roll down like waters, and righteousness like an ever-flowing stream," he cut it out. When he came to Isaiah, and he heard the prophet say, "Is not this the fast that I choose . . . to let the oppressed go free . . . ?" he cut it right out. All of the Psalms in which God is seen as the deliverer of the poor just disappeared.

In the New Testament, when he came to the Song of Mary—which promised, "The mighty will be put down from their thrones, the lowly exalted, the poor filled with good things, and the rich sent empty away"—he cut it out. You can imagine what happened to Matthew 25. He cut out Jesus' Nazareth manifesto in Luke 4: "The Spirit of the Lord is upon me, because he has anointed me to preach good news to the poor. He has sent me to proclaim release to the captives and recovery of sight to the blind, to set at liberty all those who are oppressed, and to proclaim the acceptable year of the Lord." It was all cut out. "Blessed are the poor" and "Blessed are the poor in spirit"—they were gone, too. All the beatitudes had to go.

When he was all through, the Bible was literally in shreds. It wouldn't hold together; it was falling apart in our hands.

I used to take that old Bible with me to preach. I'd hold it high above American congregations and say, "My friends, this is the American Bible—full of holes from all that we have cut out." Evangelicals and liberals, Protestants and Catholics in America—all have Bibles full of holes. The poor have been cut out of the word of God.

What we must begin to do in our day is put our Bibles back together again, restore the integrity of the word of God in our lives, in our faith communities, and in our world. Our fidelity to scripture will not be tested by our dogma and doctrine, but by how our lives demonstrate that we believe in the word of God.

The good news is that it is already happening. It's already going on. Our Bibles are being put back together. The word of God is being restored in our time.

The God of the Bible is a deliverer of the poor. God has a special love for the poor, the disenfranchised, the marginalized, those who are at the bottom of everybody else's priority list. If that isn't clear from the Bible, then nothing is clear from the Bible. It is clear from start to finish. And the poor of the world, who are the growing church all over the world, are the ones who understand this. To them it is a tremendous source of hope, comfort, and power that God is with them in their struggle for life, for justice, and a decent future for their families.

A story comes to us from South Africa, about a widow whose husband had died young and left her alone with eight children. She was poor, she was black, and she was South African. That's pretty close to the bottom in this world.

They had an old dilapidated house that she wanted to fix up, but she was a seamstress and made only two dollars a week. She worked hard, and worked extra to save enough money for four hundred bricks to fix up the old house. So she ordered the bricks and counted them when they arrived. There were only two hundred and fifty.

She asked the man who brought the bricks where the rest were. He was a wealthy and powerful man, and he told her not to bother him, that she had all the bricks she was going to get. And she told him, "I will never forget this. But that's okay; you don't have to worry about the bricks. The God I believe in is the protector of the widow and the fatherless. And somehow you're going to know that."

One of her children, a twelve-year-old boy, was listening. The words of his mother made a great impression on him.

Two weeks later, the same man pulled up to the house in a truck with his hired men to unload the rest of the bricks. "What happened?" the widow asked.

Two of the houses that he had been building had mysteriously burned to the ground, and he thought her God had something to do with it. He was embarrassed, and he was afraid. They completed the work as quickly as possible, and then he was gone. The young son was there looking on.

That young boy was Allan Boesak. Today he is helping to lead his people to freedom in South Africa. "I saw all this at age twelve," says Boesak, "and it made a tremendous impression on me; because I saw that in a very tangible way, God does take care of the poor and the meek and the lowly and the oppressed. That was something I was never to forget for the rest of my life.

"So today I am literally impassioned about these things. I keep on telling people that this is the biblical message and that it doesn't matter what the situation looks like; God will make true the promises that have been made. And there is no doubt in my mind that God will."[2]

When Allan Boesak preaches about the God who is the protector of the poor, the widow, and the orphan, he is not preaching from some text of liberation theology. He is preaching out of what he learned around his mother's table, and what he believes is so unshakable that all the might of white South Africa cannot dissuade him from that stubborn hope.

We find ourselves now at a critical historical moment. Just when it seems that everything is unraveling, that the world system is coming to the end of its rope, God is raising up something new, and from a very unexpected place.

We all remember from the history of the church something called the Reformation. It was a time when the church had lost its way. The church had forgotten essential insights of the gospel and in forgetting had become comfortable and complacent. So God raised up reformers to speak the word that had been forgotten, that was so central to faith.

In that Reformation the central insight was this: Salvation is by faith alone. It was simple and yet profound. It spoke directly to what had been lost in the church's life. That simple and powerful insight transformed the church and the world.

Today, the church is again at a turning point. I believe that we are at the beginning of something that will become nothing less than a Second Reformation in the church's life.

We have forgotten something; there is something we lack. We have been corrupted, and we have lost our way. The central insight of the new Reformation will be this: The gospel is good news to the poor. That also is an insight so simple and yet so profound. It has the power to spark a new Reformation in the church's life. Like the first, it will transform both the church and the world.

Many of us are undergoing a second conversion, a conversion to Christ whose face we see in the poor. This second conversion is essential to the Second Reformation. The call for a new Reformation is coming to us from a new place, an unexpected place: the church of the poor. The poor themselves will be the evangelists of this new word whose time has come.

Jesus has been present all the time in the poor, whom we in the affluent churches have kept at arm's length. In them—in their flesh, their lives, their history, their sorrow, their joy—in their struggle we find the invisible Christ.

We are finding Jesus again. We are rediscovering Jesus afresh. We are going back to Jesus anew. That has always been what converts the church, and that conversion is prompting a Second Reformation in the church's life.

There is an old gospel tradition, new to Western Christians, emerging in the Second Reformation. It is storytelling. The stories are mostly of the church of the poor and are also of those who are being evangelized and transformed by that story. The evangelists for this Second Reformation are ordinary people.

Today a global crisis of immense proportions is being confronted by an uprising of hope in a Second Reformation of faith led by the church of the poor. The face of Jesus is being discovered not only among the poor in Central America, South Africa, and the Philippines, but also right at home.

Everywhere you look, Christians and churches are feeding the hungry, sheltering the homeless, ministering to those with AIDS, welcoming the refugees, organizing with the disenfranchised, visiting the prisoners, and advocating justice for the oppressed. Wherever there are works of mercy and acts of justice, Christians are in the midst of them. In many places the church is heeding the gospel message to bring good news to the poor and the gospel warning that we will be judged by how we treat the least of these.

The most pressing issue today is that we really have no sense of solidarity with one another—no communion, no community, no common bond. A very telling example indeed is what is happening in my neighborhood.

A whole generation of young people is being destroyed. But for most Americans, this is just an inner-city problem, a crime concern, a drug crisis, or a violence issue. What is really happening is that a whole generation of *us* is being destroyed; but white America doesn't see it that way. It isn't *us*. It's *them*. How can we call people who are desperately poor and struggling to survive a "permanent underclass"?

In the slums of Manila, I saw whole families washing plastic and Styrofoam from the street for a living. At the end of the day you can make two dollars if you wash enough plastic. They are us, and we are them. And we are deeply connected.

If we fail to see these connections, we are simply not going to make it. All of our other problems stem from this one. At the heart of all of these issues is one single issue: We have lost our sense of being brothers and sisters, daughters and sons of God. We are the children of God, inextricably bound to one another.

And we will either live together or die as those who forgot that they were part of a common destiny.

It is time to heed the words of the prophet Amos: "Let justice roll" into the streets of oppression and drugs and hopelessness, and also into the avenues of luxury and anxiety. "Let justice roll" into the ghettos and barrios and squatter camps, but also into the affluent suburbs of comfort and indifference. "Let justice roll" into the board rooms of corporate wealth and the corridors of political power.

"Let justice roll" into a church made lukewarm by its conformity and isolated by its lack of compassion. "Let justice roll" and set free all the captives—those under bondage to poverty's chains and those under bondage to money's desires. "Let justice roll"—and let faith come alive again to all those whose eyes long to see a new day. The Second Reformation has begun.

Jim Wallis is pastor of the Sojourners Community and editor of Sojourners *magazine.*

Notes

1. Chief Seattle, from a speech called "If We Sell You Our Land, Love It," given on the occasion of the transfer of ancestral Native American lands to the federal government. "The Unforked Message of Chief Seattle," in Gamalier, *Flesh and Spirit: A Religious View of Bicentennial America* (Washington, D.C.: Community for Creative Nonviolence, 1976), pp. 72–73.

2. From an interview of Boesak by the author, 1988.

PASTOR, PRIEST, ORGANIZER:

LEADERSHIP IN

COMMUNITY MINISTRIES

David Mann

A Story of Delia and St. Boniface

The Anaheim City Council chambers were filled with Latino church people, with a good mix of Anglos present. The mayor had his head down, and the other council members were restless. This was a first. The tables had been turned. They listened unwillingly to Delia Varela, who with her six children had arrived in Anaheim from Guadalajara, Mexico, in the 1970s, describe the difficulty of raising youth in the Tijuanita barrio just behind the Disneyland tourist complex. Delia was leading two hundred members of the St. Boniface Parish Organization in a fight to win fifty thousand dollars and an acre of land as well as commitment from the city for a one-year start-up project that would lead to a mini-park and community center. They had enjoyed earlier victories in the yearlong campaign, including an agreement from the Walt Disney Corporation to put up the center, with labor provided by community residents and Disney employees.

Delia and St. Boniface won this round, too. Through the action, the leaders at St. Boniface were able to move the city to award a contract for developing and operating a mini-community center in their neighborhood to a local consortium that specializes in planning and creating self-help-oriented community centers. The consortium was given a permanent allocation of resources for the center. This skirmish made history in Anaheim. Never had the council chambers been filled primarily with immigrant Latinos. For the majority of them, it marked their first trip to the city council. After Delia finished, the pastor delivered a summary of his powerful Sunday homily on "immigrant self-help versus poor-people removal." The moving of poor people had been Anaheim's only policy for immigrants to date, he concluded; it was time to try a new approach.

Three critical ingredients for power and change were present: 1) good public theology; 2) knowledgeable, disciplined speakers; and 3) a multicultural packed house. These ingredients are expressions of a rapidly growing form of mission called *congregation-based community organizing.* A deliberate and disciplined process of leadership development and strategy lies behind this success story. Delia, the pastor, and other leaders at St. Boniface had been learning the skills of public action for change. They had also been deepening leadership qualities with the help of a professional community organizer.

Philip Newell, a national-level staff member of the Presbyterian Church (U.S.A.), writes, "People excluded from full participation in social, political, economic, and spiritual life can be empowered when they find ways of acting collectively. Local churches are natural centers for this development of community organization, for every one of them is located in some kind of neighborhood."[1]

Community organizing is a growing professional field. Organizers who work primarily with religious congregations need to combine a tough political savvy with a solid working knowledge and appreciation for the local congregation. While concepts and programs abound for renewing the urban church, the assumption here is that nothing can be more crucial than the training and retraining of pastors, for they are the key to translating what is learned through community organizing into the internal life of their congregation. A professional organizer can assist in this effort, and some pastors have turned gladly to the organizer as teacher, friend, and ally. The good organizer quickly learns that there is much to be learned from the pastor as well.

The Local Urban Congregation and Its Ailments

Before turning to the solution, however, let us consider the problem. Three dominant ailments afflict many nonethnic urban Protestant churches. First, the relationship between the congregation and the "turf" surrounding the physical church has begun to disintegrate. In the case of downtown churches, the relationship is often hostile, with increasing numbers of members staying away from night meetings, more and more trustee issues related to "security in the parking lot," and so on. More importantly, churches historically have drawn a critical part of their membership, identity, and vision from a strong neighborhood relationship; neighborhood alienation saps a critical source of vitality.

Second, the church's impact on the quality of life in the city has steadily diminished. Dieter Hessel, Presbyterian pioneer of social ministry, writes that people look primarily for two qualities in a church community: spiritual nurturance and the power to influence events in their city or neighborhood, usually concerning issues that affect their families.[2] In the absence of an avenue for creating change, churches increasingly tend to be content with hiring pastors who will provide chaplaincy services for their sick and aged, social services for the homeless and mentally ill, and spiritual services for the congregation at large.

Finally, since leadership development does not tend to be a pastoral priority, a stagnant leadership pattern develops. "Leaders" become defined as those who will do all the work and will speak up at meetings. These few sometimes become gatekeepers, resisting innovation. They overwork themselves while blaming the "apathetic many" who are, in the leaders' eyes, "irreligious and unconcerned."

Meanwhile, the many uninvolved members and potential members at the periphery of church life criticize what appears to them to be the irrelevance of the church, and they fail to involve themselves in creating change. These two groups, the "leaders" and the "periphery," are utterly out of relationship, creating a downward spiral of listlessness and inertia in the life of the church. New leaders are not developed to replace the old, and no new structures are created to involve potential new leaders in developing programs to address current issues.

From this threefold analysis of the decline of urban Protestant churches, some are seeking radically innovative mission programs. Key among these has been the rise of church-based community organizing.

Urban Clergy: Hearts and Faith, but No Method

The ability of congregation-based community organizing to take hold in the local church is closely tied to both the commitment and the skills of the pastors, at least initially. Pastors in city churches leave seminary with clear visions for change. They enter struggling churches eager to bring renewal, growth, and relevance. What they soon discover is that they lack a method that will work. They come up against their own feelings of powerlessness. They turn back to what they learned in seminary, attend denominational "professional" events, and comb the horizon for continuing education. They are seeking skills, insights, and above all a method to enact. As Donna Schaper puts it,

Clergy are drowning in the therapeutic methods of counseling—we keep trying to heal rather than change. We privatize problems and scratch our heads when that doesn't work. Seminaries don't teach us a method for social analysis or social change. Instead, they send us out with fuzzy therapeutic notions stamped on our brains by the marvelous organizing job done by clinical psychological education on the seminaries.[3]

In an intriguing book about the plight of pastors in the last decade, John Harris describes how the old methods, still taught in seminaries, no longer seem to work.

Clergy are no longer equipped with the reliable, theoretical models of their craft, that is, those practical tools for preaching, spiritual guidance, congregational leadership, and pastoral care that connect effectively with the realities of parish life in the modern world.[4]

The church-based community organization and the pastor's relationship with the community organizer can provide a laboratory for alternative new skills for pastors. The primary purpose of the congregation-based community organization (CBCO) is to build a broad-based power organization that represents the people. The power is used to bring changes that reflect the ethically based, shared values of religious traditions and to protect and improve life for low- to moderate-income families. It therefore seeks to be multi-ethnic and multi-issue. It seeks to become the voice through which congregations can take effective action on the ever-larger issues currently diminishing the quality of life in our neighborhoods and cities.

Four Critical Skills for the Development of Strong Leadership

As distinct from many church social justice groups, the CBCO focus is on developing its leadership. Four skills underlie the leadership required for this type of ministry.

Accountability

Accountability requires members of the church community to act in accordance with their faith values. Accountability is the expectation that one will carry through and do what he or she agrees to do. If a leader of an organizing committee agrees to make ten calls about an important meeting or to have ten one-on-one encounters to test feelings about the drug issue, then that person should be accountable to the larger community. Accountability is more than meeting expectations, however; it is an agreement to both support and challenge one another in community.

Evaluation

Evaluation after meetings, actions, even worship, is a time set aside for analysis, growth, and learning, a time to determine why a particular project succeeded or why it failed, to discover who did or did not accomplish an assigned task. Evaluation after a meeting is the time to share feelings, to discuss tensions that might have arisen, and to determine whether or not they were resolved. Above all, evaluation can be used for affirmation and recognition for those who have taken risks and "delivered." It is a special time when the organizer or pastor can give direct feedback to leaders about what they did well and what areas require further growth.

Relationship-Building

Relationship-building is taught most effectively by sharing models, a form of teaching by example, for healthy relationships: good listening, authentic sharing, and learning to communicate. The heart of the organizer's approach to relationship-building lies in the understanding of self-interest. Self-interest grows from the daily concerns of family, job, home, immediate neighborhood, or church. It can also grow from deeply cherished values. As the relationship deepens, leaders will learn to risk challenging people. For example, one may need to challenge an apparently too-busy person to invest some time in action about something in which he or she believes. A cynical person may need to be encouraged to persevere as an agent of change. In good relationships, priorities get challenged.

Mentoring

Mentoring is an extension of the one-to-one relationship for the purpose of intentionally developing a few key leaders. The pastor may wish to call it something else, but the purpose of mentoring is to self-consciously develop leadership skills and qualities. The "student" should be willing to be challenged and to take risks. For the mentor, the relationship requires a special investment of time and reflection, a willingness to be more open, even vulnerable. If the time is well spent, new leaders will develop and move into primary roles in the church.

A CBCO continually empowers people so that they can take on ever bigger arenas of power. The CBCO cannot afford to become a single-issue organization. It should be able to address the problem of drugs in one period and housing in another. It should be able to resolve large regional issues while always helping its local congregations fight local concerns. CBCOs don't have an "elite" group that decides on the issues to be addressed and then invites others to join. Rather, the issues emerge from the problems experienced by members of the congregation. These problems are brought to the surface by an organizing team whose members have been trained to both listen and gently agitate people's anger about problems they face. In one-to-one visits, people are invited to get involved with the organization in solving these problems. Finally, the CBCO uses its relationship-building skills to discover currently uninvolved citizens with potential for leadership. It doesn't rely on the bottleneck of an already developed and overworked leadership.

A useful symbol to describe the relationship between the community-wide church-based organization and the church itself might be that of a permeable shield. The local CBCO identifies, researches, and relieves or at least "beats back" the pressures now endangering life for families and congregations, especially in such areas as housing, immigrant rights, public education, drugs, gangs, and child care. The shield is permeable in that people pass into the congregation and out of the congregation into the community. The CBCO brings new people into the life of a church, and it invites sometimes insular church members into action for the public good.

An individual family, even an individual congregation, is powerless to create change, to defend itself against such pressures as substance abuse and gentrification. Delia Varela, of whom we spoke at the outset, was struggling to support and protect her family in the barrio behind Disneyland at the same time that St. Boniface Church was forming a community organizing team. The Varela family had learned of Anaheim's plans to "redevelop" a larger area around Disneyland, to include the certain removal of the homes of the two thousand families in her poor, working-class barrio. With the help of the community organizing team, she began visiting neighbors one by one. Subsequently, several of those visited held house meetings. In addition to their concerns about the redevelopment plans, all voiced concern about drug dealing and gang formation, into which many of their youth were being drawn.

It was out of these meetings that the strategy was born to create an alliance with the Disney Corporation. The approach to Disney was to appeal to the corporation's self-interest: An alliance could preserve the quality of the potential labor force for the tourist industry and fight drugs and gangs in Disney's backyard by creating a community center and park. Common ground was found and agreed upon. Alone, Delia's family would have been defeated; through organizing, she and her neighbors negotiated with the most powerful decision-makers in the city, redefining city priorities.

Several scholars and church leaders have studied the causes of modern disaffection from congregational life. They point to a loss of confidence in the meaning and pertinence of faith for giving direction to life in today's society.[5] One such scholar is Robert Bellah, who argues persuasively that the church has to rethink strategy for the development of people able to serve the "common good."[6] Bellah's work powerfully documents the triumph of individualism and the infiltration of psychology and the values of psychological therapy into North American culture. Individuals increasingly accept what is good and best only in terms of themselves. "The good" relates to how I feel, to what I can possess, and to the narrow confines of my particular "lifestyle enclave." This describes the choice for homogeneity and the rejection of the value of a pluralistic community—which currently affects most of Protestantism. Finally, with the powerful influence of at times shallow psychology, a twisted sense of what is right has emerged: If something feels right to an individual, then it *is* right. The concern for being part of a community that has a commitment to the "common good" has atrophied.

Congregation-based community organizing can reverse this trend. The time is ripe; the methods are clear. The challenge is ours.

David Mann, a United Church of Christ clergyperson, has been a full-time community organizer for the past seven years. He has served on the pastoral staff of First Congregational Church, Palo Alto, California, for three years and was codirector of an urban ministry in Fresno, California, for eight years.

Notes

1. Philip Newell, "Church-Based Community Organizing and John Calvin," *Church & Society* 78, no. 1 (September–October 1987): 18.

2. Dieter T. Hessel, *Social Ministry* (Philadelphia: Westminster Press, 1982).

3. Donna Schaper, "A Native's Response to Church-Based Organizing," *Cities* 5, no. 1 (Spring 1985): 16.

4. John C. Harris, *Stress, Power, and Ministry: An Approach to the Current Dilemmas of Pastors and Congregations* (Washington, D.C.: Alban Institute, 1977), p. 47. See also Harris's treatment of the issues of collaborative power (p. 48) and the pastor's varying models of influence (pp. 80–85).

5. Hessel, *Social Ministry*; Philip Murnion, "The Complex Task of the Parish," *Origins*, Dec. 1978.

6. Robert Bellah et al., *Habits of the Heart: Individualism and Commitment in American Life* (Berkeley, Calif.: University of California Press, 1985).

PART TWO

URBAN NORTH AMERICA
IN THE 1990s:
THE CONTEXT FOR MINISTRY

Urbanization has been the theme in the United States since the earliest days, says one professor of urban studies. A very high percentage of the early immigrants and African slaves began their life in North America in nonurban areas, yet each census taken after the nation's first, in 1790, indicates a population shift toward the cities. The urbanization rate escalated in the aftermath of the Civil War and under the impact of the industrial revolution that profoundly altered North American social and economic structures. By the end of World War I, half of the U.S. population lived in urban areas. Today, approximately 75 percent of U.S. residents make their homes in the city.[1]

Sociologically speaking, the inner cores of major cities in the United States have become part of the Third World. The populations of those areas are without access to basic resources of human life: food, clothing, shelter, education, work. Alongside of this poverty population in our great cities, monied people go about their lives and work. Thus the structures of poverty and those of wealth—the financial, business, governmental, and international trade centers of the affluent in our global society—reside in close proximity. On the streets and in the alleyways, the "permanent underclass"—drug lords, pimps, gangs, the unemployed and underemployed, the homeless, the hungry, the uneducated, and the elderly—is expanding. This is the social context in which the ministry of the city church must take place today. Without an understanding of the structures of life within large metropolitan areas, we are unable to plan for and carry out authentic ministry.

This section of the reader includes a series of essays on the destruction of social and cultural life in urban areas of the

United States today. The essays in this section provide important descriptive data, although not all of the critical issues facing urban communities could be addressed in one volume. The challenge is to lay a foundation for understanding the social context and the important constituencies for urban ministry. Although some essays here address the church and its ministry directly, others do not. The opening and closing essays in this section, for instance, do not speak of church communities or ministry directly. James P. Stobaugh introduces us to homeless "Jessie," the bag lady, and we follow her through her day. Elizabeth W. Markson reveals the staggering numbers of all the potential "Jessies" and other elderly women who dwell in our inner cities. If urban ministry is not about these women and their isolation, their poverty, and the violence they experience, we are missing our mission in the church today.

Clinton E. Stockwell's essay provides a brief review of some of the literature addressing the social and economic stresses of "overurbanization," homelessness, hunger, and domestic violence and challenges the church to address these issues. The next essay, a sermon by James A. Forbes, Jr., delivered at the Riverside Church in New York City, calls the church and its members to act on the Golden Rule given by the prophets, including Jesus, in its battle against "hearts infected with violence" (HIV).

The drug-dealing world, one "structured against hope and liberation," is the topic for Hal Joseph Recinos. His analysis of the background of the drug culture and the racism of our economic systems constitutes a moral imperative for the work that lies before us in the church. And Gary E. Farley draws the important relationship between the structures of poverty in rural and urban communities. Farley's work helps us guard against a naive analysis about the urban realities facing the church today as we look ahead to plan new mission and ministry for urban churches and communities.

E.S.M.

Note

1. See John V. Moeser, "The Phenomenon of Urbanization," *The Witness* 72, no. 10 (October 1989): 11.

• 4 •

A Home

for the Homeless

James P. Stobaugh

Amid the blue, acrid haze of Pall Malls and the shiny, stainless steel coffee pots sit the fallen angels of East Pittsburgh. Street people languish in the dawn of an inner-city diner, mercifully permitted by the management to stay.

A country breakfast or the deluxe waffle belongs to the clean-shaven postman, but not to the street people. They wait for their 10 A.M. mushroom soup at the soup kitchen. It is 5 A.M., so street people wait.

Waiting is a way of life for street people. If they are fortunate enough to have an address, they wait for their welfare checks. At busy emergency rooms, they wait for medical care. They wait for the dawn.

At dawn it is time to leave the diner, time to wander. The night is dangerous for street people. Always weak, undernourished, and expendable, they fear shadows that hide urban predators waiting to maim and destroy. Daylight brings safe sleep. Messy things can happen to street people at night, but daytime people won't allow messiness.

At dawn, all over Pittsburgh, street people begin to wander. By 9 A.M. they are asleep on a bench, under a bridge, or in front of the soup kitchen. "Normal" people rarely see them. Street people do not want to upset normal people; they are the providers, and street people need provision.

"Jesus loves his little Jessie," a bag lady sings as she limps out of Eat N' Park. "When she's good, and when she's bad, when she's happy, and when she's sad." With this simple

77

childhood affirmation of faith, Jessie greets each new day. She has leaned heavily on her God since her husband abandoned her fifteen years ago. Jessie unceremoniously stuffs some essential clothing, a picture of her unfaithful husband, a jar of Oil of Olay, and sixty dollars into a J.C. Penney shopping bag reinforced by a Giant Eagle grocery bag. Then she turns the corner and disappears at Penn and Negley.

Street people are created slowly. A repossessed car. An unpaid mortgage. A lost job. Eventually the street person is born, and all that remains of the former, everyday person are wistful excursions into the real world through long gazes at the televisions in Sears.

Jessie is dying, and she knows it. Two months ago her left foot was severely cut when she stepped on a piece of a Pepsi Cola bottle thoughtlessly thrown against the library wall by youths. It still bothers Jessie that kids would waste a nickel. "Kids," she growls. "Everything is given to them!"

A St. Francis Hospital emergency-room physician sutured her wound, but the root-cracked sidewalks, her oversized shoes, and too many days without a shower have doomed her. Her friend Sally suffered a similar injury last year, and her foot was amputated. Jessie would rather die, and the awful smell coming from her foot reminds her that she soon will. "Jesus loves his little Jessie . . . " she continues to sing.

Dawn is past, noon is over, and the food closet just closed. Night is returning. Commuters rush by.

Street people are moving, too. Jessie is stepping onto a downtown bus. She will sleep in a women's shelter tonight. A child on the bus is screaming. Jessie gives her a chocolate-chip cookie carefully saved in a napkin.

Night is here. Tomorrow, if they're alive, the street people will again stagger into downtown to continue the endless, empty cycle of the people of the street.

James P. Stobaugh has been an urban pastor for ten years in Pittsburgh and, most recently, in Johnstown, Pennsylvania. He did undergraduate work at Vanderbilt University and received his M.Div. from Princeton

Theological Seminary. He also did graduate work at Rutgers University in the field of history. In fall 1990, he was the Charles E. Merrill fellow at Harvard Divinity School for his work in the urban church. At present, he is working on his Ph.D. in urban policy-making at Carnegie-Mellon University.

• 5 •

THE NEW URBAN REALITY:

HOPE FOR A REMNANT

Clinton E. Stockwell

The 1980s are at an end. The United States survived, though it did so by mortgaging the next generation's future. The past decade has been characterized by privatism, individualism, and a rejection of the civic agenda of the New Deal. Simple answers have prevailed. Slogans such as "Get big government off our backs" or "Just say no" have obscured the complexity of the times. The ideology of consumerism not only plagues the United States; it has consequences for the entire world. The election of President George Bush in 1988, with one of the lowest voter turnouts in recent history, reveals the complacency of our times.

If the implicit message to "be like us" defines the U.S. foreign policy of recent administrations, the growing interdependence of nations reveals that policy's worldwide acceptance. J. John Palen's *The Urban World*[1] describes this growing globalization and internationalization. That we live in an urban world is indisputable. But less appreciated is the rapid urbanization of the Third World. Palen states that each year some 93 million people are added to the world's population, and of that number, 97 percent are people in less developed countries (LDCs) of what is referred to as the Third World. Further, three-quarters of this growth occurs in cities of these countries.

In 1950, only three cities in developing countries had populations of 5 million or more. Today there are twenty-six such cities, and by the year 2000 there will be forty-six. Cities in LDCs are adding some 1.3 billion dwellers between 1975 and

80

2000. While 188 cities in LDCs have a million or more inhabitants today, another 166 such cities will be added by 2000. In 1950, New York, London, Moscow, Paris, and Chicago were among the largest cities in the world. Of those, only New York will remain among the ten largest cities worldwide by 2000. The largest cities will include Mexico City, São Paulo, Tokyo-Yokohama, Calcutta, Bombay, Seoul, Rio de Janeiro, Shanghai, and Delhi.[2]

And to add to the sheer numbers is a phenomenon Palen describes as "overurbanization," a process in which an increase in urban population outstrips a municipality's capacity to respond economically. Overurbanization and its concomitant problems of pollution, disease, poor health and joblessness reflect a global civic agenda for the 1990s. In the developed world, one of the greatest economic transformations in history is transpiring. For Paul E. Peterson, this constitutes "the new urban reality."[3]

In an essay collected in Peterson's books, sociologist John D. Kasarda outlines the implications of this economic transformation. In just over a decade, Kasarda writes, "the transformation of older cities from centers of production and distribution of material goods to centers of information exchange and service consumption has profoundly altered the capacity of these cities to offer employment opportunities for disadvantaged residents."[4] This has created a new economy in the city.

Residents in American cities are facing a double bind. First, cities have changed from centers of production and manufacturing of material goods to "centers of administration, information exchange, and higher-order service provision."[5] Second, there has been a demographic transformation. White ethnic, middle-class populations no longer characterize the city. Rather, cities have increasingly become "reservations" of the underclass—the poor, the elderly, African Americans, Hispanics, single mothers, and recently arrived immigrants. For the most part, the new jobs being created in the service sector do not attract the poor—those members of society who increasingly characterize the city—because they ordinarily do not possess needed skills in the new economy.

Statistics highlight the dramatic demographic shifts experienced by U.S. cities. Hispanics constituted more than 50 percent of the population increase during the 1970s. By 1980, more than half of Chicago's resident population was minority; statisticians projected that that percentage would climb to nearly 70 percent during the 1990s.[6]

Racial minorities are at a disadvantage in the new economy because cities are losing entry-level industrial and manufacturing jobs, on the one hand, and gaining jobs in areas in which minorities are least prepared, on the other. Further, many of the newer jobs are now being created in areas outside central cities. Lack of transportation and skills make the poor less able to gain access to these opportunities.

The consequences for residents of central cities are devastating. Confinement of minorities and recent immigrants to cities has serious outcomes. Such people are more likely than the majority white population to become unemployed, underemployed, or dependent upon welfare. Yet unemployment statistics are misleading, as underemployed people working in the service professions are counted as employed, whereas growing segments of the population, those "out of the labor force," are not counted in employment-rate figures. In other words, these rates do not include people who are disabled, on welfare, homeless, or discouraged.[7]

William Julius Wilson, in his book, *The Truly Disadvantaged: The Inner City, the Underclass and Public Policy,*[8] attempts to show the impact of the economy's transformation upon the "underclass," those with inadequate skills and access to the new job market. Despite a 5 percent loss in net population in the nation's fifty largest cities, economic transformation caused the poverty population to increase some 20 percent in these cities.[9] For Wilson, it is not race but a complexity of structural factors that accounts for the high rate of joblessness, crime, out-of-wedlock births, teenage pregnancies, families without husbands or fathers, and welfare dependency in central cities.

In 1980, fully 85 percent of the poor lived in communities dominated by poverty. However, only 32 percent of poor whites lived in such communities. The result of living in poverty-stricken communities is social isolation as the poor, especially the racial-minority poor, tend to become more concentrated in communities with the least opportunities for jobs and to have inadequate education or training for job skills. This social isolation reflects the structural conditions of the larger society. In such communities, unemployment reaches as high as half the adult male population. "Employable males" (with appropriate job skills) are relatively scarce.[10]

Public policy must address "the social and institutional mechanisms that enhance patterns of social dislocation originally caused by racial subjugation but that have been strengthened in more recent years by such developments as the class transformation of the inner city and changes in the urban economy," Wilson writes.[11] The situation of the underclass can be altered only if universal policies are created to provide transitional employment benefits to the poor, training and retraining for the underemployed, and relocation assistance for those able to work in new industries. Wilson concludes, "Changes in the economic and social situations of the ghetto underclass will lead to changes in cultural norms and behavior patterns," not vice versa.[12]

Not all members of the "underclass" have permanent addresses. Although not counted in official statistics, the outcomes of the new economy and cutbacks in government services have been the increasing numbers at the bottom of society and the increasing intensity of their plight.

The Reagan administration argued that the big problem with the homeless (*their* problem, in Reagan's view) was that they didn't know where to go to get relief. This at best naive assertion on the part of the president reveals the major quarrel activists have with policymakers. Often, policymakers are uninformed, or it is against their political ideology to admit that America has an escalating homeless population.

Homelessness is a pervasive problem, an embarrassment for one of the wealthiest countries in the world. Groups actively involved in the issue, such as the National Coalition on the Homeless in New York City or the Community for Creative Non-Violence in Washington, D.C., estimate that the homeless population in the United States is upwards of 4 million people. Subways are full of them in New York City. Homeless people who migrate to the South seeking jobs have built tent cities in

Houston. Schools for homeless children have been opened in New York and in Salt Lake City. In Chicago, roughly four thousand beds are available for an estimated forty thousand homeless people. Hundreds try to survive all over Chicago, in abandoned houses or apartment buildings, in automobiles and under viaducts.[13]

Jonathan Kozol has documented the problem in his controversial and shocking *Rachel and Her Children: Homeless Families in America,* noting particularly the complexity of the homeless population.[14] The fastest-growing categories of the homeless are families with a single parent and children of the homeless. Kozol says that twenty-eight thousand people use shelters each night in New York; an estimated forty thousand are left unsheltered citywide. Some eighteen thousand of the sheltered are parents and their children, representing five thousand families. A growing number of the poor, and of the homeless poor in particular, are women and children. In certain parts of Massachusetts, 90 to 95 percent of the homeless are families with children.[15]

People are homeless for a variety of reasons. Over the past two decades, many have become homeless who were previously institutionalized in nursing homes or mental or penal institutions. Some few people "choose" to be homeless, because of borderline personalities or lifestyles. But many are homeless for other reasons. Some have lost their homes or apartments due to evictions, fires, or redevelopment. Others have lost jobs or have had their welfare benefits cut. Many youths, too, are homeless; some join gangs or enter underworld occupations of prostitution, drug-dealing or theft in order to survive. Homelessness among adolescents can often be attributed to "disruptive family situations, deviant parents, a lack of love and acceptance, a lack of understanding or listening."[16] Some are thrown out or pushed out of crowded housing conditions. The lack of affordable housing for the poor leaves many on the street. While 1,500 units of housing are built annually in Chicago, mostly for the middle class, thousands of units are burned or torn down, not to be replaced.[17] There is a seven- to ten-year wait to get into Chicago's decrepit public housing apartments, home to over 170,000 people. Political pressure, racial discrimination, and budget shortfalls do not allow the erection of scattered-site dwellings, a program to locate isolated dwellings for low-income people in middle-income neighborhoods. And for a Chicago alderperson to support a policy in his or her neighborhood would be political suicide.

A related and consequential problem to that of homelessness is hunger. Hunger is, of course, a worldwide problem; thousands of children die daily from hunger and malnutrition. What is less known is that this problem is widespread in the United States.

Hunger is relatively invisible to the middle class. Yet according to J. Larry Brown and H. F. Pizer in *Living Hungry in America*, there are "at least twenty million Americans . . . going hungry at some time each month" in such a wealthy nation.[18] Brown and Pizer suggest that hunger is an epidemic created by humans and spread by public policies.

In a 1987 survey of twenty-six cities, it was discovered that the demand for food assistance increased more than 18 percent from 1986.[19] In New York City just a few years ago there were about thirty organizations distributing food, but today over five hundred agencies now distribute meals in New York, averaging more than 1.2 million of them every month.[20] Hunger in the United States is further exacerbated because those who are hungry or malnourished are least likely, and least able, to articulate and make more visible the extent of their plight. These people are politically powerless; they are the invisible in U.S. society. They may be physically incapable of organizing themselves, due to the medical consequences of hunger. They are generally less prone to speak out on hunger, because that is not acceptable in a society that values self-help and individual initiative. The victims of our society are often blamed for their own plight and called "lazy," "immoral," or, worse, "not fit" to compete. They are often dependent upon government handouts or charities, with a resulting loss of self-esteem, increasing levels of guilt, and a preoccupation with survival.

Hunger is rarely the fault of the hungry; rather, it is a problem of policy, of distribution, of economic self-interest. Policy changes and structural reshaping are necessary if the hungry are to be fed in the United States and throughout the world. Hunger is not the consequence of a lack of food worldwide; it reflects a problem of economic injustice that permeates society's structures.

In a survey of users of twenty-nine emergency feeding programs in New York a few years ago, a major cause stated for increased hunger was "a job loss or cut-back in government assistance."[21] Cuts in programs such as the provision of food stamps or Aid to Families with Dependent Children have directly contributed to the hunger problem. In Chicago, malnutrition-related diseases most commonly found in the Third World have been documented. Nearly 30 percent of the city's population—some 887,000 Chicagoans—are said to be "at risk" of hunger due to inadequate income and aid.[22]

A final issue confronting the city, and society at large, is domestic violence. We are told that almost two million women are battered every year, and some form of violence occurs in 25 percent of all marriages. In 1988, 20 percent of the women seeking emergency surgical procedures were victims of wife abuse. Domestic violence also affects children. More than twelve hundred children die each year in the United States from abuse and neglect. In 1986, two million reported cases of child abuse occurred in America, up from 669,000 in 1976. At least 40 percent of all abuse cases involve alcohol or illegal drugs.[23]

Lenore E. Walker's *The Battered Woman* and Joy M. K. Bussert's *Battered Women: From a Theology of Suffering to an Ethic of Empowerment* describe this problem in detail.[24] Walker describes the psychology of battered women who are victims of a culture that legitimizes violence and oppresses women, many of whom are trapped economically with their abusers.

Psychologists and pastoral counselors often seek to keep the family together "at all costs" for reasons of cultural and religious values. Battered women, too, often internalize the values of the dominant culture. Society teaches women to be submissive and compliant, making them powerless to deal with escalating violence. According to a *Newsweek* article, women are often reluctant or unable to leave their battering husbands or male mates.[25] The *Newsweek* article reports that there are more than a thousand shelters for battered women nationwide. New strategies and programs of legal advocacy, transitional housing and skill development for battered women are much needed.

The escalation of domestic violence in the United States crosses class and racial boundaries. Bussert's book points readers to a needed "ethic of empowerment" for abused women and their children. For Bussert, the notion of the family has become an idolatry that legitimizes cultural and religious beliefs of male dominance. The religious right often blames the victim (the abused) for her abuse or gives simple answers, recommending reliance upon prayer or viewing "suffering" as a "Christian" virtue. The sanctioning of family violence, or the inappropriate counsel to remain in an abusive marital relationship regardless of the consequences, is a major issue for the 1990s.

We live in an era of escalating crises and impending apocalypse. The impasses of our time are not just nuclear or diplomatic but personal and domestic. The issues of global society require a new ecumenical vision, "the whole counsel of God for the whole people of God," as it has been stated. On the home front, domestic issues are no less critical. Hunger, homelessness, joblessness, and domestic violence all demonstrate significant tears in the social fabric, problems in the body politic.

The worldwide community of faith needs an ecumenical, global perspective on the world. Shifts in international relations create opportunities for renewed partnership and cooperation among nations and peoples who recognize their growing interdependence. Christians need a theology that embraces more intentionally the world and the "civil agenda." A theology that brings private and public worlds together is needed if the church is to recapture its relevancy. The church needs new models and means for urban or public ministries. If urban ministry takes seriously the growing concentration of people in cities, public ministry takes seriously the issues that these people, "we the people," are facing. A maintenance or business-as-usual approach to these issues will result in a church only further marginalized.

Urban and public ministry training and preparation will need to offer an open ear as well as strategies of empowerment for those victimized and marginalized in society. The capacities, not the deficiencies, of these people must be recognized and developed. Ministry to them must move beyond mere service delivery to capacity formation and the systematic analysis of the causes of pain. It must seek structural change. The pursuit of peace in society is linked to the pursuit of justice.

In Isaiah 61:1–4, it was those who mourned, those who were captive, those who were bruised and oppressed who rebuilt the city and renewed public life. By providing access to power and possible participation in the public arena to those excluded from legitimate participation in the created order, the community of faith has the opportunity and responsibility to pursue peace for the brokenhearted and justice for the oppressed of urban society.

Clinton E. Stockwell is director of the Chicago Center for Public Ministry (CCPM), a cooperative ecumenical program of the Community Renewal Society. CCPM is sponsored by the Community Renewal Society and by Chicago Theological Seminary, the Lutheran Theological Seminary at Chicago, and McCormick Theological Seminary. CCPM is an internship program in urban ministry and public policy for theology students and other graduate students in religion, art, and social work.

Notes

1. J. John Palen, *The Urban World*, 3rd edition (New York: McGraw-Hill, 1987).

2. Ibid., p. 344. Table 14:1, "The Ten Largest Cities in the World: 1950, 1985, 2000." The three cities with populations over 5 million in 1950 were Shanghai, Buenos Aires, and Calcutta.

3. Paul E. Peterson, ed., *The New Urban Reality*, (Washington, D.C.: Brookings Institution, 1985).

4. John D. Kasarda, "Urban Change and Minority Opportunities," in Peterson, *The New Urban Reality*, p. 43.

5. Ibid., p. 33.

6. Ibid., p. 53.

7. William Julius Wilson, *The Truly Disadvantaged: The Inner City,*

the Underclass and Public Policy (Chicago: University of Chicago Press, 1987), pp. 58–63.

8. Ibid.

9. Ibid., p. 46.

10. Ibid., pp. 58, 73.

11. Ibid., p. 137.

12. Ibid., p. 159.

13. Statistics available from the Interfaith Council for the Homeless, Chicago, Ill.

14. Jonathan Kozol, *Rachel and Her Children: Homeless Families in America* (New York: Crown Books, 1988), pp. 4–5.

15. Kozol, *Rachel,* pp. 4–5.

16. Dick Simpson and Clinton Stockwell, "Hunger, Homelessness and Joblessness," in *Chicago's Future: In a Time of Change,* ed. Dick Simpson (Champaign, Ohio: Stipes Publishing Co., 1988), p. 157.

17. Gregory D. Squires, Larry Bennett, Kathleen McCourt, and Philip Nyden, *Chicago: Race, Class, and the Response to Urban Decline* (Philadelphia: Temple University Press, 1987), p. 114.

18. J. Larry Brown and H. F. Pizer, *Living Hungry in America* (New York: Macmillan, 1987), p. 161.

19. Ibid.

20. Barbara Mahany, "City Facing Hunger Epidemic: Mayor's Commission Finds Major Holes in Food-Supply Safety Nets," *Chicago Tribune,* 4 November 1984, metro edition.

21. Joann Lamphere, "Hunger-New York: The New York State Hunger Watch Project," *Health and Medicine: Journal of the Health and Medicine Policy Research Group* 2, no. 3 (Spring 1984): 16.

22. Mahany, "City Facing Hunger Epidemic."

23. "A Tale of Abuse," *Newsweek,* 12 December 1988: 56–61.

24. Lenore E. Walker, *The Battered Woman* (New York: Harper & Row, 1979) and Joy M. K. Bussert, *Battered Women: From a Theology of Suffering to an Ethic of Empowerment* (N.Y.: Lutheran Church in America, 1986).

25. *Newsweek,* 12 December 1988: 56–61.

· 6 ·

Whatever Happened
to the Golden Rule?

James A. Forbes, Jr.

The sermon for today was born beside the hospital bed of one of my friends with AIDS.[1] He was disturbed about God's attitude toward people who are dying from AIDS and wanted to know whether the fact that he was gay would put a barrier between himself and the love of God. He wanted to know, will God affirm me, celebrate the uniqueness of my being, my affection, my relationships?

Now I suspect you would like to know what I told him. And I would like to know what you would have told him if you had been there. Before I tell that story, let me say this sermon comes at a time when our entire community is attempting to respond to the brutal attack of the woman jogger in Central Park while we as a people reflect upon what to do about the issues of AIDS and the increasing violence that we are experiencing in our times.

So back to the story of my friend. I came to discover that the church had in some way affected his sense of whether God could really be for him. His church, in this case, was a sensitive and caring congregation, but the wider community had made it difficult for him to trust even a biblical perspective of love and mercy and graciousness from God. Somehow the church and our society had not done what they could have done to make the passage through the perilous waters of pain and isolation more gracious for him.

It was while I was sitting by his bed that I started asking, what should the church do? And a response suggested itself,

90

like a word sent by Federal Express: The church should live by the Golden Rule. Do unto others as you would have others do unto you. I thought, "That's right." But let me confess something—I did not know where in the Bible the Golden Rule was found. And I'm a theological professor! Now don't laugh at me, brothers and sisters. Do you know where the Golden Rule is found?

I have not heard a sermon on the Golden Rule for a decade or so. As a matter of fact, I really think that rule is not the current policy of our citizens. For a period of time, it has seemed to be more and more appropriate for folks to look out for themselves—that a kind of narcissism has come to the fore in which I look into the mirror and I find myself focusing on what is good for me, what will secure me, my family, my crowd, my caucus, my group. The rule about doing unto others as we would have them do unto us has not been the major motif in our time. So I am happy to tell you where it can be found. You can find the Golden Rule in the Gospel According to St. Matthew, chapter 7, verses 7–12:

Ask, and it will be given you; search, and you will find; knock, and the door will be opened for you. For everyone who asks receives, and everyone who searches finds, and for everyone who knocks, the door will be opened. Is there anyone among you who, if your child asks for bread, will give a stone? Or if the child asks for a fish, will give a snake? If you then, who are evil, know how to give good gifts to your children, how much more will your Father in heaven give good things to those who ask him! In everything do to others as you would have them do to you; for this is the law and the prophets.

Now, two observations. Did you notice at the end of the Golden Rule—"in everything do to others as you would have them do to you"—that was not the end of the sentence? that there was a semicolon? And, following the semicolon, these words: "for this is the law and the prophets"? This suggests that the Golden Rule is not just some optional extra, added to the Ten Commandments. It is not just some voluntary principle of reciprocity; it is at the heart of the gospel. The core of Christian conduct is found right here in these words: "Do unto others as you would have them do unto you." I think it is such a strong admonition that persons who call themselves Christians who do not at least attempt to live by the Golden Rule might, in one day of harsh judgment, be required to turn in their membership cards.

What? You don't live by the Golden Rule? That is not the principle by which you order your relationships at home, in your workplace, at the church, and in the wider community? This is at the heart of it. This is almost a one-sentence requirement upon which Christian education programs are built: that we might learn how to treat other folks as we would wish to be treated ourselves.

Now there is a second thing about this text that helps to make the Golden Rule shine more brightly as we face our Christian responsibility. Notice that it was introduced with what I think is a rather staggering claim: Ask and it shall be given; seek and you shall find; knock and the door shall be opened unto you.

This text is introduced by a promise that the things we need in order to survive will be provided for us. What is this business? I think what you need to be aware of is the preceding chapter, chapter 6, where Jesus makes it clear what he is talking about: "but strive first for the kingdom of God" (Matt. 6:33) . . . what we now often call God's realm, the commonwealth of love. Seek God's kingdom and God's righteousness and all these things shall be yours as well.

In other words, Jesus is talking about a new community, a new arrangement that will obtain when God's reign has become the order of the day. In that time, people who have needs because of the quality of life in the beloved community would ask and it would be given; they would seek and find; they would knock and doors would be opened unto them. It is Jesus' projection of what it will look like when the church configures its life, or when society configures its life, according to the dream in the mind of the Creator. It is Jesus' way of saying, "This is where you learn to incline towards the inevitability of God's great reign, the beloved community." That is what Jesus was talking about: when God's reign and the principles of justice and mercy and equality have become the Magna Charta of the people of faith, when you could ask and it would be given.

It is within this kind of projection of a caring community

that Jesus then says, "Do unto others as you would have them do unto you." Jesus compares God with our parental instincts: If you, with your shortcomings, based on your human frailty, know how to show special love and care for your children, then you are like God who will provide the things we need. I think this gives deeper meaning to the word of the Golden Rule: Those who have entered the realm of God's tender, loving care will be set free from inordinate preoccupation with their own security and their well-being. One of my colleagues in the preaching class this week spoke about the problem of people being willing to extend graciousness to others who are unlike themselves. She said, it is as if people think that if God is gracious and merciful to somebody who is quite different from us that the mercy and grace will run out before God gets around to our needs. But she said, "Not so." God can love somebody other than you and still have quite an abundance of love and grace for the likes of you and also for me.

So I tried my best before I answered my friend's question to see if I could get my spirit right with the principles of the Golden Rule. I guess I tried to put myself in his place; I tried to make my response on the basis of if I were gay, if I did have AIDS, or if I happened to be a victim of the tyranny of drugs, if I had been despised, if I had been rejected, and if I had been denied a sense of comfort, if folks who used to touch me would not touch me anymore, if people were ashamed of who I was as I tried to be what I knew myself to be, what would I want somebody to say to me?

This is what I told him. I said, "We are all God's children." That is what I said. I said, "We are not the same, for God in creation was much more risk-taking to make differences. On the spectrum even of sexuality, if we'd line up, it would make an interesting rainbow coalition." I told him, "God loves us just the same. God celebrates the uniqueness of each one of us and calls us to discover the path of our own fulfillment in ways characterized by the integrity of our being." I said, "God bends from where we are and lifts us up in service of others. God forgives us when we fail to be faithful to who we are, and then God rejoices in our freedom to be who we are and encourages the community to celebrate with all people the integrity of their being. And if the beings are significantly different, then God's glory is in the diversity of creation itself."

And I said, "That does not mean we don't have problems to work through, brother; there are a lot of things I don't know, a lot of problems in the social fabric that have not been figured out yet, and I don't know how to work through them." I said, "But man, God loves you and celebrates you. You don't have to wait in dread of death, thinking that God shuts the door on you." I said, "God, in fact, has a *special caring* for those who have been despised and rejected and abused and oppressed, and maybe you'll get a more royal welcome than some who think they deserve to enter before you." That's what I told him.

But it was not immediately clear to me that I had broken through the barriers built during the days of ostracism, so if, perchance, you are not yet able to see how the Golden Rule gives us the principles by which we respond, I wish to give some pointers to help us with what I call a case study: the Golden Rule as it was lived out by the Good Samaritan.

You know the story: A man on his way from Jerusalem to Jericho falls victim to robbers. The illustration is introduced by Jesus in response to a question from a lawyer wishing to put Jesus to the test. Desiring to justify himself, he asked Jesus how he might find eternal life. And I think a clue is right there. Let me tell you this, brothers and sisters, that if you—a preacher, or a deacon, or a lawyer, or a schoolteacher, or a doctor, or whatever your profession or your vocation may be—if you constantly find yourself trying to test other folks about who they are and what they ought to be doing, if you find yourself inordinately invested in that, or if you are like the text says, always trying to justify yourself—if you find that every day you get up you are conducting a referendum as to whether you are a worthy character—it means that you have not yet entered fully into the realm of God's tender, loving care. Everybody in the realm of God's love and tender care is already somebody. You don't have to make a case for being there. By God's grace you're already in. You don't have to go around testing folks all the time, judging other folks; *you're in!*

But between Jerusalem and Jericho, hear what it says. Fell among robbers who stripped him and beat him and departed leaving him half dead. This is a description, and I think of it in two ways. I think of patients with AIDS and I think of that young woman jogging through Central Park. In the whole analysis, a victim falling among robbers who rob you of your dignity, of your personhood, who violate your very body and your spirit and your soul. This victim fell among the robbers; they stripped him and they stripped her; and beat him and beat her, and departed, leaving him and her half dead.

Now let me ask you this morning: In light of this story, who is the victim? In the case of AIDS, is it the person with AIDS? or the group to which the person belongs? or the family? or the total society? In Harlem, in Manhattan, it's the whole community that suffers every time there is an AIDS patient, for in a sense everybody has AIDS. All of us are going to die—there are just those that require specialized attention. They are the victims, but I am also a victim; you, you too, are a victim. Is the victim the young woman in the park? You know it is. There is nobody that can smooth over that dastardly deed. But again, who is the victim? Are those kids victims? (Bless their hearts—I still can not seem to identify them as a "wolf pack"; they're human beings!) Is the victim the kid who devised it from some kind of demonic impact or the other guys drawn in? Is it the mother of the victim or the mothers of the kids? Who is the victim? Is it the community itself? Is it the low-income housing project where those kids lived—the Schomburg Plaza apartment area? Who is the victim? In fact, the reason we are all so upset in this case is that we have not yet been able to identify with the attack. Was it because of poverty that they did it? The problem is we can't figure it out.

I think, brothers and sisters, that it may very well be that it is HIV—hearts infected with violence—that has broken out. I think the reason we are all upset is because there has been a break in the social contract. That you can't walk through the park, you can't walk down the street, you can't live. Something is coming unglued. And I think what is becoming unglued is *whatever it was that God had in mind* about how people ought to deal with each other as they would love to be dealt with. The Golden Rule is tarnished; some kind of acid has been poured on the Golden Rule that is strong enough to tarnish the gold. I think you and I are aware that whatever might hold our community together is coming unglued. And I think we have a right to be worried about it. A right to be frightened!

Of course, let's lay a wreath of flowers, let's have a prayer vigil, let's do the parade to show that we are together—black and white, gay and straight—and that sacred and secular organizations are working together. That's right. Let's do all of that. But you and I, looking at this story, understand that we need more than a temporary response, more than outrage. Somehow we have to recover the Golden Rule and thank God there was this person, after the preachers passed by, and after the deacons, too—after we all passed by—there was this person who came upon the fallen man and instead of bypassing him, poured oil and wine upon his wounds. He picked him up and put him upon his own horse, took him down further and put him in an inn. And the text says "took care of him." That's the word: took care of him! And this is the part that is really exciting to me: After he took care, he took out two silver coins and gave them to the innkeeper, saying, "Take care of him."

Riversiders, this is for us! Namely, we are a congregation where we do not simply take care. We do our charitable bit, but we are also people who, as we take care, find a way to engage the system in taking care. In the moving beyond charity to the analysis that leads toward system change, not only are we taking care, we are creating a take-care system that will allow us once again to live, to walk freely in our streets, and to enjoy jogging in our parks.

The question in this case study that held me up was, Why did that man stop and do that? And I think I know the answer. Why did this good Samaritan stop and give genuine care? I think I've gotten onto it! I believe he did it because he had been on that road. I suspect—it doesn't say so in the Bible, so please forgive the homiletical imagination—I suspect that he might have experienced, in one form or other, the assault of his person; he was a Samaritan, you know. He knew what it felt like to be despised and rejected, to be robbed, assaulted, and called names. He had been there. It was that capacity that I think makes possible movement into the realm of God's tender, loving care, and I think that's where I ought to end.

Jesus the Christ invites us into the realm of tender, loving care. Jesus' invitation is to the young woman, and all young women, black and white, Hispanic, Asian and Native American. Jesus says, I know what it is like. Jesus has been in Central Park—they called it Gethsemane. Assaulted, even by his friends. He had been there. He knew what it was like to be called names.

So Jesus is with our sister. Yes, and as they at the vigil stand and pray the prayer, Jesus is there. He says, "I know what you have been through; I know what it is like." And yet, Jesus says, maybe something redemptive can come from it.

So I say to my friend, "Hey, brother, in your bed of AIDS, Jesus has been there. He knows what death will be like. He knows what it's like; he's been there."

The purpose of the church in this time is to create a group of people who understand that this God created us out of the same batch of divine creativity, that we've all been there. And when you recognize in my sister and brother that we've all been there together, it will become increasingly impossible for us to engage in various forms of assault against each other.

My prayer is that we in this congregation, slowly maybe, sometimes kicking and screaming and debating and shouting about it, will become a congregation where, when we look at one another and see into the eyes of a brother or sister, we will understand their suffering and pain; we will be able to say, *I've been there,* so let me do unto this person even as I would have him or her do unto me. Amen.

James A. Forbes, Jr., is senior minister at the Riverside Church in New York City. He was professor of homiletics at Union Theological Seminary in New York City from 1976 to 1989.

Note

1. This sermon was preached April 30, 1989, at the Riverside Church in New York City by James A. Forbes, Jr., senior pastor.

RACISM AND DRUGS IN THE CITY:

THE CHURCH'S CALL TO MINISTRY

Hal Joseph Recinos

The cry of the barrios and ghettos reveals that 18 percent of infants in America born in city hospitals are substance addicted.[1] The infant mortality rate in the African American and Latino communities is higher than that of many Third World countries,[2] and drug-related crimes cause jails to fill each day with teenagers doing heavy time. There is, quite simply, a massive waste of human life in the city caused by the high levels of violence and drug-related problems. A description of the informal drug economy operating in the nation's barrios and ghettos indicates the lack of justice in society.

The violence and drugs in the city are, in part, byproducts of the structures of racism. Powerful leaders of white society have limited the structure of opportunity for people of color, forcing the people of the barrio and ghetto to find other ways to survive. For many, the drug economy provides one form of survival—perhaps for a while—in its violent world of death.

Death walks the city streets triumphantly, claiming the lives of people living in a world forgotten by most Christians. The poor and oppressed are in our inner cities, and there is no strategy within the churches to reach them politically and compassionately.

The church was called into being to continue the mission of Jesus in the context of a world structured against hope and liberation. This hopelessness today is clearly found within our drug-infested inner cities—cities that the mainline churches fled amid the "white flight" of their parishioners. What embodies the church's mission in the city under such a scenario? Whose interests are being served or not served in this ministry? Have the urban poor had good news preached to them? Do people crippled by racism walk? Do those blind to human suffering regain sight? Do those deaf to the cries of drug addicts and crack babies hear? Can the church truly present itself before wretched humanity and claim to be responding to the call of Jesus of Nazareth in our cities today? The church's struggle with drugs in the city must include answers to larger questions of racial justice and political economy.

Background to Urban Drug Culture of the 1990s

A sketch of the urban scene from the 1960s to the present provides the necessary background to the issues before us.[3] The 1960s saw the beginning of a new suburban flight, more dramatic than that of the previous decades. One result was that the poor, mostly people of color, were left to deal with the escalating problems of the city on their own. The inner city, especially, experienced mounting social tensions frequently expressed in riots—events often sparked by perceived police brutality. These riots constituted a language of social protest from enraged African Americans and Latinos that registered their denunciation of the social injustices of so-called "white" society. Ironically, those victimized by urban violence were in large part the very people already enduring human disfigurement in the larger social system.

Fiscal crisis typified urban life in the 1970s. Urban economies lost their tax bases to suburb, sunbelt, and overseas competition. For instance, New York lost six hundred thousand jobs between 1969 and 1976 alone. The fiscal situation in New York would have looked very different had the city not lost $1.5 billion in tax revenues during this time.[4] Between 1970 and 1975, the South Bronx—the national symbol of urban decay in America during this period—experienced the abandonment of twenty thousand to thirty thousand housing units each year. Buildings were burned to the ground at the rate of thirty-four a day toward the middle of the decade.[5] Many African American and Latino politicians rose to power during this period of urban crisis. The enormous task of reconstructing the social and economic structures of the urban environment—without the economic and personal support of the white community—still evades these urban leaders.

Throughout the 1970s, during a period of dramatic shifts in international capital and national urban crisis, growing numbers of immigrants, primarily from Southeast Asia and Latin America, made their way to the inner core of American cities. America's politics of race hindered the economic progress and paralyzed the social mobility of these new immigrants. To compound the problem, the Vietnam War brought an increase in heroin traffic to inner-city communities, where African Americans and Latinos were concentrated; heroin use claimed the lives of increasing numbers of this population in the form of violence- and drug-related death. Drug dealing soon epitomized the inner city's informal economy, yielding an income to the severely marginalized poor.

The 1980s may be remembered for the rise of gentrification in urban areas. This development established patterns of social relations that fueled a mounting class-based, racial and ethnic polarization in cities across the nation. The slaying of a young African American man by angry whites in Howard Beach, a neighborhood in Queens, became a national symbol of this urban struggle. The decade will also be remembered by Ronald Reagan's reassertion of U.S. hegemony in the Middle East and Central America. The '80s were the so-called "America is back" decade. Many leaders of mainline churches began discussing issues of globalization and joined the struggle for the poor by way of joining the justice struggles of the oppressed *overseas*. Meanwhile, the so-called "Crack Nation"[6] dramatically increased its membership in American cities.

Geopolitical realities have a way of directing drugs to urban streets and profits into white-collar hands. The Vietnam War put heroin on the streets. The Reagan administration's support of the contras and the war in Central America contributed to the spread of crack in North America. Drug smuggling resulted in an 8 percent drop in the wholesale price of cocaine in America by the close of the 1980s as cocaine traffic increased by 1,000 percent.[7] Today the international drug trade is a complex business with profits nearing a total of $500 billion annually.[8]

The church has failed to address the problems of drugs and urban violence associated with the international drug trade. We have failed to learn that the drug trade is an international profit-motive business sponsored outside of the barrios and ghettos. Economic prosperity for a small, urban-based power elite has developed at the cost of massive human brokenness in our cities, and the church has acted as if paralyzed in the face of this international crime against humanity.

Drug Abuse in the Nation's Barrios and Ghettos

A walk down any inner-city street tells the story of the results of the international drug business: hopelessness, hunger, economic marginalization, racism, and xenophobia haunt the inner cities of North America. Crack in the nation's barrios and ghettos creates conditions of violence that destroy human life. By the mid-'80s, Puerto Ricans between the ages of fifteen and forty-four in the state of New York, who represent 5 percent of the total population, constituted 22 percent of the victims of murder.[9] Many of these deaths were associated with drug-related violence. Drug-related murders have increased for Latinos and people of color in all of the nation's major cities. In 1989, violent crimes such as murder, rape, robbery, and aggravated assault in thirteen metropolitan areas across the nation totaled 25,931.[10]

In the United States, between 500,000 and 750,000 poor people are IV drug abusers, and AIDS has been rapidly spreading among this population. The disease is striking more IV drug abusers in the post-industrial urban centers of northern New Jersey—home to large African American and Latino underclass populations—than any other group. According to a *New York Times* report,[11] IV drug abusers constituted 69 percent of the AIDS cases in Newark and 53 percent of the AIDS cases in cities such as Jersey City and Paterson.

George Bush's "war on drugs," which has been characterized by interception strategies, prevents only 5 to 7 percent of the total amount of drugs being smuggled into the United

States from actually entering the country. It is increasingly apparent that the role of military and police agencies is unlikely to dismantle the international drug trade. If just one cargo plane penetrates the interception net, it will succeed in bringing into this country a huge amount of cocaine. The risks are high, but so are the profits: pilots are said to earn an estimated $500,000 for each flight.[12] Meanwhile, thousands die yearly in the United States from the terrorism of crack and the resultant pervasive violence in society. Death has become reality for too many people in the city.

A Public Ministry is Needed

Jesus engaged in a public ministry that made followers critically aware of the structures of systemic oppression operating in Roman-occupied Palestinian society. The church called to continue Christ's mission is required to embody a Christian ethical practice capable of making the faith community critically aware of the oppressive structures at the root of human suffering. God's parenthood and the equality of all people means that human injustice, economic exploitation, racism, sexism, and poverty are scandalous in the created order. The drug trade and the violence associated with it are contradictory to the vision God has for humanity.

Drug-plagued ghetto and barrio streets invite the church to a life of prophetic mission characterized by commitment to the task of humanizing all dimensions of life at every level of the social order. Crack addiction is a sign of extreme oppression. For a whole generation of urban poor, and especially African Americans and Latinos, crack has become a present-day symbol of death. Yet the church's response pales in comparison to the magnitude of the problem, and the good news of the gospel is not reaching the street where the junkie exists in the midst of what appears to be an indifferent society. Local church communities now must develop strategies to incarnate themselves in history—in our cities—as Christ-centered institutions of social criticism and agents of community change. Only then will it be possible for the struggle against drugs and violence in the city to be won.

Where Is the Church?

The cries of young people—who make up a large number of those most heavily struck by drugs and violence in the city—have fallen largely on deaf ears. The silence of the church to date can, perhaps, be blamed on its overly privatized brand of Christianity. This must change. Church silence on urgent matters such as drugs in the city leads to the sacrifice of human lives to the violence of drugs and the politics of addiction. The church dare not forget that Jesus suffered in order to save. In urban America, Jesus cries out from the rooftops where junkies ritualize despair by getting high on dope. The Galilean Christ experiences the anguish of IV drug users suffering from AIDS. He feels the pain of prostitutes who hustle to feed children and drug habits; he weeps with the terrified mothers of the nation's cities who lose little ones to stray bullets, crack, and drug-related murder.

Christians who pay attention to these cries will discover that barrio and ghetto youths have evolved a culture of protest and resistance on the streets. The junkies in the city know instinctively that they are in a violent argument with the powers and principalities of the society that has produced their poverty.[13] Christians need to spend considerable time listening to rap and salsa music, reading the writing on the tenement walls in the barrios and ghettos, and interpreting the murals on the sides of abandoned buildings. All of these forms of cultural discourse manifest a critique of society that identifies and questions systems of structured oppression.

The church must walk with the oppressed in the service of justice by engaging in action directed toward the structural transformation of society in the direction of God's reign.[14] The church in the United States cannot afford to interpret the faith tradition in light of established society's requirement of submissiveness in history. Jesus of Nazareth took upon himself the flesh of poverty and historical rejection (Phil. 2:5–9). Christ summons local church communities everywhere to breathe the stale air of abandoned tenements and to transform the anguish of crack-reality in the city.

A series of questions is before the church as it engages the fight against drugs and violence in the city. How will the church begin to understand the relationship between Third World debt and the coca trade? Can the church understand the difference between crack cocaine and the role of coca in indigenous cultures in South America? Will the church hear that children are the poorest members of society, bearing in their flesh the despair of parents pushed to the margins of a post-industrial social order? What will the church do once it hears the cry of the oppressed in the inner city?

The church can help to broaden the terms of discourse defining the so-called "war on drugs" beyond a standard law-enforcement policy. Methods of curtailing the spread of drugs and violence must include examination of the economic conditions constituting the framework of human existence for persons at home and in nations where coca is grown. Churches should send a clear message to international banking institutions demanding an end to the laundering of drug monies.[15]

The Church Incarnate in Community

A powerful strategy presents itself for the church to use to broaden its understanding of the fight against drugs and violence: an immersion program that places the church members in direct contact with the lives of the urban poor and oppressed. The local church could organize an action-reflection group of six to ten people. This group would have the task of relating to a particular community and issue of urban life for an extended period of time. For instance, the group might relate to street-corner drug society by daily contact with that community. This could lead to greater understanding of the dynamics of junkie life. While it will prove difficult to establish initial contact with street-junkie society, it is not impossible.

Initial contact with any group about which the church has little or no knowledge is best accomplished with the help of a local group or mediating person. Ex-junkies committed to the fight against drugs and drug-related violence in their communities can be tremendously helpful to the action-reflection group. After adequate orientation to a local community's fight against drugs, group members can begin to walk the streets and learn about the ways people talk about their world and problems. The early stage of immersion can include reading of local community newspapers, literature, and other available published material. Organized events and informal conversations with local people will also help the action-reflection group develop an insider's perspective on community life.

Junkie society always includes people who have spent a great deal of time reflecting on their social situation. The group may collect life stories of such people. Life stories that juxtapose junkies' experiences with local community history, set in the context of larger economic and political processes, will cast an important light on the politics of drugs in the city. Life stories will enable group members to understand and appreciate situations that exist in the local community from the perspective of the addicted. Life stories will both humanize the junkie and point to structural factors sustaining the system of life at the margins of the inner city.

The action-reflection group can then communicate these life stories to the larger church membership, using both their own words and the words of the junkies themselves. Immersion in the stuff that constitutes local community life will enable people in the church to develop a greater appreciation for the context in which people must struggle and live their lives.

Moreover, understanding the fight against drugs from the "inside" changes the terms of reference by which people in the church define community. Because the junkie is humanized in the eyes of the church by the action-reflection team's immersion in junkie life, the church—even the church of the poor in the city—will not be able to define itself as a community set apart. Instead, local churches will seek to incarnate themselves as communities of faith seeking the transformation of junkie society by embodying an ethic of struggle that promotes local daily contact with those termed "non-persons" (junkies) by society.

A Personal Note

The church everywhere has a profound role to play in terms of action aimed at ending the madness of drugs and violence in the cities. Clearly, violence has increased in the city to levels previously unimaginable. I was a junkie living for the most part on the streets of New York, Los Angeles, and San Juan, Puerto Rico, in the late '60s and early '70s. Violence and death were very much a part of junkie life then; however, the pattern of violence and the instruments of death used then pale in contrast with today's reality in the inner city. The knife was the weapon dominating life on the streets. Few junkies possessed handguns of any kind. Pervasive violence was not the common denominator of life on the streets that it is today.

Now firearms of every kind can be found in the hands of young people in the inner city. Teenagers are walking about with semiautomatic pistols, Uzis, AK–47s, and assault rifles. Handguns are the most widely used weapon in extinguishing the lives of young African American men.[16] African American men between the ages of fifteen and twenty-four would have stood a better chance of surviving combat in the Vietnam War, and were far safer on duty in the Persian Gulf War, than in the inner-city streets today.[17] The situation for Latino men in America is no less scandalous. A whole generation of young African Americans and Latinos is dying violently. The blood of these children of God covers the streets of the city, passionately imploring the church to help seek a solution.

God walks the city streets, calling the church to committed Christian service. Christians eager to proclaim the good news of God-in-Christ or discover the means capable of laying the foundation for the contemporary renewal of the church must immerse themselves in the life of the city. Jesus weeps with the marginalized and drug-plagued humanity of the city, providing inspiration and courage to those children of God who struggle to realize a radical transformation of their world. The church must hear the cry of the city and respond to the structure of death and violence, beginning in the nation's barrios and ghettos. Today, the suffering endured by Jesus is in the cries of the so-called "Crack Nation," in which people are crushed daily by the culture of junkiedom. Jesus calls all Christians to heal his broken body by entering the world of the outcasts. Clearly, God is calling upon the church to heal the shattered bodies of the barrios and ghettos. Surely Christians will follow Christ into service at the fringes of society out of a deep commitment to the vision of "the city which is to come" (Heb. 13:15).

Hal Joseph Recinos is associate professor of theology, culture, and urban ministry at Wesley Theological Seminary in Washington, D.C. He is the author of Hear the Cry! A Latino Pastor Challenges the Church *(Westminster/John Knox Press, 1989).*

Notes

1. See T. Berry Brazelton, ".Why is America Failing its Children?" *The New York Times Magazine,* 9 September 1990: 42.

2. Figures available from Children's Defense Fund and National Coalition of Hispanic Health and Human Services, Washington, D.C. See also Recinos, *Hear the Cry* (Louisville, Ky.: Westminster/John Knox Press, 1989), p. 134.

3. Parts of this section are drawn from a forthcoming work on urban ministry: Recinos, *And Who Is My Neighbor: Global Encounters in the City* (Nashville: Abingdon Press, 1992).

4. Howard P. Chudacoff and Judith E. Smith, *The Evolution of American Urban Society,* 3rd ed. (Englewood Cliffs, N.J.: Prentice-Hall, 1988), p. 301.

5. Jon C. Teaford, *The Twentieth-Century American City: Problem, Promise, and Reality* (Baltimore: Johns Hopkins University Press, 1986), pp. 142–143.

6. See Jerry Adler et al., "Hour by Hour Crack," *Newsweek,* 28 November 1988: 64–75.

7. See Bill Teska, "The Covert Connection," *Christian Social Action* 3, no. 6 (June 1990): 16.

8. As quoted by Eva Bertram, "It's Worth the Risk," *Christian Social Action,* June 1990: 13.

9. Joan W. Moore and Harry Pachon, *Hispanics in the United States* (Englewood Cliffs, N.J.: Prentice-Hall, 1985), p. 85.

10. Steven D. Kerge, "How Safe Are You?" *Washingtonian,* December 1990: 142.

11. John Terney, "In Newark, A Spiral of Drugs and AIDS," *New York Times,* 16 December 1990, p. 1.

12. See Eva Bertram, "It's Worth the Risk," p. 13.

13. To explore the concept of culture understood as argument, see especially William Brett, ed., *The Politics of Culture* (Washington, D.C.: Smithsonian Institution, 1991).

14. See Jon Sobrino, *Spirituality of Liberation: Toward Political Holiness,* trans. Robert R. Barr (Maryknoll, N.Y.: Orbis Books, 1988), pp. 80–86.

15. See especially Eva Bertram, "It's Worth the Risk," p. 13.

16. Anthony A. Parker, "U.S. Drug Trade Sparks Record Violence," *Sojourners* (March 1989).

17. Statistic published by the Centers for Disease Control, Atlanta, 1991.

· 8 ·

POVERTY:

THE URBAN-RURAL LINKAGES

Gary E. Farley

The geographic pattern of poverty in the United States is revealing. The drastically poor counties, by and large, are rural. However, the top metropolitan population centers—New York, Chicago, Los Angeles—can also be found on the map of poverty in the United States. This essay will trace some of the structural linkages between poverty in urban settings and the rural clusters of persistent poverty.

The 242 rural counties classified by the U.S. Department of Agriculture as persistently poor are clustered in four areas of the nation: central Appalachia, the Mississippi Delta, the Rio Grande Valley, and Western Native American lands.[1] (See fig. 8.1.)

Appalachia

In Appalachia, the poor are the remnant of small highland farmsteads and abandoned coal camps. Most are white. They have been called "yesterday's people"[2] and "the people left behind."[3] Less flattering labels, perhaps, are "briar" and "hillbilly." Large numbers of people from this region migrated to the industrial cities of the Great Lakes during World War II, and the stream continues, although many are now retiring and moving "back home," creating a reverse or alternate current.

Appalachian agriculture in the prewar era was of the "kitchen-garden" variety, meaning that a family produced most of its food for itself. Until after World War II, little cash was needed. A few hundred dollars gained from the sale of

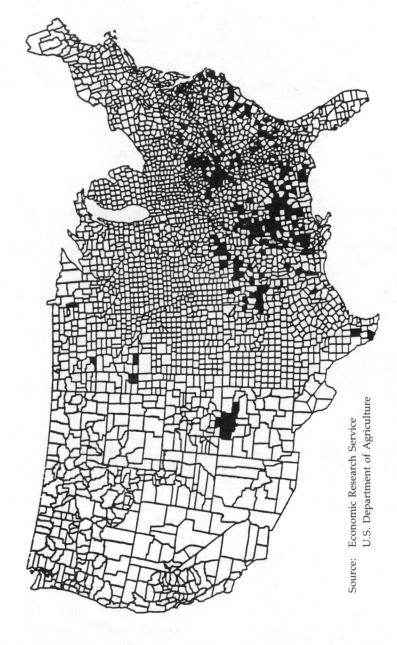

Source: Economic Research Service
U.S. Department of Agriculture

Figure 8.1. Persistent Poverty Counties (Nonmetro United States)

tobacco, timber, illegal whiskey, or cattle or earned through a few months of public work provided for those things that had to be purchased from the larger economy. TV's Walton family provided a dramatized view of such a lifestyle.

Coal mining has been a traditional mainstay of the Appalachian economy. Before 1950, there was work for hundreds of thousands of miners. But then the railroads switched from coal to diesel fuel, postwar homes turned to natural gas heating, and the mines were mechanized. Demand fell. Jobs were lost. In time, coal used to generate electricity brought production back to wartime levels. But by then, advances in mining technology meant that one or two people could produce as much coal as a hundred miners had dug a generation earlier.[4]

The response of millions was to migrate to the cities, with their promise of factory jobs. By 1960, when presidential candidate John F. Kennedy made their plight a national issue, Appalachian communities had become bifurcated: old and young, unemployed miners and wealthy mine owners, uneducated and educated, powerless and powerful.[5]

The plight of Appalachian migrants in the industrial cities was often a sad one. Their schools had not prepared them for the better-paying urban jobs, so they had to take the dirty, dangerous, unstable ones. Often their religion was other-worldly and fatalistic, leading them to accept unjust social institutions rather than trying to change them. Their experiences in retail buying had not included modern consumer credit; thus, they were vulnerable to exploitative salespeople. Their cultural values were attuned toward being comfortable and having enough, not amassing and consuming things conspicuously, so they were ill-prepared for the urban rat race. And their experience of dealing with elected officials "down home" on a personal basis did not equip them to deal with city government bureaucrats.[6]

They settled first in the "briar" ghettos of Dayton, Detroit, or Columbus, Ohio. Some were "successful" and partially urbanized. They moved on to blue-collar suburbs. But many were injured in job-related accidents and sank deeper into poverty; their situation was often compounded by alcohol addiction, violence, and crime. John Egerton has done a service to those who seek to minister to the Appalachian poor by chronicling the multigenerational life of a typical family in *Generations*.[7] He tells the story of plain people struggling to survive in an increasingly urban world.

The Mississippi Delta

A second cluster of poor counties is concentrated in the Mississippi Delta and scattered through the so-called "Black Belt" of the Old South. Here cotton was king, indeed, and the poor were mostly African American field hands and sharecroppers. Children of slaves, still poor and tied to the land, they performed mostly seasonal work for the planters. But the introduction of new technology, including tractors and mechanical cotton pickers, and the replacement of cotton with synthetic fibers following World War II made the sharecropper family economically obsolete.[8]

African Americans left the Delta by the thousands for Memphis, St. Louis, Chicago, and other industrial cities. Growing consumer demand, fueled by an expanded money supply, meant more factory jobs, more construction jobs, and more work in the service industries. Soon the old African American ghettos of the industrial cities exploded across traditional barriers into working-class neighborhoods. Before long, the central cities became mostly African American. As with the Appalachian rural-to-urban migrators, some of these workers, now in retirement, are moving back to the Delta. Yet the stream of young African Americans continues to flow to the cities.

Many parallels can be drawn between the Appalachian and the African American experience in the cities. The immigrants from the Delta, too, were exploited, used up, and discarded by impersonal urban institutions. However, some prophets appeared among their pastors. And their churches took on a social ministry and a stance for social change not found in the urban church of the migrators from Appalachia. Unfortunately, the urban African American church did not have the economic base "back home" that characterized the churches of the nineteenth-century immigrants from Europe to the cities of the United States. There were no African American Baptist or Methodist equivalents of Jesuits or Franciscans to build schools and colleges so that their youth could acquire the knowledge and skills needed to move into the professions. There was no program for the construction of churches to provide employment and skill development. There was no large cadre of urban-raised ministers to model an appropriate lifestyle for urban living.[9] Consequently, the experience of the African American immigrant to the city has not mirrored that of the European ethnic in urban America.

Because of these and other social forces—including slavery—the African American family structure has always suffered. The experience of urban poverty has weakened it further. Some contend that well-intentioned social welfare programs have done little to help it.[10] African Americans had experienced a structure of discrimination in the economic, educational, and political systems in the rural South. In the urban North, discrimination was more informal and obscure but equally real.

Some African Americans from the Delta managed to escape poverty, or made it possible for their children to do so, in their move to the cities. Government programs that provided for job training and college education helped. So did reform laws that struck down structural discrimination. But most Delta emigrants did not find the pot of gold at the end of the urban rainbow. The situation of many is desperate. Intraracial urban crime is a growing problem. Drug use is widespread. The African American ghetto is an increasingly dangerous place.

The situation of the rural African American is also grim. African American ownership of farmland has dropped alarmingly. The rural industrialization that characterized the 1970s did not reach the Delta or the Black Belt counties. The private-academy movement has resegregated schools. Many African Americans who remain in the rural South are physically or are mentally disabled.[11] Delta counties tend to be bifurcated as well: African American and white, poor and "comfortably off," powerless and powerful. And while many more African Americans now hold public office in rural and urban communities, all too often the tax base is so weak that significant structural problems cannot be addressed aggressively.[12]

The Rio Grande Valley

A third concentration of rural poverty is found along the Rio Grande Valley, especially in Texas, south of Interstate 10. Here, a labor-intensive agriculture continues its existence in fields, groves, and orchards. Emigrants from Mexico are drawn to the region for work—hard, dirty, stoop work. After a few seasons, many move on to better-paying work in the cities of Texas and elsewhere. They are quickly replaced by others fleeing Mexico's poverty.

The Hispanic poor share a distinct and rich cultural heritage. They have access to a powerful church with considerable resources. Typically, they have strong family bases. However, cultural discrimination and a lack of knowledge of English place them in a position of great disadvantage.

In the valley, at least three classes of Hispanics can be identified. The first consists of the "old" families. Many are wealthy and share the prejudices of the Anglos toward the newcomers. The second group includes the multigenerational immigrants, some of whom are being assimilated and are escaping poverty. Third are the new arrivals. Most of them are very poor and are exploited for their labor.[13]

Given current farm security acts, it is likely that this arrangement will continue for many years. Developments in mechanization of harvesting may have an impact on the labor market, but the demand for workers will continue to be high in the vegetable fields, where mechanization generally lags behind. Meanwhile, those who have left the farm for the city barrios tend to have received education (albeit limited) in Mexico or during their migrant farm labor years and are usually motivated to improve their economic lot.

In his studies of Hispanics, anthropologist Oscar Lewis advanced the concept of the "culture of poverty." He contended that poor people are poor not simply because of physical or mental handicaps, inferior educational institutions and opportunity, lack of political power, discriminatory laws, prejudice, weak family support, lack of experience with the dominant economic system, or the failure of their church to motivate and aid them. He declared that some poor people have been raised in a culture with attitudes, values, and skills that run contrary to those held by the dominant society.[14] If they are to escape poverty, they have to "convert" to the dominant culture or become "bicultural," able to move back and forth between the cultures as the context demands. That alternative is common among "successful" African Americans and Hispanics. "Conversion" is more common among Appalachian migrants and Native Americans.

From this perspective, those who remain poor in either a rural or an urban context may not only lack support from the institutions of their society, they may also hold beliefs, attitudes, and values that place them at a disadvantage. To acknowledge this possibility is not to make a moral judgment concerning the values of the poor. It is simply to note that their values often deviate from the standards of their society. Those who minister among such peoples in urban areas must understand these cultural elements.

Western Native American Lands

The fourth cluster of poverty, as revealed by figure 8.1, is really not a cluster. Rather, it includes a set of rural counties in New Mexico, the Dakotas, and Oklahoma, where Native Americans were settled by the federal government a century or more ago. The poverty in these counties reflects the policy of taking a people from a hunting-and-gathering economy and training them to live in a commercial agricultural economy. Two factors spelled failure for this effort: The tribes were often placed on land that was not suited for commercial agriculture, and their cultural values did not support such a lifestyle.[15]

In spite of some well-intended programs in more recent times, the plight of Native Americans is a serious one. Poverty abounds. Tribes have turned to bingo and the exploitation of tourism as economic enterprises. Tribal government is often corrupt and split into factions. The corporate cooperation that one might normally expect in a "tribe" has been lost under the impact of relationships with the larger society.[16]

Increasingly, Native Americans are leaving the secure poverty of the rural reservation or enclave to try to better their lot in the city. Some have been reasonably successful. They have overcome the prejudice of other Americans, built up over thousands of hours of watching cowboys-and-Indians movies and television shows. But they are the exceptions. Most are found in terrible poverty on the "bad streets" of the city. Alcohol abuse is almost universal. Anger is alternately suppressed and vented. Like other rural-to-urban migrants, the Native Americans have not been prepared by their schools, churches, tribal governments, economic institutions, or families for this transition. Those who seek to minister to and with Native Americans find the task a most difficult one.[17]

Rural Poverty and the Urban Ghetto: Conclusions

The four major concentrations of rural poverty and their impact on urban poverty have been described above. Two important disclaimers follow:

First, not all rural poverty is limited to these four areas. Most rural communities have poor people.

Second, since most of the 242 persistently poor rural counties outlined in the Department of Agriculture's study have low population density, there may be other rural counties that actually have more poor people but are hidden by the statistical process.[18] An example would be the Hispanic poor in California's central valley.

However, by focusing on these four concentrations, we can identify some very significant facts.

First, all four areas have an economy that draws upon natural resources. Mechanization in agriculture and mining has caused the loss of jobs or has made a region noncompetitive economically.

Second, the abundance of the natural resources of energy, food, and fiber for clothing has kept prices relatively low. The industries of processing, transporting, and distributing natural resources have provided the largest share of the income and the better jobs. To this point, these "value added" jobs have been clustered mostly in urban areas. Increased and permanent poverty for rural areas has been the inevitable result of these patterns—putting these four clusters of poor counties, it has been argued, in the same camp with Third World developing countries.

Third, World War II brought the nation and the world out of an economic depression. In the restructuring of the economy, money became the primary means of exchange of goods, labor, and services. Each of the four areas suffered because of this change.

Fourth, the world is now in the process of moving toward a global economy. This economy is having a negative impact on poor Americans by transferring industrial jobs overseas, by expanding the number of low-paying, part-time, often seasonal jobs in the service industries, and by strengthening the dominance of money over barter, shared labor, and home industries as a medium for the exchange for goods and services.

Fifth, the migration of the rural poor to the cities in the 1950s was a response to postwar industrialization. Alvin Toffler called it the second great wave of American migration.[19] It brought the cities new affluence by providing cheap labor and expanded markets, but it also brought them a new underclass. Whites from Appalachian rural areas, African Americans, Hispanics, and Native Americans replaced Eastern Europeans at the bottom of the class-status ladder. In more recent times, we have seen a new wave of immigration from Asia. Tension is resulting as many of them pass the American-born poor on the ladder. Whether because of the "culture of poverty" or a changing economy that seems to be shrinking the traditional middle class, any possibility for upward mobility for the American underclass seems unlikely in the near future.

Sixth, each of the four migratory groups discussed in this essay has been the object of prejudice. Consequently, societal attitudes have weighed against their upward mobility.

Seventh, each group came to the city with a set of beliefs common to rural people, beliefs that placed them at a disadvantage in dealing with the urban context. Table 8.1, which contrasts rural and urban culture, illustrates this point. Those who are from rural cultures experience a certain vulnerability when thrown into the radically different urban culture. In the city, these groups have tended to cluster together in certain

Table 8.1. Rural and Urban Culture

	Rural Culture	*Urban Culture*
Social Unit	The family. Works, plays, and visits together. We are known in community as a family.	The individual. Those with whom we work do not, by and large, know our families.
Social Contacts	We know people in their whole context. We have known the postman from birth.	We know people only in their roles. We usually do not know their names, families, problems, hopes, dreams.
Social Bond	Custom. Unwritten leases. One's word is one's bond. There is a concern for quality of product. Craftsmanship.	Contract. Signed leases and contracts. Concern only for fulfilling terms of the written contract.
Social Values	Tradition. "We've always done it this way." Respect for the past.	Novelty. What is the new way? Paul at Athens: "They spent their time in nothing else, but either to tell or hear one new thing" (Acts 17:21, KJV alt). Concern for the future.
Social Control	Direct action. If a neighbor is sick, the neighbors pitch in and plant or harvest his or her crops.	Agencies. Problems are referred to agencies. Response to a new need is to create a new agency.
Social Environment	Nature. The setting is nature, and the concern is with the weather, the soil, and the animals.	Technological. Laboratories. Weather is controlled, and most concern is only for the weekend. A setting of bricks, cement, and machines.
Social Focus	Kinship and locality. We move in circles depending upon whom we are kin to and who our neighbors are. The focus is on the family. We see the same people in a variety of activities.	Common interest. We work with one group, worship with another, bowl with another, fish with another group—and there may be few if any persons who are common to two or more of these groups.

This table was developed by and is used by permission of Rockwell Smith.

areas. In part this is motivated by a desire to reestablish the qualities of a rural community in a different setting.

Eighth, our economic institutions have been exploitative rather than developmental. Our economic system seems to need an underclass—people available for the dirty, mindless jobs. Their condition motivates us to work hard so that we will not join them. They offer us at least some social status in being "better off than some folk." They are the object of our charity and thus may salve our consciences. As a flexible and mobile work force, they save management labor costs and make the economy more elastic.

Ninth, some from the poor—those without access to other forms of economic well-being—become entrepreneurs of vice; they resource the passion, greed, and avarice of those in the upper classes. For example, a large portion of the drugs sold illegally in the United States are consumed outside the ghettos, but it is in the ghettos themselves that communities are being destroyed and lives lost due to the drug traffic.

The theme sounded here over and over is that those who live in areas of deep poverty are hard pressed to find ways into new life.

Modern American urban poverty is grounded in the social and cultural structures of rural America. The social structures of Appalachia, the Delta, the reservation and the Rio Grande Valley have not prepared their citizens for life in the cities. Families have become fragmented and quarrelsome. Schools often seem irrelevant, and vocational training prepares its students mostly for vanishing jobs. The churches have proclaimed an otherworldly message. Government has not addressed injustices. Once rural immigrants arrive in the city, most urban social institutions do little as well.

The biblical message of the Social Gospel about the problems of assimilating European immigrants at the beginning of the twentieth century remains relevant for the rural immigrant at the end of the century. Its demand—that business and government deal justly with people—needs to be sounded again. Martin Luther King, Jr., tried, but he died too soon. It is time for his call to justice, righteousness, and love to be proclaimed once more. The consequence of not taking this message seriously has been the development of the "culture of poverty" described above. Personal attitudes, self-concept, family weaknesses, inept social programs, exploitative economic institutions, and warped theology have all contributed to the emergence of what seems to be a permanent underclass. The Western social system falls under the judgment of God. We continue to ignore the structural causes of poverty at great peril to society and life itself.

The urbanization of modern society has been identified by social scientists as the second great social revolution, rivaling the shift from a hunting-and-gathering economy to a food-cultivation and production-based one about ten thousand years ago.[20] The way people make their living, relate to their environment, interact with one another, learn, love, and worship have all been changed by urbanization. In the process, the traditional patterns and bonds of community have been lost.

How to respond to and give shape to these changes in order to reestablish community is the crucial question that gave rise to the discipline of sociology just over a century ago. The founders of sociology—Auguste Comte, Karl Marx, Max Weber, Ferdinand Tönnies, Émile Durkheim, and George Simmel—all analyzed the impact of urbanization on people, their culture, and their institutional structures.[21] These issues continue to confront contemporary theorists such as Robert Nisbet, Jacques Ellul, Peter Berger, and Anthony Giddens.[22] While some contemporary futurists may question the continued utility of cities, none denies the continued significance of the consequences of urbanization.[23]

The case of poverty is illustrative of but one of such consequences. When a community had an agricultural base, poverty was typically the result of bad weather, insect infestation, marginality of land, personal tragedy, rapid population growth, laziness, or conquest by a tyrant. The natural causes were usually cyclical. Kinship and clan networks eased the impact of personal tragedies such as disease, disability, or widowhood. This is not to suggest that poverty was not a constant problem in rural society. Jesus was speaking at the village of Bethany when he declared that the poor would always be with us (Matt. 26:11). However, poverty in the agriculturally based community was sometimes alleviated by the years of plentiful harvest. Memory of a better time provided hope that could carry a community through the bad times. In our contemporary urban setting, poverty is an unabating experience for many people. Many lose hope.

Micah was not the first or only native of a farming village to be lured to Jerusalem in the eighth century B.C. (Micah 1:1–5; 3:8–12). But until the nineteenth century and the Industrial Revolution, which spurred modern urbanization, cities remained relatively small, compact, and scattered around the world. Today they have become massive, and their problems seem unmanageable. We seem to have failed in creating "livable" cities based on classic sociological theories. Perhaps it is time to reconsider the possibility of basing urban community on the gospel of Jesus. This theme is found in the writings of urban theologian Harvey Cox, and before him, of the Niebuhrs.[24] The institutions and structures of society must be reformulated so that hope will be the heritage of all people— rural, urban, and rural-to-urban immigrants.

Urban ministry must aggressively evangelize: witnessing, teaching, baptizing, and making disciples (Matt. 28:19–20). We must minister to the hurting, work to change public policy, and demand quality performance from government, schools, churches, businesses, industry, and social organizations. As social theorist Richard Quinney contends, this was the position taken by Roger Williams in the establishment of the city of Providence in the new colony of Rhode Island.[25] Today, we have an errand in the urban wilderness to reformulate community. Only when new communities have been established can we hope that urban life will approximate what God wills it to be. Only then can we truly address the needs of the poor.

Gary E. Farley is associate director of the town and country missions department of the Home Mission Board of the Southern Baptist Convention. He came to this position in 1984 after nineteen years as professor of sociology and social work in Tennessee and Oklahoma. He has lived in three of the areas discussed in this essay and works in all of them now.

Notes

1. Lloyd D. Bender et al., "The Diverse Social and Economic Structure of Nonmetropolitan America," *Rural Development Research Report: An Occasional Paper* 49, Economic Research Service, U.S. Department of Agriculture (1985): 14.

2. Jack E. Weller, *Yesterday's People: Life in Contemporary Appalachia* (Lexington, Ky.: University of Kentucky Press, 1965).

3. *The People Left Behind,* Report of the President's National Advisory Commission on Rural Poverty (Washington, D.C.: U.S. Government Printing Office, 1967).

4. Thomas R. Ford, ed., *The Southern Appalachian Region: A Survey* (Lexington, Ky.: University of Kentucky Press, 1962).

5. Harry M. Caudill, *Night Comes to the Cumberlands: A Biography of a Depressed Area* (Boston: Little, Brown & Co., 1963).

6. Todd Gitlin and Nanci Hollander, *Uptown: Poor Whites in Chicago* (New York: Harper & Row, 1970).

7. John Egerton, *Generations: An American Family* (New York: Simon & Schuster, 1983).

8. Pete Daniel, *Standing at the Crossroads: Southern Life since 1900* (New York: Hill & Wang, 1986).

9. E. Franklin Frazier, *The Negro Church in America* (New York: Schocken Books, 1963), pp. 52–71.

10. Robert Staples, "The Black American Family," in *Ethnic Families in America: Patterns and Variations,* ed. Charles H. Mindel and Robert W. Habenstein (New York: Elsevier, 1976); Andrew Billingsley and A. T. Billingsley, *Black Families in White America* (Englewood Cliffs, N.J.: Prentice-Hall, 1968).

11. Thomas A. Tyson and William W. Falk, "Two Sides of the Sunbelt: Economic Development in the Rural and Urban South," in U.S. Congress Joint Economic Committee, *New Dimensions in Rural Policy: Building Upon Our Heritage* (Washington, D.C.: U.S. Government Printing Office, 1986), pp. 158–165.

12.William F. Winter, "Charting a Course for the Rural South," in *The Rural South in Crisis: Challenges for the Future,* ed. Lionel J. Beaulieu (Boulder, Colo.: Westview Press, 1988).

13. James Stuart Olson, *The Ethnic Dimension in American History* (New York: St. Martin's Press, 1979), pp. 320–323.

14. Oscar Lewis, *La Vida: A Puerto Rican Family in the Culture of*

Poverty—San Juan and New York (New York: Random House, 1966), pp. xlii–lii.

15. Efforts were actually made to train Native Americans for a commercial agricultural economy at Shawnee Mission (Mission, Kansas).

16. Anthony Gary Dworkin and Rosalind J. Dworkin, *The Minority Report: An Introduction to Racial, Ethnic, and Gender Relations* (New York: Holt, Rinehart & Winston, 1982), pp. 233–261.

17. John A. Price, "North American Indian Families," in Mindel and Habenstein, *Ethnic Families*, pp. 248–270.

18. Bender et al., *Research Report*, pp. 12–13.

19. Alvin Toffler, *The Third Wave* (New York: Bantam Books, 1980).

20. Leslie White, *The Science of Culture: A Study of Man and Civilization* (New York: Grove Press, 1949), pp. 363–393.

21. Jonathan Turner, *The Structure of Sociological Theory*, rev. ed. (Homewood, Ill.: Dorsey Press, 1978).

22. Robert Nisbet, *The Social Bond* (New York: Alfred A. Knopf, 1970); Jacques Ellul, *The Technological Society*, trans. John Wilkinson (New York: Alfred A. Knopf, 1964); Peter Berger, *Facing Up to Modernity* (New York: Basic Books, 1977); Anthony Giddens, *The Constitution of Society: Outline of the Theory of Structuration* (Berkeley, Calif.: University of California Press, 1984).

23. John Naisbitt and Patricia Aburdene, *Megatrends 2000: Ten New Directions for the 1990s* (New York: William Morrow & Co., 1990).

24. Harvey Gallagher Cox, *The Secular City: Secularization and Urbanization in Theological Perspective* (New York: Macmillan, 1965); H. Richard Niebuhr, *Radical Monotheism and Western Culture* (New York: Harper & Brothers, 1960); Reinhold Niebuhr, *Man's Nature and His Community* (New York: Charles Scribner, 1970).

25. Richard Quinney, *Providence: The Reconstruction of Social and Moral Order* (New York: Longman Group, 1980).

Further Reading

Realizing the Dream . . . Fulfilling the Potential, a report by the Lower Mississippi Delta Development Commission.
Irma T. Elo and Calvin L. Beale, *Natural Resources and Rural Poverty:*

An Overview, Rural Development, Poverty, and Natural Resources Workshop Paper Series (Washington, D.C.: National Center for Food and Agricultural Policy, Resources for the Future, Inc.).

Linda M. Ghelfi, *Poverty Among Black Families in the Nonmetro South,* Rural Development Research Report 62, Economic Research Service, U.S. Department of Agriculture, August 1986.

Nina Glasgow, *The Nonmetro Elderly,* Rural Development Research Report 70, Economic Research Service, U.S. Department of Agriculture, June 1988.

• 9 •

OLDER WOMEN IN THE CITY

Elizabeth W. Markson

It is no longer news that the American population is aging rapidly. About 29 million Americans—one in eight—are now sixty-five years of age or older; by 2030, one in every five Americans will be in this age category. The population explosion among the elderly is particularly evident among the "old-old" segment of the population: Americans are surviving to age eighty-five and older in unprecedented numbers and proportions.[1]

By the year 2000, the majority of elderly families will be composed primarily of women. Women sixty-five and older now outnumber their male age peers in the United States three to two—a considerable change from a scant thirty years ago, when the ratio of women to men in old age was almost equal (six to five). Among the very elderly (eighty-five and older) there are five women to every two men. Clearly, old age is primarily women's territory.[2]

In 1900, the average life expectancy at birth for white women was 48.7 years; for nonwhite women, 33.5. By 1988, the average life expectancy at birth was 78.8 for white and 73.8 for African American females. The percentage of women living to age sixty-five has also increased dramatically. By 1988, 86 percent of all white and 78 percent of all nonwhite women could expect to reach that age. Obviously, changes in patterns of female life expectancy have had marked effects on the demographic profile of the United States.[3]

Contrary to popular belief, the majority of elderly women do not live in rural and small-town areas and retirement communities. About two in three of those sixty-five and older live

in metropolitan areas. Whether in the inner city or on the urban fringe, the majority of elderly women have "aged in
place" and are the least likely of any age group to move. The
graying of suburbia is a relatively new phenomenon. Older
women are maintaining their long-term residences in suburbs
that are most often characterized by lower average per capita
income, lower home values, and higher population densities
than the more affluent suburbs or gentrified city areas to which
their children may have moved. Although many elderly
women in suburbia—and in some areas of the city itself—may
own their own homes, they are nonetheless burdened by the
costs of utilities, real estate taxes, insurance, and home repairs
and maintenance.[4]

In general, elderly African American women and Latinas
are more likely to live in the inner city than are their white
counterparts. Seven in ten African American elderly men and
women and almost three in ten Latina elderly live in metropolitan areas. Latinas in the Northeast are concentrated in inner-
city areas of New York, Philadelphia, Boston, and Hartford,
Conn.,[5] and share the Spanish language as their major common bond; their migration histories vary as widely as do their
countries of origin. For example, Mexican Americans have migrated from rural areas to Los Angeles, San Francisco, San Antonio, Houston, and Chicago; they include both new
immigrants and elderly women whose families colonized the
Southwest centuries ago. The majority of Puerto Rican, Cu-
ban, and Central and South American elderly women are relatively recent immigrants.

Older women immigrants from Asia and the Pacific Islands
are also a very diverse group, including Chinese, Korean, Viet-
namese, Laotian, Hmong (hill people from Vietnam), and Fili-
pino, among others; like Latinas, recent immigrant Asian and
Pacific women are most often concentrated in the city in low-
income minority neighborhoods. Despite their variations in
language and country of origin, Asian and Pacific Island immigrants may share the common themes of rigidly defined
age- and gender-linked roles, lesser authority of women, and
precedence of the needs of the family over those of any individual member.[6] As the foreign-born Latina and Asian population

ages, it will swell the ranks of the growing urban underclass unless there are dramatic changes in the opportunity structure of the economy to provide avenues out of poverty.[7]

The older female population in metropolitan areas, like the elderly population in general, is very diverse. There are rich widows (most often white with inherited wealth) as well as homeless older women who rely on subways, public buildings, and shelters as residences;[8] elderly women with college and professional degrees, elderly women who are illiterate. Despite their diversity, older women in metropolitan areas face similar social and psychological hazards. Paradoxically, our very success as a postindustrial nation has produced special problems for the elderly, both male and female. High levels of productivity and automation make their economic contribution unnecessary. The labor of neither group is needed for economic growth, and their wisdom has been largely replaced by formal education and communication technologies. In later life, both sexes are victims of ageism, a term coined more than two decades ago to denote "the systematic stereotyping and discrimination against people because they are old . . . to see older people as different . . . [and] subtly cease to identify with . . . elders as human beings."[9]

Women are doubly stigmatized as they age—victims of ageism coupled with sexism. Once past menopause, females are more likely to be both denigrated and feared than their male counterparts. Consider, for example, the numerous unflattering words for elderly women—for example, *hag, old bag, crone*—and the numerous mother-in-law jokes and comic strip depictions of menacing, ugly, or absurd old women. Far fewer old men are similarly portrayed. Our contemporary distaste for older women is at least in part a remnant of those bleak chapters in European Christian history when suspicion of witchcraft "fell on every old woman with a wrinkled face"[10] and as many as two million women, primarily poor widows no longer able to work, were executed as witches. Similarly, in Puritan Massachusettes, those most likely to be condemned for witchcraft were poor older women, usually single or widowed, who had a reputation of annoying their neighbors![11]

Combined with ageism and sexism is another problem for

older women: their economic designation as "dependents." The now-old woman has had relatively little formal control over goods and resources; her status has most often been defined by her position in the family. Even those women who are or were employed tend to be defined more by their roles as wives, mothers, grandmothers, and if married or widowed, by their husbands' status. Designated as dependents and relying on Social Security (the most common source of income for elderly women),[12] these women are not only unimportant parts of the metropolitan economy but are perceived as a cause of lower income for younger families. During the current period of fiscal restraint for human services, "generational equity" has become a popular theme,[13] and elders are often described as "greedy geezers," getting rich at the expense of the young. Most immediately, it is elderly women who live longer and are more likely to be poor that are affected by the premise that the old are self-ish, unable or unwilling to pull their own weight, and a drain on social resources that belong to the next generation.

Contemporary Problems of Urban Women

Increasingly, poverty in the United States has become feminized, with single mothers with young children and elderly women among the poorest in the nation. Compared to old men, elderly women have lower incomes, a fact largely associated with a pattern of lifelong economic dependency on men and with widowhood in old age. In 1987, 80 percent of elderly women in the United States had incomes of less than $13,000 per year, and elderly women comprised 73 percent of the elderly poor.[14]

In interpreting poverty levels, it is important to keep in mind that the federal government uses different income standards to classify the poverty level among those sixty-five and older than among the rest of the population. The elderly are considered to need less money; in 1988, for example, the poverty index for an elderly couple was calculated at $800 less in annual income than that for a couple aged fifteen to sixty-four. For unmarried people sixty-five or older, the poverty index was $481 less per year than that for their younger counterparts.[15]

Not surprisingly, the proportion of elderly females living below the poverty line is much higher among minorities; in 1987, 40 percent of African American females and 30 percent of Latinas sixty-five and older lived below the poverty level, compared to 12.5 percent of their white counterparts. Especially vulnerable to poverty are widowed women who have little formal education and live alone in the inner city.[16] The highest poverty rate—59 percent—is among minority women age eighty-five and older who live alone.[17] Many of these women are unaware that they qualify for Supplemental Security Income (SSI), an income maintenance program for the elderly and disabled that has been characterized by low participation rates since its inception. According to a recent Harris survey, only 37 percent of all elders know how to apply for SSI. Moreover, for many minority older women in the inner city, adherence to the work ethic, cultural and familial traditions, and family pride make applying for a means-tested program especially degrading.

American elderly have derived a smaller proportion of their incomes from social insurance programs such as Social Security than elders in several other developed countries. Poverty rates among the American elderly in general and older women in particular have been among the highest in the developed world. In one recent study by the Bureau of the Census, in which incomes were adjusted on an equivalent basis for seven industrialized nations, only Israel had a higher concentration of low-income elderly.[18] Despite the financial help of Medicare and Medicaid, poverty among American elderly increases after medical expenses; this is especially true for very old and frail women living alone.[19]

A second problem that plagues the urban elderly woman is fear of crime. From a variety of studies, a portrait of the elderly urban woman victim may be drawn.[20] First, although for every thousand people, men are at greater *proportional* risk than women, more older women are victimized than men due to the greater absolute numbers of women in the population. Second, the elderly female victim of crime is most likely to be poor, living alone, and widowed. She is also disproportionately likely to be a member of a minority group and to be physically handicapped.[21] All other factors being equal, offenders indicated they would prefer younger, wealthier victims. Older women are chosen as victims primarily as a kind of "training ground" for youthful offenders to perfect their mugging, robbery, or burglary skills.

A third major problem confronting urban older women is widowhood. Of the 8.5 million older Americans who live alone, almost four-fifths are women. The majority are widows, accounting for three out of four women aged sixty-five to seventy-four living alone and more than four in five of those aged seventy-five and older.[22] While most widowed African Americans and Latinas live with other family members, most widowed whites maintain separate households,[23] a difference that reflects both cultural tradition and socioeconomic status, for minority widows are among the poorest of the poor. Yet, like all older people, widows are a diverse group. The inner-city widow is especially disadvantaged. In poor areas of New York City that are characterized by high crime rates, poverty, and deteriorated housing, the highest proportion of single-person households is found among the most frail segment of the white population: old people in their seventies or eighties, primarily widows.[24] At special risk in New York and urban areas of New Jersey are Latinas, who live in substandard housing and have the smallest incomes, the least education, and the most health problems of all women.[25]

Asian women represent diverse nationalities and must deal with language and cultural barriers, poverty, physical and mental stress, and loss of family ties.[26] Many foreign-born Chinese elders, uncertain about their status in the United States due to past restrictive immigration policies, reside with their children but feel unhappy at the lack of filial respect they receive;[27] their fear and mistrust of the dominant society also reduces their likelihood of applying for legal entitlements such as SSI and Medicare.

Unless uprooted by immigration, most women, regardless of marital status, enter old age with a convoy of social support accumulated through social exchange throughout their lifetimes.[28] Never-married older women, contrary to popular belief, are not socially isolated and are no less likely to be socially active than married, widowed, or divorced women of the same age.[29] Indeed, the never-married report a higher level of interaction with friends than do married elderly and are the most likely of any marital group to have siblings or other relatives in the household.[30] Being married has different consequences for men throughout the life course, and in old age, marriage appears to be more crucial for social interaction, life expectancy, and general well-being of men than it is for women.[31]

A fourth area of concern for elderly urban women is in relationships with their children. Despite the prevalent myth that the elderly are abandoned by their children, numerous studies indicate the contrary. Family members remain the primary source of assistance to one another throughout the life course, with resources flowing from the more able to the less able. Although the recent trend toward smaller families has left elders with fewer family members on whom to rely for assistance, study after study has shown the persistence of family bonds, demonstrated by high rates of writing, phoning, visiting, and children's expressions of concern for their parents' well-being.[32] Despite the trend to greater residential mobility, especially among upwardly mobile adult children, about eight in ten elders with children live within one hour's driving distance from at least one child.[33] Expectations of support from adult children vary by characteristics such as ethnicity, religion, and race. Low-income, elderly Puerto Rican women in Boston, for example, value respect from their children as the most important aspect of social support and more important than affection.[34] Despite racial and ethnic variations, urban elders typically prefer "intimacy at a distance": maintaining their independence, living near but not with their children.[35] Indeed, longitudinal data show that older people perceive living alone as more desirable now than they did three decades ago and, to maintain independence, are more willing to sacrifice the income they might gain from moving in with others.[36]

However, many elderly women living alone have no living children, a situation more common among African Americans than among whites. For most elderly women living alone, relatives are the main source of help. More than two-thirds feel they can depend on help from relatives—most often their children—for a few days, and most can count on relatives' help for a few weeks. Although other relatives may be available to help them, childless widows are especially vulnerable when health problems arise and are at greater risk of institutionalization than are widows with children. Indeed, about three-quarters of the patients in a nursing home at any given point in time are women. The typical nursing-home resident is an eighty-five-year-old white widow with multiple disabilities who was admitted from a short-stay hospital and who lived alone in a metropolitan area prior to admission.[37]

A final problem for the older woman in the city is her inability to take advantage of all its riches. Although the city has better transportation, more social and health services, and more recreational and cultural facilities than do nonurban areas, not all urban women are able to enjoy these advantages. Low-income elderly may not be able to afford buses and subways, nor are buses or subways easy to negotiate for an even mildly disabled person. A study of Washington, D.C., elderly who were eligible for special transport services showed that less than 15 percent used the services; non-users tended to be less active and in poorer health than eligible elders who used the services. Reasons for non-use included lack of knowledge of existence of the services; dissatisfaction with the types of services available; and pride.[38] Access to the various facilities of the city may also be limited by language barriers, unfamiliarity with other neighborhoods, and fear. With rampant crime in their neighborhoods, many older women are afraid to leave their homes. Poverty, lack of education, and poor health can severely limit a person's access to the resources of her city. That a higher proportion of urban than rural elderly feel bored, depressed, and lonely—as well as independent, excited, and interested—is perhaps a reflection of the contradictions of urban life as well as of the general sense of relative deprivation that many older people feel amidst riches they admire but cannot afford.[39]

Although much is written about the anonymity of the city, the urban setting is in many ways conducive to friendship. For all of the perils of the inner city, for example, the neighborhood is an important place for socializing with family and friends. Paradoxically, income is not the primary factor in social contacts with family and friends in urban areas; for example, whereas social contacts increase with higher income among whites, social contacts increase among African Americans as income decreases.[40] There are strong social networks among urban elderly women, although those networks, like the women themselves, will vary immensely. Shared work experience, shared values, shared language or ethnicity, shared religion—these are just a few of the bases for friendship and social connectedness of older women in the city.[41]

Despite the hazards and problems facing urban elderly women, such women are hardy. Although oppressed by ageism, sexism, and poverty, frightened by crime and neighborhood change, and largely ignored by both the women's movement and the old-age movement, they remain irrepressible. They are our mothers, our grandmothers, our aunts or distant cousins, our sisters, and perhaps one day our daughters or granddaughters or ourselves. What is needed now is public and private action to better their lives today and in the future.

Elizabeth W. Markson is associate director of the Gerontology Center, research associate professor of sociology, and adjunct associate professor of socio-medical sciences and community medicine at Boston University. She has written extensively on women and aging.

Notes

1. AARP, *A Profile of Older Americans 1990* (Washington, D.C.: American Association of Retired Persons, n.d.), p. 1.

2. Ibid., p. 1.

3. U.S. Bureau of the Census, *Statistical Abstract of the United States: 1990* (Washington, D.C.: U.S. Government Printing Office, 1990).

4. Senate Select Committee on Aging, *Aging America* (Washington, D.C.: U.S. Government Printing Office, 1990).

5. Kyriakos S. Markides and Jeffrey S. Levin, "The Changing Economy and the Future of the Minority Aged," *The Gerontologist* 27, no. 3 (1987): 273–274.

6. Barbara W. K. Yee, "Gender and Family Issues in Minority Groups," *Generations* 14, no. 3 (Summer 1990): 39–42.

7. Ibid.

8. Jennifer Hand, "Shopping Bag Women," in *Older Women: Issues and Prospects*, ed. Elizabeth W. Markson (Lexington, Mass.: Lexington Books, division of D.C. Heath, 1984), pp. 155–177.

9. Robert N. Butler, "Ageism: Another Form of Bigotry," *The Gerontologist* 9, no. 14: 243–246.

10. Antonia Fraser, *The Weaker Vessel* (New York: Alfred A. Knopf, 1984), p. 113.

11. See John Demos, *Entertaining Satan: Witchcraft and the Culture of Early New England* (New York: Oxford, 1982).

12. Beth B. Hess, "Gender and Aging: The Demographic Parameters," in *Generations* 14, no. 3: 14.

13. See, for example, David Durenberger, "Education and the Contract Between the Generations," *The Generations Journal* 11, no. 1: 5.

14. ICF, Inc., for the Commonwealth Fund Commission on Elderly People Living Alone, *Old, Alone, and Poor: Technical Analyses* (Baltimore, Md.: Commonwealth Fund Commission on Elderly People Living Alone, 1987).

15. U.S. Bureau of the Census, *Statistical Abstract 1990*, p. 423.

16. U.S. Bureau of the Census, Current Population Reports, Series P-60, no. 161 (Washington, D.C.: U.S. Government Printing Office, 1989).

17. Jennie D. Kasper, *Aging Alone: Profiles and Projections* (Baltimore, Md.: Commonwealth Fund, 1988).

18. Barbara Boyle Torrey, Kevin G. Kinsella, and Cynthia M. Tauber, *An Aging World* (Washington, D.C.: U.S. Bureau of the Census, 1988).

19. Midwest Research Institute, *Crimes Against Aging Americans: Kansas City Study* (Kansas City, Mo.: Midwest Research Institute, 1976).

20. Midwest Research Institute, *Crimes Against Aging Americans;* D. A. Grossman, *Reducing the Impact of Crime against the Elderly: A Survey and Appraisal of Existing and Potential Programs* (New York: Florence V. Burden Foundation, 1977); J. E. Burkhardt, *Crime and the Elderly: Their Perceptions and Their Reactions* (Rockville, Md.:

National Criminal Justice Reference Service Microfiche Program, 1977).

21. Michael P. Connelly et al., "Crime and the Hispanic Elderly," (paper presented at the American Criminology Society Meetings, San Diego, Calif., November 1985).

22. Kasper, *Aging Alone*.

23. Senate Select Committee, *Aging America*.

24. Marjorie Cantor, *Study of the Inner-City Elderly* (New York: Office of the Aging, 1978).

25. Ibid.

26. Elzbieta Gozdziak, "New Branches—Distant Roots: Older Refugees in the United States," *Aging*, no. 359 (1989): 2–7.

27. J. E. Lubben and R. M. Becerra, "Social Support Among Black, Mexican and Chinese Elderly," in *Ethnic Dimensions of Aging*, ed. Donald E. Gelfand and C. M. Barresi (New York: Springer Publishing Co., 1987), pp. 130–144.

28. Toni Antonucci and H. Akiyama, "Social Networks in Adult Life and a Preliminary Examination of the Convoy Model," *Journal of Gerontology* 42, no. 5: 519–527.

29. Rita Braito and Donna Anderson, "The Ever-Single Elderly Women," in Markson, *Older Women* (Lexington, Mass.: Lexington Books, division of D.C. Heath, 1984): 195–225.

30. D. E. Stull and A. Scarisbrick-Hauser, "Never-Married Elderly: A Reassessment with Implications for Long-Term Care Policy," *Research on Aging* 11, no. 1 (1987): 124–138.

31. Beth B. Hess and Joan Waring, "Family Relationships of Older Women: A Women's Issue," in Markson, *Older Women*, pp. 227–251.

32. K. Seccombe, "Financial Assistance from Elderly Retirement-Age Sons to Their Aging Parents," *Research on Aging* 10, no. 1 (1988): 102–118.

33. D. J. Dewit et al., "Physical Distance and Social Contact Between Elders and Their Adult Children," *Research on Aging* 10, no. 1 (1988): 56–80.

34. Melba Sanchez-Ayendez, "Puerto Rican Elderly Women: The Cultural Dimension of Social Support Networks," *Women and Health* 14, nos. 3–4 (1988): 239–252.

35. Hess and Waring, "*Family Relationships of Older Women: A Women's Issue*," in Markson, *Older Women*, pp. 227–251.

36. Kasper, *Aging Alone;* Fred Pampel, *Social Change and the Aged: Recent Trends in the United States* (Lexington, Mass.: Lexington Books, division of D.C. Heath, 1981).

37. National Center for Health Statistics, "Use of Nursing Homes by the Elderly: Preliminary Data from the 1985 National Nursing Home Survey," *Advance Data from Vital and Health Statistics* 135 (Hyattsville, Md.: U.S. Public Health Service, 1987).

38. Deborah L. Lyons and Isaac Lipowitz, *The Nonutilization of Special Transport Services by the Elderly in Urban Areas: A Case Study and Executive Summary* (Springfield, Va.: National Technical Information Service, 1982).

39. Alfred P. Fengler et al., "Correlates of Dimensions of Happiness in Urban and Non Urban Settings," *International Journal of Aging and Human Development* 16, no. 1 (1983): 53–65.

40. Jacquelyn Wolf et al., "Distance and Contacts: Interactions of Black Urban Elderly Adults with Family and Friends," *Journal of Gerontology* 38, no. 4 (July 1983): 465–471.

41. Doris Francis, "Friends from the Workplace," in *Growing Old in America,* 4th ed., ed. Beth B. Hess and Elizabeth W. Markson (New Brunswick, N.J.: Transaction Publishers, 1990), pp. 465–480.

PART THREE

PASTORAL DIMENSIONS
OF MINISTRY
IN CITIES

Pastoral ministry is often thought of in individual terms: A parishioner has a pastor who ministers to him or her or to the family. What urban ministers know so well today is the interdependence of all those who live in the city. Individual requests for isolated pastoral assistance cannot meet people's needs, for what they require for life and health and wholeness of spirit includes needs to which city governments, schools, neighbors, relatives, or other church members or faith communities must respond.

The interdependence of the pastoral dimensions of ministry in the city today signals both spiritual and ethical themes. Members of the Urban Ministry Collective address these two aspects of the pastoral work of urban ministry in this section of the reader.

The New Spirituality and Empowerment

Pastoral ministry in the city can not survive without a deep and lively spirituality. The section discussing the new spirituality and empowerment opens with Robert Michael Franklin's essay about the culture of the African American urban church, exemplified by "dignity, beauty, creativity, and collective power." Franklin underscores how African spirituality nurtures the "counterculture consciousness," thus enabling transformative, healing, and enabling relationships with the city. Letty Russell, in asking "what the Spirit is saying" to the churches in the city, discovers the anguished cry of battered women to which the church is called to respond. Janet Walton and Eleanor Scott Meyers investigate the role of ritual and worship in the processes of social change in urban churches and their neighborhoods. They describe for us their work with members of the worship committee of a congregation in a changing neighborhood.

The essays in this section are about capacity-building or empowerment through a process that engages spirituality. Philip Amerson makes this strategy specific as he describes the leadership style of the storyteller in public ministry. Amerson calls us to see more deeply into the souls and trust more fully the talents and stories of the folk who are part of our urban parishes. Barbara Brown Taylor's moving meditations in the unsafe city whose protective "walls have fallen," suggest urban ministers look beyond the perils we have never been able to control to discover "how much God" we can find in the city and its people.

Valerie E. Russell's work on urban spirituality combines hard-hitting social analysis with moments of "grace needed to heal broken places." She challenges us to think about how we might prepare ourselves for the "terrifying task of being channels of God's power" in our cities today. Russell develops basic elements of a strategy for spirituality in the urban church rooted in the compelling statistics of poverty.

Ethical Foundations for Urban Ministry Strategies

All urban ministry strategies must be built on ethical foundations. Six authors suggest areas of program development for urban congregations, strategies that address central ethical issues presented by the context for metropolitan ministry in the 1990s. The astounding outlines of the urban health-care crisis are detailed by Kent C. Miller and Janice L. Burggrabe. In their essay they suggest a set of criteria by which urban churches can develop a strategy for healing ministries. The essay by Dennis Hollinger and Joseph Modica continues to develop one of the themes of this reader: the particular vulnerability of women in these times when the church often fails to fulfill its role as women's advocate. Suggestions for ministerial strategies accompany their analysis of the issues surrounding the poverty of women.

Katie Day, in her work on the church and public policy, invites us to see how the work of ministry is related to policy development in urban areas. Carol S. Robb takes a specific policy issue, child care, and spells out in detail why the church must be involved in this basic justice work. This section of the reader is full of examples illustrating why these issues of public policy and the needs of children must be addressed by urban ministry today.

The final two essays in this section address two key issues facing urban communities today: homelessness and AIDS. They ask, "What can the churches do?" The answer is, plenty. But we must be informed first. Valerie E. Russell says we must develop a theology that empowers; we must fight stereotyping "the Poor" and perpetuating the deepening gap of the them-versus-us dichotomy. Her call for our participation in public responsibility and public policy takes a confessional stance: We must see how we are part of the problem. William A. Doubleday and Suki Terada Ports describe AIDS as an "epidemic of poverty" and speak of the failures of the church to respond. We must learn, they suggest, to view this phenomenon not as a result of "individual moral failure" but as a "syndrome of societal breakdown." They describe the vision of an "AIDS-friendly congregation" as a powerful model for envisioning not only the church but the city itself.

E.S.M.

THE NEW SPIRITUALITY AND EMPOWERMENT

CHURCH AND CITY:
AFRICAN AMERICAN
CHRISTIANITY'S MINISTRY

Robert Michael Franklin

While more than half the African American population in the United States resides in central cities, popular images rarely provide accurate depictions of the warp and woof of urban African American life. In particular, they tend to overlook the heroic humanizing role played by its religious communities, especially churches. Were it not for the multifaceted ministries of these inner-city African American churches, urban life would degenerate into something resembling the Hobbesian characterization—it would be "nasty, brutish and short."

In 1893, African Americans' most influential spokesperson, Booker T. Washington, publicly and forcefully urged newly freed members of his race to resist the temptation to migrate north. "Cast down your buckets where you are!" he bellowed to former slaves within the racially mixed audience of the Cotton States and International Exposition in Atlanta.[1]

His words were futile, though Washington did not live long enough to see the dramatic urbanization of the African American population after 1915, the year of his death. The combined incentives of expanded employment opportunities created by the world wars, intensifying racial oppression in the South, and more available public relief during the Depression led 75 percent of the African American population to have moved to cities by 1965—half of these people to the urban North. By

1980, New York had the largest African American population of any city (1.7 million), followed by Chicago (1.2 million), Detroit (760,000), Philadelphia (640,000) and Los Angeles (500,000).[2]

But the urbanization of African American Christianity was not entirely a twentieth-century phenomenon. During the earliest years of our nation's history, free African Americans founded independent churches in northern cities. For instance, Richard Allen established the Bethel Chapel African Methodist Episcopal Church in Philadelphia in 1794. Nevertheless, the rapid migration of southern African Americans in this century opened a new chapter in African American church urbanization. For the first time, the churches faced the challenge of resettling and reorienting hundreds of thousands of newcomers. This ministry was performed vigorously by mainstream, middle-class, institutional churches such as Bethel Chapel AME Church and the Abyssinian Baptist Church of Harlem as well as by the numerous storefront churches then typical of the Church of God in Christ.

African Americans arriving in urban centers were economically poor but spiritually rich. They were products of a church culture that emphasized their dignity, beauty, creativity, and collective power. This culture was itself the result of a transformed, evolving system of traditional African religious belief, which maintained the sovereignty of a monotheistic God, the kinship of human beings, the sacredness of family and community networks, and the significance of oral culture. At the core of this spirituality was the quest for harmony with God, spirits, ancestors, other people, oneself, and nature.

African spirituality has found expression through four distinctive conventions: preaching, prayer, music, and shouting. Together, these help to nurture the counterculture consciousness enabling the church to enter into a mutually transforming relationship with the city. This consciousness includes a commitment to creating a nonracist church and a just society, no matter what obstacles are posed by the cultural status quo.

In the hands of skillful African American pastors, preaching seeks to empower the powerless by telling the stories of God's preferential care for the disadvantaged. "It is no secret what

God can do. What he's done for others, he'll do for you" is a common refrain. This empowerment is an essential task for city preachers facing parishioners who are on the bottom rung of the political and economic ladder. In turn, African Americans implement this power through organized civil rights activism, voting, and running for elective offices.

In 1926, Chicagoans sent Oscar DePriest to Congress, the first African American to occupy a House seat since Reconstruction. In 1945, New Yorkers followed suit by sending Adam Clayton Powell, Jr., to Washington. In 1963, Martin Luther King, Jr., preached the century's most memorable sermon, "I Have a Dream," moving Congress and the nation closer to embracing the ideal of equal justice for all. Since the passage of the Voting Rights Act of 1965, nearly all of America's largest cities have elected African American mayors. The church and, specifically, liberation preaching have been instrumental in this political movement. When African American preachers are not satisfied with the laity's leadership record or potential, they run for office themselves, as ministers Jesse Jackson, Andrew Young, Walter Fauntroy, William Gray III, and Floyd Flake have done.

Whereas African American preaching mobilizes public activism, prayer nurtures the personal hope and courage necessary to sustain such action. Prayer is an opportunity for intimate communion with the divine. African Americans are constantly urged to "call God up and tell him what you want." In the church, prayer is a highly ritualized sacred time of healing and care, given by talking through the pain felt by the people as a whole. Typically, corporate prayer includes naming the new corrupting influences of the city: the street gangs that make it unsafe to attend weeknight services, the thieves who repeatedly steal the public address system, or the dope dealers seeking to corrupt the youth.

One of prayer's most distinctive features, especially in African American Baptist culture, is its eschatological conclusion. Following the ritual articulation of praise, thanksgiving, confession of sin, petition, and intercession, the prayer leader (usually a deacon) "takes the prayer home" by poetically characterizing life as a fleeting pilgrimage that will soon end:

"Heavenly Father, may your children find rest on the other side of Jordan, where every day will be Sunday and sabbath will have no end." Such death-defying prayer instills hope for a better future and empowers people to take risks here and now in behalf of God's kingdom of justice and peace.

Volumes have been written on the extraordinary character of African American sacred music. This music reinforces the sense of power engendered by preaching and prayer. Its artistic wealth has given birth to a vast number of musical traditions, including spirituals, jazz, blues, gospel, soul, funk, and rap. The music African Americans hear on Sunday morning often is a complex blend of these traditions. Indeed, many people no longer can discern a distinction between sacred and secular melodies, harmonies, and rhythms.

One of the most dynamic features of the rapidly growing African American urban churches is the enormous, magnificently dressed gospel choir. Such well-rehearsed and -choreographed choirs perform both in the church and on the concert circuit. Many of them have recorded albums and spawned stars.

Shouting is the practice of worshiping through ecstatic utterances, weeping, speaking in tongues, spontaneous singing, dancing, running, and other forms of behavior associated with revivalistic piety and with some African traditional religions. It is the most controversial and least retained feature of rural southern African American religion. Acculturated African Americans look upon it as unnecessary and embarrassing. But shouting has been a common feature of the piety of poor and working-class African Americans. As the larger culture has developed greater sympathy for religion's mystical and charismatic dimensions, and as African Americans have relaxed their embrace of white Christian piety, educated and affluent people have begun to tolerate and even encourage spontaneous, emotion-filled worship. For people who labor long hours in restrictive work environments, exciting worship is a liberating refreshment.

Nearly all African American churches express in varying degrees and forms the above characteristics, which constitute the core of urban African American church culture. Because of its resistance to assimilating the character and customs of mainstream American Christianity, the Church of God in Christ, a predominantly urban church, embodies these features in a more authentic and deeply rooted manner than other African American denominations. The church was founded, like other Pentecostal denominations, at the turn of the century. Its cofounder, Charles Harrison Mason, was a brilliant organizer and spiritual virtuoso who prepared energetic young male preachers and female missionaries to plant churches in northern cities.

Among them was the denomination's most influential and charismatic theologian, Bishop Ozro Thurston Jones, Jr., of Philadelphia. According to Bishop Jones, the church's urban ministry was rooted in Luke 4:18. In that passage Jesus proclaims that the Holy Spirit anoints and empowers ministries directed toward the poor and brokenhearted. Jones believed that the church's message is especially appealing to the urban underclass because it treats evil and sin as tangible realities and offers deliverance from the power if not the presence of sickness and evil. Because there are no incurable conditions or irredeemable states, the church offers hope to everyone.

In the Church of God in Christ, worship is organized into three distinct but interconnected sacred frames or movements: devotion, formal worship, and the ritual of fellowship. The devotional frame is the prelude to formal worship and varies in length and character. Usually it is conducted by laypeople, often women. During this time, members may claim the floor to offer testimonies of God's deliverance, exhortations to the congregation, or extemporaneous singing and prayer. Here the rich oral culture of African American religion is given free expression.

An announcement or a musical introduction signals the transition from devotions to formal worship, presided over by the predominantly male religious elite. The service is balanced between congregational singing and dynamic performances by gospel choirs, usually accompanied by a band, especially by drums. The presence of drums, tambourines and other percussive instruments indicates that the church takes seriously both the psalmists' injunctions and the effort to retain African spiritual expression in Christian worship.

Formal worship does not mean rigid worship. Worshipers feel free to interact with the music or sermon by talking back, shouting, standing, clapping, walking, running, or dancing. According to Church of God in Christ Bishop Ithiel Clemmons, a denominational historian and theologian, part of Bishop Mason's genius entailed the re-Africanization of modern African American Christianity.

Some of the best preaching in America emanates from Church of God in Christ pulpits, where it is understood as a narrative art form. The best preachers tell the story in a manner eliciting communal participation and evoking ecstatic praise.

Because worship is sacred time, it is never rushed. At the appropriate moment, it ends, and the ritual of fellowship begins. Usually, this entails sharing a meal prepared by church members. For people who lack adequate family support or housing, it can be refreshing to spend the entire day (and evening) at church with the extended church family. During these long days, both the congregation and the pastor can care for members. Christian education classes are held before devotions and again before evening worship services.

This denomination has enjoyed dramatic growth in urban areas not only because of its rich corporate life but because of its heavy emphasis on personal evangelism. While its language of soul-winning is similar to that of white fundamentalist churches, the Church of God in Christ weds evangelism and home mission work—attending to the total needs of those who are being proselytized. Often, home missionaries go into tenements and public housing projects to teach home economic skills, to care for children whose parents are sick or incarcerated, and to conduct street worship services challenging the hegemony of drug dealers and street gangs.

Through its ministries of lively, contagious worship and deliverance-oriented evangelism, the Church of God in Christ illustrates the urban genius of African American church culture. Despite the enormous challenges faced by all Christian churches in the city, the spirituality and ministry of African American churches remind us that the liberating power of Christ can transform and humanize life in the city.

Robert Michael Franklin, assistant professor of ethics and society at Candler School of Theology, is director of the Program of Black Church Studies. He is the author of Liberating Visions: Human Fulfillment and Social Justice in African-American Moral Thought *(1990).*

Notes

1. John Hope Franklin, ed., *Three Negro Classics* (New York: Avon Books, 1965), p. 147.

2. *America's Black Population* (Washington, D.C.: Bureau of the Census, 1983), p. 1.

• 11 •

THE CITY

AS BATTERED WOMAN

Letty Russell

A few years ago, Sara Coxon, one of my students, showed me a paper she had written, titled "Battered Women: Hearing the Silent Screams." As I read it, I got a familiar feeling in the pit of my stomach—a feeling of desolation, of pain, of horror at what sexism looks like in one of its more virulent forms. I recognized the feeling in part because I'm a woman. I also recognized it because I have often had that same feeling in the pit of my stomach in sharing the pain and desolation of what oppression looks like in the midst of the city.

Those parallels led me to believe that in seeking out "what the Spirit is saying to the churches" (Rev. 3:13), we would do well to reflect on and uphold an image of the city as battered woman. Like a battered woman, the city suffers through cycles of violence, isolation, and fear. Like a battered woman, in suffering through those cycles, the city often cries out to us in silent and not-so-silent screams.

A battered woman is caught in a cycle of violence. She is often not only powerless to break out of that cycle, she is often blamed for it: accused of being unfaithful, neurotic, or masochistic. She is seen as anything but a victim of violence, abused by the very man to whom she has looked for protection and love.

The city also is caught in a cycle of violence, powerless to break out. Blamed as sinful, immoral, decadent, and dirty, the city is seen as anything but the victim of violence, abused by the very forces of economics and politics that have been the source of her strength and culture.

152

At the same time, a battered woman is caught in a cycle of isolation. Her husband, himself also victimized, cuts her off from all other sources of help and comfort. She's punished for leaving the home. And very often she is forced to see herself as a failure, as having fallen short of the mythical image of the nuclear family as a center of community and comfort.

Just so, the city suffers the same isolation. It fails to find support and solidarity from the region or nation that feeds off of it. Corporations control its economy, which slowly collapses under the myth that the city will endure regardless. Like a battered woman, the city is rejected by those who have caused its poverty for fear that they too will catch the disease.

For a battered woman, these cycles of violence and isolation produce an endless cycle of fear: fear of more and more pain, fear of further destruction of her home through the "help" of police, courts, and agencies. This fear produces the ultimate paralysis: the belief that she no longer has the power to break out.

The city, too, is often in the grip of just such a fear. Its inhabitants are afraid of violence and destruction from one another and from those so-called helpers who float loans and produce new fears of bankruptcy and increased poverty. Such fears similarly bring the ultimate paralysis: the belief that the city can no longer bring life out of death.

In the face of those sexist, racist, and classist structures that batter women and city alike, what is the Spirit saying to the churches? I can't speak for all of the church. But I can say that I hear churches being called to share in the work of the Spirit as paraclete or advocate for those oppressed by racism, sexism, and poverty.

The Spirit herself is described in the Gospel of John as paraclete, which refers to a person of high standing who gives personal support to defendants by intervening with a judge on their behalf. The urban people of God are called to join the Spirit as advocates. We are to be those who put our reputations on the line for the oppressed.

Whether by taking to the streets to protest Washington's distorted budget priorities or by working for better social control of investments or by binding up the wounds of those already battered, the church is called to hammer out the message of hope. Amidst despair, we are called not to mouth words of cheap hope but to perform concrete actions of solidarity with all who, though victimized repeatedly, struggle to break the chains of that cruel cycle. Empowered by the divine paraclete, we are to devote ourselves to seeing that there are no more battered women—and no more battered cities.

As my student Sara Coxon put it in her paper, "Every time a woman screams 'No!' to violence, the New Age breaks in our midst. Hearing her scream is hearing the Spirit's awful and wrathful protest against oppression. Hearing that scream is hearing the voice of the Spirit, which is moving in all of us from death into God's new life." The Spirit calls us to give voice to those whose screams have for so long been silenced in cities across this land and around our globe, for the cries in our own cities are not so very different from the cries of the poor around the world.

One reason the cries of pain have not been heard is that for too long the city as battered woman has been denied a human face. The Spirit of the God who was willing to take on even the most disfigured form of a suffering servant (see Isa. 53:2) calls us as the urban people of God to reveal the human form of those victimized by the distorted and objectifying myths of sexism, machismo, success, and power.

As Elizabeth Dodson Gray once said, cities and battered women have been "mythed upon."[1] They have been named "whore of Babylon" or "Bride of New Jerusalem." They have been named "city of sin," "city of death," or "city of light and life." Cities, like battered women, suffer from a dualistic myth. As long as they are first named "virgin bride," they will soon be victimized as "battered whore." How easy it is for us to ignore the Spirit standing at their side, crying out to us, "For God's sake, they're human!"

Cities, like battered women, are human beings—human beings in whom God hopes and with whom God stands. We as the church are called to respond to the city, to share in making and keeping human life human. If we are to be a sign of the hope to which God has called us, we can do no other.

Letty Russell is professor of theology, Yale Divinity School and author of Feminist Interpretation of the Bible *(Philadelphia: Westminster Press, 1985) and* Household of Freedom: Authority in Feminist Theology *(Philadelphia: Westminster Press, 1987).*

Note

1. Elizabeth Dodson Gray, *Patriarchy as a Conceptual Trap* (Wellesley, Mass.: Roundtable Press), pp. 17–36.

• 12 •

RITUAL EXPRESSION

IN THE URBAN CHURCH

Janet Walton and Eleanor Scott Meyers

The Problem

Something is missing in our churches. The images, symbols, sounds, narratives and forms on which the church bases its worship do not connect with the experiences of many of its members. People of color (primarily in "old-line" denominations), people of different social backgrounds from those that founded these churches, and women in general are the objects of liturgical amnesia. Their heritage and their contributions are rarely identified and named, and they are forgotten as members of the church. Liturgical amnesia is a serious concern in the church today.

This concern is the focus of the story of one urban church that has experienced class-, age-, and race-based transitions in its neighborhood, a story that describes a brief, monthlong exploration of the relationship between a changing church population and its liturgical expression. Working with a group of urban church members,* we designed a project based upon our belief that rituals do not build community and are not liberating when their forms and symbols are tied to authoritative images and structures that have lost their significance for the participants.

Three assumptions undergirded this study:

---

*Names in this essay have been changed.

1. There is a particular quality of power inherent in ritual activity. Ritual offers a form of nonmanipulative power that stimulates activity and morale in its participants without using psychological pressure.[1] Leaders have power to define symbols and assume certain hierarchical roles. The power of ritual to overcome structures of domination will therefore depend upon new forms of shared leadership within faith communities.

2. The experience of "strangerness" is a reality in contemporary churches. Urban congregations, frequently tossed by social and economic upheaval, must deal with this "strangerness"—these differences in background that engender fear—on a regular basis. Audre Lorde urges us to "... reach down into that deep place of knowledge inside (yourself) and touch the terror and loathing of any difference that lives there. See whose face it wears."[2] Exposing differences and naming this fear in the midst of worship help to free groups to move away from "strangerness." Such movements, begun in worship, can continue to develop toward justice and love based on new solidarity among various peoples within urban neighborhoods.

3. Storytelling is a vehicle for initiating social change. It is through the simple ritual act of storytelling that communities can discover a structure of meaning that binds groups together across socially constructed barriers.[3] We understand that the struggle to change oppressive social structures must be supported by the struggle to change symbolic and ritual structures that have, over time, provided the psychological and spiritual foundations of material oppression.[4]

History of the West End Community Church

This congregation traces its history to a prestigious church established in 1834 in a wealthy residential neighborhood. Trying to stay ahead of transitions in racial, ethnic, and commercial populations, the church moved to a new location in 1856 and again in 1897. The latter move placed the church once more in the heart of the newest and one of the finest residential regions of the city. Neighborhood transition took about thirty years at this location. The Depression witnessed the previously elite, affluent Protestant population losing jobs and leaving the neighborhood. A Jewish neighborhood developed around the church building. The sanctuary, built to seat twelve hundred, was never full again.

Another, smaller congregation was located ten blocks away. During the mid-1940s, as both groups experienced dramatic declines in membership, a merger was worked out, and a new church name, West End Community Church, was adopted.

By the 1970s the neighborhood surrounding the church had experienced great economic decline. The few members could no longer pay the bills required to support the decaying building, but with the financial support of the denomination, the average Sunday attendance, which by 1980 had fallen to about thirty-five, slowly began to increase.

The transition in the 1980s was one of gentrification. Single persons now comprised over 50 percent of the households in the neighborhood. The census reports indicated declining diversity in economic, ethnic, and social levels as the population of young white professionals between the ages of twenty-four and forty-five grew. But the statistics did not identify the large and growing numbers of homeless people who populated the streets of the neighborhood.

One of the challenges facing this small congregation was, then, the integration of two very different worshiping groups, the "old" congregation and the "new": students, artists, young professionals. Each of these constituencies valued a different mode of sharing and participation in worship. It was time to put to the test our belief that community worship emerges, ideally, from community needs.

The Project

After initial meetings with the pastors and a member of the worship committee, we agreed to introduce the project—a process for planning a Sunday service that acknowledged and honored social changes in the worshiping community—to members of the worship committee. We talked about our ideas and addressed their questions. Once encouraged, we began by forming a small planning group that represented the cultural diversity of the congregation. In addition to the senior (male), associate (male), and student (female) pastors, eleven others, ten of whom were female and one male, joined the process. All were open to telling their own stories. The worship committee overseeing the project agreed not to put limits on our planning for worship.

First Planning Session

Our goal for the first gathering was to acknowledge our differences and build a sense of community through the process of naming those differences. We assumed that the work with individual stories and life circumstances would enable people to get in touch with their deepest needs and longings—significant components of authentic ritual. Understanding our shared needs would also be one way to begin to overcome the barriers of class, race, and gender.

We began by introducing the project and ourselves, emphasizing that knowing one another—our similarities and our differences—would contribute powerfully to community worship. A presupposition concerning a fear of differences guided the beginning point: "We are going to divide according to clearly defined categories in order to bring ourselves together." We asked the group to move near a set of stairs and suggested that the men move up onto the stairs (representing dominance) and the women remain down on the floor. There was much laughing with an undercurrent of unease. It was quickly noted that there were few men in the planning group and that they were mostly clergy.

Other divisions included those who lived a paired ("up the stairs") versus a single ("down on the floor") lifestyle; those who were under forty-five ("up") versus those forty-five or over ("down"); white persons ("up") versus people of color and/or ethnic background; members of the congregation who had been there four or more years ("up") versus nonmembers or those who had joined more recently; clergy ("up") versus lay members; people whose church background was in the original denominational tradition ("up") versus those for whom this was an "adopted" church home; and those who had six or more close friends within the congregation ("up") versus those who were not that well connected.

The one person of color in the planning group was an older woman who lived alone. Amid the nervous laughter as she continued to be left on the "down" side, finally to be isolated altogether, she said, "I don't know whether I should have come to this session." Participants were seeing, feeling, and saying things in a new way.

Following this exercise we discussed how differences— which we had just experienced—relate to the worship experience. Individuals talked about "status," which created barriers around worship leadership, and about ways in which various kinds of participation can lead to styles of "insider" communication that only longtime members understand, leaving visitors and relative newcomers out of the worship experience. They mentioned that the predominance of male ordained pastors can reinforce hierarchy and patriarchy to the detriment of the whole community, even though many expressed great appreciation for the present clergy. They agreed that power had shifted to the newer, younger members in some ways. They understood that this church was really "white" and that the economically privileged worshiped on Sunday morning, while the less privileged came to church at other times, usually seeking assistance.

As the conversation turned to issues of race and economics, we invited the group to spend time in pairs to talk about their own family and class backgrounds. This opportunity elicited new understandings about the class-based barriers we sense but rarely name. Such understanding can help identify meaningful symbols to be used in transformative worship. We learned from these discussions that what we have come to view as essential in worship often comes from the class background of the "founding fathers" of the church: academic garb on the preacher and white linen on the table; leadership from well-educated white males. Over time such ideas tend to achieve a kind of morality: Linen is correct and cotton print is not. These traditional liturgical symbols suggest that we all share the values that emerge from these class backgrounds when perhaps we do not. In order to discover the deepest longings and needs of those in our worshiping communities and potentially in urban neighborhoods, we want to honor our differences and dispel the notion that we are all alike.

Finally, we asked the members of the group to speak briefly about their decision to join this church: "What drew you here and what keeps you here?" They named the importance of being connected intentionally to people in the congregation and of being open to a variety of ethnic and racial backgrounds. (The woman of color mentioned that the spiritual sung on the day she first visited influenced her decision to become a member.)

Our first planning session concluded with a short service. We began with a litany on brokenness, an acknowledgement of ways our differences affected our understanding of God and one another. As various forms of brokenness were named (closed-mindedness, insensitivity, stereotyping), members of the group were invited to step out of the circle as a way of identifying their experience. After each naming of brokenness, we responded together, "broken to be healed," and reformed the circle. Over and over again we broke the circle and recreated it as we reflected on our experiences of apartness.

We then experienced the positive value of difference. To the tune of "Jacob's Ladder," we sang "We are standing in God's circle" and invited people to offer various names for God. We sang it repeatedly, pausing to listen to one another name God. The worship concluded with a blessing and the passing of the peace.

Our closing conversation centered on what each had experienced as significant in the service: "Brokenness was made real by moving my body." "I had to listen carefully, be really present in order to respond." "Worship often feels too complex; this wasn't. The children would love the candlelight, the moving around. We have no children in our services and I miss them." "We touched each other." "We are finding ourselves being revealed to ourselves."

Second Planning Session

Our goal for the second planning session was to shape a meaningful service for the congregation. As leaders, we had analyzed our first meeting with the planning group, especially the issues raised by the group members about what they needed in worship. Using these assessments, we prepared a Sunday-morning ritual based on the Eastertide scripture of the Emmaus walk (Luke 24:13–35) for their review.

We began the evening with prayer, using pieces from our proposal for the Sunday service to follow. We shared a litany that had been adapted from West End Community Church's official mission statement. Then we read the Emmaus story, in which two disciples discuss their loss of hope: "We had so hoped that our time of freedom was at hand" (vs. 21, authors' translation). Having read the text, we invited the group to take a walk in the neighborhood. "The task is to be observers. The disciples didn't see Jesus in their despair. Today, look and listen with these questions in your mind: 'Where do you see God? And how does God's presence or absence encourage you or discourage you today?' "

Following the walk, we discussed the Sunday service, including the possibility of an "Emmaus walk" in the neighborhood as the core of our proposed plan. We were encouraged by the enthusiasm of this small group of planners, just back from their own Emmaus walk. But even so, they had to be convinced that the walk would be well received as part of the Sunday service. We reasserted our commitment not to pressure people into participating. Options were always possible: for example, visiting with a friend in the sanctuary or spending the time in meditation while others were on the walk.

We struggled with the plan, which, in fact, would mean changes in almost every aspect of the service. Many in the planning group had to be "converted" to a new idea or a new way to do a familiar thing. In the end, however, we reached a consensus about the shape of the Sunday service, and all took assignments.

The Sunday Ritual

We began with a time of hymn singing, gathered around the organ. The choice of music included a variety of ethnic styles, and there was an invitation for the congregation to call out suggestions spontaneously. The people were then invited to take their seats, and the associate pastor led them in an adapted confession—an acknowledgment of some of their differences. He asked people to stand by categories, such as older or younger than forty-five, born in the United States or in other countries, new or old members, single or coupled lifestyles. The congregation clearly reflected a wide diversity of backgrounds and choices.

A passing of the peace followed. There was more conversation than usual. People identified with each other in new ways. A hymn, "We Gather Together," from a new hymnal[5] followed. It was chosen for the appropriateness of the text and for the purpose of exposing the congregation to a hymnal written in language that included women as well as men, African Americans as well as Euro-Americans, and images of collaboration rather than of dominance. The hymn was followed by the scripture for the day, the Emmaus walk, presented in a dramatic reading by some of the young actors in the congregation.

A sermon did not follow the reading. Rather, the litany adapted from the parish's mission statement and used with the planning group was read. The litany served to remind the congregation of the strong commitment this parish has historically made to the physical and spiritual needs of the neighborhood community.

After five minutes of exegetical interpretation, the pastor invited the congregation to take a ten-minute walk, in pairs, through the neighborhood. He explained that the planning team felt that this activity was an appropriate and unique way to reflect on the meaning of the scriptural text and suggested that the congregants identify the places where they saw God present in their neighborhood.

Most people cooperated, many eagerly. A few who were physically unable did not go outside but visited together in their pew. When the people returned, they were given cards on which they recorded where they had seen God, which were collected during the offertory as all were invited to bring their offerings to the front of the sanctuary. This part of the service concluded with the doxology.

The service then continued with a traditional sharing of joys and concerns by members of the congregation, a hymn, and community prayer. There was a higher level of participation than usual in this part of the service (undoubtedly influenced by the time spent in pairs), which was concluded with a recitation of a contemporary version of the Lord's Prayer, printed in the bulletin.

As in the story of the disciples on the road to Emmaus, the service continued around the table for Communion. For the first time in the history of this congregation, a female minister (the student pastor) led the congregation in blessing the gifts and the community. Instead of remaining in the pews, the congregation gathered around the table, where they could give the bread and cup to one another. The thanksgiving prayer began with the final verses of the Emmaus text, which recounts the story of the shared meal, and continued with a responsive litany, in which the people recited: "Take and eat . . . drink this all of you"—words usually reserved for the minister. After the congregation received Communion, the service concluded with a closing prayer, a familiar hymn, and the benediction.

Conclusion

The aim of this research project was to look at how change might be brought about in oppressive social structures through the use of symbolic structures. We chose to look at an urban congregation since the economic, political, and social crises of this historic moment can be addressed directly in such a setting. The work with the planning group was dynamic and appeared to empower the members within the group as a whole.

The Sunday service shared with the larger group was assessed as "successful" by the planners who met after the service.

When we returned to visit the congregation at worship several months later, however, we noted very little difference between what we had observed on our first visit with the congregation and what we observed on our return visit. Although painful, acknowledging this fact has been important for our ongoing work in other churches. The power of dominant traditions implemented by those who define the values of the church is embedded in cement, stone, words, and wood in that corner of that city and will not easily be left behind. Building on the "everydayness" in the lives of people in this congregation will remain a challenging task. With these limitations in mind, we make the following observations.

1. There is minimal recognition of the social change within the congregation and little corresponding change in the content and form of its worship. For example, much of the congregation consists of young, single, working women, whose daily concerns focus on career and friends. They come to the church to be part of a larger "family." Yet the predominant language and images of the hymns, scripture, and prayers excludes their experience, emphasizing male metaphors and male dominance. God is "father," a "king" whose will controls lives. These metaphors are hardly liberating for young, eager, committed women.

2. Though the mission statement of the church guides its members to active service in the community, it does not influence the Sunday service. Though street people eat at the church, they do not come for services. Though there is a significant Hispanic population in the neighborhood, they have separate and marginalized services. *The* event in the church each week is the "white," English-language service in the sanctuary on Sunday morning.

3. Hardly a single member of the congregation is from the upper class, yet the remnants of upper-class priorities remain. The altar is covered with a lace tablecloth for Communion; the containers are sterling silver. (For our Sunday service we invited people in the congregation to bring their own cups for Communion and to use textiles to cover the table)—perhaps multi-

colored cloths or simple handcrafted materials, the handiwork or heritage of the people who now make up the congregation and neighborhood.)

4. The arrangement of space emphasizes a hierarchical model that minimizes the responsibility of the whole community, poor as well as rich, illiterate as well as literate, in caring for each other and for the people of our world.

5. People in the church do not know each other well. In this small community where fewer than a hundred people gather on Sunday, a walk in pairs introduced unknown dimensions of people's lives to each other. It impacted the community prayer that followed; the prayers were concrete and inclusive.

6. When properly introduced, people will cooperate with new forms and new components of services if they can see the direct relationship these suggestions have with their own lives. Though some of the suggestions for this service had seemed quite radical, there was hardly any resistance. Rather, the response was gratitude, enthusiasm and anticipation.

Something is indeed missing in the Sunday service at this particular church. What we surmised—that there is often a gap between what people feel they need in a Sunday worship service and what they find—was borne out in this study. To our delight, the congregation seemed willing to acknowledge these gaps. However, changes must be implemented *on a consistent basis* to break down the race-, gender-, age-, and ethnicity-based barriers to community in this urban church. Constant vigilance and unrelenting education would be required to enable such an ongoing conversion.

Janet Walton is professor of worship at Union Theological Seminary in New York City.

Eleanor Scott Meyers is president of Pacific School of Religion, Berkeley, California. She was formerly professor of church and society at Union Theological Seminary in New York City and academic dean at Saint Paul School of Theology, Kansas City, Missouri.

Notes

1. D. Emmet, "The Concept of Power," *Proceedings of the Aristotelian Society* 54 (1953–54): 18.

2. Audre Lorde, *Sister Outsider: Essays and Speeches* (Trumansburg, N.Y.: Crossing Press, 1984), p. 113.

3. Lonnie Kliever points out the important use of autobiography within primitive Christianity as the means of social cohesion used by strangers—those without a deeply rooted, commonly held memory or hope. See his "Confessions of Unbelief: In Quest of the Vital Lie," in *Journal for the Scientific Study of Religion* 25, no. 1 (March 1986): 102–114.

4. Gregory Baum, *Religion and Alienation: A Theological Reading of Sociology* (New York: Paulist Press, 1975), pp. 227–237.

5. Ruth C. Duck and Michael G. Bausch, eds., *Everflowing Streams: Songs for Worship* (New York: Pilgrim Press, 1981).

• 13 •

PUBLIC MINISTRY:

CHRONICLES OF CAPACITY BUILDING

Philip Amerson

City Chronicles: Michael and Bess

With two stories we begin. Lessons from Michael and Bess: two stories from two radically different people. Michael, sixteen, grew up on the streets of our parish. Bess, eighty-three, now in a retirement community, is a longtime member of the congregation.

Two stories, yet one. Different actors, different circumstances, yet common themes. The day came when I recognized what they held in common: their common vocabulary. Michael was in the office. I had just returned from a visit with Bess in the hospital. Bess had told me about the folks, her friends in the retirement community. Then I heard Michael talk of "folks in the neighborhood who know what is going on." I found myself thinking, "There's that word again." Bess and Michael both use it, and often. They speak of the folks.

Bess and Michael are my teachers, my pastors, even though I am one of the "professional" pastors of the parish. They are the unelected, undesignated representatives of the folk of the parish. They are not the *laos* (the nonprofessional church leaders) in the recognized sense, yet they are among the "genuine articles," the ones who call for authentic new ways of living the gospel. Folks don't need to be elected. They are the subjects of action—beginning points. They act whether officially recognized or not.

Here is an anomaly, a puzzle: public ministry requires upfront, officially recognized leadership styles that must at the same moment be shaped by the "folk leaders." That's the paradox. In seeking to do the work of public ministry, the pastor must lead, interpret, and monitor, act in visionary, even audacious ways—tasks that cannot be done effectively apart from the authority, insight, and vision of ones like Bess and Michael.

Many who would analyze, fix, solve, save, develop, intervene, and compensate are surprised to learn that such folk gifts exist. If we have eyes to see, we will be astonished to learn of the potent resources, the capacities already in place among the folk, young and old.

Michael told of the violence he experienced daily as a teenager in the city. We knew about the fighting; it was, after all, on our doorstep. But from Michael's lips it was a litany with poetic and powerful clarity of street gang goings-on, of friends shot or stabbed. As a child on the playground of the church, he saw a young man with a handgun shoot another dead. He carried the memory, for himself and for others who would hear. When we listened to Michael, we heard social and political analysis far more sophisticated and precise than that shared by the educated of the surrounding service institutions, the church included.

A young man of enormous talent, Michael worked on the church's "Bridge House," a neighborhood center and gathering place. He was dependable. What a surprise to hear school counselors and teachers speak of him as "incorrigible," as a "problem" best solved by encouraging him to leave school early. Whereas we experienced him as bright, thoughtful, and trustworthy, other "professionals" spoke of him in such different tones that the dissonance was beyond explanation.

Rather than school, it could as easily be the welfare department discounting Michael's gifts, or an employment training program, or, yes, the church. Big-city institutions are easily caught up in management styles that ignore the folk gifts of the "clients" being served. It is a story of community lost and community broken. It is about the dominance of a foreign culture, a culture of service bureaucracies with their forms, regulations, and policies, imposed on "impoverished" neighborhoods.

In such circumstances, pastors are needed to lead, but first to listen, to hear others who can teach about the imposition of outside expectations. Michael shared his story one day waiting to go to "Saturday School." Saturday School is one of the disciplinary approaches used by the suburban school corporation to "teach a lesson" to the youth under suspension. The school is forty minutes away. This city, like dozens of others, is under a court order to desegregate the schools. Of course, this means "one-way busing"—from the core city to the suburbs. The school corporation provided no Saturday School buses, and public transportation to the distant school was nonexistent. It was mandatory for students being disciplined to appear at the suburban location, no matter what transportation was available in their family, or else they were to be permanently expelled from school.

The church was offered as a neighborhood site for Saturday School. During many sessions with school officials, folks from the parish offered to volunteer as staff for such a center. The answer to the request for a center in the neighborhood was no. In an interesting twist of bureaucratic logic, the folk were told that a Saturday School located in their neighborhood would be considered "resegregation." The folk knew that this and many other such decisions contributed to the dropout rate—more than 40 percent—among their high-school-aged youth.

The stubbornness of the school administration resulted in a call for organizing strategies on behalf of the youth. Michael, however, was not in favor of a protest march or the circulating of petitions. He suggested a concert by the neighborhood youth to unite the community. He knew the neighborhood needed the Bridge House, whatever the suburban school corporation could or could not be coaxed into doing. He knew the need for a "safe place," a place away from the violence, the violence of the streets and the violence of systems for domination unable to hear the voices of the folks. He suggested that neighborhood dance groups, the "Naptown Boyz," the "Gamma Rays," and the "Home Girls," put on a concert, the proceeds going toward operation of the Bridge House.

Michael knew the need to organize, but he identified deeper and more urgent issues: the provision of a safe place in the neighborhood and the strengthening of the sense of community among the folk. Michael had his own gift to give, one that did not fit the categories of expectation brought by the "service" institutions that claimed him as a client. He knew that before organizing could be effectively undertaken, the folks needed to succeed in doing something for themselves, where they lived. Michael gave his gift by sharing his vision and providing leadership for the concert. It built community. It was a gift of poetry and song. It was an alternative for those who get stuck looking for ways to confront or improve delivery systems. Michael offered the gift of his "folk culture."

The concert took place; the struggle for educational access goes on. Buses are now provided for Saturday School, and neighbors are ever more organized, successfully bringing changes to some of the more flagrant discriminatory practices of the suburban school corporation. When asked to talk about the time when the congregation and neighbors began to effectively address the educational concerns of the children, many of the folk of the parish don't speak of petitions circulated, or of meetings with school officials, or even of the election of new school board members; instead, they speak of the concert for the Bridge House.

Had we pastors followed our training and instincts, we might well have rushed to the strategies of community organizing. Michael knew better. This time, something else was required. He helped us start by recognizing the community already present. This was done, as he taught us, by sharing and valuing the "folk culture."

Bess, too, knows systemic violence. She had to struggle with the staff of her retirement community to get the medical care she needed. Bess knew her health, her body. The nursing staff was reluctant to send her to the hospital. Perhaps they didn't want the bother or to appear to overreact, or perhaps they might lose medical benefits income for care provided away from the home. Bess understood. With the help of another resident who served as lookout, Bess escaped in an ambulance she called for herself.

I visited Bess on the day she had, for a second time, overruled the retirement center nursing staff and admitted herself to the hospital. She was diagnosed as being in the midst of a heart attack. Bess knew herself; she acted. When I visited her, she was still in the emergency room, in a gown too short and on a table too hard. She had been in the emergency room for six hours. The hospital was full, the emergency room hectic. Bess looked pale and under much stress. Who wouldn't be, after dealing with nurses who refused to believe her, an ambulance ride, an overcrowded and noisy emergency ward and the diagnosis of a coronary in progress!

I wanted to help, but there seemed little to do. She held my hand. We talked. Her attention was on her family. "Tell them not to wait for me. They need rest, and I'll be all right." We prayed, but only after she teased me about giving her the "Methodist last rites."

The next day I visited her in the intensive care unit. She was sitting up in bed, comb in one hand and mirror on the table. She was primping. I said, "My, you look wonderful. Getting ready for a heavy date?"

She laughed and replied, "I'm feeling better, so I ought to look it." We took time to talk. She told me stories, stories of the way she survived the discrimination she faced every day. Her stories were full of whimsy and touches of humor.

Near the end of our conversation she turned to me and said, "Don't you just hate whiners?" I nodded. She continued.

"You know at the retirement community—that's our fancy word for nursing home—I get out and visit the old folks." I laughed at her good humor and vision of herself as a youngster. "Some of those folks do nothing but sit around and whimper. They're whiners!" she asserted. "Some of those folks are just wasting away for no reason."

By now Bess was looking straight into my eyes. "They think they can't do anything about their situations. Why, one woman the other day went on about how lonely she was and how she had no family or friends.

"I said to her, 'Don't you believe in Jesus?' And the woman said to me, 'I'm not that kind of Christian.'"

Bess continued, "I looked her in the eye." (I'm certain it was with the same steady gaze that Bess had now focused on me.) "And I said, 'That's too bad, because if you had that kind of friend in Jesus, you wouldn't need to be lonely. You'd have lots of brothers and sisters. In fact, you'd have one of your sisters visiting with you right now.' "

Bess giggled and looked away. I was aware again that I was being taught by my friend, one of the folks of the parish. I was being pastored by the unlikely ones. Bess and Michael, doing the folk ministry of our parish, were slowly bringing me along, helping me be pastor, helping the parish toward community.

Strategist and Scop

It was from Lutheran theologian Walter Wangerin that I first learned of the notion of a *scop*.[1] *Scop* (pronounced "shop") is a medieval term for the poet, the reteller of the epic struggle of the folk. The *scop* goes with the people into their daily lives, their battles, and then in the evening, in the mead hall, retells their story.

The contemporary urban pastor, Wangerin argues, plays a role most analogous to that of *scop*. She or he is to hear the stories of the people and then retell them in terms of the larger epic. The role of the pastor, according to Wangerin, is to live with the people, sharing, observing, and listening, and then to "whisper into the ears for the people" what is true from the great epic story as expressed in terms of their daily stories.

As Wangerin points out, *scop* is the root of the modern word "shape." The *scop* is a shaper. The shaper's work is to "story" the events of the day in terms of the larger meaningful history of the people, or "to sing into the everyday events of the folk, the old, old story."[2]

Our culture gives primacy to statistic, strategy, and syllogism over story. Like most people schooled in modern "scientific" disciplines, we have learned how to measure and categorize. We can report on the dimensions and densities of an objective social "fact." Measuring, quantifying, and analyzing is the way we search for dimensions of reality.[3] We practice the philosophical maxim, "It may be measured, therefore it is." Wangerin suggests that we need chroniclers rather than census takers, storytellers rather than strategists,[4] for we have failed too often to learn the value of hearing the stories behind, around, and under the "facts."

All of our measuring, our statistics, our calibrations are inadequate tools for understanding other realities. For example, how does one measure spirit? Where is the formula for paradox? Who can analyze and predict friendship, commitment, irony, or sacrifice? As we have been recently reminded, there are "habits of the heart" that are genuine human phenomena, though difficult to quantify or reduplicate.[5] Our scientific tools may measure the great achievements of a people, but they are impotent to catch the shape of the goodness of a people.

City ministry is shaped by the stories of the people. More than by any scholastic paradigms, it is the parable, metaphor, and drama—the witness and testimony of the people—that sustain the congregation and pastor. We too easily forget the teaching style of Jesus. How often he began by saying, "Which of you . . . ," or "A certain man . . . ," or "The realm of heaven is like . . . ." Rather than the one-way traffic from scientific measurement to new strategies, perhaps we need to see story as the footbridge between ways of knowing.

It is not easy to be open to both story and syllogism, but it is crucial for mission in our cities. The moment we begin to "bring closure," develop "the plan," or move to "the strategy," we find ourselves distressed by someone from the neighborhood or congregation who wants to interrupt with a story. Truly listening to the story is often the beginning of a genuine mutual endeavor of ministry.

The stories don't always come quickly; we must relearn the difficult task of waiting with expectancy for story. This is Advent time for ministry. As children we knew how to do this. Eudora Welty writes:

Long before I wrote stories, I listened for stories. Listening for them is something more acute than listening to them. I suppose it's an early form of participation in what goes on. Listening children know stories are there. When their elders sit and begin, children are just waiting and hoping for one to come out, like a mouse from its hole.[6]

Stories are heard before they can be told, lived out before they can be appropriated for living. As one cannot adequately capture the grandeur of stained glass by walking the perimeter of the cathedral or taking exterior photographs, so one misses the potency of narrative by viewing stories as valuable for illustration but little else. The preacher is tempted to believe that she should be the "teller" of story and must learn good "storytelling techniques." This, however, is not our primary task. We must instead first listen and seek the port of entry into the stories all around us. By telling the story too soon, we betray the arrogance of drawing conclusions for others.

The practiced storyteller is reluctant. She will wait for the right occasion. Story is not a joke or an anecdote that one can't wait to tell. Just as it takes patience to hear the story, one must display some patience in waiting to tell the story. Delay is appropriate. It allows room for humor and freedom for the unexpected and for another story. As much as we may become the carriers of a story, story is ultimately God's gift. We often must wait for it, in the hearing and in the telling. I am learning to mull over stories of the past, to be confronted by the escapades of the present, knowing that it is in the listening and telling of story that we find the bridge toward future odysseys. I can't measure that bridge and prove its existence; all I can do is share stories with you, stories like those of Michael and Bess.[7]

Where is the Public in "Public Ministry"?
A Few Hunches

Where did the idea of public ministry emerge? The term appeared in several denominational documents on ministry in urban areas in the early 1980s. Donna Schaper, formerly at the Urban Academy in Chicago, and Don Benedict, formerly of the Community Renewal Society in Chicago, were among the initial advocates for a change in language away from categories such as "urban" or "inner city" and toward "public" ministry. A significant pioneering effort at public ministry beginning in the 1950s in the United States was centered in the work of the East Harlem Protestant Parish.[8]

Why is there a need for new language, for a redefining of categories? Certainly the terms *urban* or *inner city* were too narrow in scope, limiting metropolitan ministry to "ghetto ministries" or failing to recognize the political and class relationships throughout a metropolitan area. These terms also carried a measure of separation, stigma, and prejudice, too often "urban" ministries were categorized as ministries of charity and predestined to paternalistic patterns. These labels tended to identify city people as the "have-nots" or "deprived" or "clients" and did not take into account the resources of the people, the folk.

While the founders of the clinical pastoral education (CPE) movement did not intend it to be a training ground in privatized and individualized approaches to ministry, this is nonetheless what much of such education tended to stress. CPE became another way of turning the folks into clients, a way of "numbering the people,"[9] a way of devaluing community. Ministry that included understandings of structural evil, of community organizing, and of the need to move away from paternalistic notions of working with "deprived clients" requires training in PPE, or public pastoral education.[10]

The Ochlos, *The Folks*

The North American church interested in engaging in ministry with and for the "folk" would profit through exposure to and study of the ways in which the pressing need for public ministry has manifested itself throughout the world.

From Korea, for instance, comes minjung theology. In contrast to the ruling elite, the *minjung* are the folks of society.[11] The biblical word for the *minjung* is *ochlos*, or the crowd. Looking at the Gospel of Mark, Ahn Byung-mu suggests the *ochlos* form the background of all Jesus' activities.[12] Mark uses the term *ochlos* in preference to the other often-used word for the people, *laos*, when he speaks of them as the sinners, the outsiders, and the tax collectors. The *ochlos*, like the *minjung*, is not the ruling class. It is the alienated class, and Jesus is criticized by the temporal powers for being among its people.

Capacity Building

Another resource for better understanding of the "public" in public ministry comes from the work of John McKnight and his colleagues at the Center for Urban Affairs and Policy Research at Northwestern University. McKnight has long suggested a shift in mentality from support of the service institutions, which make people into clients and low-income neighborhoods into "client neighborhoods," toward "capacity-oriented strategies for neighborhood development."[13]

According to McKnight, the typical pattern in low-income neighborhoods over the last generation is for human-service industries to seek to build on deficiencies, with "needs assessments," rather than building on the capacity of a community. He argues that client neighborhoods have resulted. They are "dominated by systems which have institutionalized degraded visions for devalued people. They have become barriers to opportunity, walling people in from citizen territory."[14] McKnight calls for a journey from "client to citizen"; at the crux of this "regenerating journey" is the belief in the capacity of every person to contribute to the improving of community life.[15]

Those struggling to discover the character of public ministry are brought to the question, 'How may congregations and congregational leaders work as capacity builders and not needs collectors?" The suggestion implicit and explicit in the earlier section on Bess and Michael is that one begins with stories. This is not meant to be a call to passive "storytelling strategies." It is intended as a political manifesto: To begin with stories is to begin with the currency of the streets; it is an effort to acknowledge and affirm the capacities, and in many cases the abundance, of the people.

Communities of the Base, and the Tabernacle and People Movements

For yet other examples in which community is built on the foundation of "*ochlos*-capacity building," we might turn to the tabernacle and people movements[16] and the base communities of Latin America. Such communities require a perpetual currency of exchange among leaders within traditional institutions and the folks who struggle at the margins of a society. *Faith of a People*, the small work by Pablo Galdámez, is a very effective tool to encourage discourse and new consciousness with people involved in mission or praxis/reflection activities in the parish.[17]

We must not assume that the leadership skills, stories, dreams, and visions of the folk, the *ochlos*, will inevitably emerge and find voice over against the temple religions and client institutions of our society simply because it should. Folk culture is by nature highly conservative, even reactionary. There is risk called for, public risk: the risk of assuming leadership, of acting with emerging communal authority. This is the risky business of the *scop*, work so risky it may be done only within the context of repentance.

How, then, will power and authority be developed among the folk? If minjung theology is right, the people are already acting as subjects. What is the role of the congregation, and of the pastor in particular, in providing a forum and focus for new leadership development and community-building activity? It is, we posit, for the congregation to assume the role of "repentant risk-takers."

The New English Bible's translation presents Jesus' sending out of the disciples (Mark 6:7–13) in an especially fascinating manner. After the disciples are given authority over unclean spirits and receive their instructions for the journey, it is reported that the disciples "set out and called publicly for repentance" (v. 12, NEB).

This public call for repentance, this public word, this publishing of the authority of Jesus and his disciples, is related in the accounts to the healing of people, especially the casting out of demons. It is also connected to the painful healing of the community. People who were outcasts are made acceptable to the community. The public publishing is occasioned after the healing as a way to demonstrate the unity and commonality among the people. Persons healed become public voices, even when they are warned not to speak.

What may one draw from this? What type of leadership development is appropriate? These are, I believe, among the most difficult questions for those involved in public ministry. It has been suggested[18] that there are two images of power presented in the gospel: one in which power belongs to the leader (Jesus gives power to the disciples, Luke 9:1–2) and the other in which power is discovered in the interaction of the group ("stay here in the city until you have been clothed with power from on high" [Luke 24:49]). Power is available through the "everyday, practical interplay of the group's life."[19] This is the lesson taught by Bess and Michael. The congregation and the pastor must take the risk of listening for the folk.

These hunches will, I suspect, help public ministry find definition. There are new roles for the pastor to play: mentor, artist, and healer. There are new ways congregations may practice ministry as communities of mentors, artists, and healers. The beginning point I would suggest is listening to the folk. Perhaps something will be "whispered in our ears" that our years in academia and in ministry have not taught us. We may then risk exploring those whispers in a more public way.

Philip Amerson is a pastor at Broadway United Methodist Church in Indianapolis. He is the author of Tell Me City Stories *(Seminary Consortium for Urban Pastoral Education, 1988).*

Notes

1. Walter Wangerin, "The Holy, Human Weave of Community" (Keynote address for the SCUPE Urban Congress, Chicago, April 1988).

2. Ibid.

3. Philip Amerson, "Inside Story: A Parable," *The Other Side* 195 (September 1988): 14.

4. Wangerin, "The Holy, Human Weave."

5. Robert Bellah et al., *Habits of the Heart* (Berkeley, Calif.: University of California Press, 1985).

6. Eudora Welty, *One Writer's Beginnings* (Cambridge, Mass.: Harvard University Press, 1983), p. 14.

7. For more on the value of narrative for urban or public ministry, see Philip Amerson, *Tell Me City Stories* (Chicago: Seminary Consortium for Urban Pastoral Education, 1988) and "The Miracle on Twenty-Ninth Street," *The Other Side* 192 (March 1988): 32–35.

8. George W. Webber, "The Struggle for Integrity," *Review of Religious Research* 23, no. 1 (September 1981): 3–21.

9. Wangerin, "The Holy, Human Weave."

10. But how will we understand the public? Several recent authors have written of the "public," though not always fully reflecting the views of those who would support PPE. See, for example, Richard J. Neuhaus, *The Naked Public Square: Religion and Democracy in America* (Grand Rapids: Wm. B. Eerdmans, 1984) or Martin Marty, *The Public Church: Mainline, Evangelical, Catholic* (New York: Crossroad, 1981). Parker Palmer's *The Company of Strangers: Christians and the Renewal of America's Public Life* (New York: Crossroad, 1981) is much closer to urban pastors' notion of "public ministry." Palmer is especially helpful in exploring the spirituality and hospitality necessary for public ministry.

11. Kim Yong-bock, "Messiah and Minjung: Discerning Messianic Politics over against Political Messianism," in *Minjung Theology: People as the Subjects of History*, ed. Commission on Theological Concerns of the Christian Conference of Asia (Maryknoll, N.Y.: Orbis Books, 1981). See particularly pp. 183–184.

12. Ahn Byung-mu, "Jesus and the Minjung in the Gospel of Mark," in *Minjung Theology*, pp. 138–152.

13. John McKnight, *The Future of Low-Income Neighborhoods and the People Who Reside There* (Evanston, Ill.: Center for Urban Affairs and Policy Research, Northwestern University, 1988), pp. 3–9.

14. Ibid., p. 14.

15. J. McKnight, "Regenerating Community," *Social Policy* 17 (Winter 1987): 56.

16. See Leonard Sweet, "From Catacomb to Basilica: The Dilemma of Oldline Protestantism," *The Christian Century* 105 (2 November 1988): 981–984; Wade Clark Roof and William McKinney, *American Mainline Religion* (New Brunswick, N.J.: Rutgers University Press, 1987); and Robert Wuthnow, *The*

Restructuring of American Religion (Princeton, N.J.: Princeton University Press, 1988).

17. Pablo Galdámez, *Faith of a People: The Life of a Christian Community in El Salvador, 1970–1980,* trans. Robert R. Barr (Maryknoll, N.Y.: Orbis, 1986).

18. James D. Whitehead and Evelyn Eaton Whitehead, *The Emerging Laity: Returning Leadership to the Community of Faith* (New York: Doubleday, 1986), pp. 35–49.

19. Ibid., p. 36.

• 14 •

LOOKING FOR GOD IN THE CITY:

A MEDITATION

Barbara Brown Taylor

From the very beginning, cities have been the best and the worst of places, vessels for a concentrated humanity that is capable of the best and worst under God's sun. For most of us, the city we love is also the city we sometimes hate, but it is the city to which we have been called and the city that we want, somehow, to save.

I landed in the city by chance, not by plan. When I was ordained a few years back, the only parishes open to deacons of my gender were urban ones, parishes full of people who leave their harmonious neighborhoods and drive downtown because they want the discord or at least the diversity of the city. They will put up with the racket for the richness of the place and are willing to be disturbed by it all.

Before long I, too, was disturbed—by how much there was to do, by how complicated the problems were and how elusive their solutions, by how hard it was to measure any progress at all, never mind success. I was especially disturbed by the people who came tapping at my doors and yelling through my open windows, wanting food, wanting money, wanting chiefly to be reckoned with. I set aside time every day to see those I could and found myself defenseless in the face of their intricate stories. Even if I did not believe them, I was astonished by their inventiveness and found it hard to deny them anything.

My discretionary fund dwindled, but I clung to the notion that I was helping people, that if I gave them what they said

182

they needed then they would go forth from the church better able to solve their problems. I thought I was fixing them, or helping them to fix themselves, and I bid each of them good-bye as though I was releasing a young bird I had raised.

They began to return, with new stories or variations on the old ones, and brought their friends. My name got loose in one low-income housing development, and I spent a whole week dealing with half a dozen eviction notices from the same land-lord. Slowly and painfully it dawned on me that the harder I worked, the more work there was to do. It was the beginning of my wisdom about urban ministry. Forget what your parents taught you about how a job well done stays done. In the city, a job well done simply earns you ten more, and none of them stays done.

That hard work breeds more work is only one of the para-doxes of the city. There is a theological one as well: The city is, at one and the same time, the object of God's historical wrath and of God's promise. Jesus weeps over Jerusalem more than once, as Jeremiah and the others did before him. Their prophe-cies against the city are thinly veiled torch songs, the songs of lovers who have offered themselves and been rebuffed. God has been half crazy in love with Jerusalem since first laying eyes on her, but she has been unfaithful. Thus God's prom-ise—and wrath.

According to holy writ, there are three chief places where God reveals God's self to us: on mountaintops, in the wilder-ness, and in the city. The air is thin in the first; there are wild beasts in the second; but the city may be the hardest place of all to recognize the presence and activity of God. There is a lot of sin, for one thing, a lot of sadness and lostness and disorder. And there are a lot of distractions, not least of which is our busyness, our scrambling efforts to feed all the hungers we meet. It is hard to stay attentive to God's activity when we are half dead from our own.

But this is not a new dilemma. Sometime around the begin-ning of the fourth century, there were Christians who began leaving their cities for the deserts of Egypt and Palestine and Syria. They decided they were not strong enough to remain in the city without conforming to its appetites. They looked upon urban society as a shipwreck from which they must swim or lose their lives. So, led by a farmer's son named Antony, they moved into the desert, where they disciplined their own appetites. Their stories come down to us as the stories of the desert mothers and fathers, and they are frequently misunderstood as life-denying ascetics.

Instead, they were holy gypsies, pilgrims in search of that heavenly country hinted at by the author of the letter to the Hebrews. In faith, the desert mothers and fathers moved to the desert looking for a *verbum salutis*, a saving word, but what they really hoped to find was the new Jerusalem. They lived in caves and supported themselves by weaving baskets. They kept their mouths shut, for the most part, but people were constantly seeking them out for their wisdom accumulated from lives of unceasing prayer. They ate little and loved a lot and were known for their charity toward everyone.

My hunch is that they have something to teach those of us who have refused to abandon ship, who are still bailing water and patching holes and looking for God in the gorgeous wrecks of our cities. At first glance, we do not have much in common. The desert folk left their cities, after all; we are still in ours.

What defined a city in ancient times were its walls. The very word "city" in Hebrew means "an enclosed place," and what a city was good for was defense. Under attack, people fled their fields and villages and headed for the nearest city. The gate of any city, though on its perimeter, was in fact its center, the place where access to the city was controlled, where vendors sold their wares and beggars begged for alms.

The desert, on the other hand, was a place without walls, a place of desolation or ruin where demons roamed, a lonely place populated by jackals, vultures, ostriches, and wild asses that brayed at the moon. To live in the desert was to live undefended, to expose yourself to the elements and sleep lightly, surrounded by a whole crowd of spirits that might wish you well but more likely wished you dead.

I believe that the city and the wilderness have swapped places these last sixteen centuries, or at least have drawn closer together. The city's walls have fallen; it is no longer a place to go to be safe but a place to go to be challenged, to wrestle the modern-day demons of corruption and excess, the beasts of homelessness and despair.

So maybe the desert mothers and fathers have something to teach us after all. Their motto was "flee, be silent, and pray," but that is the "what" of what they did. The "how" may matter more for us, because everything they did was characterized by a kind of light-handedness, an ease and buoyancy that made them saints in their own time, although sainthood was the last thing they would have desired or thought they deserved.

Detachment, laughter, and humility, three practices that sustained the desert mothers and fathers so long ago, may preserve our urban lives even now.

Detachment may be the most troublesome of the three, since most of us have learned the word to mean something like coldness or indifference. Detached? *Au contraire!* We are involved, committed; we are Christ's body on earth, bearers of the Holy Spirit, commissioned to make disciples of all nations. But that is where the problem begins, because the opposite of detachment is attachment—to our own expectations, for instance, or to our own compulsive way of doing things, to the satisfaction of our own needs and our own ideas about the way things and people and cities ought to be. Above all, we tend to get attached to our results, to the elusive fruits of our labors, and that is not good for us.

What the desert folk knew that we have largely forgotten is the value of a certain *apatheia*—not the absence of care but the presence of so much care that we give up our own desires and disappointments for the sake of those whom we serve. With a little detachment, we meet them not where they ought to be but where they are, and we meet them with no thought of how we can fix them, but only, perhaps, of how much God we can discover in them. This kind of detachment is a kind of indifference, insofar as it ceases to matter to us whether or not the world conforms to our requirements; we cease to choose our chores on the basis of how effective they are likely to be; we become careless in the accounting of our rewards. We do what we can and then we rest, waiting to see what God will reveal to us next.

Abbot Pastor, one of the desert elders, was asked by a brother: "How should I conduct myself in the place where I live?" The elder replied, "Wherever you may be, do not desire your word to have power before you and you will rest."[1]

We have been called not to swim away from the beautiful, battered ships of our cities but to stay with them and to look for the presence of God in them at all times and in all places. It requires a certain detachment, a certain independence from all the perils that have never been under our control. But above all it requires a certain freedom from our own hopes and wants, however noble they may be. "You did not recognize God's moment when it came," Jesus says to Jerusalem (Luke 19:44, NEB) but it is hard to recognize God's moment while we are consumed with making the most of our own.

Abbot Lot came to Abbot Joseph and said: Father, according as I am able, I keep my little rule, and my little fast, my prayer, meditation and contemplative silence; and according as I am able I strive to cleanse my heart of thoughts: now what more should I do? The elder rose up in reply and stretched out his hands to heaven, and his fingers became like ten lamps of fire. He said: Why not be totally changed into fire?[2]

Fire versus burnout

Those of us in urban ministry read and hear a lot about professional burnout, that creeping deadness of the soul that narrows our vision and extinguishes our energy until it is all we can do to get out of bed in the morning. We are sitting ducks for it, the trade journals tell us, for at least four reasons: 1) our jobs are never done; 2) our results are hard to measure; 3) our expectations are high—not to mention the expectations others have of us; and 4) most of us do not get to choose whom or even how we will serve. We are not psychotherapists who may stop when our forty-five minutes are up or physicians who may decline new patients when our case loads are full. We are baptized Christians who have promised to seek and serve Christ in all persons. On what grounds do we turn away from someone in need, and to whom do we say no? Given the ubiquity of our Lord, it is a sobering question.

And yet we know well the consequences of *not* saying no: Our tempers flare, our health fails, our cynicism grows like a weed, and the quality of our service begins eventually to stink. We spend a lot of time planning vacations and sabbaticals still a long way off; we do not sleep well at night; sometimes we have trouble breathing. Worst of all, we lose the knack of hope. We see the dark side of things and shield our eyes from the light. Spring arrives, and what we notice are the baby birds dead on the sidewalk or the fading of the flowers. What we hear in church on Sunday or what we say there begins to sound like wishful thinking, whistling in the dark. Something has to give.

While the word *burnout* is a new one, the phenomenon is as old as time, as old as Psalm 55. The psalmist is panic-stricken and speaks of a heart torn with anguish because of violence and strife in a city filled with trouble, mischief, rumor, scandal, and spite. The psalmist wants a refuge in the wilderness, a sanctuary in which to hide from the storms of life: "Oh that I had wings like a dove! I would fly away and be at rest" (v.6).

Detachment is one of the virtues of the desert mothers and fathers that allowed them to hold their lives lightly, to surrender their expectations of the way the world ought to be, to give up their striving to get what they wanted in favor of learning to want what they got. It is one of the cures for burnout. Modern-day clinicians tell us about a few more.

The phrase they use is "hardiness," a frame of mind exhibited by people who seem immune to stress, who function well under the worst of circumstances and bounce back fast when they are laid low. I have heard it said that these people have some things in common: chiefly, a sense of purpose and belonging. They are people who have found something to love, something to which they can commit their lives; they are people with strong ties to others. They work hard but they do not work alone, and they believe in what they are doing. Loners and cynics do not, apparently, rate very high on the hardiness scale.

Then, clinicians tell us, there is self-esteem. Hardy people, so we are told, have a realistic notion of their strengths and weaknesses and seem satisfied with the balance. They have found the fertile ground between thinking they can do nothing and thinking they can do everything. When they sit down at the end of the day, they look first at what they have accomplished and only then at what still waits to be done. They treat themselves at least as kindly as they would treat a stranger.

Empathy is another characteristic of hardy people, according to researchers. They are forever giving their adversaries the benefit of the doubt, forever trying to see things through other people's eyes. They are not half as interested in how they are different from other people as in how they are the same. They say "us" a lot and "them" not much at all. They tend to greet people they do not know like long-lost kin.

Finally, experts say, there is humor, which we may define as an acute sense of proportion. Hardy people do not take themselves or anyone else too seriously. They laugh a lot, at least partly because they are good at seeing the cartoons we all make as we live our lives. But their laughter is more radical than that; they also laugh to make outrage tolerable, to defy the powers that be, and to remind themselves that who they are is not dependent on how the world treats them. By choosing to laugh when they might just as well cry, they have the last word, and what they proclaim by their guffaws is that there is more to everything than meets the eye.

It is this kind of anarchic laughter that the desert mothers and fathers did so well. They never tired of tricking the sightseers who sought them out; they did everything they could to ruin their own reputations. If the tourists came to see ascetics, then the hermits would rustle up a banquet worthy of a Southern Baptist Sunday school picnic. If, on the other hand, visitors came to collect some wisdom, the hermits would begin to weave their baskets, muttering nothing more profound than, "Pass the scissors, please."[3]

They may have been mischievous, but they were never mean. They simply could not stand to be revered, and they enjoyed themselves immensely as they tarnished their own images. One of my favorite stories from the desert goes like this:

Once there was a disciple of a Greek philosopher who was commanded by his Master for three years to give money to everyone who insulted him. When this period of trial was over, the Master said to him: Now you can go to Athens and learn wisdom. When the disciple was entering Athens he met a certain wise man who sat at the gate insulting everybody who came and went. He also insulted the disciple who immediately burst out laughing. Why do you laugh when I insult you? said the wise man. Because, said the disciple, for three years I have been paying for this kind of thing and now you give it to me for nothing. Enter the city, said the wise man, it is all yours.[4]

We have been through the same gate; we too collect our insults for free, but, please God, we are able to laugh about it, to recognize the exquisite if sometimes painful humor that drenches all our days. The psalmist hankers for wings with which to fly away, but these are not the wings that are offered to us. What we are offered instead are the wings of a broody hen who longs to gather us as her own dear children. Beneath her life-giving breast there is room for all Jerusalem. All we have to do is to let her gather us and to recognize her for who and what she is. All we have to do, with joy that rises up and spills out of our mouths, is say, "Blessings on the one who comes in the name of the Lord."

Barbara Brown Taylor is a priest in the Episcopal Diocese of Atlanta. She is the author of two volumes of sermons: Mixed Blessings *(Atlanta: Cherokee Publishing Company, 1986) and* The Seeds of Heaven *(Cincinnati: Forward Movement, 1990).*

Notes

1. Thomas Merton, trans., *The Wisdom of the Desert: Sayings from the Desert Fathers of the Fourth Century* (New York: New Directions, 1960), p. 53.
2. Ibid., p. 50.
3. Ibid., p. 27.
4. Ibid., p. 39.

• 15 •

A Lesson
on Urban Spirituality

Valerie E. Russell

Urban spirituality is more than vague platitudes about caring about one another in the "God loves you; so do I" mode. It
means, rather, radical engagement with the stranger, resembling more the attitude of "God loves you, and I'm trying!" A
strong spirituality for the city requires a theological belief system that stems from hard-hitting critical social analysis, a process that seeks harmony between the discipline of meditation
and commitment to an action-based agenda—the mind and
heart seeking to "know" God and act accordingly. Such action
is at its most sustainable when we do our spiritual homework,
because in urban ministry, struggle is a constant companion.
Acquiring a spiritual resiliency is a mighty faith task for empowering people to sustain caring and action. Burnout and
cynicism are two of the most powerful realities of our times—
not only among the poor but among those who would minister
to them.

Urban spirituality boldly affirms that each person is unique
and worthy of respect. Otherwise "the poor" are merely stereotyped categories, figures on charts, "them" as opposed to
"us." Our American culture idolizes individualism in the
mainstream in ways that often undercut a sense of common
bonding or "peoplehood." But when it comes to the marginalized, we rapidly shift that criterion and lump folks into categories that enable us to depersonalize them and thus relieve our
consciences of any sense of responsibility. An "urban spirituality" raises serious questions about the relationship between

the "haves" and the economically marginal. It can radically transform lives.

How do we define "successful" urban spirituality? With struggle as our constant companion and moments of grace manifesting themselves very unpredictably, indeed, we must live with the unknown. An urban spirituality fully aware of the demonic power of human greed and fear knows that the new world we seek may well not happen in our lifetime.

Urban spirituality has at its heart concerns about both power and powerlessness. What is power? How do we use it, and toward what ends? God's power? our power? empowerment, shared power? It asks also, What constitutes true powerlessness? When is it vital to acknowledge powerlessness as a reality as opposed to claiming it as a defense against commitment and action? What are the limits of power, not only in terms of the world's agendas but in light of the acknowledgment of the power of God? When is it important to get out of the way so that the Spirit can move beyond us? And how do we prepare ourselves for the terrifying task of being channels of God's power?

The question of power and spirituality in the urban context is one of the most difficult of our time, but transformation is what we dare to dream and do in ministry. We seek keys to unlock doors to new visions. Such visions are the epoxy glue determining how my spirit is bonded to yours and how one effort on behalf of justice is bonded to other efforts. Ultimately the power question connects us to questions about our relation to God and the Holy.

The Context for Urban Spirituality

There is a weariness at the heart of our contemplation of present realities for the urban poor. Weariness grows more profound as we contemplate specific solutions to meet the challenges. As William Sloane Coffin has stated, this is the kind of bone-centered weariness that leaves you too tired to get your rocking chair going when you finally find the time to sit down. Consider the statistics. Estimates of the rate of poverty in the United States suggest that it hovers around 33 million—*nearly one out of every seven people live below the poverty line.*[1] Consider, too, the following:

• Between 1979 and 1985, the number of people living in poverty in the United States rose by 4.3 million.
• Almost two of three poor adults in the United States are women. Their vulnerability to poverty is increased by lack of access to jobs and equitable salaries, divorce and separation, inadequate welfare benefits, and insufficient support services such as child care for those able and willing to work.
• Of all children under the age of six, 22 percent live in poverty. For African American children under six, the rate is 45.6 percent; for Hispanic children, 40.7 percent; for white children, 17 percent. It is, however, important to remember that though poverty rates are increasingly racial in character and proportions (including both adults and children, 31.9 percent of all African Americans and 29 percent of all Hispanics live in poverty), in absolute numbers, poor whites outnumber poor African Americans two to one.[2]

In the face of these devastating statistics, we find that the prognosis for the creation of new jobs in the service sector does not bode well for the correction of the problem. Of the 8 million new jobs created in the United States between 1979 and 1984, nearly 60 percent of that growth came in jobs paying less than $7,000 a year—only $583 a month before social security and tax deductions!

Sociologically speaking, the implications of these statistics are devastating for the future. They predict quite clearly an institutionalization of the growing "permanent underclass," a euphemism for the chronic, unchangeable poor. The impact is felt across the board: in health care, in housing, in the integrity of the family. Our government has no national health policy, and access to health insurance is increasingly limited to those who can afford large premiums. Little preventive health care is available to the urban poor, the consequences of which will be borne by future generations. Public and private housing policies also seem to discriminate against the poor: Requests for public housing units in the Boston area alone rose from seven thousand in 1950 to over seventeen thousand in 1980. Regentrification has meant rapid conversion of affordable housing into expensive condominiums, depleting the supply of decent affordable housing. The median price for a single-family dwelling in Boston in 1987 was more than $180,000; monthly rents, nearly $800.

In addition, our family structure is falling apart. The number of teen pregnancies and single-parent families is ever on the rise. Teens, especially African American youth, are facing critical unemployment pressures, and drug use and crime are on the increase.

Add to these alarming reports some facts about the decline of churches in the Boston area (similar to declines across the country): seven major Protestant denominations have experienced a devastating combined net loss of churches in local urban neighborhoods since World War II, representing a loss of tens of thousands of members. Roman Catholic membership has dropped substantially as well, and far fewer people identify themselves as practicing Jews than before World War II.

It appears that the mainline churches have all but abandoned the city and the matter of human survival in the urban setting. They certainly do not show much evidence of spiritual "praxis muscle" in the face of dire need. Furthermore, many of the mainline churches that do remain in urban neighborhoods have tended to become reactive rather than proactive. This often results in passive, dependent behavior. Internalizing their fear of change, they often hold on for dear life to their remaining members. Perceiving themselves as victims, they blame the victims of social disease for the fact that their church has fallen on hard times. Focused on a personal salvation, they often separate issues of faith and politics from the ethos of what it means to be a religious community in such a context.

Developing a New Spiritual Base

Observation and experience have demonstrated that there are several factors—not intended to be exhaustive—that should be integrated into the church's strategy to enable a more dynamic spirituality in such a context. They include: 1) revaluing experience as knowledge base; 2) fighting despair, amnesia and silence; 3) creating new symbols and metaphors for "the Holy"; 4) reclaiming a "tough tenderness"; and 5) learning from Exodus and liberation theology.

Revaluing experience as knowledge base.   Urban church people and the poor in urban communities suffer from a lack of validation of their experience—they rarely value what they already know. We live in a society that idolizes expertise and devalues common experiential wisdom. In poor communities, such wisdom has been referred to as "mother wit." Streetwise poor people appear to be functionally obsolete in our computerized technological age.

Many who are marginalized sense that the "experts" who have so much control over their lives are hovering over them and cannot be challenged. Such a devaluing of experience as usable knowledge creates a deep despair and massive sense of powerlessness among poor urban people. Part of the function of urban ministry must be, in the midst of such an assault, to help people rediscover survival strategies for self-determination and decision-making power.

Institutions, particularly the institutional church (which a secular society often also diminishes in an age of technology and specialization), must develop a similar methodology as a response to the despair it often feels in the midst of urban chaos and present-day socioeconomic arrangements.

Fighting despair, amnesia and silence.   We must kindle and give expression to a prophetic and incisive humor that fights despair and creates a broadened perspective on events and issues in the midst of the struggle. Agents of serious change rarely talk about humor. Mainline religion in particular has tended to define a style of deadly seriousness as a sign of true engagement. Celebration, joy, and laughter have seemed incongruous with full involvement with people's pain and survival and therefore as childish. But a study of the great movements of our time, from labor and civil rights to the feminist movement, demonstrates salient examples of the very strong and proactive function of laughter in empowering people to move into threatening situations with power.

In our time, people such as Dick Gregory and Lily Tomlin have creatively used humor that emerges from the struggles of the marginalized for power. To use humor intentionally to fight despair is to learn how to stand back and put life into a perspective that enables one to tolerate the pain of struggle.[3] Spirituality embodies a form of humor and joy that acknowledges that despite the wonderful gift of creation, the human condition is a mess.

Spiritually, fighting against despair is an exercise in exodus and wilderness journeying. It is moving out of Egypt—not allowing victimization to control the mind or behavioral patterns any longer. To fight against despair is to see life as a journey: a journey that will be full of ambiguity and vulnerability but also of grace and hope and humor and joy.

As in the struggle against despair, when we tell stories of the movements of people from one exile to another, we also fight amnesia. Amnesia emerges from the fact that our present culture tends to be ahistorical. Just as we do not tend to value our experience, neither do we value our history.

The white mainline church is mired in this problem. If many of the present-day denominations were aware of and took to heart the radical stands of their ancestors, both positive and negative, they would generate a more concrete and accurate agenda in the present context. As it is, the church suffers from denial of its negative role in shaping present social pathology and is similarly cut off from a sense of its rich history. The social movements of these churches played a major role in mobilizing bold, moral responses to social and political realities throughout United States history, going back to the days of slavery. An awareness of historical involvement with the poor, both positive and negative, makes the present passivity of church life incongruous.

Conversely, the African American church has spent decades recovering the legacy of slavery and of those in the post-Reconstruction era who worked in service to society. It thus recaptured the strengths born from the struggle: the religion, songs, and lifestyle that learned to celebrate grace in the midst of suffering.

The problem with many of today's poor is that they have forgotten or repressed that history, if they ever knew it. In a fifth-grade summer class at the Boston City Mission Society's tutoring program, several students insisted the teacher was lying to them about slavery; they believed it had never happened at all. The teacher challenged them to go home and ask their parents about it, to inquire why it was that their ancestors came to this land and how it was that they now lived in Boston. They returned the next day chagrined; their parents had said it was so! When the teacher asked them why African Americans were so depressed economically, why it was so difficult to find integrated housing or live in suburban communities, one student replied, "I guess I thought that was just the way it was!"

Amnesia enables people to believe that they are poor, depressed, and in despair because that's "just the way it is." Amnesia also enables whites and those who participate passively in perpetuating unjust social relationships to believe the same thing.

Urban ministry needs to practice telling the ancient stories of the wilderness journeying, the exodus, and the great triumphs of the human spirit as a constant and ever-present theme in the practice of ministry. In relating the stories of how the exodus experience has been lived over and over again, not only can we discover grace in the midst of the struggles of our lives, but as feminist theologian Nelle Morton tells us, we can also honor each other's journeys as valid and heroic; we can "hear one another into being."[4] It is in the actual telling of the story that we find the determination and power to break free of our sense of despair and victimization.

And what of silence? Silence in and of itself is not necessarily negative. While our often extroverted society and liturgical forms have not valued silence as a positive mode of discernment, it certainly must be affirmed as such. Often, God's presence in our midst cannot be heard because of all the noise that drowns out the still, small voice and distracts us from careful observation. Our consumer mentality pervades our lives, including our religious and faith expectations, and the value of silence is consequently underrated. We do not enjoy sufficient silence in our lives, nor in our electronic age do we use well the small quantities of it at our disposal.

Of equal concern is the silence of assent, which allows the hidden oppressive arrangements of the rich and powerful in the society to continue and suggests to the poor and oppressed that they must tolerate their victimization. Silence as muteness against the outrageous injustices in the world is a major sin of our time among churches and their people. Synonyms for the word "mute" include voiceless, inarticulate, dumbfounded, repressed, and subdued, all of which aptly describe both the urban poor and urban churches in the context of scandalous need.

Creating new symbols to capture our experience. New religious symbols that have a meaningful content in an urban technological age must be created. I saw in an editorial once the story of a woman reflecting on the death of her father. As a child she had climbed on his feet and held onto his belt, and he had "danced" her around the room. Now that he had died, she speculated that for the first time in her life, she would truly have to "get down off her father's feet" and claim her own ground. The urban poor are very much in the same position as they inherit the spiritual symbols from an agricultural, rural cultural past. "The Lord is my shepherd" is a beautiful symbol—unless you live in a world that is totally devoid of shepherds! Contemporary symbols of faith in the urban setting are in danger today of being reduced to "artifacts" rather than remaining as living, pulsing symbols of "God with us."

A Catholic seminarian told me recently that he felt exhausted after leaving mass each week because the more ambiguous life became, the more the liturgy tried to fill the ambiguity with words. "I'm exhausted because I feel as if I've just spent the last half hour distorting the truth, and in a language that is not my own." It is time, liturgically, to get down off our father's shoes, to create new liturgies and new symbols which invoke our meaning, not that which we have inherited.

At an inner-city mission populated by a sizable community of alcoholics and chronically poor, the pastor asked the community—primarily African American—to create their own symbols of oppression, both external and self-imposed. These would be placed on the altar each week as signs of brokenness that needed healing. By the third week, the congregation had placed on the altar a whiskey bottle, a lynch rope and a crutch as signs of brokenness. During the fourth week, considerable time was spent trying to discern if the cross truly belonged in the middle of those contemporary symbols. On Easter Sunday, the decision was made that the story about the crucified and risen Lord had some relationship to the whiskey bottle, the lynch rope and the crutch. What a great affirmation of faith! That Easter was no disembodied event; that Jesus rose into the midst of that community's pain. Few of us have ever forgotten the power of that Easter. It is a powerful paradigm of the way in which people could revitalize ancient symbols and restore meaning to the metaphors.

Joseph Campbell, in his nationally televised series of interviews on public television, tells us that we cannot borrow God—that every generation must discover God for itself. We must get down off our father's shoes and participate in recreating religious symbols that have meaning for the urban poor in the midst of their daily experience.

Reclaiming a "tough tenderness."   In order to create a different urban spirituality, we must strive to live in the tension between tenderness and toughness. Underneath our psyches and throughout the tapestry of our society, there live demons of anger and cruelty that are so deep and insidious they can hardly be faced. The Ku Klux Klan no longer wears sheets; publicly avowed Klanners sit in board rooms dressed in business suits. Many of our urban schools have become police combat zones. And in many places in our country, guns have come to be regarded as a precondition to liberty! The assassinations of Martin Luther King, Jr., and Robert F. Kennedy in 1968 forever changed our understanding of the power of such violence in the public arena. Added to the dramatic assassination of John F. Kennedy in 1963, these events shattered the deeply held, desperately prayed-for theory that we could reconstruct a free, democratic, and inclusive society based on the notion of nonviolence. As I have heard William Sloane Coffin say many times, "Would we keep destroying the best amongst us if we hadn't already destroyed the best within us?"[5]

We need to uncover a new gentleness amongst us, one full of an active passion that calls us to become more human. A number of writers are beginning to address this issue. Audre Lorde powerfully addresses the question of gentleness in violent contexts:

we have learned to be at home with cruelty because we have survived much of it within our own lives. . . . Until now, there has been little that taught us how to be kind to each other. . . . It would be ridiculous to believe that this process is not lengthy and difficult. It is suicidal to believe it is not possible.[6]

In many ways such tenderness is embodied in what some are now calling the theology of accompaniment. It is a way of being in gentle, strong solidarity with the poor and enabling the poor to find ways to be in strong solidarity with one another. Within this form of solidarity, the non-poor will avoid becoming voyeurs of others' pain. The poor, in the meantime, will avoid the competitive game of trying to climb out of their victimization on the backs of other victims.

Liberation theology methodology. Finally, as we strive in urban ministry to snuff out despair, to help people to recover from amnesia, to break silence, to tell our stories to one another, to build new symbols of the Holy, and to recapture our gentleness, we need a theological construct that makes some clear assumptions and a methodology that will enable these things to happen. Liberation theology as it has emerged in oppressed communities around the globe is a paradigm for this mode of journeying, a journeying toward a sense of the Holy as inextricably bound to the issue of politics. And for the marginalized, the exodus story is a meaningful model. As Michael Walzer writes:

Wherever you live, it is probably Egypt;
. . . there is a better place, a world more attractive, a promised
    land;
. . . "the way to the land is through the wilderness."
There is no way to get from here to there except by joining
    together and marching.[7]

He goes on to state that the key question for the journey toward liberation is a spiritual one: "Can God furnish a table in the wilderness?"[8] Harvey Cox addresses the fact that the mainline church often fears such affirmations and journeying. He asserts that secularism tries to "expel God and quarantine religion to the heart of the individual." Like the secularists, the church also fears a bubbling, uncontrollable spirit:

the dilemma now is no longer how to revive a comatose piety in an age of unbelief, but how to cope with fresh voices of faith that do not conform to old patterns. Church leaders are faced not with a decline in spirituality but with a new outburst of religious energy.[9]

In reference to the awakening of the Latin American church in a revolutionary situation, Cox discusses how liberation theology represents grassroots religious energy boiling up from the bottom and the margins of society.[10] But this bubbling is threatening to the heart of a clergy-dominated, catechism-oriented hierarchy. Most of us who know church institutions, from denominations to seminaries, know this is true, and we know that part of the enemy is the part of us that desperately seeks to keep control over the ways we symbolize and name God. We are often the ones guilty of impeding the outburst of the Spirit.

Liberation theology, as methodology, challenges us to discern this bubbling Spirit in our midst and to clear the way for it to do its work in the world. Liberation theology is essential for urban spirituality as it is an attempt to interpret the Bible and Christianity from the perspective of the poor. It promises to answer the question of where and when God prepares a welcome table in the midst of the struggle.

If we are to heal a broken world and communicate the good news in the midst of the bad, we must find dramatic new ways of practicing faith and spirituality and enable people to practice a spirituality that addresses the tragic places where life is split asunder. This new style of urban spirituality will convince people whose lives are informed, it seems, only by hopelessness to believe that they have the power to transform lives, to energize the exhaustion in their bones, to deal with the feelings of betrayal and abandonment that they so often experience as marginalized people. It is a spirituality that embodies political and psychic struggle. It is a spirituality that embraces the urban poor and those of us who would be seen in solidarity rather than as voyeurs of those in economic and social distress.

Valerie E. Russell has taught urban ministry at Harvard Divinity School, Yale Divinity School, and New York Theological Seminary. She is a nationally known lay leader in the United Church of Christ. Currently she is president of the City Mission Society of Boston.

Notes

1. Economic Justice and the Christian Conscience, "How Poverty Mars U.S. Society," *The Witness* 71, no. 6 (June 1988): 8.

2. Ibid.

3. My favorite example of the use of humor to fight despair is the story of the great comedian Dick Gregory, who at the height of the civil rights struggle wrote his first book, which he titled *Nigger.* In the introduction, he dedicated it to his mother so that if she ever heard that word again she could "rest easy," knowing that the speaker is just talking about his book!

And another: In Williamston, North Carolina, at the height of the first freedom marches, a crowd sat inside an African American church praying and singing to prepare their hearts for marching. Circling outside was a vocal, abusive truckload of armed members of the Ku Klux Klan with a bullhorn, threatening all forms of violence the minute one marcher set foot on the pavement outside the church. When it came time to move out, the tension was palpable. All of a sudden, from out of the congregation, which sat stark still listening to the threats from outside, one of the congregants muttered just loud enough to be discernible, "Well, Lord, here I am . . . but please send him"—pointing to his neighbor. The silence was broken with a thankful laughter that someone had given voice to his inner feelings, and the crowd gathered with a sense of determined willingness and went forth with power.

4. Nelle Morton, *The Journey is Home* (Boston: Beacon Press, 1985), pp. 127–128.

5. This quotation is used frequently by William Sloane Coffin, senior minister of the Riverside Church in New York City from 1979 to 1989.

6. Audre Lorde, *Sister Outsider: Essays and Speeches* (Trumansburg, N.Y.: Crossing Press, 1984), p. 175.

7. Michael Walzer, *Exodus and Revolution* (New York: Basic Books, 1985), pp. 148–149.

8. Ibid.

9. Harvey Cox, *The Silencing of Leonardo Boff: The Vatican and the Future of World Christianity* (Yorktown Heights, N.Y.: Meyer Stone Books, 1988), p. 288.

10. Ibid.

ETHICAL FOUNDATIONS
FOR URBAN MINISTRY STRATEGIES

• 16 •

A Health Crisis
and a Healing Ministry

Kent C. Miller and Janice L. Burggrabe

A cartoon shows a patient lying on a gurney being pushed down the hallway by a nurse. Worried astonishment appears on his face as the nurse says, "Don't worry, Dr. Smith has had many patients at death's door, and he's brought them right through."

A similar theme popped up unexpectedly when a newspaper article stated, "He collapsed on the sidewalk and died without medical assistance."

The ambiguous meaning of medical care in these images gives rise to a certain morbid humor. But the ambiguity of urban health care in the 1990s is far from humorous.

For every medical benefit available in this technologically advanced society, there is a barrier that denies those options to the poor and disenfranchised. For example:

- We know from research that infant mortality rates are lowered by providing care early in pregnancy. Yet neighborhood clinics and family practice centers are unable to provide malpractice insurance to obstetricians, so prenatal services are discontinued.
- In our cities, public hospitals face growing numbers of individuals with urgent medical needs and lack of medical coverage. Yet shrinking public resources and lack of payment mechanisms for public hospitals today curtail many critical services.
- We in the United States spend more money on medical expenses than any other country in the world. Health ex-

penses average over twenty-five hundred dollars a year for every American.[1] Yet in many cities and neighborhoods people do not have resources for even basic health care needs. Public funds are shrinking, and health facilities are forced to consolidate programs, cut hours, and close sites, leaving the poor even fewer options for medical treatment.

- Millions of employed people enjoy the benefits of medical insurance and the high-tech medical care it can provide. Yet there are growing numbers of working people who are "medically indigent": working part-time, or even full time, but underinsured or without any insurance. Many who do have insurance cannot afford the expenses left unpaid by Medicare or Medicaid.
- We have an elaborate array of medical services and technology with the ability to provide highly specialized treatment, including providing patients with new hearts or otherwise keeping them alive with extraordinary medical procedures. Yet there is no locus of accountability and no set of guidelines for equity in treatment: Who receives these services? How much is to be spent on expensive treatments for a few, and how much is to be spent on basic health care costs for everyone?

In short, the picture of our urban health scene is of a place of burgeoning health-care needs with a diminishing capability to meet them despite awesome medical know-how. America's cities are places of unnecessary health-care injustice.

We live in a situation we never intended but find difficult to change. In the early 1990s, the health industry is a *$600 billion* mountain of resistance to change. At current rates of health expenditures, it is estimated that by the year 2000, the health costs in this nation will rise to $1.5 trillion, or $5,551 for every person in the United States, for a system of health care plagued by unintended consequences.[2]

The medical industry has become a multi-tiered health care process offering highly advanced medical care to those who can pay the price and no care at all to indigent people who cannot pay. It is inefficient, because no orderly rules or processes exist to connect the parts. High-tech treatment available only to those with resources is emphasized instead of the promotion of health for all. As a nation, we are still uncertain as to whether health care is a right or a privilege.

The many forces that plague our health-care industry are made worse in urban areas through other conditions: poverty, high-density population, violence, widespread substance abuse, deteriorating housing, minimal education, unemployment, wide variations in ethnic traditions and language. As an example of the impact on health care of these related factors, surveys of thirteen hospitals in eight cities by the inspector general of the Department of Health and Human Services found that in 1989, 8,794 newborns exposed to crack cocaine before birth were treated at a cost of $300 million more than the cost of normal deliveries. Nationally, this translates into more than $3 billion in medical care for the hundred thousand crack babies born in 1990. By the year 2000, this figure could increase tenfold, with between one million and four million children born to mothers abusing drugs.[3] And drugs are only one problem in the urban medical crisis. Each of the other conditions listed above has a major impact on medical care and its delivery in the urban setting.

Many in the United States agreed with Walter Cronkite when he said that our health care system is not very healthy, it is not caring, and it is certainly not a system.[4]

Looking for a Diagnosis

The scriptures and traditions that define the Christian church provide many resources and compelling reasons for the church to become a place of healing in the midst of the health crisis in the urban United States. Whether one starts with the ancient practice of offering hospitality to the stranger or the injunction to do justice, to love kindness, and walk humbly with God, or seeks to live out the meaning of shalom as peace and wholeness, one is confronted with the truth that all are central to our identity as a church called to be healers.

The good news of the gospel writers leaves no ambiguity about God's healing presence and the church as a place where healing can be found. Each story that tells of Jesus' healing is made even more meaningful by the use of a form of the Greek verb *sodzo*, meaning "being made whole," "being healed," "being saved." God offers wholeness, healing, salvation. And today during the Eucharist, upon receiving the elements, members of some traditions respond by saying, "But say the word and I shall be healed."

With such richness to draw upon, how does the urban church begin to understand the urban health crisis and position itself to offer healing to the people of the city, to become a source of wholeness where there is so much brokenness?

The church can begin to foster wholeness by untangling the urban health crisis in an orderly way. With well-defined criteria, we may be able to see more clearly what problems exist and what particular actions the church might take.

Five words—which we call the "five A's"—offer a set of criteria for beginning to understand the current urban health crisis. A set of questions flows from each word's meaning. There is, of course, spillover from one category to the other, but the scheme is simple, and we offer it as a tool for ministry development. With these criteria in mind, local congregations and groups of churches can meaningfully address the need for health and wholeness in their respective settings.

Availability

The services necessary for basic medical care should be available to all. Are there such services in the community? Which are missing? What happens when medical services are not available to all people? The infant mortality rate, a common measure of health status, is illustrative for urban areas. Nationally, the mortality rate for infants is ten deaths for a thousand live births. Yet in cities with 100,000 to 250,000 people, thirteen babies in every thousand live births died within a year, with the ten "worst" cities having mortality rates of seventeen to twenty for every thousand.[5] Low birth weight is a major contributor to infant death and disability. Infants born at low birth weight are forty times more likely to die during their first month of life and two to three times more likely to suffer from chronic handicapping conditions such as blindness, deafness, and mental retardation.[6]

If prenatal care were available to all, many of these deaths could be avoided. The people in urban settings least likely to have access to prenatal care are minority teenagers with low income and little education. You can look at the statistics or simply walk through the neonatal intensive care unit of any inner-city hospital. Enormously expensive technical wizardry is required to rescue tiny, fragile infants from a crisis that should be preventable.

After years of successfully reducing the occurrence of measles, the United States now faces new outbreaks of that disease as well as of whooping cough and rubella. There were 26,520 cases of measles in 1990, eighteen times more than in 1983. The immunization budget grew each year from 1981 to 1991, but it could not keep pace with the cost of the vaccines needed to immunize a child in a public clinic, which grew from $6.69 to $91.20 during that time period, a thirteenfold increase. Nationally, about 70 percent of two-year-olds are immunized, but only about half of two-year-olds in U.S. inner cities are immunized. This rate is lower than that for *one*-year-olds in twenty-eight out of thirty-eight countries in Latin America![7]

How can a church check its community for the availability of necessary medical care, not only for children but for people of all ages? It can begin by listing the known services and asking questions such as these:

- Do public or private providers, or both, offer prenatal care? immunizations for communicable diseases? primary care for routine health problems? treatment for diseases such as AIDS, Alzheimer's disease, mental illness, drug and alcohol addiction?
- Are both inpatient (hospital) and outpatient (office or clinic) services offered in our area?
- Are prescription and over-the-counter medicines affordable and available to low-income patients?
- What emergency services exist?

Other questions about the availability of needed services must be added as is appropriate for the community. For each "no" or "not available" answer, the follow-up question, "why," must be asked, with both the providers' perspective and the potential consumers' perspective sought in the answer.

Adequacy

While some or most services may be *available*, they should also be *adequate* to serve the basic health and medical needs of the population. Adequacy indicates the ability to deliver up-to-date medical services and the capacity of services to meet the needs of the population, whatever its size.

In many cities, homeless ill people and other victims of violence and accidents, drug-induced crises, and AIDS crowd available emergency centers and public hospital beds in spiraling numbers. Personnel and financial resources are stretched, and aging facilities and equipment remain in use. A recent story in a Dallas newspaper illustrates this reality.[8] A 30 percent rise in the number of patients seeking help in recent years, with almost half having serious injuries, threatens Dallas's system of emergency care with collapse. The article points out that the situation is even worse in Houston and is critical for every urban area in the country.

In many urban emergency rooms, these scenes are common: a person with "moderate bleeding" waits several hours while the doctor treats accident victims in critical condition; a patient with drug-induced psychosis becomes violent, injuring the attending nurse; a teenager who has attempted suicide repeatedly loses consciousness; a pregnant woman with delivery imminent has no insurance and no obstetrician.

In many hospitals, the costly services of intensive care units are tied up with long-term care of older persons who may not recover but for whom we have no other long-term care options. The hospital system has care units available, but they are inadequate to meet the increasing need.

How can a church check its community for adequacy of medical and health care services? It can begin by asking questions:

- Is immunization available for all children? Can sick people see a physician promptly? Can crisis care be obtained twenty-four hours a day?

- Are there enough staff persons to deliver the services offered? Are the facilities large enough for the population?
- Are the necessary equipment and supplies on hand?

For each negative answer to questions such as these, the church must ask why. Answers must be viewed critically from both the providers' and the users' perspectives, since all too often providers would preserve the status quo whereas users would work for change, particularly in the area of priorities for limited health-dollar investments.

Accessibility

The basic health and medical services must be accessible to all members of the population. A system is accessible if the people have the means to reach the service, to be introduced into the service delivery system, and to receive the services in a timely way.

In many urban areas, private and public health care services are arranged more for the needs and priorities of the providers than of the users. In recent years, for instance, medical centers have been placed on the periphery of the city to lower costs and to facilitate access by doctors and providers. Services are easiest to access and most convenient for use by those who have insurance or some ability to pay, know their way into and around the system, and can negotiate the hurdles they encounter. Access is also easier if the patient understands medical terms, is of a socioeconomic and/or ethnic group similar to that of the provider, and fits into the "boxes" (diagnostic categories and payment channels) that determine how medical care is dispensed.

Economic factors (lack of insurance, unemployment, poverty) are the most common barriers to access to medical services; however, age, marital status, and minority status are also important. For example, elderly people are typically "screened out" of treatment through stereotypical diagnosis (physicians expect certain illnesses in elderly people while ignoring treatable conditions such as malnutrition.[9] Children living with uninsured parents (especially unemployed single mothers) or with grandparents (Medicare will not cover grandchildren) are at particular risk. Fully 90 percent of all Hispanics live in urban areas, and one study shows that two-thirds of poor Hispanics are not covered by private or public health insurance.[10] Many earn too much to qualify for welfare (and Medicaid) yet not enough to pay for the cost of insurance or the cost of medical treatment.

What are the consequences of these barriers to access? Lacking a car, families face long bus rides or walks to the city outskirts to get medical care. People forgo early care for health problems, which leads to emergency-room visits when the condition worsens. Parents must decide whether food or medicine is the highest spending priority for available cash. Children lack immunizations because preventive care isn't covered and seems less urgent than care during illness.

When churches consider the issues of access to care, they need to ask questions about barriers:

• What distances must people travel from home or work?
• Can physically limited people enter and move through buildings easily?
• Do minority groups encounter language and cultural barriers in communicating with care-givers? Have the providers hired persons of linguistic and ethnic background similar to the users of the service? Do health and medical training programs recruit such minority persons?
• Are services offered during days and hours when most people can avail themselves of services needed?
• What are the perceptual barriers experienced by potential users of the services? For example, do medical personnel talk down to clients? Does the clinic use rigid rules of punctuality to exclude clients?
• Are there barriers of eligibility (such as residency or income)?

For each negative answer to such questions, the church must ask why and view the responses from the point of view of the users of services. Accessibility to users should be a higher priority than convenience or routines of the providers.

Affordability

Basic health and medical services must be affordable to all members of the population. Mechanisms of coverage, fee setting, or funding methods must exist that include everyone so that all are able to obtain basic medical care and health service.

Affordability plays a significant role in access to services, often determining limits to the type and level of care obtained. Many services are offered only when it is clear that the providers will be reimbursed by government programs or major insurers.

Medical costs—and therefore affordability—are influenced by several system-wide factors such as advances in technology for diagnostic purposes, increased use of services, more sophisticated treatment techniques, and rising administrative costs. Administrative costs alone, if the present growth rate persists, will consume one-third of all health-care spending by 2003. Strategies to contain these expenses are beginning to be put into operation. But for the present, the inescapable fact is that a continually growing gap exists between charges and available funds: Fewer and fewer people can afford to be sick.

Medical insurance is the avenue to medical care, and today a large percent of the U.S. population has no insurance, a fact that affects medical service delivery for 37 million people. A study of 592,598 patients hospitalized in some of the nation's hospitals in 1987 found that uninsured patients received significantly less care than insured individuals. Death rates were found to be significantly higher among uninsured patients in most groups.[11]

A recent article describes how the inability to afford mammograms, routine examinations, and early treatment dramatically lowers the survival rates of the poor, whatever the illness. Poor women in urban centers fare particularly badly. In a study at a hospital in Harlem, only 25 percent of women afflicted with breast cancer were alive five years after diagnosis; nationally, the expected survival rate is greater than 60 percent. Also profiled in the article was a seriously ill fifty-eight-year-old woman who was turned away by two private Miami hospitals because she had no insurance or money and her situation was not deemed an emergency. Publicity finally opened doors to care, but treatment came too late and the delays proved fatal. While other factors caused delay as well, money was the major problem.[12] Such stories are commonplace in cities all over the United States.

The major public hospitals in our cities are caught in the middle of spiraling costs. Hospital administrators and boards often fail to control costs internally; however, hospitals today are often victims of rising expenses beyond their control due to the large numbers of uninsured patients. In 1988, more than 30 percent of inpatient and 52 percent of outpatient visits to one hundred metropolitan public hospitals were by uninsured patients.[13] The hospitals report that bad debt and charity work rose from 22 percent of charges in 1982 to 42 percent of charges in 1988. Most of these hospitals were operating at a deficit.

The church must ask these questions about affordability:

- Are the charges for service within the reach of most of the residents who would use the services? Consider those with private insurance or Medicare/Medicaid and those who need subsidized or public services. Which services are too costly for many of the residents?
- Who is left out of the service?
- Who cannot afford to pay for the charges not covered by insurance?
- Are people being billed accurately for services offered?
- Are questions and problems with bills handled promptly? fairly?
- Are patients being asked to pay for expenses that should be billed directly to Medicare—to "float" the cost (for three to six months) until they are reimbursed?

For each answer, the church can ask why this is so and seek to discover the source of the problem that places services beyond the reach of certain segments of the population. We must seek health-care fee arrangements that ensure that care will not be denied or postponed.

Accountability

Basic medical services must be offered equitably and fairly to all members of the community. Providers must exercise responsibility for quality and cost of care. Means should exist for resolving problems regarding services. Is there accountability in the provision of health and medical services?

This may be the most important "A" for churches, because it raises fundamental questions of ethics and justice as well as concern about the "response-ability" of providers of medical services. It is a basic fact that our nation's technical medical capability far outstrips our ability or willingness to provide even minimal care to many people.

In a recent newspaper column, William Buckley raises the important ethical issues of accountability in the delivery of medical care in the United States.[14] The issues include the millions of dollars spent each year to maintain the marginal lives of unresponsive, terminally ill people; the prevalence of "defensive medicine" (the practice of providing costly but unnecessary and unhelpful treatment to guard against malpractice charges); and the unrealistically high payment levels for high-tech medical services. Meanwhile, churches, schools, and community groups hold bake sales and car washes to help desperate parents obtain lifesaving surgery for their children; ghetto residents sit on hard chairs in crowded storefront clinics for a half day or more, waiting to see a doctor; neighborhood delegations petition city officials to restore services cut from the public hospital budget; pregnant women make dozens of calls before locating a doctor who will accept Medicaid payments.

There is no locus of accountability, no place where ethical issues are scrutinized within the medical delivery process. When issues are forced into the courts it is often of significant ethical importance, but even more important, the process becomes a symbol of the lack of accountability in addressing these issues within the medical industry itself. Amid this scrambled, chaotic scene, the church can focus upon accountability of medical services by asking questions such as the following:

- Are services provided fairly and equally to all?
- How do providers show responsibility for the quality and cost of the care they offer?
- What standards are used by which to assess the quality of the services delivered?
- What options are available for resolving problems or dissatisfaction about a service?
- Is the quality of care at public or charitable settings the same as in private, fee-for-service facilities? Does it differ significantly? In what way or ways?
- Who sets the priorities that determine quality of service in the medical facility? What impact do patient or user needs have on these priorities?
- Do publicly funded facilities have mechanisms of accountability to local residents and potential users for the quality and type of services?

In each case, the follow-up questions should be, Why? and Who is (or should be) accountable? Those with vested interest in specific health-care services within a community will not usually be the voices of conscience. The church may be the only credible organization willing and able to raise these questions.

The Church as Advocate, Healing Agent, and Health Provider

Even though the North American church has largely given away its traditional role in offering health and wholeness, now may be the time to reclaim it. We easily transferred the responsibility for our individual health and for the use of the healing arts to the medical community. We trusted hospitals to be places of care and healing for the sick—rich or poor. (Hospitals had their beginnings as places of hospitality for poor, sick people who had no one else to care for them.) And we trusted health professionals to keep us healthy and cure us when we became ill.

Now may be the time for the church to reaffirm its belief in the wholeness of the person and to seek to heal the unnatural split between body and soul—a split that led us to assign the task of curing the body to medical institutions and curing the soul to the church. Once we affirm our wholeness and address each person holistically (physically, spiritually, mentally, socially, and emotionally) we can reaffirm our place in a ministry of health and wholeness.

The church can fill three roles as it develops a response to its diagnosis of the urban health crisis: that of advocate, of healing agent, and of health provider.

The church should need no instruction about its role as advocate—it need only study the health issues for which it should become an advocate. Standing on the side of the poor, the disenfranchised, the marginal is our ancient tradition. After careful analysis of the health-care situation, a group of advocacy targets should emerge, ranging from individual providers and local clinics to regional boards and state or federal agencies and legislatures.

The church must talk with its urban residents who are not well served and work with them to raise questions for medical service providers. The church might inaugurate its role of advocate by keeping a clinic open in the evening or by arranging commitments to fund immunizations or more responsive emergency services. It may offer its "neutral office" as a place of negotiation with providers. Members may need to develop certain skills required to bargain with board and councils.

In addition, churches should be part of the national church advocacy effort working toward universal access to health care, toward the development of a national health-care plan that would leave no one out. Religious groups across the spectrum have joined in the effort to promote, even demand, of Congress an equitable national health-care plan.

The church can also become a healing agent, a role at the very heart of the church's identity. All worship should be healing. It should learn to ask, "Do people leave our worship more whole than before? Do they experience healing from the brokenness in their lives?" This may require some substantial rethinking of worship. It may be time to incorporate liturgies of healing (laying on of hands, anointing with oil, prayers for healing) in each service. The language of brokenness and wholeness may need to replace traditional language of sin and salvation. Infant baptism may be an occasion to enroll the child in a process for regular "well-baby checks" at a local clinic as part of the church's baptismal pledge to nurture the child.

The program of mission and outreach to the residents of the community may need to become more holistic. Support groups for a wide range of problems can begin as part of the ministry—not merely providing space for twelve-step groups, but incorporating these and other support groups into the life and ministry of the church. Those who take the Eucharist to homebound persons can be trained to be more perceptive and active in ministry to all the needs of those visited.

Church school classes and evening programs can teach about health and healing and can present our faith in ways that restore to it the meaning of wholeness. This can be as general as Bible study or study of issues or as particular as offering classes to help people quit smoking, lose weight, or cope with stress.

Another natural role for the church is as provider of health care. Churches of various traditions are adding parish nurses to the staff to offer health education, support groups, health screening, health counseling, and referral. This can be an especially important way to help people gain access to medical services.

Churches often have space that can be used as a setting for such services as a dental or medical clinic. This could be staffed with volunteers or serve as an extension of other medical facilities. Such clinics could be funded from public or foundation sources. They can also be aimed at certain groups, such as well babies or the elderly.

Today, especially, our urban churches are plagued with the untenable reality that in a land of medical plenty, the disenfranchised in their neighborhoods starve. The discovery of the gap between the promise and the reality of our health care can be the occasion for transforming and healing grace. The church understands what it means to live between the reality of what is and the promise of what is yet to be. It is imperative that we respond with a ministry of healing to the brokenness we find in our cities.

Kent C. Miller, an ordained Presbyterian minister, has worked in health-related ministry programs in Texas for the past two decades, including eleven years in San Antonio as an urban minister. He has edited and written a series of manuals, A Healing Presence: The Congregation's Ministry in Health and Wholeness *(San Antonio: Benedictine Resource Center, 1991).*

Janice L. Burggrabe, a Presbyterian elder from St. Louis, Missouri, is a nurse and health educator. She has taught in several colleges in St. Louis, been a consultant for area businesses, and written on health management.

Notes

1. "Health and Medical Services," *U.S. Industrial Outlook*, U.S. Department of Commerce, International Trade Administration, January 1991, pp. 44–51.

2. Document #S/N003-009-586-8, Health Care Financing Administration, U.S. Department of Commerce. Documents are available from Superintendent of Documents, Government Printing Office, Washington, D.C. 20402-9325.

3. Merit C. Kimball, "Crack Babies Exacting Heavy Toll on U.S. Hospitals," *Health Week*, 26 March 1990.

4. Walter Cronkite's statement was made in "Borderline Medicine," produced by Public Policy Production, Inc. (New York: WNET, 17 December 1990).

5. National Center for Health Statistics data as reported by Children's Defense Fund, 122 C Street NW, Washington, D.C. 20001, February 1991. See also *The Washington Post*, 21 March 1991, metro edition.

6. *Troubling Trends: The Health of America's Next Generation*, National Commission to Prevent Infant Mortality, Room 2006, 330 C Street SW, Washington, D.C., 1990.

7. Susan Oakie, "Vaccination Record in U.S. Falls Sharply," *The Washington Post*, 24 March 1991, metro edition.

8. Terry Box, "Hospital's Caseload Reaches Critical Mass," *Dallas Morning News*, 15 June 1991, metro edition.

9. Theresa Tighe, "Ignored Elderly: Doctors Accused of Poor Diagnosis," *St. Louis Post Dispatch*, 15 July 1990, metro edition.

10. Sarah Henry, "Barriers to Access," *Modern Maturity* 33, no. 5 (October–November 1990): 33.

11. Jack Hadley et al., "Comparison of Uninsured and Privately Insured Hospital Patients," *Journal of the American Medical Association* 265 (16 January 1991): 374.

12. Dorothy J. Gaiter, "Although Cures Exist, Poverty Fells Many Afflicted with Cancer," *Wall Street Journal*, 1 May 1991, Midwest edition.

13. National Association of Public Hospitals, "America's Safety Net Hospitals," January 1991. Reviewed in *Medical Benefits*, 15 March 1991.

14. William Buckley, "In Search of a Cure for Medical Woes," *St. Louis Post Dispatch*, 10 June 1991.

• 17 •

THE FEMINIZATION OF POVERTY: CHALLENGE FOR THE CHURCH

Dennis Hollinger and Joseph Modica

Hunger and poverty in the Third World have captured the attention of Americans in recent years. Through the news media and appeals of relief organizations, millions of dollars have been raised for famine relief and economic development.

While global hunger and human need have been raised to our consciousness, there is another poverty that remains subliminal to most Americans: the growing poverty of women and their children. The "feminization of poverty," as many sociologists now label it, is a growing phenomenon that has not enlisted the compassion and response of many who have sent their twenty-five-dollar checks for world relief.

Americans' ignorance of the situation is no doubt to blame for part of the failure to respond, but one cannot overlook the heartless apathy that arises from a mixture of economic satisfaction and rationalization in U.S. culture. As economist John Kenneth Galbraith puts it:

[They] . . . find a reason for separating themselves and their consciences from the . . . poverty of the . . . poor. The capacity for rationalization that has, in the past, so well served indifference, noninvolvement or other forms of denial of poverty, remains fully available.[1]

Profile of Feminization of Poverty

The term "feminization of poverty" was coined by sociologist Diana Pearse in 1978. From a demographic study in the

221

late 1970s, she concluded that an increasing number of poor in the United States are single women and their children. Recent statistics of this phenomenon are revealing:

- Two out of three poor adults are women, and almost four-fifths of the poor are women and children.
- Women head half of all poor families.
- The poverty rate for female-headed households is nearly three times that of male-headed households.
- More than half the children in female-headed households are poor (50 percent of white children, 68 percent of African American and Latino children).
- A woman over sixty years of age is almost twice as likely as her male counterpart to be impoverished.
- One-fifth of all elderly women are poor (among elderly African American women, 43.5 percent; among elderly Latinas, 27.4 percent).[2]

While the percentage of poor families headed by women has remained fairly constant throughout the late 1980s and early 1990s, the situation continues to create major problems for these women and their children. An overview of data from previous decades gives us a helpful perspective on the intensity of the problem.

In 1960, 61 percent of poor families were headed by a man, and 27 percent were headed by a woman.[3] However, in the span of two decades (ending in 1980), the percentage of poor families headed by a male had dropped to 29 percent while the number that were female-headed increased to 50 percent.[4] (Ironically, this occurred during the years after the declaration of the War on Poverty.) The trend has been particularly acute in the African American community, for during the 1970s "the number of black families in poverty who were maintained by men declined by 35%, while the number maintained by women increased by 62%. In the course of one decade, black female-headed families increased from one-half to three-fourths of all poor black families."[5] Michael Harrington notes that in 1981, of the 859,000 people on welfare in New York City, 519,000 were children—498,000 of whom lived in female-headed families.[6] The evidence is clear that poverty in the United States is becoming increasingly lodged among single-parent women and their children.

The Causes of Feminization of Poverty

What factors have given rise to this phenomenon? The answers are complex and intricate, but we must examine historical processes and social, economic, and political factors.

Historical Overview

The genesis of this problem can be traced to the period following World War II (late 1940s to early 1950s). Two significant patterns emerged: internal migration of African Americans and an increase in the number of women in the work force. Among African Americans, there was a momentous shift from southern to northern cities, which were perceived as the "promised land" for natives of the agricultural South. As Claude Brown so aptly described it in his foreword to *Manchild in the Promised Land*:

Going to New York was good-bye to the cotton field, good-bye to 'Massa Charlie,' good-bye to the chain gang, and most of all, good-bye to those sunup to sundown working hours. One no longer had to wait to get to heaven to lay his burden down: burdens could be laid down in New York.[7]

But the "promised land" turned out to be a ghetto of despair. Declining job opportunities (too many workers and not enough jobs) coupled with an abundance of children (a pattern inherited from the past) placed immense pressures on these migrants searching for an economic exodus.

The second pattern noted above may seem contradictory to the rise of female poverty: How could an increase in the female work force accompany an increase in female poverty? The vast increase in the percentage of working women took place during World War II, when businesses recruited females to replace drafted males in the war industries. After World War

II, many women remained in the work force but had available to them typically "female" jobs: as typists, clerks, and workers in the service sector.[8] These service occupations were among the lowest-paying jobs. Women were almost always paid less than male counterparts, even when their qualifications were the same. Harrington notes that even when women entered the professional sector, they tended to be segregated within the professions themselves. Those who got M.D.s were pediatricians, gynecologists, and psychotherapists, not surgeons. These specialties, it will be noted, are appropriately "feminine," involving taking care of children, women, and emotional problems, as opposed to the "masculine" functions of repairing broken bodies or performing miraculous transplants.[9] Women, who held positions in the work force within an already disadvantaged occupational structure, were at the same time increasingly becoming single heads of household. The percent of the overall population living in women-headed families therefore increased within the poverty population. Hence, the seeds of female poverty were planted.

The 1960s began with an intense focus on the "War on Poverty," as echoed in President Lyndon B. Johnson's message to Congress:

But we have never lost sight of our goal: an America in which every citizen shares all the opportunities of his society, in which every man has a chance to advance his welfare to the limit of his capacities. . . . To finish that work I have called for a national war on poverty. Our objective: total victory.[10]

However, an external war distracted the fight against this internal struggle. The Vietnam War, with its accompanying internal dissension, quickly overshadowed the War on Poverty. Poor people on the television screen were replaced by images of the bombing of Hanoi, and thus the War on Poverty was short-lived. It is true that assistance programs were developed and some poor people were served. However, the U.S. government tended to adhere to a crisis mentality that addressed emergencies but never got to the root causes and long-range measures that might prevent poverty.

Social Factors

The social dimension of female poverty is related to the dissolution of the nuclear family. The number of divorces tripled between 1962 and 1985,[11] and for many women, poverty may be only a divorce away. Moreover, between 1950 and 1979, the number of children born out of wedlock in the United States quadrupled for both African Americans and whites. In 1979, more than half of African American births in the United States were out of wedlock (the figure for whites was 17 percent). Among African American women, teenagers accounted for 45 percent of those pregnancies out of wedlock.[12] What is the plight of the teenage parent?

Michael Harrington suggests that

these young women will, in almost every case, become single parents and will receive little or nothing from the fathers of their children. That happens to them before they are even out of high school, and they therefore come into the already disadvantaged women's labor market with much less training than anyone else. Some of them will despair of ever finding a job—not an irrational response—and will simply drop out altogether, becoming welfare cases. The "lucky" ones will find a menial, poorly paid job somewhere.[13]

Thus the increasing rates of divorce and teenage pregnancy produce an increasing number of single women, many with children, trying to establish themselves in society. Large numbers of them will experience intense poverty, as evidenced by the fact that between 1960 and 1982, the average income for families headed by females fell from 77 percent to 62 percent of the average income of white husband-and-wife families.[14]

The breakdown of the family social structure and the increasing levels of poverty experienced by women are not merely about divorce rates or having children outside of wedlock—as they are so often portrayed. The real story is particularly evident with regard to the African American family. Until World War II, the two-parent nuclear family was the dominant pattern for such families, but drastic changes have occurred since 1960. The incidence of female-headed African American households increased from 22 percent in 1960 to 42 percent in 1983.[15] This is closely related to the number of teens having children outside of marriage. Noted author Marian Edelman states that "the crux of the problem facing the black family today is that young black women who become pregnant do not marry nearly as often as they used to."[16] When marriage rates of African Americans and whites are compared, the problem becomes striking: While 27 percent of white males aged twenty to twenty-four have married, only 12 percent of African American males in the same age group have done so; among males aged twenty-five to twenty-nine, 65 percent of whites have married, but only 44 percent of African Americans.[17]

Why are these men not marrying? Various analysts have concluded that the problem of male joblessness is the single most important factor underlying the rise in the number of unwed mothers.[18] The proportion of African American males in a position to support a family has declined significantly—and thus the rise in female-headed households, many of which are poor. The African American child in a female-headed household has a two in three chance of being poor, and if the family is headed by a mother under twenty-five years of age, the child has a four in five chance of being poor.[19]

The significant factor in both the beginning and ending of poverty is change in household earnings. However, a predominant factor accounting for the development as well as the maintenance of poverty among women and their dependent children is "the difference in household structure between a married household and an unmarried household."[20]

Economic Factors

In the economic sector, women are at a disadvantage regarding job opportunities, salaries, pension plans, and Social Security benefits. Sociologist David Claerbaut has suggested that poverty is not a lack of material possessions but rather a lack of options.[21] The reasons for this include the facts that 1) women often begin work at younger ages than men—thus the lack of proper educational and employment prerequisites; 2) women usually interrupt their work for raising children, which diminishes the qualifying time for employee benefits such as pension and Social Security; and 3) women usually receive lower-paying jobs that lack child-care and health benefits.

In addition to these factors are clear acts of discrimination. A 1977 governmental study discovered that if working women were paid what similarly qualified men earn, the number of poor families would decrease by half.[22] Despite the fact that women's participation in the labor force has increased significantly in the past several decades, a full-time, year-round female worker earns only 62 percent of the salary of her male counterpart.[23] Anthony Downs writes: "The most obvious cause of poverty in these households is the need of mothers to stay home and care for their children, which prevents them from working full-time, or at all. Furthermore, for those who are able to work, available jobs are mostly at the lower end of the pay scale."[24] One way to remedy women's increasing rate of poverty is to provide equal pay for work of comparable value.

While equal pay is an important dimension, we should recognize that it is only one aspect of the solution. Offering equal pay does not guarantee correction of institutional ills that sustain the cycle of female poverty. For example, necessary governmental services need to be offered to encourage family cohesion. Yet many need-based services are being discontinued in today's economic structuring: "A compensatory-education grant program for the schools that disadvantaged students attend has lost seventeen percent of its funds, [and] a child-nutrition program which subsidizes meals at schools and day-care centers has lost twenty-eight percent."[25] Offering a single mother a salary comparable to a man's, while at the same time withdrawing or reducing needed support services, places that woman in a catch-22 situation. Equal pay will not produce equal options if necessary medical, child-care, and other services enabling her to work are not in place.

Political Factors

The feminization of poverty is based in part on political factors in the form of ineffective or absent public policies. One of the problem areas is the low priority given to poverty issues in terms of the national budget and federal efforts to address the problem. Numerous social analysts have contended that efforts at alleviating poverty are limited by defense interests and expenditures. Nancy Amidei, writing in the mid-1980s, noted, "A few years ago two-thirds of general federal tax revenues were spent on two items: military spending and interest on the debt. Today, that applies to nearly three-fourths of all federal spending."[26] Today, the cuts made in poverty programs during the 1980s have still not been redressed. Moreover, "in no state in the United States does any family on AFDC [Aid to Families with Dependent Children] receive a cash grant or non-income transfers sufficient to bring its total income up to the poverty level."[27]

There are also specific political regulations that combat family provisions (termed "anti-family provisions"). In twenty-nine states, two-parent families, no matter how poor, cannot receive welfare payments or Medicaid. Thus, specific public policies force family dissolution.[28] Such policies also engender illegal activities such as prostitution, dope peddling, bootlegging, and gambling, since income earned in this way is not reported to public assistance authorities.[29] Therefore, the growing population of poverty-stricken females is trapped in a no-win situation: The political system penalizes families for going to work or observing the rules. Harrington offers an insightful statement regarding the cause-and-effect relationship of public polices to the poor: "The psychological agony of the poor is not simply a characteristic of the interior life, but, in part at least, a public product that could be changed by different policies."[30] The above observation can be extended by stating that female poverty is not a simple product but the interweaving of historical, sociological, economic, and political factors. These interwoven contexts have contributed immensely to the feminization of poverty.

Responses to the Feminization of Poverty

On a corporate level, two institutions have demonstrated lethargy concerning female poverty: the government and the church. Since World War II, the government has tended to give military and defense concerns priority in both attention and spending. The assumption has been that high levels of military spending will not only maintain peace within the world but will provide jobs and hence alleviate poverty. But as Marjorie Tuite has noted:

Contrary to widespread belief, military spending is not good for the economy. It does not increase employment; it generates unemployment and the unemployment generated falls heavily upon women. . . . [I]n 1980 . . . every time $1 billion was given to the military rather than spent in domestic programs, 9,500 jobs for women disappeared or failed to be created.[31]

Poor females and their children are increasingly aware of the government's failure to address their fundamental plight and have been further alienated from the mainstream of American society as they have advocated for their rights. Attention to their needs calls for much more than monetary transfers; it calls for creative analysis of the situation and new ways to name and respond to the issues that lie behind their problems.

The church has also been negligent in addressing this issue. Many Christians interpret empathy for the poor with placing a few extra dollars in the Sunday offering. There are certainly those who do identify with the poor by use of their time, talents, commitment, and money. However, public complacency is a significant factor in the spiraling effect of female poverty. Jim Wallis, editor of *Sojourners* magazine, interprets the acceptance of the status quo as complacency:

There is a biblical mandate to support the cause of the poor against the abuses of wealth and power. In America, to accept the *status quo* means to support the rich against the poor. We pursue our material comfort at the cost of impoverishing others. In fact, our life styles and our consumption directly support the suppression of the poor, at home and around the world.[32]

The church needs a radical reversal regarding the blind acceptance of the status quo and material lifestyles. A revitalized sensitivity must emerge for the poor through a change of attitude, awareness, and action.

Attitudinal Changes

First, we must dispose of the stereotype that welfare mothers are promiscuous and immoral women who have large families in order to obtain more money from welfare. Such attitudes conveniently blame the victim for her predicament. Similarly, we must combat the false conclusion that "if only the poor would work hard, they wouldn't be poor anymore." Robert Bell cites the results of a Gallup poll, which inquired:

In your opinion which is more often to blame if a person is poor— lack of effort on his own part, or circumstances beyond his control?
Thirty-three percent answered, 'lack of effort'; twenty-nine percent 'circumstances'; thirty-two percent 'equal'; and six percent had 'no opinion.'[33]

Generally, society blames the poor for being poor, but such blame focuses on the effects, not the causes. Poverty is a lack of options, complicated by the depletion of indispensable goods and services. The church must stop blaming the poor and begin assuming concern for their circumstances and the causes of poverty. This will be difficult as long as we in the church hold a "we-they" attitude and do not welcome those who are poor into our worship and communities.

On issues such as the feminization of poverty, the church needs to assume a prophetic role, much like the Old Testament prophets who were representatives of God in addressing societal problems. Too often the church has focused primarily on its priestly role. As such it is primarily a place of nurturance, not responsibility; a place of passive acceptance rather than active questioning of social injustices. The priestly functions of the church are essential in reminding people of God's presence and power for all of life. But only when the church also assumes a prophetic stance will attitudes and structures begin to change.

Awareness

Second, our awareness concerning female poverty must be elevated. Awareness of the problem best begins with a biblical understanding that God has a special concern for the poor. This can be accomplished in two ways. First, the church must broaden its conception of mission to include both personal salvation and social justice. Without this holistic view of mission, social issues—such as the feminization of poverty—are easily dismissed as problems that are the responsibility only of government. A gospel message that concentrates solely on "saving souls" is fragmented and incomplete, for even a person's physical and social conditions are a barometer of his or her spiritual receptivity. Spiritual and physical needs cannot be divorced from each other.

Church people must become aware of the issues surrounding female poverty before they can become responsible. Clergy and other church leaders need to provide education about the facts of poverty and its conceivable solutions as well as biblical teachings on the issue. This might be done in several possible forums that could help create an awareness of the needs of the poor and motivate Christians to action: 1) a weekend seminar led by an organization involved in poverty-related issues, such as Bread for the World; 2) a weekly Bible study dealing with social and ethical issues; or 3) an adult Sunday school class focusing on the specific problems of poverty.

Action

Finally, a change of attitudes and the development of awareness will help pave the way to productive action. Amidei offers an insight regarding the role of public action in effecting change:

Our government has never acted on behalf of poor people without pressure, and thus far no sector of society has moved effectively to create the pressure for positive change: not the private charitable groups, not the state or local governments, and not the business community.[34]

The question that remains is: Who, then, will do it? Who will take the necessary action to combat poverty among women and children? Christian responsibility must begin with the church, for governmental programs alone are ineffective. The church is to be light and salt in the world, but it must also become a storehouse of social services and advocacy for local communities. The development of food and clothing pantries can help meet the basic needs of poor families. The development of day-care and after-school programs can render vital services to women with children of school age or younger. The development of parenting and family life skills classes can do much to help young single mothers cope with their situations as well as meet others facing a similar plight. In addition, services such as English-as-a-second-language classes and job training programs can encourage women to search for jobs, which may assist them in breaking out of the vicious cycle of poverty. The church can also address the problem by encouraging business leaders to hire women who are trapped by poverty and have few options. Each of these programs can help the church become a visible presence in the community, and all of these services can easily be integrated with evangelism and proclamation ministries.

One church that has attempted to respond to the problem of poverty in female-headed families is the Shiloh Baptist Church in the inner city of Washington, D.C. The many single mothers and children plagued with poverty, crime, and drugs in the neighborhood became the focus for the mission of the Shiloh Baptist Church and, at the urging of the senior pastor, the church built a $5 million Family Life Center, funded by the members themselves, to address community needs. The center provides scholarships, counseling, tutoring programs, family recreation, day-care services, and other programs. This congregation is truly committed to urban ministry. Although most of its more than six thousand members have chosen to take up residence away from the church's neighborhood, the great majority has elected to retain its membership and to continue work on behalf of those caught in this desperate cycle of poverty. This church has not waited for government to "solve the problem" but has taken action with the conviction that the church can make a difference through its own mission and ministry.

Dennis Hollinger, Ph.D., is associate professor (church and society) at the Associated Mennonite Biblical Seminary in Elkhart, Indiana.

Joseph Modica, a former pastor in New York City, is currently a Ph.D. student at Drew University in Madison, New Jersey.

Notes

1. John Kenneth Galbraith, "The Heartless Society," *New York Times Magazine* (September 1984): 40.

2. Martha S. Hill, "The Changing Nature of Poverty," *The Annals of the American Academy of Political and Social Science* 479 (May 1985): 35; Janice Peterson, "The Feminization of Poverty," *Journal of Economic Issues* 21 (1987): 329-337; Karin Stallard et al., *Poverty in the American Dream: Women and Children First* (Boston: South End Press, 1983).

3. The remaining percentage of poor consists of those not living in family arrangements of two or more people.

4. Hill, "The Changing Nature," p. 36.

5. Peterson, "Feminization," p. 329.

6. Michael Harrington, *The New American Poverty* (New York: Holt, Rinehart & Winston, 1984), p. 35.

7. Claude Brown, *Manchild in the Promised Land* (New York: Signet Books, 1965), p. vii.

8. Harrington, *Poverty*, p. 197.

9. Ibid.

10. Lyndon B. Johnson, "Message to Congress on Poverty," in *Poverty in the Affluent Society*, ed. Hanna H. Meissner (New York: Harper & Row, 1966), p. 202.

11. Vicky Cahan, "The Feminization of Poverty: More Women Are Getting Poorer," *Business Week* 28 (January 1985): 84.

12. Harrington, *Poverty*, p. 193.

13. Ibid., p. 197.

14. Peterson, "Feminization," p. 331.

15. William J. Wilson, *The Truly Disadvantaged: The Inner City, the Underclass, and Public Policy* (Chicago: University of Chicago Press, 1987), p. 66.

16. Marian Edelman, *Families in Peril: An Agenda for Social Change*, (Cambridge, Mass.: Harvard University Press, 1986), p. 6.

17. Ibid.

18. Wilson, *The Truly Disadvantaged*, p. 73; Edelman, *Families in Peril*, pp. 10–13.

19. Edelman, *Families in Peril*, p. 3.

20. Hill, "The Changing Nature," p. 42.

21. David Claerbaut, *Urban Ministry* (Grand Rapids, Mich.: Zondervan, 1983), p. 69.

22. Stallard, *Poverty*, p. 9.

23. Bureau of the Census, "Money Income of Households, Families and Persons in the United States," *Current Population Reports*, Series P 60, no. 51 (Washington, D.C.: U.S. Government Printing Office, 1986), p. 155.

24. Anthony Downs, *Who Are the Urban Poor?* rev. ed. (New York: Committee for Economic Development, 1970), p. 33.

25. Nicholas Lehmann, "The Culture of Poverty," *Atlantic* (29 September 1984): 29.

26. Nancy Amidei, "Poverty, 1965–85," *Commonweal* 21 (June 1985): 365.

27. Peterson, "Feminization," p. 335.

28. Harrington, *Poverty*, p. 198.

29. Downs, *Urban Poor*, p. 35.

30. Harrington, *Poverty*, p. 202.

31. Marjorie Tuite, "Poverty, Thy Name is Woman," *Church & Society* (January–February 1983): 39.

32. Jim Wallis, *Agenda for Biblical People* (New York: Harper & Row, 1976), pp. 86–87.

33. Robert B. Bell, *Contemporary Social Problems* (Homewood, Ill.: The Dorsey Press, 1981), p. 138.

34. Amidei, "Poverty, 1965–85," p. 365.

• 18 •

THE URBAN CONGREGATION
AND PUBLIC POLICY

Katie Day

In the autumn of 1987, the Community Renewal Society in Chicago—a hundred-year-old United Church of Christ city-wide service organization—came under harsh criticism by *The Chicago Tribune* for its support of a congregation-based effort to resist the relocation of a football stadium in a poor African American neighborhood. The organization had provided funding and technical assistance to a Baptist church which was spearheading the effort to "block the Bears" from overwhelming their parish area and setting the stage for gentrification. For this, CRS—which serves as an umbrella coalition to provide structure, empowerment, and advocacy for local congregations—had been lambasted as being "anti-development."

Pastor Art Griffin of the Baptist church had emerged as a leader in the effort, which had brought congregations and community groups together. He declared that their neighborhood was literally under siege, that those in the neighborhood were fighting for their own survival. He described the "on-the-job training" that had occurred formally and informally in their grassroots organization. The resulting strategies for opposing the "principalities and powers" were impressive; their analyses of power-brokering in their city, sophisticated. They had produced their own development plan for the neighborhood, called "A Better Alternative," which had been delivered to the state capital in Springfield by two busloads of concerned neighbors.

There is much that is remarkable about this situation. But

235

underlying the particulars of the approach taken and the strategies used is a stunning reality: *the city was taking the religious community seriously enough that it challenged their position in the public forum*! From the Community Renewal Society to the First Baptist Church in the local ward, the church was considered a credible and formidable player in the shaping of urban policy. In fact, CRS has developed a unique role for itself in Chicago. It has come to be identified as a valuable resource in policy development—providing both tangible research and the more intangible "soul" to the policy questions that engage city hall and neighborhoods alike. Staff people from the central office and members of the congregations with whom CRS is in partnership frequently testify before the city council. Investigative reporting and in-depth research by CRS on issues such as AIDS and homelessness have been utilized in the development of urban policy. CRS had worked closely with the administration of Mayor Harold Washington, and at the time of his death, it was called upon to coordinate his memorial service.

The Community Renewal Society is atypical not only for Chicago but for other urban areas as well. The church has simply not expanded its vision of urban ministry to embrace the area of policy formulation. While focusing its energies on the *impact* of urban policies, the community of faith is rarely represented—through voice or vote—in the boardrooms and washrooms where policies are hammered out that will directly affect the quality of life in our cities. Why?

When urban pastors gather, there is often an enthusiastic swapping of stories and description of programs of which they are justifiably proud. Yet often lurking not far from the surface is a cynicism and depression about the long-term effectiveness of the church in the complex setting of urban America. Poverty, racism, and displacement have been reincarnated in different forms, especially related to the drug culture, and are creating new generations of victims despite our best stabs at urban ministry. Pastors and laypeople feel overwhelmed by the resiliency and enormity of urban problems. Further, the skills and power needed for social change seem beyond the access of the religious community.

For those who daily confront such realities as youth unemployment and high school dropout rates, which hover around 50 percent in African American neighborhoods, a sense of helplessness seems understandable. Ministering in a parish area that has a persistent infant mortality rate comparable to that of a Third World country logically breeds despondency. How can the community of faith seriously speak of transformation in these contexts? One coping mechanism is to narrow the focus of transformation; we can still speak of changing the heart, the congregation, the church building, or even the neighborhood. But addressing the policies that perpetuate economic injustice, for example, seems beyond the boundaries of our hope.

Further, urban congregations have necessarily needed to focus attention on their own survival in the 1970s and '80s. Running a parish consumes most of the energy of struggling congregations. Endeavors not perceived to have a direct payoff in terms of new members are not high priorities. This breeds a fragmentation in the broader religious community. In many places, once thriving ecumenical ventures have deteriorated to the lowest level of cooperation: the proverbial Thanksgiving service. Under these conditions, the lack of engagement with urban policy issues is understandable.

What is Urban Policy?

The immediate image that springs to mind is the formal decision-making power of municipal governments: to raise property taxes, increase the school board budget, cut back on services, or build a convention center. But urban policy has a much broader purview. It can be defined as any meaningful course of action that has a direct impact on the quality of life in a city. One urbanologist has defined policy as the "mobilization of bias."[1] Urban policy would include any organized and realized plan of ordering our public life. *Court decisions*, through the interpretation of the law, essentially set policy. *Public bureaucracies* are often the hidden policy-makers: By developing the plan of implementation, they often have more of an influence than the actual passage of a law. Urban policies are often the result of the *interaction of federal, state, and munic- ipal levels of government.* (The federal budget cutbacks of the 1980s were critical factors in policy formulation at the local level, for example.) However, not to be overlooked is *privatiza- tion*: the crucial role played by the private sector in the devel- opment of public policies. Banks, for example, could virtually direct residential patterns in cities through redlining. Within the climate of privatization, the boundary between the public and private sectors is blurring. One result is that private devel- opers can have as much impact on the life of a city as do its elected officials.

There are also less obvious, more informal ways that bias becomes mobilized into policy. Since Max Weber described the symbiotic relationship between "the Protestant ethic and the spirit of capitalism,"[2] there has been a healthy respect for the rule of a cultural climate, or ethos, as the fertile ground out of which more formalized policies emerge. Cities have his- tories, "personalities," if you will. Like other cultures, a particu- lar urban ethos is shaped by its own cast of characters, its sacred rituals and spaces, its stories and scandals, its location and even its image of itself. The ethos continues to change, to be pro- duced and reproduced, challenged and reinforced by its inter- preters. While religion served as a primary interpreter for generations in many cities, civic leaders and now particularly the media play a dominant role. It is here, in the creation of the urban ethos, that bias takes shape. It can then be mobilized both through and outside of the political process.

Chicago's Community Renewal Society is the rare organiza- tion that appreciates the role it can play in both formal and informal dimensions of policy formulation—an appreciation that undergirds the confidence and sense of empowerment that leads them as much into lobbying in city hall as into lead- ing the people in grieving the loss of their mayor. Their pres- ence in the city is both "sacred" and "secular," and both of those functions have an impact on the shaping of policies that in turn affect the quality of life for the people of Chicago.

If we in the religious community are, for the most part, ham- strung in taking an active and effective role in shaping urban policy, we have ourselves largely to blame. We either subconsciously relegate policy analysis to the "experts," believing it to be an amoral, "objective" science, or we trust the moral intentions of policymakers. We do not want to appear naive by introducing the language of faith into the public forum. We abdicate our power in both the formal and informal arenas in which bias is indeed mobilized. Caught in our own powerlessness, our agenda becomes loaded with programmatic responses to the victims of misguided urban policies: homeless people, teenage mothers, unemployed workers, addicts. Except for some isolated efforts, the religious community has not had much impact on the larger policy areas these victims represent: housing, economic development, education, and health care.

A new strategy is needed. A new language is needed. A new vision is needed both of the city and of our presence in it. It is clear throughout the biblical witness that the welfare (shalom) of the city and of the people of God are inextricably interrelated (Jer. 29:7). Our present health and our futures are caught up with each other.

Privatization: A Closer Look

The Chicago Bears stadium issue is illustrative of the growing influence that privatization has had on the development of urban policies and their impact on life in the big city. Privatization is not a concept associated with the sort of media-drawing drama that attracts moral outrage and fuels a public response by the religious community: "Black youth killed by white police officer," "Homeless shelter cut from city budget," or "Bomb dropped on MOVE house: 11 killed." *But it has more impact on the urban policy formulation and the quality of everyday life than any of these more dramatic events*. It would be harder to organize a community around the issue of privatization than around those issues that capture headlines and the moral imagination. Perhaps because it seems so amorphous and dispassionate, the public does not feel threatened by it. But without public accountability, policies driven by the private sector can undermine the economic base of a community, redefine its way of life, and in fact displace it altogether.

Privatization cannot be conceived of as a singular, mono-lithic concept but refers to a continuum of approaches in which private sector resources are incorporated and utilized in the sphere of services generally overseen by government. The discussion of privatization is essentially an ethical one, striking at the heart of some of the most basic values and assumptions about life together: What is the role of city government as pro-vider of services? By what criteria should this distribution of services be evaluated? And by whom?

Privatization became commonplace in municipal govern-ments during the 1980s. Currently, approximately 80 percent of municipalities have contracts with private companies for ve-hicle towing, 50 percent for legal services, and 40 percent for solid waste collection.[3] There is seemingly no limit to what is "privatizable." Transportation, health care, corrections, police services, building inspection, fire protection, street repair, and even civil litigation settlement have all been subcontracted to private companies by various municipalities.[4]

The most basic motivation for privatization is cost-efficiency, the assumption being that due to the driving force of the profit motive, the private sector is capable of delivering services of better quality at a lower cost. In a Department of Housing and Urban Development report on the benefits of contracting out services to private companies, the cost compar-isons were dramatic; for example, the asphalt construction of streets is 96 percent more expensive if done by a public agency; janitorial services are 73 percent higher; and traffic sig-nal maintenance is 56 percent more costly when supplied by the city.[5]

In the growing body of literature on privatization, a distinc-tion is often made between the role of local government as *provider* of services rather than producer. It is usually asserted by those in favor of privatization that while government might subcontract out the production of services, it is able to main-tain its role as provider. Rather than actually delivering the services, the government instead acts as broker and man-ager—still insuring as it did before that lights will light, fires will be put out, prisoners will stay in jail. Privatization is seen as one more management tool enabling government to do its job more efficiently. As such, it is presented as a politically and morally neutral strategy:

Privatization is no longer an ideological issue. It is not a matter of Democrat versus Republican, left versus right, liberal versus conservative. It is basically an economic efficiency issue. Local governments at all levels need the type of economic relief that can be provided by private enterprise.[6]

In this view, the only point of evaluation should be efficiency. Since this continues to be demonstrated as the strong suit of privatization of services, efficiency-conscious government officials are utilizing this strategy at ever-increasing rates. In cost-saving terms, privatization has been undeniably positive. However, communities are more than economic units; they are also "moral associations."[7] Their purpose is not just to provide quality services as cheaply as possible but to protect just relations and democratic participation for the whole public. For this reason, evaluation of any program or policy has to undergo more complex scrutiny than just a cost-effectiveness analysis. A number of other political, social, and ethical questions need to be brought into the discussion: Who benefits? at what cost? Who controls the program, and who is accountable for it? What are its future implications?

Philadelphia: A Case Study of Privatization

Now we will turn to a situation in Philadelphia that will directly and indirectly affect the quality of life for many of its citizens—especially the poor. Yet it is the type of policy decision that typically has not been engaged by the religious community. First, we will consider how the church might have evaluated such policy—by what ethical standards. Second, we will ask how the religious community could affect such urban policies.

The city of Philadelphia has been pursuing a strategy of public-private partnership in the development of its waterfront area, Penn's Landing, a project that represents a hybrid of privatization strategy. Public and private investment dollars will be used to transform the area into a tourist attraction—

complete with new upscale stores and restaurants as well as museums, a newly landscaped promenade, and access routes from Interstate 95. It will be managed by a public-private corporation that will provide services for the public spaces (trash collection, security, and capital improvement). These services will most probably be contracted out to private companies.

Penn's Landing is considered a critical piece in a larger economic development strategy that is projected into the next century. Public officials expect it to affect the entire city by magnetically attracting jobs, more business investors, and tourist dollars, thereby expanding the tax base. An important question, however, remains. How might the church evaluate such a project, which will have so great an impact on the life of the city? What follow are five questions which must be asked of this or any other urban policy guided by the commitment to privatization.

How efficient is it?   No doubt the city administration understands the privatization approach to represent substantial cost savings compared to a purely public approach to the development project. However, despite the wealth of research confirming cost savings, the *assumption* of efficiency can be a costly one. Subcontracting by public providers to private producers does not automatically translate into increased efficiency of services. Perhaps the greatest example of privatization, the defense industry, is marked by the greatest degree of inefficiency and cost overruns.

While competition within the marketplace has the effect of lowering costs, it does not always exist in the private sector. Monopolies develop; larger companies outbid smaller businesses. Cost overruns result well after contracts are signed. The Penn's Landing project could thus drain more resources from Philadelphia than is currently projected. The religious community should approach glowing financial projections from the position of a "hermeneutic of suspicion." How competitive is the bidding? What guarantees are there against cost overruns? While there are urban planners whose services could be employed to evaluate the claims of efficiency, one does not need to be a professional to ask these questions in the public forum.

Who benefits? While, ostensibly, local government and taxpayers will be the primary beneficiaries of the development of Penn's Landing, in fact it is the consumers drawn from outside the city, especially tourists, who are the target populations, not the local residents of the city.

The second major group to benefit from the project is the private businesses located in the area. However, these will not necessarily be local entrepreneurs; most retailers pursued for this type of urban recreation area are national chains. While robust business does generate jobs, these nonlocal companies are not likely to plow their profits into local expansion but will likely take their profits out of the local economy for investment elsewhere.

The privately owned corporations will further benefit through the public-private management corporation, which will concentrate the contracts for sanitation and security services. The private corporations will also have a large voice in the aesthetics of design of public spaces.

At what cost? In calculating the cost of any policy, it is important to look beyond the bottom line of the spread sheet to the distribution of the "savings." Often, the savings of one group represents the cost to another; within the community, fiscal savings for a few can create social costs for many.

Not surprisingly, the major voices of opposition to privatization of municipal development and services have been those of public employees.[8] The cost cuts in moving from public- to private-sector service delivery occur primarily in labor expenditures. This disproportionately affects the minority community, for whom public employment has been a primary vehicle for upward mobility. (In 1980, over 27 percent of all employed African Americans in the United States worked for government, compared to 16 percent of white workers.)[9]

A 1986 study compared minority employment patterns in ten cities that had privatized services. They found that the private service deliverers in fact hired about the same percentage of minority employees as did the public agencies. *However, there was a large discrepancy between wages and benefits offered by the private companies, with some employers paying only about half the compensation available in the public sector.*[10] Further, these cities did not subcontract with minority businesses.

All of this adds up to another bottom line: The move toward privatization will contribute to the growing polarization between the lower and middle classes and between white and minority workers.

Who is in control?   In the urban environment, the question of control (and its corollary, accountability) is both perceptual and political. If our street is consistently unplowed during winter snows, we know whom to call, whom to blame, and finally whom to vote against if there is no change. Responsibility and channels of response are clear when the public good is serviced by public agencies. It is less clear in the public perception or political process who is responsible in a privately managed area such as Penn's Landing or within a privately subcontracted agency. There are no established lines of communication or accountability for the public. Privatization creates a hidden and unreachable bureaucracy, thereby undermining the democratic participation essential to a healthy city government. While the government should still be accountable to the public, it is not unusual for it to lose control over the service producer.[11]

What are the implications?   Both the Bears stadium and Penn's Landing represent development strategies in which public funding, support, and risk-taking will enable the private sector to manage a parcel of urban space for the purpose of generating a profit. It is part of a downtown-oriented approach to urban development that promises job creation and an economic "trickle-out" effect that will benefit all. Currently, city officials across the country are being seduced by such claims from a private sector intent on developing skyscrapers, convention halls, and waterfront entertainment centers. Yet questions must be raised of this public-private partnership strategy. The claims of dramatic urban economic rescue must be challenged and the implications of the strategies delineated, especially when resources are being drawn away from other strategic policy options. Is it important that there be yet another urban aquarium when small businesses are struggling and safe, affordable housing is only a memory for many city dwellers?[12]

There are obvious questions to be raised on behalf of the public interest. These questions are about economics and ethics; they are both complex and profoundly simple. They are questions of public policy and of public conscience.

Displacement. Downtown development usually means that through the exercise of eminent domain, the government will take over residential and commercial property. Generally those who are ordered to sacrifice their neighborhoods and places of work are poor and without the political clout of more affluent neighborhoods and commercial strips. When displacement occurs, not only are individual homes lost, but social networks are irrevocably destroyed as well.[13] The human costs of such policies must be factored into the evaluation of any policy formulation.

Jobs. Advocates of privatization often make job creation the centerpiece of their argument, predicting how many jobs will be generated for how many dollars invested. These figures are somewhat arbitrary, based as they are on speculative projections. If, in developing a convention center in San Francisco, a hundred jobs were created, can similar results be expected in Peoria or Rochester? Other claims need to be scrutinized: How many jobs were lost to begin with? Are the new jobs permanent? Do they match the needs of the local labor market in terms of wages and benefits offered, and skill levels of available workers?

Services. Private-public development projects have serious implications for the distribution of services: fire protection, sanitation, police, and maintenance. Privatized management bodies serve to institutionalize inequity, drawing much-needed services away from neighborhoods. One journalist speculated that projects such as Penn's Landing will create urban environments marked by "spotless islands in a sea of filth."[14]

Public space.   As policies take hold in which the role of the private sector is enhanced through investment, service provision, and management, the meaning of public space is called into question. Will public parks and walkways continue to be places where musicians can perform, homeless folks sleep, demonstrators assemble and dissenters soapbox?

Tax base.   City officials hope that as corporations locate in new office buildings and create new jobs, new sources of tax revenue will be created. This is a critical concern, since federal aid to cities was so radically reduced in the '80s that an enormous burden was placed on cities to generate income. Cities are thus caught in a no-win situation. In order to compete with suburban locations, they must offer reduced taxes for corporations considering relocation. In addition, the increased revenue needs and decreased social services make middle-class workers less willing to accept the tax burdens and social challenges of city life. And these will only increase as cities gamble their limited resources on downtown development, diverting funds away from housing, education, and services that maintain the quality of life in the neighborhoods.

Urban policies that depend on strategies of privatization and particularly on public-private downtown development have an optimistic long-range perspective that makes assumptions about the economic benefits that will eventually trickle out to the poor and working-class residents of the city. Indeed, believers in such policies have to take a giant leap of faith to accept such glowing long-term projections. The problem with the long run, as John Maynard Keynes reminded us, is that we'll all be dead.

Conclusion

How can the religious community respond to the momentum of current urban policy, which bends toward privatization of both services and economic development strategies? While we often cower at the prospect of such involvement, interviews with city officials indicate that they would welcome and indeed expect the church to participate as a moral presence and critic in the policy formulation process. Here are some suggestions for how we might begin:

1. We need to address our own sense of powerlessness—its sources and expressions—before jumping into the fray.
2. We need to create opportunities for clergy and laypeople to learn the skills of policy analysis. This should be an ecumenical project that utilizes the resources of universities, policymakers and policy watchers.
3. We must support research and analysis at the local level. Perhaps positions for "urban ethicists" could be created to monitor policy-making downtown.
4. We should encourage and support church-based community organizing efforts. There is no better source of public accountability than an informed organization of citizens who will be directly affected by policy decisions.
5. In our role as mythologizers and interpreters, let us not underestimate our call and ability to affect the urban ethos, especially the destructive values of privatism and profits-before-people. We should target cultural biases *before* they get mobilized into policy.
6. Finally, we must hold accountable those policymakers who are members of our congregations: union leaders, city council members, bureaucrats, and bank officials who are active in their churches and synagogues yet find that their values and actions in the workplace are not challenged by their spiritual community.

Our cities are in crisis, and privatization processes will continue to expand the problems. Today we are responding to issues that were not even on the agenda a decade ago, such as homelessness, drug-related crime, and AIDS. Privatization can draw resources away from these critical and developing crises. Services to those individuals and groups affected by such crises will never be profitable and so will never be subject to the practice of subcontracting. Therefore, those who suffer most in our cities could fall into even bigger cracks in light of the privatization frenzy unless we insert ourselves prominently and effectively into the process of urban policy-making.

Katie Day is a Presbyterian minister currently serving on the faculty of Lutheran Theological Seminary and as parish associate at Tabernacle United Church, both in Philadelphia. She is coauthor (with John Raines) of Modern Work and Human Meaning *(Westminster Press, 1986).*

Notes

1. E. E. Schattschneider, *The Semisovereign People: A Realist's View of Democracy in America* (New York: Holt, Reinhart & Winston, 1960).

2. Max Weber, *The Protestant Ethic and the Spirit of Capitalism*, trans. Talcott Parsons (New York: Charles Scribner's Sons, 1958).

3. David Seader, "Privatization and America's Cities," *Public Management* 68 (December 1986): 6.

4. Privatization can take several other forms: for example, selling off public properties, supplying vouchers to consumers for housing, transportation, and food, and co-opting volunteer services.

5. Seader, "Privatization," p. 9.

6. Robert Spann, "Public versus Private Provision of Governmental Services," in *Budgets and Bureaucrats: The Sources of Government Growth*, ed. Thomas E. Borcherding (Durham, N.C.: Duke University Press, 1977), p. 88.

7. Hadley Arkes, *The Philosopher in the City: The Moral Dimensions of Urban Politics* (Princeton, N.J.: Princeton University Press, 1981), p. 269.

8. See *Passing the Bucks*, published by the American Federation of State, County, and Municipal Employees (AFSCME).

9. Robert Suggs, "Minorities and Privatization: Issues of Equity," *Public Management* 68 (December 1986): 14–15.

10. Ibid., p. 15.

11. As reported in *Business Week* (10 March 1986), p. 14, the Massachusetts Taxpayers' Foundation (a conservative group) found in their study of contracting out by the state government that the "state had lost fiscal and program control to a provider-dominated system."

12. In the summer of 1991 the Penn's Landing controversy is still unresolved. The city is essentially going broke and is not in a position to carry forward with such projects to attract business. Due to this, some of the developers have withdrawn from the project. The

project has not been rejected or abandoned, but some aspects have been left behind—such as the "super service" concept.

13. Both research and experience have continued to confirm Herbert Gans's findings in his epic study of the "urban renewal" of Boston's North Side in the early 1960s: *The Urban Villagers* (New York: Free Press, 1962).

14. Thomas Hine, "What is the price to pay for a developed Penn's Landing?" *Philadelphia Enquirer* (2 August 1987).

• 19 •

What We Owe Women and Children: Reflections on the Church and Economic Justice

Carol S. Robb

Over the past several decades, our society has been grappling with the effects of an economic transformation that has encouraged and depended upon women entering the paid labor force in large numbers. In 1950, 28 percent of all women were in the paid labor force; by 1970, the figure was 43 percent, and by 1985, 55 percent. More significantly, a major impact of this household transformation has been on married women with children. In 1950, about 24 percent of married women with children were in the paid labor force, while by 1985, that figure had risen to 61 percent.[1] A large percentage of these women live in our cities.

There is a social expectation that women, whether or not they work outside the home, take most of the responsibility for child care and housework. All children have fathers, yet fathers have not moved to take responsibility for child care and housework to an equivalent degree to which women have moved into the rest of the economy. Although some fathers have made efforts, fathers have not experienced the qualitative shift in their identities and responsibilities that mothers have. Individually, families have made adjustments to the new situations brought about by the working status of the majority of mothers—some positive, some negative. But the stresses or strains experienced in such families, particularly with regard to child care, are typically viewed in the United States as private matters to be solved in

250

individual ways. As a nation, we have not yet grasped child care as an issue that has a bearing on the common good to the extent that we must take collective responsibility. We must develop a shared commitment to make it possible for all adults to combine work and family responsibilities.

The church has been working to fill this need, though not because of denominational policy. Congregation by congregation, churches have become landlords to child-care centers or have developed child-care programs in response to the needs of their congregants and neighbors. In fact, 50 to 55 percent of all children in child care spend their days in church-owned real estate.[2]

In 1988, a bill known as the Act for Better Child Care (ABC), which would have made available large amounts of money to subsidize child-care programs across the country, was defeated in Congress. It should be instructive for the church to know that, in the minds of many secular advocates for children, a major reason for the defeat of the ABC bill was that religious bodies did not agree that churches should have to conform to federal standards to qualify for child-care subsidies. This issue is complicated further by undercurrents within the church about what is the morally justifiable role of substitute care for children.

Rural as well as urban churches are facing questions of whether or not to support child care on their premises: if so, how to fund it; if not, how to find other ways to support caregiving for children. The accelerated breakdown of the extended family in urban areas necessarily makes this question more urgent for urban churches that are attempting to clarify their perspectives on the relationship of child-care programs and public policies to their mission.

There are several honorable motivations for viewing the support of child care as a mission of the congregation. All involve wanting somehow to buttress the child-nurturance needs of church and neighborhood families and to satisfy the requirements of economic justice for women. Churches as well as secular agencies ought to be involved in supporting multiple approaches to child care insofar as they have resources to offer.

Certainly they have something to contribute to the conversation about why society in general should be more involved in child-care policies. But they, like all contemporary societal institutions, should be apprised of the major concerns that account for our national ambivalence about ways of caring for our children other than by full-time care given by the mother; they should also be aware of arguments in favor of a more extensive and publicly supported child-care system. Such arguments should be grounded in the view that a necessary condition for social and economic justice for women and their children is the possibility of choosing a life plan, choosing it without coercion, in accord with values we women as moral agents hold to be true and consistent for a moral community and a just society.[3]

The reason I have developed a sensitivity to the structures of child care is, of course, autobiographical. I had been teaching at a seminary for one year when I became pregnant. Work had been the center of my identity for a long while, and I had a very ill-formed notion that a baby would fit around the edges of my work life. I informed my colleagues that I wouldn't need much time off and that nothing much would change. In fact, I had no idea how significant a new child is in the configuration of one's life and how deep would be the emotions linking me to parenting. Duncan was six weeks old and just beginning to smile when I went back to bare-bones teaching responsibilities. Together, my partner and I arranged our hours at work so we could limit Duncan's substitute care, and we continue to do so, though it requires more cooperation than our colleagues can easily offer.

Even so, I felt robbed of time with my new baby, time to heal and recover a sense of groundedness. How much more difficult must it be for those many women who have no such support. The stress and love involved in childbirth and parenting are the personal experiences that linked me psychically with millions of women, allowing me to identify with them and their partners in a deeper way than had been possible before.

Social and material conditions are necessary to support people's life plans. For women, those supports will include procreative choice, including maternity or parental leave and high-quality child care. But the moral agency of women is not perceived here to be a collection of individual women's private reflections. Rather, in a culture that promotes guilt among mothers in the paid labor force, solidarity among women and visionary men is the context in which women can move out of privatism and atomistic individualism and into autonomy, defined as the freedom to be responsible. In turn, this autonomy requires and is nurtured by communities in long-term efforts to change social structures in the light of the values we have chosen, consistent with a vision of an economy that meets the requirements of justice.

I use a particular perspective on justice that is an extension of recent theological reflections on the problem of how to know what is one's due. The standard means of measuring justice—according to equality, merit, works, needs, the law, and rank—yield conflicting answers to this question. The tendency in U.S. culture is to emphasize justice by works, argue for equality, but expect only what the law requires. But several people have argued in recent work that U.S. culture should be confronted by biblical norms for justice in which need receives primary emphasis, as in the just entitlement of the poor, as a corrective to the ideology of liberalism that promotes both individualism and atomism.[4] I concur with this assessment, and to make the case for more social supports for child care, I specifically build on the work of Margaret Farley, Beverly Harrison, and Mary Daly.

Margaret Farley claims that justice requires attention to the specific conditions of autonomy for each person. Far from being an abstract and distant procedure, justice requires that we understand the concrete details of people's lives, including their needs and capabilities.[5] Beverly Harrison understands justice to be the heart of religious promise and the passion of re-creating the world in a way that gives dignity to women. She develops a theory of human rights—rights language being justice language—wherein rights are defined as the minimal conditions for participation in community with dignity. She says that if bodily integrity for women is to have any content at all, we must have rights to procreative choice.[6] In speaking to what women need, she agrees with Farley's perspective on the positive value of the principle of justice.

Finally, Mary Daly claims that justice is a male norm and that women do not have a stake in what justice requires. Justice is abstract, ignoring the social conditions that make people different from each other. In defining justice, men have excluded women and our subjugated status from moral consideration.[7] Although Daly herself does not appeal to principles of justice, by saying that women have never been included in the morally relevant community when "the boys" have meted out justice, she is telling us something about what justice requires. Now we must add to the list of measures of justice a measure called *justice as participation*. Or at the very least, participation in the discussion of the meaning of justice should be a procedural requirement, much as is due process.

Justice in our time must give priority to what women *need* as minimal conditions for participating in our communities with dignity. In addition, women must participate in the discussion of what justice requires. Our participation is required at every level. Otherwise, justice as participation will not have been satisfied.

The Argument

What we have come to call child-care policy, then, is an important component of procreative choice. Economic justice for women requires the nation to make a commitment to high-quality child care in the form of day-care centers, maternity leaves, parenting leaves, and flex-time, when possible, in the paid labor force. There are at least four reasons that *all* families should be entitled to child care—those families that cannot afford it as well as those that can.

First, women currently pay a heavier cost than men for what should be a common effort: the support and nurture of children.

Second, we owe women rights to family support systems because we can afford to provide them. The examples given to us by other industrialized nations indicate how slow our own nation has been to support women and families in these ways.

Third, we owe such supports to women because we can find no convincing argument that, when done with quality controls, the supports will cause harm to our children.

And finally, we owe these supports because a significant section of our population in poverty needs them to attain minimal conditions of well-being for women and children.

Bearing the Cost of Child Care Fairly

In several ways, childbearing and rearing exact a higher cost from women than from men. Women are segregated by sex in the labor force. They are concentrated in low-paying jobs that are clumped in the service sector and are sparsely unionized. Just as affirmative action was beginning to result in the hiring of more women in the traditionally male smokestack industries, those industries began to lose their share in the world markets and lay off workers. When that happened, racial-ethnic and women workers were the first to lose their jobs, and when they went to search for new jobs, they found that the only type of jobs experiencing growth in the economy were low-paying service sector jobs. In addition to sex segregation, women also suffer from the wage gap. In 1987, women earned sixty-five cents to a male dollar.[8] Therefore, when women (including women with children) work, they do not bring home the same paycheck to support their families as did their male colleagues. Both job segregation and the wage gap have been legitimated by employers who claim that women are not singlehandedly supporting their families or are not as reliable as men because of family responsibilities. In this way, women pay for our child-bearing past or potential in ways that men do not.

There is in our culture the expectation that women receive their fulfillment primarily in marriage and child-rearing. This expectation is internalized across class, resulting in a failure on the part of women and men to think of women as having a major stake in the quality of their jobs. There seem, in addition, to be inadequate organizing movements for sectors of the labor force in which women are clustered. Yet, women in the United States, like men, work primarily for economic reasons.

Fully 43 percent of the women in the labor force are single, divorced, separated, or widowed. Another 25 percent are married to men earning less that $15,000 a year. Married women who work contribute 39 percent of the family income.[9] It would be in women's best interest to demand education and training before entering the paid labor force, insist on higher pay scales and benefits, and support collective action. Otherwise our identification with our families results in unfair compensation for our work.

Divorce in the United States has a greater negative impact on women than men, and it usually *benefits* men financially. Because married-couple families have two potential adult earners, and because the husband is likely to have higher earnings than the wife, women who head their own families are much more likely to be poorer than married-couple families. When marriages end, the women get poorer, while men's economic standing usually improves.[10] One reason is that women typically receive custody of the children after divorce, and over two-thirds of mothers of children with an absent father receive either no child support or less than the agreed-upon amount.[11] Marriages that began in the 1970s have a 50 percent chance of ending in divorce. This rate has stabilized, but what it means is that women can no longer (if they ever could) assume their only life's work will be housework and child care. These are the economic costs that women pay. There is also a spiritual cost to women who are full-time parents and homemakers whose work is not valued as real work and who feel judged by their peers who enter the paid labor force. It is the spiritual cost of the loss of self-worth. Everybody has a stake in healthy childbirth and good child-rearing. Women should not bear that responsibility unfairly.

Affording Child Care

We owe women rights to family support systems because we can afford to provide them. The claim that "can implies ought" is not a sufficient argument for anything, but our society needs to be disabused of the idea that the cost of benefits and services required to support high-quality child care is so high as to make their implementation irresponsible. The examples given to us by other industrialized nations indicate how slow our own nation has been to support women and families in these ways.

Investigations of Germany, France, Hungary (prior to 1990), and Sweden demonstrate that this issue hinges on political will rather than on availability of resources. These countries have policies to attenuate the negative health aspects as well as the income loss involved in *childbirth* through a variety of maternity benefits and maternity and parental leaves. There are cash and in-kind family income supports for *child-rearing* in all countries. All countries provide a benefit that assures *income replacement*, totally or in large part, for the loss of earnings by women at the time of childbirth and for some time immediately thereafter. This benefit is wage-related and covers about 90 percent of wages, and, with rare exception, the costs fall not on industry but on the society at large.[12]

Of course, the question is raised, how do these countries finance their child-care policies for very young children? Costs do not appear to be a deterrent to the development of out-of-home care for children under three. Societies that want to offer care are able to do it by combining national, state, and local subsidies with parent fees.[13] The costs of failure to be intentional about child care also have effects on children and families, and these must be considered and weighed in the balance. At stake is economic justice for women and a nurturing environment for our children. These are high stakes.

The principle of subsidiarity stipulates that social issues should be handled at the lowest possible level of society at which they can be handled effectively. If child care can be handled in the home, it should be. If it cannot, however, it is our moral responsibility to involve increasingly higher levels, such as the neighborhood, the school, the parish, the town, the state, the region, and finally the nation until it can be adequately taken care of. Thus parents, school districts, and churches have to be involved with the issues of early child care. Municipal and state support is also needed. The national government, too, should have responsibility for child care as a national priority, unifying and buttressing state standards and providing some subsidy to local and state levels. This is the lesson I derive from looking at other industrialized nations, which, like the United States, by virtue of industrialization have experienced a significant shift of women from the household economy to the paid labor force.

Effects on Children

Since well over 50 percent of all mothers are either working or seeking work,[14] the society needs to know that we can provide supports for high-quality child care without doing an injustice to our children, our future. Substitute care for children three years and older is not a major issue because we have relatively long experience with school and preschool nurseries and know that there are ways to assure our children's well-being in those situations. Our primary concern is with the effects of infant day care, since with few exceptions, such as in Hungary, there is no large-scale effort to provide parental leave for either mothers or fathers for an extended period of time.

Evidence gathered in the early 1980s indicates that good-quality infant day care has no adverse consequences on maternal attachment or intellectual or social development. It appears to have a neutral effect on development.[15] The policy implications of these findings seem to point consistently to the need to devise standards assuring stability and education of care-givers, low ratio of children to care-givers, adequate compensation for care-givers, and high-quality environments. But the factors associated with high-quality child care are all costly. If we can provide them, we will not commit developmental injustice to our children in the effort to sustain economic justice for women.

Nor will we commit social injustice to the child-care workers. According to 1987 census figures, child-care workers, teachers, and aides earned an average of $9,952 a year. Their turnover rate is conservatively measured at 35 percent annually, and their average length of stay in a job is 2.7 years. The average U.S. worker in all occupational categories stays in a job for 6.6 years, so child-care workers' turnover rate is considerably higher than average.[16] If we want a stable environment for our children, one in which they can form relationships in which to build trust, then we will have to increase salaries and provide the benefits commensurate with the professionalism required to provide that environment.

It would *not* be a signal of a just society to re-create a stigmatized, low-paid role for working women in which women do for low pay and for other people's children what we previously did for no pay but for our own children. In such a situation, caregivers would be carrying the major burden of decent-quality child care. To avoid exploiting other women, we must secure adequate public subsidy and mandated minimum standards, recognizing that they will constitute a major expense.

On the other hand, alternatives to infant day care should be available to those working parents who would prefer to be with their babies during the first months, or even years, of life. Minimally, we should be able to guarantee paid parental leave for four to six months[17] and extended leaves with job security for two years. However, we should not stint in our efforts to shorten work weeks for parents with young children.

Fathers should have equal responsibility for seeking adjustable work weeks as mothers have. There is a good possibility that child care will remain undervalued as work as long as it is seen as "women's work."

Commitment to Those in Poverty

Finally, we owe these child-care supports because a significant section of our population in poverty needs them to attain minimal conditions of well-being for women and children. The percentage of the U.S. population that is poor declined dramatically during the 1960s, changed little during the 1970s, and then began rising in the early 1980s, after the War on Poverty Programs were dismantled. Using the official definition of poverty, the percentage of the population poor in 1960 was 20.2; in 1970 it was 12.6; by 1987 it was 13.5.[18]

In order to understand who is in poverty in this nation, we need to explore the feminization of poverty. The feminization of poverty does not mean that the poor are now predominantly adult women, for that is not the case. Women are a somewhat larger fraction of the poor now (1960: 33 percent;

1980: 38.7 percent), but not much. The fraction of the poor who are adult men has remained unchanged (1960: 20 percent; 1980: 21.8 percent), and the fraction who are children has decreased (1960: 47 percent; 1980: 39.4 percent), so the slight decrease in the fraction who are children accompanied the slight increase in the fraction who are women.[19]

What is now different, and what the feminization of poverty signifies, is that there is now an increased proportion of poor women who head their own households. Whereas in 1960 the majority (60.8 percent) of poor individuals were in families with a male present, by 1980, this figure dropped to less than one-third (28.7 percent). As of 1980, half of all individuals in poverty were in families with a female head of household. Thus, poverty has become feminized because the poor have come to depend more on women as the main breadwinners, and poor women now have more financial responsibility for rearing children, while the wage gap has remained relatively unchanged. The general growth in female-headed families has been due to several demographic factors, notably a sharp increase in the incidence of divorce and separation and independent living by unmarried mothers.[20]

Accessibility of high-quality child care, then, is a key piece of strategy to address the structural components of poverty. Statistics underscore the importance of child care to the women who are heads of households: The poverty rate for single mothers with earnings is about one-third that for single mothers with no earnings. Moreover, the poverty rate for single mothers of children under the age of six, when those women worked full-time all year, was one-tenth that of nonworking mothers. The main reasons given by nonworking mothers in poverty for not being in the labor force are child-care responsibilities and the lack of adequate and affordable child-care services.[21]

The Church, Working Parents, and the Need for Child Care

The church is already active in the child-care arena. Day care centers have gone to churches asking for space, and the churches have, in many instances, been generous landlords providing it. Some churches have decided, on the basis of the needs of their congregants, to start day-care centers on their premises. Church-housed programs probably constitute the largest group of day-care providers in the nation.[22]

Ninety-nine percent of all church-housed programs are open to all members of the community and do not require church membership. The main motivation for the churches' involvement appears to be desire to provide service to the community, whether the program is operated by the church or only housed on the church property. It is not primarily Christian education or evangelism, narrowly conceived. By general standards, church-housed programs measure up rather well. Programs developed by the churches themselves tend to run larger group sizes than "for-profit" programs *housed* in churches, and we should monitor this aspect, as the greater number of children can sometimes mean less individual care. But overall, the quality of programs is something of which the churches can be proud.

One rough spot in church involvement in child care is the value placed on that care as measured by the church's treatment of staff members. Staff members are not considered church employees, even when the program is operated wholly by the congregation. Consequently, child-care workers do not ordinarily receive health-care benefits, nor are they eligible for extensive pension programs operated by national church agencies. The average annual salary of church-based child-care staff is deplorable. In 1981, directors' salaries averaged $12,486; the teachers', $9,000; teachers' aides, $7,380.[23] Most directors (87 percent) and teachers (74 percent) have college degrees.[24]

If we take seriously the findings that stability among care-givers is one indicator of high-quality day care, the church must look again at the salary structure for child-care workers. If we want care-givers to be able to commit themselves in the long term to a particular center with our particular children, we must increase their job stability. In this respect, rather than challenging the rest of the nation, the church is now *like* the rest of the nation.

The church and the nation will have to face the question of economic justice for care-givers in order to provide quality care for our infants and children and to support families whose parents are in the paid labor force. It is a matter of the common good: what is good for our nation as a whole, and what is good for individual women, men, and children. No policy that defines "good" at the expense of the dignified participation of women and children in the community can be considered consistent with the common good.

There are two further considerations that we as members of churches and neighborhoods should address. One is the care of so-called latchkey children between the ages of six and thirteen, whose parents are working outside the home when school is dismissed. A related issue is that of parents, particularly mothers, who are *not* in the paid labor force and are at home when their children get out of school. These mothers often become the unofficial care-givers of the neighborhood, a mixed blessing. On the one hand, they may prefer their children to play with friends at home so they can have confidence that their own children are not getting into mischief. On the other hand, it becomes next to impossible to have time with their own children and to supervise their chores and homework when numerous friends with working parents have congregated. This is also a justice issue, particularly when parents in the paid labor force presume that the at-home mothers will fill in the gaps not only for unscheduled time but for school outings and related responsibilities. On what basis can we build just community relations if we undervalue work in the home, yet depend on it?

The church has another arena of responsibility in addition to the programmatic and political arenas, and that is in reconstructing our theological perspective with respect to the value of women and what we have considered women's work. The image that emerges as I reflect on the enormous size of the theological task is one of women baking bread, whether at home or in the back of the bakery, and men breaking the bread before the congregation. As women move into the professional ministry, they struggle with the paradoxical requirement in mainline denominations that only the ordained can break the bread in the liturgical memory of the Passover meal of Jesus and those who participated in his new way of radical egalitarianism. The church is ill-equipped to revalue women and women's work if it must spend enormous energy repressing women's energy and influence, as it seems to have done since the very earliest forms of the church. Yet the revaluing of women and their work is the church's task, by virtue of its confessed identity as the community who bears witness to the new life of freedom and responsibility, whose outlines were drawn by Jesus of Nazareth.

In the process of revaluing women and women's work, the church must be willing to encounter several layers of idolatry that are nearly impervious to criticism. The first layer is the assumption that the common good is constituted by the aggregate of individual goods, defined by each individual independently. Rather, a biblically based economic ethic will witness that the material conditions necessary for participation in community with dignity are binding on the whole community and have priority over other goods, particularly the freedom to enjoy luxuries. In effect, the first theological task is to disentangle the church's thinking about justice from its assumption that justice means freedom. Freedom is a high value and will be a mark of a just economy, but it is only relative to a higher value, the satisfaction of fundamental need.

Another layer of idolatry is the assumption that sexuality is dirty because of our embodiedness and the experience of pleasure and that if we are going to have sexual pleasure, we should pay for it. Sexual negativity is directly related to the privatization of child-rearing: "You played around. You got pregnant. Now you deal with it." This same attitude buttresses many anti-choice perspectives, and it is no accident that many people who are opposed to the licensing of churches for child care, which would guarantee standards for the stability and safety in care, are also opposed to procreative choice with regard to abortion. The church has an immense theological task in disentangling sexuality from our notions of sin; it is a task that is fundamental to revaluing women and our work.

Justice for women and children has structural implications for the organization of our economy. The concerns of millions of mothers and fathers about the care of their children are more than individual issues—they amount to a social agenda. The moral component of this social agenda is not gender equality alone, although that is a component of gender justice. The moral issue, in addition, is to satisfy the requirements of justice by attending to the concrete needs of women and children and incidentally to the men whose work lives have been structured so that they cannot be parents to their children. Child-care policies appear to be foundational for the participation of women and children in the community with dignity. The church has an obligation to play a pivotal role in this transformation.

Carol S. Robb is associate professor of Christian social ethics at San Francisco Theological Seminary.

Notes

1. Nancy Barrett, "Women and the Economy" in *The American Woman 1987–1988: A Report in Depth*, ed. Sara E. Rix, for the Women's Research and Education Institute of the Congressional Caucus for Women's Issues (New York: W. W. Norton & Co., 1987), p. 107.

2. Eileen Lindner, address to the conference, Religion and Government: The Fine Line, Implications for Child Care in Churches, at San Francisco Theological Seminary, March 2, 1989.

3. I am using language here that is historically used by the Boston Personalists, specifically Walter Muelder, *Moral Law in Christian Social Ethics* (New York and Toronto: The Edwin Mellen Press, 1966). The law of the most inclusive end, as well as others, requires a life plan, a notion without much substance for many women for whom the culture has a plan that they only be supportive to families and others.

4. I think particularly of Karen Lebacqz's *Justice in an Unjust World: Foundations for a Christian Approach to Justice* (Minneapolis: Augsburg, 1987), in which the dominant themes are to discover what justice requires by listening to the people who suffer injustice, and that justice is restorative of genuine human community. In reading

Lebacqz, however, one is drawn to the question of what people suffering injustice *need* to enable the community to be restored. See also Daniel C. Maguire, *A New American Justice* (Minneapolis: Winston, 1980); David Hollenbach, *Claims in Conflict: Retrieving and Renewing the Catholic Human Rights Tradition* (New York: Paulist Press, 1979); and Prentiss L. Pemberton and Daniel Rush Finn, *Toward a Christian Economic Ethic: Stewardship and Social Power* (Minneapolis: Winston Press, 1985).

5. Margaret A. Farley, *Personal Commitments: Making, Keeping, Breaking* (San Francisco: Harper & Row, 1986), pp. 82–83.

6. Beverly Wildung Harrison, *Our Right to Choose: Toward a New Ethic of Abortion* (Boston: Beacon Press, 1983), p. 196.

7. Mary Daly, *Pure Lust: Elemental Feminist Philosophy* (Boston: Beacon Press, 1984), pp. 272–279.

8. There have been attempts to explain the wage gap, in large part, as the result of women taking time out of the paid labor force to have and nurture children for a few years. However, a recent study by the Bureau of the Census reports that work interruptions account for a tiny part of the earnings disparity, which is 31 percentage points. The bureau found that even if women's education, experience, and interruptions were the same as men's, the earnings gap would be reduced by only about 5 percentage points. See Barrett, "Women and the Economy," in Rix, ed., *The American Woman 1987–1988*, p. 130. The specific figure I use for the 1987 wage gap is demonstrated by Heidi Hartmann, director of Women's Policy Research, in "Briefing Paper #1: The Wage Gap," for the National Committee on Pay Equity, 1201 Sixteenth Street Northwest, Suite 420, Washington, D.C. 20036, April 1989, p. 2.

9. Sheila B. Kamerman and Alfred J. Kahn, *Child Care, Family Benefits, and Working Parents: A Study in Comparative Policy* (New York: Columbia University Press, 1981), p. 25.

10. One year after a divorce or separation, adjusted family income for all women had dropped by 9 to 25 percent of its pre-divorce level (depending upon the exact method of calculation) and had risen 13 percent for men. These averages conceal large variations. The fall in living standards was much sharper for women whose families initially had been in the top half of the income distribution: 29 percent of women from these affluent pre-divorce families had experienced a drop in adjusted income of more than half by one year

after the divorce. In contrast, 19 percent of women from less affluent pre-divorce families had comparable income drops, and 38 percent of less affluent women actually experienced a rise in adjusted income by one year after the divorce. See Andrew Cherlin, "Women and the Family," in Rix, ed., *The American Woman 1987–1988*, p. 89.

11. This latter phenomenon is the reason many women now look askance at no-fault divorce laws. The changes in divorce laws from fault-based grounds to no-fault grounds have hurt divorced women economically. The new laws assume that husbands and wives are equals, while in reality most wives have far less earning potential than their husbands. Older wives may not have worked for wages in decades. Younger, better educated women may have worked only part-time or withdrawn from the labor force when their children were young, thus forgoing the opportunity to develop a career. Settlements that award the wife half the family's property leave the wife and children dependent on her earning power and her ex-husband's child support payments, the latter of which is often unreliable and quite insufficient. See Rix; *The American Woman 1987–1988*, pp. 87–88.

12. Kamerman and Kahn, *Child Care, Family Benefits, and Working Parents.* Another source that used Sheila Kamerman's research and extends her purview to include Britain and Italy is Sylvia Ann Hewlett, *A Lesser Life: The Myth of Women's Liberation in America* (New York: Warner Books, 1986). Hewlett couches her work in terms of a criticism of the priorities of the contemporary women's movement in the United States. That agenda is not one I share, but the inclusion of Italy, which is primarily Catholic and yet is still more intentional than the United States about supporting women in the labor force with children, is instructive.

13. Kamerman and Kahn, *Child Care*, pp. 106–119.

14. For a good review of the uneven standards that apply to day care in the different states and a discussion of why there is an inherent contradiction in letting market forces be a major mechanism for providing child-care services, see Deborah Fallows, *A Mother's Work* (Boston: Houghton Mifflin, 1985), pp. 142–182. She thinks the development of the large chains of for-profit day-care centers illustrates a special case of market failure. What the chains need in order to maximize profits is often incompatible with what children need in order to thrive.

15. See Kamerman and Kahn, *Child Care, Family Benefits, and Working Parents*, particularly pp. 122–129.

16. Sheila B. Kamerman, "Child Care Services: An Issue for Gender Equity and Women's Solidarity." *Child Welfare* 64, no. 3 (May–June 1985): p. 268.

17. Thomas J. Gamble and Edward Zigler, "Effects of Infant Day Care: Another Look at the Evidence," *American Journal of Orthopsychiatry* 56, no. 1: 29; and T. Berry Brazelton, "Issues for Working Parents," in the same volume, p. 23.

18. Martha S. Hill, "The Changing Nature of Poverty," *The Annals of the American Academy of Political and Social Science* 479 (May 1985): 35.

19. Ibid., p. 37. The feminization of poverty has not been due to rising poverty incidence for the expanding group of female-headed families. Poverty incidence for female-headed families *declined* significantly between 1960 and 1970 and slowly declined further between 1970 and 1980. The poverty population came to be increasingly composed of female-headed families because there was a larger relative decline in poverty incidence for male-present families and there is an increase in the proportion of people in the overall population who are living in female-headed households. Such statistics appear to contradict the assertion that two out of three adults in poverty are women, but in fact it does not.

20. Ibid., p. 38.

21. Kamerman, "Child Care Services," p. 264.

22. For this section on the church's role in child care, I am drawing from the research of the National Council of Churches study whose results are published in Eileen W. Lindner, Mary C. Mattis, and June R. Rogers, *When Churches Mind the Children: A Study of Day Care in Local Parishes* (Ypsilanti, Mich.: High Scope Press, 1983). Among the authors' findings: 53 percent of the day-care programs in churches are operated by the parish itself, while 47 percent are independently operated on church premises. The church is thus a major direct provider of child care in the United States.

23. Ibid., p. 65; and Susan Garland, "America's Child Care Crisis: The First Steps Toward Solutions," *Business Week*, 10 July 1989: 65.

24. Lindner, Mattis, and Rogers, *When Churches Mind the Children*, p. 65.

• 20 •

THE UPROOTED POOR:

MANDATE FOR MISSION

Valerie E. Russell

After the heroic global struggle in Alaska in the autumn of 1988 to save three stranded whales, the *Boston Globe* ran a cartoon picturing two homeless people dressed in whale costumes sitting on a heating grate in a city street, one saying to the other, "Now maybe people will pay attention to *us*." This cartoon gives us startling and painful commentary on our times. As people of faith, we are haunted by the specter of poverty and the challenge to faithfulness in times such as ours. We sadly admit that we often seem to be more responsive to the dramatic than compassionate to those caught in the daily humdrum struggle of survival.

After eight years, as he prepared to leave the office of president, Ronald Reagan asserted in a Christmas interview that he believed that many of the homeless chose to be homeless. This is significant not only because, as president of the United States, he should have known better, but because his attitude is all too prevalent in our society today. The old myth that *any* in our society can pick themselves up by their own bootstraps, if they desire, is alive and well and at the heart of our attitudes about economic survival.

We do make exceptions for those whom we consider mentally and physically incapable of keeping pace with the mainstream. But for the most part, those whom we have labeled the "permanent underclass" or the "chronically unemployed" are poor, we too often think, because of their own choices.

This bootstrap theory prevails because of the lack of a basic

268

understanding of many of the dramatic economic and social shifts that have occurred in our society over the past ten to twenty years. The most dramatic sign of our economic crisis is the devastating degree of homelessness now evident everywhere in our land, particularly in the cities.

Michael Harrington, author of *The New American Poverty*,[1] suggests that the word "homeless" is not a particularly accurate term to describe this phenomenon and suggests that we ought to think about such people as "the uprooted." Hence, in this article I shall try to analyze this uprootedness as we in the church seek to understand and respond to the profoundly systemic causes of poverty as experienced in the United States today.

Poverty in the United States is increasingly caused by systemic forces, as is "homelessness." To understand it any other way is to underestimate the issue. As Harrington notes, the concept of homelessness implies that the poor's problem is a lack of physical shelter. It is much more profound than that. "Rather the 'homeless' are victims of a bewildering transition . . . sufferers of a kind of social shell shock, totally unprepared for coping with a society whose economy and social arrangements have dramatically shifted."[2]

The statistical base to support this analysis of such uprootedness and "social shell shock" in devastating. Thousands of jobs have disappeared from society in our age of technology. The creation of mega-companies and superconglomerates has all but wiped out small family businesses and mom-and-pop operations. We have witnessed this dynamic not only in cities but in rural areas with the dissolution of small family farms. Further, millions of *new* jobs created in the United States offer workers only 60 percent of the salary they were making in their previous employment.[3] Such incomes do not allow individuals and families to survive in these times of escalating rents. During the winter at the City Mission Society in Boston, we have an average of 125 calls a week from the working poor in crisis, faced with a choice between "meat and heat."

Covertly, or perhaps overtly, we have abandoned the hope held by many until the early 1980s of regaining a "fully employable" economy in which minimally skilled individuals could earn a sustainable, living wage. There is little to suggest that the United States will turn away from the comforts of technology and move back toward a labor-intensive economy in which minimal-skill jobs are plentiful. Nor have we seen any serious advocacy for federal subsidies for the lowest-paying service-sector jobs. Even government-funded job-training programs are at the same level as they were in the 1960s and 1970s.

While minimum-level skilled jobs decreased, federal spending for the poor did increase between 1961 and 1976 from $4.46 billion to $197.8 billion, the poverty portion of the federal budget moving from 4.7 percent in 1961 to 9.4 percent in 1976.[4] This dramatic rise caused many conservatives to charge that the federal government was *creating* poverty by encouraging dependency, a position many still hold. Yet in actuality, much of this increase went to raise Social Security and Medicare payments for the aging. "In each case," Harrington points out, "the nonpoor, who are roughly 85 percent of the people over 65, got much, much more than the [traditional] poor." Indeed, in 1976, only 10.8 million of the 25 million Americans officially defined as poor were receiving Aid to Families with Dependent Children (AFDC).[5]

Riding the crest of the conservative wave, the Reagan administration made many cuts in entitlement programs that had aided the "chronic" poor. Despite the rhetoric about providing a safety net, estimates as of June 1988 were that *one in every seven persons* in the United States was living below the poverty line (ten thousand dollars a year for a family of four). This equals nearly 33.1 million people, 4.3 million of whom were added between 1979 and 1985. Today 22 percent of all children, including 45.6 percent of all African American children and 40.7 percent of all Hispanic children, live below the poverty line. Also hardest hit are women, as almost two out of three poor adults in the United States are female.[6] One natural result of this dramatic rise in numbers of those who live below the poverty line, accompanied by a decrease in jobs providing a livable wage, has been the kind of radical uprootedness resulting in the homelessness of which Harrington speaks.

In addition, the trend of the middle and upper-middle classes moving back into the core cities (regentrification) has obliterated formerly affordable housing. According to the Department of Housing and Urban Development, thousands of units of low-income housing have disappeared since 1980. Housing prices have risen dramatically in the past eight years; at the same time, federal support for subsidized housing was slashed from $32.2 billion in 1981 to $7.5 billion in 1988, a cut of 77 percent.[7] Thus today there are more than half a million people in the United States who have become homeless (uprooted).[8]

This is not a new phenomenon. There have always been homeless in the United States, mainly the mentally ill and deinstitutionalized. But such vast numbers of people cannot be hidden away any longer. And because they increasingly represent families and younger people unable to find work, they cannot so easily be cast aside as part of the "permanent underclass" of dysfunctional individuals. The grave danger is, of course, that they will become such a dramatic mirror of society's dysfunction and of our dehumanized lack of compassion that we will "adjust" our thinking and accept such uprootedness, homelessness, and poverty as a given—a norm in our age.

What Can the Churches Do?

The United Church of Christ has a priority on homelessness voted by the 1987 General Synod. Many of our local parishioners work in soup kitchens and shelters and are beginning to construct permanent affordable housing. All our actions, however, must be put into a theological and spiritual context that defines mission in dramatic terms.

As Christians, we are under a practical gospel mandate to respond with care and compassion in the midst of such a time. The Magnificat of Mary, Jesus' sermon in Luke 4, and other biblical injunctions are quite clear in their message that God is especially concerned with the condition of the poor. This same God also calls us to be astute and deeply committed to working toward a more just society. Our response to this crisis must be theological in nature and mission oriented.

First, we must be careful not to romanticize suffering. As Christians, we affirm the powerful and dramatic suffering of Jesus' life and death, culminating in the cross. Yet over the centuries Christians have struggled with doctrines of suffering. While in our contemporary society we have become more oriented toward self-fulfillment, and our theology is not as laced with concepts of a just earthly suffering, the idea that suffering is either natural or a consequence of God's punishment resides nevertheless within much of our religious psyche.

Thus we tend to confuse the *reality of suffering* that results from our separation from God and each other with the *judgment of a God* who rewards and punishes people through either economic security or suffering. I hear church people articulate it often: "The Bible says the poor will always be with us—it's just the way life is"; or "Jesus was himself homeless"; or "God helps those who help themselves"; or "If Jesus *himself* died on a cross because he was persecuted by the powers of his time, why do you think life will be so different in ours?"

At the World Council of Churches meeting in Los Angeles in January 1989, a Maori layperson raised a critical question for the U.S. delegation in this regard. Noting that North Americans too often use Jesus to justify the suffering of others, he asked, "What would happen if, as well as the image of Christ dying for us, the cross also symbolized an invitation for us to die with him?" Perhaps then our subconscious idealization of suffering would be transformed into an acceptance of a mandate of "accompaniment," that is, a standing in solidarity with those who suffer.

Christian consciousness knows that Jesus' ministry sought to heal the broken places and to discern God's grace, power, and transformation in the midst of suffering. In no way did Jesus seek to romanticize suffering. He always sought to empower into wholeness those who suffered.

So must our theology seek to empower. Accompaniment with the uprooted enables the non-poor to share resources with the poor, but it also keeps us from becoming voyeurs of others' pain. A theology of accompaniment likewise conveys a sense of journeying in a *direction*. We cannot afford merely to leave people where we find them, which so much of our mission often does.

The future of our society, as well as the integrity of Christian discipleship, requires a journeying response. Therefore it requires our advocacy for and solidarity with those who suffer. Our end goal is to join God in breaking the bonds of suffering and to be agents of healing.

Second, as Christians we must fight the stereotyped categories that reduce "the poor" and "the homeless" to mere charts and statistics—"them" as opposed to "us." Our U.S. culture, which tends to idolize individualism in the economic mainstream, shifts that criterion when it deals with the economically marginalized, lumping folks into categories that enable us to depersonalize them and thus relieve our consciences of a sense of responsibility. Christians, believing in the uniqueness of *each person* created by God as worthy of respect, will not allow the systems of the world to rob any class of people, particularly the poor, of dignity and personhood.

Finally, as a people of faith we must take responsibility for our complicity in the plight of the poor as long as we remain silent and allow uncompassionate public policy to exist in one of the wealthiest nations on earth. Mainline Christians must become active in connecting faith to the public-policy sphere. Not only our religious leaders but we ourselves must raise the normative questions regarding what level of human existence we will tolerate in our society. As Christians, we have a responsibility to place at the heart of both the political and the church agenda the questions about the quality of human life. Who is to live and who shall be sacrificed into economic wastelands of poverty? Who shall be condemned by our indifferent system of triage to an anonymous hopelessness? Certainly Jesus had quite a different response to these questions than did Darwin, with his view that only the "fit" will survive.

In raising these issues we must also realize that we advocate not only for the poor and the homeless/uprooted but essentially for the survival of all humanity. Such advocacy likewise becomes a measure of our own faithfulness to the gospel.

In his book *The Politics of Spirituality*, William Stringfellow says that when, during his childhood, adults spoke about the

Holy Spirit, it was always an "utterly obscure, unspecified, literally spooky allusion."[9] Later, when reading the Bible as an adult, he discovered that the Bible is "quite definitive and lucid as to the identity, character, style and habitat of the Holy Spirit."[10] Stringfellow concludes that the spirituality and openness to the Spirit in the Bible is "no hocus-pocus, but a harsh leading of people from bondage, through bondage and toward resurrection."[11]

It is not only the poor and the homeless/uprooted who are in need of resurrection; it is we ourselves as well. Our theological understanding and mission stance with regard to empowering the economically uprooted constitute a very concrete place for encountering anew the incarnate, ever-present God. Such encounter can bring us life-renewing change in our mission commitment. It can roll the stone away.

Valerie E. Russell has taught urban ministry at Harvard Divinity School, Yale Divinity School, and New York Theological Seminary. She is a nationally known lay leader in the United Church of Christ. Currently she is president of the City Mission Society of Boston.

Notes

1. Michael Harrington, *The New American Poverty* (New York: Penguin Books, 1984).

2. Ibid., p. 100.

3. Ibid., p. 47.

4. Ibid., p. 27.

5. Ibid., p. 28.

6. Economic Justice and the Christian Conscience, "How Poverty Mars U.S. Society," *The Witness* 71, no. 6 (June 1988): 8.

7. Figures detailing cuts in federal support were confirmed orally by a HUD official.

8. Interagency Council on the Homeless, "How Many Homeless People Are There?" April 1991, #1–1.

9. William Stringfellow, *The Politics of Spirituality* (Philadelphia: Westminster Press, 1984), p. 17.

10. Ibid., p. 18.

11. Ibid.

• 21 •

FIGHTING AIDS AND HIV

TOGETHER

William A. Doubleday and Suki Terada Ports

Soft rice with pickled plum and green tea, chicken soup, or hot brandy with rum and lemon from a recipe handed down by grandmother—these are recipes not only for healing the sick person but for making him or her feel loved. Whatever their origins, traditions of caring within the family and community meant that a sick person was simply cared for—whatever the source of his or her illness. In recent decades, this caring has been accompanied by a readiness to draw upon the seemingly ever-expanding resources of modern medicine. Then AIDS came along. Caring broke down. Families sometimes fled; communities were often idle or indifferent; churches and clergy frequently stood in judgment; and the once idealized medical establishment initially had little to offer and in some places even less inclination to provide it.

Early in the AIDS pandemic, personal and institutional homophobia, along with a widespread fear of the disease and its carriers, prompted many people in U.S. society to stand by while members of the gay community alone provided much of the care and most of the advocacy work on behalf of those affected by AIDS. It is reasonable to say that without the massive mobilization of the gay community for political pressure, volunteer work, and social services, there would have been little response to the AIDS crisis in the United States in the 1980s.

The mobilization of homosexual communities, along with their political allies, friends, and families, brought about the development of a network of AIDS professionals who became experts overnight. The many deaths among lovers and friends hastened the work and created an ongoing sense of urgency. Unfortunately, the loss of life was often accompanied by the experience of overt prejudice: the loss of jobs and income, of health insurance and life insurance, of family support or lover's involvement. Sometimes the loss of home not only created situations of grief and struggle but also turned AIDS into an issue of civil and human rights.

AIDS became news and was covered by the media in both constructive and sensational ways. While many stories were positive in creating awareness in the gay and lesbian communities, others exacerbated homophobia and were catalytic in promoting the parallel pandemic of AIDSfear or AFRAIDS (Acute Fear Regarding AIDS). The media coverage tended to foster the misconception that only gay transmission of the virus was possible or likely, and thus the risk to the partners of bisexuals, to IV drug users and their sexual partners, and to the unborn went unpublicized. Occasionally the cases of "innocent" hemophiliacs or transfusion recipients would be sensationalized, as were the cases of the Ray family, whose home was burned in Florida, and Ryan White, who became a nationally known figure in his attempt to continue attending public school in Indiana.[1] Surely the media cannot be held solely responsible for the general public's reaction, since much of the fault clearly lay with the slow reaction of health and educational agencies as well as with the inadequate response and preparedness of social-service providers.

Many of the problems regarding HIV infection and AIDS care developed because of the persistent mistaken belief that it was a disease facing only gay, and particularly white, men. This misconception has created problems worldwide. The enormity of the pandemic is only partially reflected by the cumulative global total of 266,098 cases reported to the World Health Organization as of July 1, 1990. During the 1990s, for instance, the World Health Organization expects 10 million children to be orphaned in developing countries as a result of AIDS. In some African urban areas, up to one-third of people between the ages of fifteen and forty-nine are infected.[2] Due to the rampant malnutrition and malaria already plaguing the health of many developing nations, early intervention or significant treatment in HIV-related illness is not even a possibility. No section of the globe is unaffected. The AIDS pandemic runs the gamut, touching everyone. Recognition of the epidemic in Asia, Oceania, Latin American countries and Caribbean islands is unhappily accompanied by a dearth of education about the source of HIV infection, by military and tourist use of prostitution, by pedophilia, and by a general lack of adequate medical facilities and preventative devices.

There is growing evidence that AIDS care in the United States manifests our deeply rooted system of social stratification in which racial and ethnic minorities, women and children, and the urban and rural poor often have drastically limited access to the health care system. National newspapers suggest that they are diagnosed later, are cared for less effectively, and die sooner than their economically and sociologically advantaged neighbors. Even the middle-class, educated, initially employed and well-insured person with AIDS is likely to experience some level of poverty when benefits are lost while living or dying with AIDS. But the disparities of AIDS care do not simply reflect the socioeconomic makeup of the sufferers. In significant ways, AIDS care and services continue to reflect the prejudices and social values of the particular communities, states, and regions in which an individual is affected by the disease.

Recently there has been a growing tendency in the media and among some politicians to compare AIDS funding with funding for cancer, Alzheimer's, or other diseases, often with the spoken or implied suggestion that people with those other illnesses are more innocent, more deserving, or more in keeping with mainstream society's values. While the gay and lesbian community's efforts have been valiant, over time the needs for care, services, and advocacy for many different populations have continued to explode while resources have grown more scarce. Throughout the Reagan and Bush administrations, the political climate around AIDS has remained essentially hostile, and the funding environment has become increasingly more competitive. Research for treatment, development of a vaccine, medical intervention for the acutely ill, palliative care for the dying, support for the newly diagnosed, psychiatric care and supervision of those with dementia, housing for the homeless and food for the hungry, family services for the newly orphaned, and social services and pastoral care for all affected by the disease—these components of AIDS care compete for funding in what really should be a comprehensive and complementary system of holistic care.

AIDS is but one more devastating wrinkle in the midst of countless social problems in the United States today. State and national governments fail to address the need for programs of health insurance for all, even as AIDS care increasingly demonstrates that there are two radically different health-care systems in the United States: one for the rich and insured, the other for the poor and uninsured or underinsured. Some of our finest hospitals are in serious financial trouble because AIDS has become the straw that is breaking the health care camel's back. Municipal hospitals already overburdened before the onset of AIDS are now facing disaster. Access to hospital beds becomes more scarce, and in some neighborhoods, waits in the emergency room stretch into week-long ordeals. The uninsured may be turned away, referred to understaffed "free" clinics, or left undiagnosed or inadequately treated. While some more prosperous AIDS patients have access to new treatments and medications, poor patients frequently receive only a bare minimum level of care. Medical, counseling, and other social services, including housing, are frequently denied to the poor, especially to adolescents, whose age and status cause them to fall through the cracks in the system.[3]

Around the nation, the prison system, already overloaded and overcrowded, is failing to provide care to those infected with AIDS or precautions for those in danger of infection. A conspiracy of silence often surrounds the drug use and unsafe sexual behavior that continue within the prison walls. Drugs are often available, but clean needles are not. Condoms are frequently considered illegal by prison officials, who may base decisions upon moral idealism rather than upon what puts people at risk, including wives and other sex partners during conjugal visits. Those who are infected may even be released or paroled into the care of families who do not understand the disease or onto the streets, where they join the ranks of the homeless.

In 1989, the Coalition for the Homeless in New York City estimated that at least eight-thousand homeless people were infected with the AIDS virus in New York City alone, including not only former prisoners but addicts, the deinstitutionalized mentally ill, teenage runaways, and some who had simply fallen on hard times. Such a statistic does not begin to reflect the "invisible" homeless: families who live daily with severe overcrowding due to lack of available and affordable housing, shortfalls in income, and life catastrophes such as fires, urban violence, and family illness.

The HIV/AIDS education process, usually targeted at gay males, has created a multitude of problems for women, especially those in less affluent communities. Often women with detectable symptoms have gone undiagnosed when physicians have failed to consider them HIV-related. Ironically, the issue of abortion also arises for women who are pregnant and infected. Some who do not wish to abort are coerced or urged to do so, though only some babies are actually infected with the HIV virus during pregnancy.[4] When their mothers become seriously ill or die from AIDS, "boarder babies" are left in institutions, orphans are left in the custody of unprepared relatives, and overwhelmed aged grandparents are left caring for infants as well as their sometimes previously estranged adult children.

AIDS: An Epidemic of Poverty

Many commentators and preachers continue to categorize AIDS as a "gay disease," though increasingly—on the East Coast and in a growing number of other metropolitan and rural areas—it is an epidemic of poverty. It is an epidemic compounded by society's racism and transmitted through behaviors related to drug use, through all kinds of sexual relations, and through the birth of babies to already infected mothers. Though no community is exempt from the impact of AIDS, the epidemic has had and will continue to have a particularly devastating effect on the people, the creativity, and the vitality of our cities, where a disturbingly large proportion of African American and Hispanic men, women, and children have been stricken with this disease. The rapid growth of cases among Asians and Pacific Islanders and among Native Americans, both on and off reservations, exemplifies what happens when ethnic-, language-, and tradition-specific education is not implemented and adequately funded.

The heterosexual transmission of AIDS is still widely ignored by many Americans all too ready to see AIDS as somebody else's problem. Government leaders, educators, and pastors alike have failed to coordinate a massive and comprehensive mobilization toward education for prevention and treatment to stop the genocidal implications of AIDS in the poorer neighborhoods of the United States. Unfortunately, moralistic pronouncements about traditional family values, abstinence from drugs and from nonmonogamous and nonmarital sexual behavior, and "just saying no" have represented the principal strands of educational messages to have emerged from most governmental and religious leaders. There has been widespread resistance to speaking candidly about safer forms of sexual behavior and about the correct use and distribution of condoms to reduce the spread of infection, particularly among adolescents entering an almost inevitably sexually active part of their lives. The risk of AIDS infection for teenagers and young adults who are exploring their sexuality and experimenting with drugs represents the next wave of the epidemic, especially within communities already heavily affected by alcohol, drug addiction, and AIDS. This is a wave whose statistics may not manifest themselves for nearly another decade, given the long incubation period of HIV infection.

Some communities and their officials that I am aware of have actually tried to forbid the distribution of explicit AIDS-education materials in the language of the streets. In several cities, campaigns to teach addicts about cleaning their needles and "works" with bleach have encountered a wave of indignant condemnation even as the infection rate of the addicted, their sexual partners, and their babies continues to rise at an alarming rate. The gay community in the United States and in parts of Western Europe represents one of the few social sectors in which massive AIDS education seems actually to have curbed the spread of the disease, at least for a time.

The Failure of the Church to Respond

The church, once a force for quality health care in the United States, appears to have divested itself of such a role. It seems to have little interest and even less influence in the health-care arena, which seems at times to be dominated by profit-making institutional bureaucracies and misguided government regulations.

Although a decade has passed since U.S. society was first confronted with the AIDS crisis, many churches have remained strikingly ineffectual, not recognizing the extent to which the epidemic mirrors the broader problem of our culture: poverty.

Some voices within the churches have asked, When will we stand up and truly join hands in compassionate response to the AIDS crisis? When will we speak out for those who cannot speak for themselves? When will we rise up in behalf of those whom many in our society would condemn to death? In some sectors of the churches, in some denominations, in some regions of the country, in some parishes and judicatories, the "gay-identified" or "gay-sympathetic" clergy and laity have been left almost alone in the forefront of AIDS care-giving. Many clergy have held back from genuine pastoral involvement—even from involvement with the troubled or bereaved families of people with AIDS.

As long as one's own parishioners are not directly affected, such indifference in terms of caring and education for prevention is perhaps understandable, but it is surely shortsighted in terms of the human and financial costs that face us as a nation dealing with the AIDS epidemic for decades to come. More difficult to comprehend is the response of some churches in communities heavily impacted by AIDS, when the clergy and parishes stand in judgment, casting, perhaps, a few stones of moralistic condemnation.

Whatever the causes of church indifference or noninvolvement with people with AIDS, there remain many religious leaders who see pastoral care in the AIDS crisis as either one last opportunity for condemnation of the sinful or as one brief occasion for simple kindness toward the soon dead. Most clergy have missed the complexity and nuances of AIDS and its diverse sufferers. AIDS is not only about dying, it is about living with an often brutal disease that may span many years of an individual's life. AIDS is about "the worried well" and the HIV-antibody positive. AIDS is about healing and support for people continuing to work and play as they live with AIDS and about the need for hospice-type services for those who are dying from it. AIDS is about hemophiliacs and transfusion recipients, women and children, prisoners and prostitutes. AIDS can be about disfigurement and dementia, about hunger and homelessness, about depression and despair. AIDS is too often about rejection and neglect by families, friends, employers, or health and social-service workers. AIDS, too often, has been about rejection and neglect by our churches and our clergy.

Why cannot the AIDS crisis be the motivation for seeing drug use not as a symptom of individual moral failure but rather as a syndrome of societal breakdown? Why is education about drugs and sex taboo or low priority in our churches and schools and on the agendas of local, state, and federal government? Why are drug treatment programs so scarce, so underfunded, so inaccessible? Is it time to legalize and regulate drugs, rather than to continue to pursue failed policies of prohibition and criminalization? Could people, money, and resources then be redeployed toward education and treatment? Can the churches do more than moralize in the arena of addictions? Can we see addiction not as a symptom of depravity but as a sign of spiritual brokenness in a troubled world?

The Church's Potential for Constructive Response

We can, however, be encouraged that a growing number of churches, both at the denominational and parish levels, have in fact responded to the AIDS crisis in diverse and essentially positive ways. Several denominations have developed educational materials directed toward the young about drugs, sex, and AIDS. A variety of religious leaders have promulgated statements and preached sermons calling for care and compassion for all who are affected by AIDS. Around the country, clergy have responded with sensitive pastoral care, and lay-people have enrolled as lay pastoral care-givers, as hospital and hospice volunteers, and as friendly visitors or "buddies" in secular and religious AIDS service organizations. Churches have played a role in developing comprehensive AIDS services in communities, in providing meals and housing for those in need, and in making space available for programs that serve people affected by AIDS. Somewhat less forcefully, the churches have sometimes also been heard in the public square calling for a more effective and more compassionate response from government in terms of funding for research and medical and social programs.

But clearly the churches can and should do more. In October 1989, the Rev. Connie Hartquist, Episcopal chaplain at San Francisco General Hospital, addressed the National Episcopal AIDS Coalition meeting in Cincinnati. She reported that she had been proposing to parishes where she did AIDS education that they might designate themselves as "AIDS-friendly congregations." Although she had received few takers on her proposition, she said that her vision encompassed a parish that recognized its call to pastoral servanthood to all affected by the disease, its call to effective education for prevention, and its call to be a prophetic voice in troubled times. Pastoral servanthood would serve as a model of inclusivity and compassion that would be antidotal to the judgmental voices raised by certain representatives of the church in the midst of the AIDS crisis.

The vision of an "AIDS-friendly congregation" seems a powerful model for fighting AIDS in the city. Such a congregation would be hospitable to those who suffer, to those who grieve, and to those who struggle. It would require courageous and well-informed clergy and lay leadership. These days of AIDS epidemic are not the occasion for knee-jerk activism but rather a time for education and discernment. When should the parish start a particular AIDS ministry? When might it network with other religious or community groups? When could it deploy its people into already existing programs? When does it recognize that at a particular moment its energies must go into caring for the sick, the dying, and the bereaved in its midst?

People may need assurances about the safety of the common cup at Communion. Parishioners may need to be educated and reeducated about how AIDS is transmitted: by intimate sexual contact and shared needles, not by casual social relations or care-giving in which proper precautions are taken. In time, people may be ready to discuss the more difficult theological and ethical issues of human sexuality and addiction that inevitably arise when they being to listen to the stories and understand the pain of people living and dying with AIDS. Even parishes and individuals that initially resist embracing a compassionate response will likely be converted when they begin to experience relationship with people affected by AIDS. But will they and their leaders be ready when the need for care arises in their very midst? AIDS is not somebody else's problem; it's everyone's problem. As one button puts it, "Our church has AIDS."

AIDS has been in our midst for more than a decade. When will we open our eyes and see? When will we open our ears and hear? When will we open our mouths and speak the gospel language of love, truth, and justice in the midst of this grave human crisis?

The Rev. William A. Doubleday is associate professor of pastoral theology and director of field education, the General Theological Seminary, New York.

Suki Terada Ports is director of the Family Health Project, New York, and member of the board of directors, the National Minority AIDS Council.

Notes

1. Ryan White and Ann M. Cunningham, *Ryan White: My Own Story* (New York: Dial Books, 1991).

2. "AIDS: The Economic Trauma," *South: Emerging World Review*, no. 123 (June/July 1991): 12.

3. *AIDS in Children, Adolescents and Heterosexual Adults: An Interdisciplinary Approach to Prevention*, ed. Raymond F. Schinazi and Andre J. Nahmias (New York: Elsevier Science Publishing, 1988).

4. Ronald Bayer, "Perinatal Transmission of HIV Infection: The Ethics of Prevention," in *AIDS and the Health Care System*, ed. Lawrence O. Gostin (New Haven, Conn.: Yale University Press, 1990), p. 69.

Part Four

Case Studies
of Congregations
and Education for Ministry

The church has always understood the power of a story. Jesus taught through the telling of stories. Today when we read the gospel we are invited into new worlds of faithfulness and hope through the stories from our Jewish and Christian beginnings. Preachers preach using narrative, and teachers teach through illustrations from real life. Real stories, ones teeming with the passion and power of everyday life, are remembered and stored away in our hearts. Such stories become resources for the creating of new visions for our lives.

Case studies are a bit like stories, for in these illustrations of churches and educational programs, we are invited to see new possibilities for our institutions, given the challenges faced by the church today. These are "ways in the wilderness" of our cities today (see Isa. 43:19). The stories tell something about what these folks have discovered while on that journey.

Local Ministries and Church-Based Community Organizing

Mary Lou Porrata and the members of the San Lucas UCC church in Chicago know that they must hold onto a vision, yet they—like many urban residents—dwell and labor in the midst of a setting where people are often denied the resources to dream. However, as members of a faithful community, they know well the text: Where there is no vision, the people perish (Prov. 29:18, KJV). Porrata shares the story of her urban Chicago congregation and stimulates a new vision for the church in the city. Urban missioner Sam Appel describes the hellish life of the inner city of Camden, New Jersey, and a model for authentic urban ministry there. David C. Bloom reminds us that the renewal of urban life calls on the witness of faith in our cities. A brief incident in the life of downtown Seattle illustrates the power of prayer and gospel word as church folks work together in the city. All three of these case studies of urban ministry describe challenges, struggles, and victories of church-based community organizing, a method for ministry aimed at revitalizing churches, people's lives, and their communities.

Theological Education and the Preparation for Public Ministry

The institutions of theological education must develop curriculum and methodology to prepare the future leaders of the church. A seminary education today should include the teaching of a method for ministering in settings such as those described in this book, a pastoral and healing ministry in urban communities where most of the U.S. population resides. Leaders in theological education today are working to address what is called the "globalization" of the seminaries, pulling them toward the year 2000 and out of the stereotypical, narrow, Anglo and male models of theology and church. In the future of the Christian church, "white" is but one of the stripes in a racial-ethnic rainbow, with a wide variety of cultures and traditions to enhance the vitality of Christian spirituality and community. The new pluralism present in the United States puts the old mainline church and its educational programs on notice: Change or your institutions will die while others take up the worship and mission of the church of Jesus Christ.

The case studies of theological education presented here attempt to give some direction to these processes of institutional change. We globalize our educational institutions and programs when the content and methods we use in teaching and learning give voice to the contributions and issues raised by those outside the traditional structures of the institutional church and dominant structures of society. Glenda Hope and Penny Sarvis introduce the problems encountered in developing an on-site alternative education program for seminary students in San Francisco. Tex Sample introduces us to the "cultural right," whose adherents constitute a major segment of any urban church, and helps us think about how to prepare ministerial leaders who can share ministry with this cultural group in the United States. And Lynn Rhodes and Nancy Richardson lay out the theoretical structures for an educational program integrated with the context of ministry—their strategy for effective ministerial preparation in the city and elsewhere.

It is our hope that the strategies and processes of *Envisioning the New City* will find their way into the agendas of both churches and seminaries. We need a new "job description" for the work and worship of the church today if our cities and those who reside there—more than three-fourths of our nation's population—are to survive. If our cities and their constituencies are not healed, everyone, everywhere is put at risk. The needs are urgent; the time is now. The church cannot abandon the cities without abandoning its faithful call to be the church. We must take this uncharted journey with courage, knowledge, determination, celebration, and faith.

E.S.M.

Local Ministry and Church-Based Community Organizing

• 22 •

SAN LUCAS: *PRESENTE!*

Mary Lou Porrata

San Lucas is a small Hispanic United Church of Christ congregation in the Humboldt Park community of Chicago. There are approximately seventy or seventy-five members, but usual Sunday morning attendance is between forty and sixty. San Lucas was founded in the late 1970s with the express purpose of being *presente* in the community; it is not only a house of spiritual worship and prayer on Sundays but a place where the rhythm of worship goes on all week long. People come and go daily, bringing and defining needs, searching for and finding resources.

When San Lucas sought a permanent home, it settled upon an area facing the northern edge of the two-hundred-acre Humboldt Park, which, since the early 1960s, the Puerto Rican people have been proud to claim. This area was the scene of riots in the 1960s and '70s, and today it is the site of innumerable episodes of violence and crime, often drug-related. But Humboldt Park also is an area of recreation and a place where community bonding happens among the residents in the Hispanic neighborhoods that surround it.

This is where San Lucas staked out its claim by purchasing an old three-story building that already had a community history, some of it unknown. When the congregation, led by its pastor, Jorge Morales, bought it, the Puerto Rican community knew it only as the Polish Veterans' Hall. Many remember dances and celebrations of relatives' receptions there. A bar still in the back of the sanctuary stood as a reminder of its former use.

Thus, from the start, context and commitment were clear.

The congregation was intended to be a vital part of the wider community, present in body, mind, soul, and spirit. Social action and programs offering a variety of ministries to spiritual and physical needs have put this commitment into action over the years. Reasonably stable and expanding only slowly throughout its first twelve years, the congregation has remained remarkably true to its calling.

San Lucas: A Small Church

San Lucas readily fits a number of characterizations of small churches as outlined by Carl Dudley.[1] For example, the congregation loves to celebrate its Puerto Rican culture, especially through food—eating is a true cultural-social event. I tell students who visit our church, "You'll find out we love to eat together!" Communion, the first Sunday of every month, is always followed by a meal. Easter morning and afternoon services include a potluck meal; Mother's Day, Father's Day, and Memorial Day Sunday all include a meal or picnic in the park. Monthly special activities such as bowling/pizza night and family night include a communal meal. Thursday evening Bible studies held in homes are always concluded with coffee and snacks. When I hesitate to ask families on public assistance to host Bible study because of the hardship of providing food for the occasion, I must remind myself that to suggest we forgo the post-study snack would be insulting.

Along with eating, special events are important for the small church. Every occasion is turned into an event, some of which now have become traditions: producing the Christmas drama "Martin the Cobbler," Epiphany gift-giving every Three Kings' Day, dramatizing the resurrection story every Easter. And naturally, the major events—Communion Sunday, Good Friday, Christmas Day, baptisms and the reception of new members—constitute highlights on San Lucas's church calendar.

These are the important regular events, but there are equally important anniversaries of onetime events that are also regularly celebrated: our move from Armitage Street to North Avenue and the transformation of the Veterans' hall into a sanctuary (including the discovery of beautiful boarded-up stained glass windows and a baptistry under the large stage), the founding of the youth center, and a demonstration against Post Office hiring policies.

The celebration of event after event was overwhelming at first—I wondered if we would ever be free of planning for major events so we could get on with the church's regular business. But I've come to recognize that celebrating events important to the life of the church and its people is an integral part of the worship cycle.

People are the most important ingredient of a church's makeup. This is especially true for our small church. Some folks attend services two or three times a year; they are warmly greeted when there and accepted as family even when not there. Others attend sporadically and are accepted either way, while the "regulars" have their accustomed places in the sanctuary and are very much missed when not there. For this "regular" group, "How are you?" is more than just a greeting. People know that Cecilia, one of the founding mothers of the church, has not been well, not only because of the way she answers the greeting but also because of her unusually subdued behavior during worship. We also know that when there is time for prayer petitions, Cristina will always share several family needs with the group.

Sometimes the in-group feeling described above wears thin. People know too much about each other—a typical small-church phenomenon. They are impatient with each other and become easily irritated over the idiosyncracies of the others. The group is intimate and closely knit, but intimacy and confidentiality sometimes erupt in conflict, which can threaten to be destructive. How to transform this potential for destruction into constructive energy remains a challenge.

San Lucas: A Relational Church

The San Lucas congregation displays and lives out a relational faith as opposed to a rigorous faith. The people belong naturally to the church body. While "belonging" may be a difficult process because it's hard for a new person to break into the small, close group, theoretically anyone can belong through baptism or transfer of membership. One doesn't prove oneself through a whole list of right doctrines, strict adherence to a predefined creed, or a designated conversion moment. One is part of the church family because one wants to be and because one shares a common faith. In fact, actual membership is rarely a valid criterion for whether one really belongs or participates. Some very dear "members" are not members at all!

The San Lucas congregation is made up of all the individuals and their needs, and all are important because they belong to the family in one way or another. Over the years, many people have come because they have been cared for and prayed for. In short, San Lucas has taken on a culturally comfortable, people-oriented relational style rather than an ordered, impersonal, directional, ambition-oriented style.

San Lucas: A Church that Combines Faith and Action

San Lucas doesn't fit easily into a neat slot. We are not a church open for Sunday morning worship only, nor are we a one-dimensional community organization. Our specific intent has been to combine faith and action as a faithful living out of the gospel. As a member of the mainline United Church of Christ denomination, San Lucas describes itself in the following way:

The San Lucas United Church of Christ is an evangelical church and a community of believers that believe it necessary that faith be maintained through action. This congregation celebrates the grace of God in its life in victory over sin and all the oppressive forces that try to dehumanize the people of God.

. . . We have been called to be witness of the love, power and justice of God. Our ministry is directed to make an impact not only on the lives of individuals [but] also on institutions and power structures. Our ministry extends to the community in the organizations we have created to serve the people.[2]

As I have participated in carrying out this mission, I have felt a bit of ambiguity as to where to place the church on H. Richard Niebuhr's Christ–culture continuum. Perhaps it

best fits as a Christ-*in*-culture church, an area located somewhere between Niebuhr's "Christ above culture" and "Christ,
transformer of culture." San Lucas is a

synthesis . . . [of the] willing and intelligent cooperation of Christians with nonbelievers in carrying on the work of the world, while
yet maintaining the distinctiveness of Christian faith and life.[3]

Yet San Lucas goes a step beyond this synthesis into experiencing Christ as transformer. Emphasis is not only on our responsibility to the whole community but also on the fact that Jesus
Christ makes the difference in our individual lives and how we
live. Although the church practices infant baptism and confir-
mation of youth, there is not the traditional talk about an evangelical "conversion." Sermons and Bible study often include the
concept that a choice to follow Christ means an openness to his
redeeming work in our lives, something that should change or
"convert" us in comparison to how others live.

Practical details about exactly what this change entails are
not usually spelled out, however, and there are no church rules
such as prohibition of divorce, drinking, or smoking, or adherence to dress code. There is no feeling of horror toward or
withdrawal from the cultural environment that other, more
radical positions might require; there is belief that in the deepest spirit of each person, Christ dwells, loving and forgiving,
making a difference, even protecting one in the midst of all the
surrounding tragedies.[4]

Furthermore, there is a strong sense that without this personal transforming Christ who is on my side, I would not make
it. Doña Carmen, for example, has repeatedly thanked God
fervently for faithfulness and answers to prayer even though
her welfare check covers so little of her actual needs; even
when her adult daughter's brain tumor puts her in the hospital
once more; even though that daughter's death, whenever it
occurs, will leave Carmen with four young grandchildren to
care for or parcel out; even when her son, recently jailed for
drug trafficking, is sentenced to two-and-a-half years in
prison.

Can the gospel at San Lucas be divided into a social gospel
and a spiritual gospel? Not so readily! For us, the gospel is good

news in a bad-news situation. The good news is not only that there is heaven down the road for those who believe but also that the kingdom is at work right now, bringing hope and justice and change. It is a single message. At San Lucas, we cannot preach revival unless it also works for justice and relief from oppression.

San Lucas leans, then, toward a social gospel perspective. Our mission is in reaching out to community needs and concerns and in joining with other organizations in the struggle against the injustices of the system, particularly against the poor and minority groups. This isn't simply a humanitarian mission to one's fellow humans; it is a result of Christ's gospel: His followers are commanded to follow him in feeding the hungry and freeing the oppressed—in short, in carrying out the kingdom of God on earth. San Lucas would lose its particular mission if it were to become only another community development organization or only another storefront gospel church. Faith and action continue to be held in critical and creative tension at San Lucas. Faith without action is dead. And action without faith is only humanitarian service. San Lucas is called to be unique: to promote well-being, to struggle for justice for all, to provide pastoral care to encourage people, to be the embodiment of God's Spirit in this place.

"San Lucas *Presente*": Guiding Symbols

Presente.   There could not have been a better word chosen to symbolize what San Lucas has been about ever since its first worship services were held in February 1977. The church was founded to be *presente* in the community, not only as a house of spiritual worship and prayer on Sundays but as a house where worship occurs all week long: community people coming and going daily, bringing needs, and finding resources.

Community.   Second only to the word *presente* as a symbol for San Lucas, and in very close connection to it, is the word *community.* San Lucas is closely tied to the community in which it is located. The Puerto Rican community is relatively new in the Humboldt Park area, having arrived in the area in the early 1960s. They have already established a strong sense of pride and ownership in the area. Although other Hispanics are present in both the community and the San Lucas congregation, Puerto Ricans make up the largest concentration.

San Lucas was born to take a stand in its community and to take risks. People in the community take a holistic view of ministry, and the church's doors are open daily with activities for youth, advocacy work, an anti-hunger network, and other programs. In 1978, Central Unidad Latina, a youth center, was founded by San Lucas and community residents. It is housed in the church basement and in other spaces as well for its various tutoring, cultural, educational, and recreational programs for community youth.

Although continuing to be small in numbers, the congregation has spoken out about large-scale community issues such as equal employment opportunities, police brutality, infant mortality, hunger, welfare advocacy, and housing. The congregation has worked on other national and international issues such as nuclear arms, Central American policy, assistance to refugees, and immigration laws. We admit, though, that it's hard to take positions with the larger problems while nearly drowning in our own local issues.

The sanctuary.   Even the arrangement of the sanctuary itself is an in-house attempt to work out the emphasis on community. The benches form a semicircle focusing on the pulpit and Communion table. The Communion table used to be brought out only on the monthly Communion Sundays, but now it is a permanent part of the sanctuary. There is a sense that the people are called to gather around the table to participate and worship.

The wooden cross behind the altar was made by hand by several people in the church soon after the church was opened. It represents a personal contribution of time, talent, and resources on the part of church community members, but it also represents a church that, at that time, had no money to buy a cross. Most of the furnishings have been donated by the larger church community.

A trip several years ago to visit churches in Nicaragua led me to make another important change in the sanctuary. At the time the pulpit was on the highest level of the platform, but I was able to win the congregation's vote to have it physically lowered to the level of the sanctuary. We used this issue as an educational event for the congregation, to help break down some of the mystical construal of the pastor as a high priest over the people, standing between them and God. The move demonstrated solidarity with some of the more revolutionary churches in Nicaragua and especially signified a sense of community and oneness between all people, including between clergy and laypeople.

Balance.   Since the very beginning, there has been at San Lucas an emphasis on maintaining a balance between spiritual ministry and outreach, "faith" and "action" as stated above. The church was founded about the same time as the West Town Coalition, a grassroots community organization, but from the start the congregation felt that the church was to be different from the coalition. Several organizations existed to promote change in the city, but San Lucas has maintained its distinct identity apart from the community action groups.

This difference is symbolized in three banners made by the women of the church. The first banner is of a scale balancing faith and action. And lest there be doubt that faith was as important as action, the second banner depicts David dancing before the Lord, placing emphasis on worship. A third banner represents the women's group itself. It includes the words *Christian Women in Action* and emphasizes cultural aspects of the Puerto Rican community. All three banners are prominently displayed in the front of the sanctuary, along with a fourth banner: "San Lucas—Friendship, Community."

In San Lucas's quest for continuing ministry in the Humboldt Park–West Town community areas, it must maintain constant awareness of this need for balance. Some do not find spiritual depth here because the church is too issue-conscious and action-oriented. Too little emphasis is placed, they say, on Christian education, faith development, and discipleship. But others who would not ordinarily attend service in a traditional church feel at home at San Lucas. Their desire for a lived-out gospel is met through the church's espousal of social action ministries throughout the community.

San Lucas, the name.   Finally, there is much in a name, and "San Lucas" (St. Luke) was not chosen randomly. Luke was not a follower of Jesus in only a spiritual sense; he was also a doctor, a healer. In his Gospel account he seems to take more notice of the despised and the outcast and of Jesus' response to them than do any of the other Gospel writers. Luke takes note of Jesus' inclusion of women among his disciples (chapter 8) as well as of other recognition and acceptance of women. San Lucas takes pride in following that model by being the first Hispanic United Church of Christ congregation to have a Hispanic woman as pastor.

Only Luke records Jesus' sense of mission and completion of Old Testament prophecy (chapter 4) to preach the good news to the poor and the captives. Likewise, only Luke records Jesus' trip, at the age of twelve, to the temple where he confronted the teachings and questions of the religious elders. For San Lucas, this story provides ample evidence for an important emphasis on ministry to our youth.

San Lucas *Presente*: How Do We Do It?

In answering this question, we can only go by our own experience. Leadership, networking, and advocacy are the ingredients helping us realize our ministry. These ingredients are essential to all ministries and must be present as part of the transforming process as we all participate in the building of the kingdom.

Leadership.   The Bible is full of examples of the need for leadership training. Several notable instances show Moses turning over the leadership to Joshua (Deuteronomy 31ff.), Paul nurturing Timothy (2 Timothy), and Priscilla and Aquilla taking Apollos aside to instruct him more accurately (Acts 18:26). Belief, conviction, and commitment were crucial to these leaders, and it was important that their successors also develop these qualities for themselves. To do so, they needed instruction and guidance.

People need to be prepared; we do not learn well or remain committed in complete isolation. At the same time, individuals carry a lot of resources already within them, and the church must be creative in finding ways to develop those resources. Teaching, encouraging, challenging, preaching, modeling relationships, playing, sharing experiences are all part of the nurturing process. The goal is for individuals to develop their own inner qualities so they are prepared to meet with strength the various situations with which they will surely be faced. At San Lucas we encourage people in the area to become leaders in their families, churches, and communities.

Networking.   San Lucas does not pretend to carry out the mission in the community by itself. I have marvelled at the wisdom of the congregation in bonding together with other churches and organizations because there is strength in numbers and because cooperative efforts are often better than single-handed attempts. The Humboldt Park Ministerial Association is one concrete result of such networking. The Hispanic churches in the area have not always worked together. The numerous Pentecostal churches differ quite radically in theology from many other denominations and tend to be more isolated in their activities. In 1984, however, ninety-four citywide gang-related deaths brought Humboldt Park ministers together over a common cause that concerned them all: the lives and safety of their people, particularly the youth. Out of this the Ministerial Association was formed. Through its influence and that of other concerned groups, CIN (Chicago Intervention Network) was formed.

Other networks also exist. The Center for Community and Leadership Development (formerly the Center for Theological Education) was begun out of San Lucas, but in cooperation with numerous other groups. It serves as a resource and training center for various churches and other organizations in the area.

Similarly, the Anti-Hunger Network is a cooperative effort

of area churches to provide centrally located distribution points for food, clothing, and a variety of services and to coordinate the hours each location is open. In this network, San Lucas does referrals and advocacy with the State Department of Public Aid and other programs.

Within our network program we developed a concern about inadequate distribution of commodities. After many consultations with Illinois Department of Pubic Aid officials from both city and state levels, the local network got the contract to distribute food commodities for this area. A larger group of thirty-five churches is involved in this aspect of the Anti-Hunger Network.

The West Town–Humboldt Park Infant Mortality Reduction Initiative programs and the Monsignor Romero Christian Center, which works with Central American refugees, are other current examples of San Lucas's instrumentality in beginning programs in cooperation with other churches or agencies. In addition, San Lucas members represent the church on boards or councils of various other community programs such as Centro Unidad Latina, Public Aid Advisory, Interfaith Council for the Homeless, University of Illinois Cooperative Extension Service Advisory, and others.

In these ways, San Lucas holds hands with others around its community, forming a network that attempts to shrink the gaps through which too many people have slipped unnoticed in the past.

Advocacy. San Lucas serves as a connecting link. We pride ourselves on being the one church in the Anti-Hunger Network that does referrals and advocacy. The church itself doesn't have all the answers, but we have good connections and will get people in touch with groups we have been instrumental in forming or with other agencies with which we have contact.

Advocacy does not remove control of the situation from those people in need. Rather, it connects people to available resources and stands beside them in the struggle for justice. It is a step toward empowerment: giving people the resources to permit them to take control over their own destiny.

"Where There Is No Vision, the People Perish" (Prov. 29:18, KJV).

At San Lucas, God is recognized as immanent, not distant and removed. God is *presente* in the daily lives of all our parishioners. God cares in the midst of the suffering. The people of San Lucas are broken people; none of them has been spared from the hardest knocks of life. Neither is any one member of the church perfect; nor does one member have all the answers for anyone else. In fact, there are sometimes serious conflicts within the church body, among members and leaders, even with outside groups. These conflicts at times threaten San Lucas's sense of balance and its ability to serve. A sense of futility sometimes creeps in as we fight the injustices of being a minority group in a domineering society.

But in the midst of this near hopelessness and anger there is a commitment and a flame of hope. Shared hopelessness in a faith community takes on a dimension not available elsewhere. Hopelessness—unless it disintegrates in despair—can spur hopeful people to action. Although instant resolutions are rare, people participate and offer what they have. And God's Spirit is there.

My experience is that Sunday morning worship is the highlight of our week. It is the time to formally acknowledge and give praise for God's constant presence among us. Though worship follows a liturgical form, it includes spontaneity and creativity. Singing with piano and tambourine, clapping and moving, celebrating our joys and sharing our sorrows, needing and receiving, giving to each other in the presence of God— that is what San Lucas is about.

We will go only as far as we see. If we do not prepare that vision as individuals and within our congregation, we will cease to move ahead. The church must impart this vision to its people. The church must be prophetic about its mission in today's urban situation. These prophetic words will not necessarily be easy words to hear or live out, but if the church can offer meaning and belonging and purpose to its people, it will continue to carry on and grow. Where people are challenged to commit themselves, even sacrifice for what they believe, they will be *presente* to each other as God is *presente* to each of us. San Lucas will continue in the struggle.

The Rev. Mary Lou Porrata, a former community organizer and a seminary graduate, is pastor of the San Lucas United Church of Christ in the West Town–Humboldt Park community of Chicago.

Notes

1. Carl S. Dudley, *Making the Small Church Effective* (Nashville: Abingdon Press, 1983).

2. Excerpt taken from the current statement of faith of the San Lucas United Church of Christ in Chicago.

3. H. Richard Niebuhr, *Christ and Culture* (New York: Harper & Brothers, 1951), pp. 143–144.

4. Ibid., p. 190.

• 23 •

AN ECUMENICAL APPROACH
TO URBAN MINISTRY

David C. Bloom

On a Tuesday in April of last year, one hundred people from local churches, community groups, and the local service employees union met for a noontime prayer service in downtown Seattle. The service was in the multilevel atrium of one of the city's largest bank buildings, surrounded by upscale boutiques and restaurants. The coalescing issue that had brought this diverse crowd together was economic justice. Downtown building owners and maintenance companies were attempting to force the fifteen hundred janitors for the offices in Seattle's booming, high-rise commercial core to accept a new labor contract with significant wage and benefit cuts.

About half of the janitors were minorities. About half were women. Many had families. On the average, their incomes were just above the official poverty level. They were being asked to accept a contract that would have placed many of them near or even below the poverty level. They were the working poor. They had few allies. The prayer service was an attempt by the religious community to provide a conspicuous demonstration of public support for the janitors—on the business community's own turf. As hundreds of office workers on their lunch hour looked on, the participants prayed together, sang hymns, heard the biblical word of justice, and listened to the testimony of the janitors themselves.

Ultimately, the contract issue was settled favorably for the janitors. The fifteen Protestant, Catholic, and Jewish clergy who had convened the prayer service had also met with building owners, written letters that were published in the daily newspapers, attended workers' rallies, and encouraged their congregations to give support to the janitors. The president of the service employees union, in thanking the churches, spoke of the effectiveness of their ecumenical effort:

The religious community was an essential element of our success. By defining the building owners' efforts to impoverish local janitors as a moral issue, and one of concern to the community as a whole, Seattle's religious community sent the building owners a message that their efforts were an attack on the community as a whole and its moral standards.

The religious community's work on the janitors' issue demonstrates both the importance and the effectiveness of developing ecumenical strategies for urban ministry. When religious leaders spoke as a group, the building owners, unaccustomed to being challenged, were forced to listen; the issue was aired in public; and the workers were supported. Even more important, the church was perceived as speaking with one voice, not several—or worse, not at all. The moral issue of economic justice for the working poor—an issue of growing concern in cities across the country as the prevalence of low-paying service-sector jobs increases—was set in bold relief against the backdrop of the growing affluence of Seattle's business community. The public articulation of God's vision of hope and justice for the people of the city actually made news.

Another example of ecumenical activity has been the growth of community-based ministries that have been organized to provide emergency relief through feeding programs, shelters for the homeless, and financial assistance for rent and utility bills to out-of-work or underemployed families. At least ten such ecumenical ministries have formed in the Seattle area since the late 1970s to assist local congregations in responding more effectively to the growing human need in their communities. Some of these groups have also been effective in pushing for local public policy changes to benefit low-income people.

There is considerable evidence that our experience in Seattle is not unique. David Bos of St. Matthews Area Ministry in Lou-

isville, Kentucky, has tracked the community ministry movement and in 1989 estimated that there were more than five
hundred such ministries across the United States. Most developed in the 1980s. Those of us in the Church Council of
Greater Seattle have recognized the value of such urban ministry:

- It provides a more diverse and comprehensive forum for the
  identification of critical community concerns.
- It provides a broader base and an important catalyst for organizing around those concerns.
- It draws on the numerical strength and the collective wisdom and experience of several congregations at once.
- It increases the opportunities for church members and
  neighborhood residents to experience the reality of community.
- It empowers people at the local level to take responsibility
  for issues that directly affect their lives and the lives of their
  neighbors.
- It provides a broader platform from which to set forth God's
  vision of justice for the poor, the alienated, and the dispossessed.
- It gives visible and tangible expression to the unity of the
  church.

The continuing and increasing problems of urban poverty,
the resurgence of racial injustice, the destruction of low-
income neighborhoods to make way for urban redevelopment,
the attacks on low-income people in service-related industries,
such as Seattle's janitors—these and other pressing issues confront our cities. It is into this arena that the urban church is
called to proclaim God's vision for the city as a just, inclusive,
and peaceful community. We shall express that vision most
authentically and powerfully when we engage in this ministry
ecumenically.

David C. Bloom is an ordained minister in the American Baptist Church.
He has been associate director for urban ministry for the Council of

Churches of Greater Seattle for the past ten years and has worked for the council for the last fourteen years. He spent eight years in local parish ministry in the Washington, D.C., area. He continues to be involved in a wide range of urban issues.

• 24 •

METROPOLITAN MINISTRY

IN JERSEY GHETTOS

Sam Appel

Urban missioners who are in the church as well as in the world for Christ's sake must take their environment with utmost seriousness.

Walter Rauschenbusch was right when he observed that the original sin he saw in the people of his parish in Hell's Kitchen wasn't inherited: it came from Hell's Kitchen. Our environment is a major factor in determining what happens to us, and the saving of souls has to take environment into consideration. What worries us more than anything else today is the quality of environment both in our great cities and in rural areas hard hit by urbanization. What we are only beginning to realize is that the people who live in favorable circumstances cannot possibly hold fellowship with God unless they are involved in correcting environmental conditions that cripple persons at birth and mutilate them throughout their lives. Anyone who seeks to save his soul without being involved in the conversion of the contemporary cruelty systems is anti-Christian.[1]

Camden: Apartheid American Style

Camden, New Jersey, is an old city, dating from colonial times. In the early part of the twentieth century, the city was a bustling little manufacturing center. It is the home of the Campbell Soup Company and the Radio Corporation of America (now General Electric). Today, very few Camden residents work for Campbell Soup—the plant closed in 1990.

312

General Electric is almost totally involved in defense contracts and employs mostly professional personnel. Camden also once included the New York Ship Yards, Boscul Coffee, Ester-brook Pen Company, Evans Leather, Knox Gelatin, and Standard Tank and Seat. All of these industries have either expired or moved out of Camden.

Today, the largest employers include city and county government and the public school system, and most of the people who work for these entities live outside the city. The majority of Camden's police and firefighters do not reside in the city, nor do most public school teachers. During World War II, Camden boasted a population of 125,000 people, and in 1960 it numbered 117,000. Today the population hovers around 85,000. Most of its white residents have left; the vast majority of residents today are African American and Hispanic. Fully 55 to 60 percent of Camden's citizens are on some kind of governmental subsidy: Aid to Families with Dependent Children, Social Security, Supplemental Security Income, or General Assistance.[2]

In short, in Camden it is apartheid, American style. While the highways carry growing numbers of Porsches, Jaguars, and Mercedeses, buses are also in motion taking the poor to work in jobs that leave them poor. While new condominiums and houses rise in the most luxurious regions of our county at prices of three hundred thousand dollars and more, thousands of Camden residents have no access to decent, affordable housing. The result is a separate and unequal society, one distinguished by income inequality and blatant racism.

Certain institutions that serve so many well are, for the poor, cruelty systems: education, housing, food production, health care, banking, business, church and political structures. For example, our food production system, which ranks among the greatest of U.S. technological advances, is a system that feeds the majority of citizens well, yet imposes hunger on a significant minority. It is the same system for the victors and the victims in the struggle for food, but for the victors it is steak and potatoes while for the victims it is beans without bacon.

Because unemployment and underemployment are consistently high, a permanent underclass is maintained. A large majority of poor people are trapped, especially racial-ethnic folk, the elderly poor, and single women with children, to whom economic justice has been particularly denied. By the late 1970s, religious leaders understood that more than half the children in Camden were living in poverty. By the mid-1980s, Camden leaders were suggesting that that figure had risen to more than 60 percent and were well aware of the fact that around 75 percent of Camden's public school pupils were eligible for a free lunch. The level of poverty in Camden is painfully obvious.

In more ways than one, Camden is a dumping site for the region. The process is called, irreverently, NIMBY—Not in My Backyard. Camden residents have been forced over the years to put up with trash disposal sites, sewage treatment plants, prisons, prostitution, and junk in *our* backyard. Drugs, violence, and crime run rampant in Camden.

In 1963, the Presbytery of West Jersey (a governing body of sixty-five churches in seven counties in southern New Jersey) was prompted to plan for new ways of doing mission in Camden. The Camden Metropolitan Ministry (CMM), a new structure supportive of and supplemental to the work and witness of congregations in the city of Camden, thus began with three ordained missioners on staff, each of whom provided part-time pastoral leadership to three local Presbyterian churches. The CMM was separate from the congregations and provided a way for the Presbytery to be present and prophetic in the metropolitan region. Less than a year after its founding, the ministry had set up permanent headquarters in an old tavern, which served also as a metropolitan training center and as the meeting place for numerous church and community groups. The Presbyterian policy statement that informed our work from the beginning emphasized that our mission would include strategies to stand with and for the poor, the dispossessed, the rejected, the ostracized, the oppressed, whoever and wherever they are in the city.

It was agreed that authentic urban ministry in such an environment would require five essential ingredients if it were to be faithful and effective:

Confession. Confession includes both the admission of our failures and faithlessness and the annunciation of who we are as the people of God. In the case of the CMM, we stated publicly that we were "a mission of the West Jersey Presbytery to the people of the metropolitan area in obedience and witness to Christ's Lordship. We understand our task to be that of discerning, exposing, and sharing Christ's redemptive presence at specific times and places. This task we thankfully and joyfully discharge through a ministry of proclamation, of prophecy, and of service."

Centering on the Word of God. Because the biblical witness is the foundation of urban ministry and is vital to it, we intended to work for the deliverance of those presently held captive by the principalities and powers of this world, to "bind up the brokenhearted" (Isa. 61:1), to "raise up the former devastations" (61:4), to "give a garland instead of ashes" (61:3). We believe that God's agenda compels us to work on behalf of a just community wherein the needs of the poor, the alienated, and the dispossessed are the first priority.

Congregational and metropolitan ministry. We pledged to work with others because no one congregation could command the funds, personnel, facilities, or knowledge to address urban conditions. In the case of CMM, a structure was created so that ministry could work through both congregations and the presbytery. The latter allows staff not only to deal with metropolitan issues that impinge upon the urban center (for example, sewage treatment, trash removal, employment, housing, education) but to tap the resources, both financial and human, or more than thirty-five suburban churches in order to address urban issues.

Coalitional networking. We worked to establish a coalitional network. Working with others who had similar purposes, including those who work outside of the church, would help to assure long-term success.

Church-based community organizing. We viewed organizing as a central function of ministry because it is a way of effectively and powerfully living out our faith in the church and in the city.

The first three ingredients of urban ministry—confession, centering on the Word of God, and a congregational and metropolitan structure—are foundational. The last two, coalitional networking and church-based community organizing, are strategic. They require a somewhat more detailed explanation.

Coalitional Networking for Christ's Sake

Compliments often come in strange ways from strange quarters. In the late '60s a city council member made this bald assertion to Dr. Ulysses S. Wiggins, president of the National Association for the Advancement of Colored People: "Those guys down at CMM, they're communists." The president responded, "Come on now, they're three white, middle-class, Presbyterian clergy. Why do you say that?" The retort: "They're everywhere!"

It seems to me that if we are in the world, in the urban world for Christ's sake, we must be visible, we must be "everywhere!" And to be "everywhere" on behalf of rightness, justice, community and shalom requires us to hook up, to network, to merge, to fuse with others who have similar purposes and are willing, even eager, to unite to achieve those ends.

Little ever happens as a result of exposure unless action is organized. Wherever cities have become a dwelling place for a large number of poor and oppressed people, an urban mission must organize, unite with, and link up with any and all who would address issues and attempt to make profound social change. One reason for the effectiveness of the CMM was its variety of ecclesiastical and secular alliances that together addressed Camden's multitude of problems. This listing of CMM organizations over the years, albeit partial, will demonstrate the extraordinary empowerment potential of coalitions:

- *Ecumenical Program and Outreach Committee* (EPOC)—a coalition of Presbyterians, Baptists, and members of the United Church of Christ committed to responding to racial

strife in Camden. This group sponsored much of the metropolitan training for CMM and served as a crisis network so
that congregations in the city and suburbs could respond
appropriately to events in Camden.

- *South Jersey Religious Leaders*—an interfaith group that conducted seminars on metropolitan issues and initiated and
supported some ecumenical ministries.
- *Inter-Faith, Inter-Racial Council of the Clergy*—a large group
of religious leaders that organized to develop housing for
the working poor in Camden.
- *Protestant Chaplaincy Services Center*—provides and supports three Protestant chaplains at the Camden County
Health Services Center. The Health Services Center provides intermediate care, long-term care, and psychiatric care
for more than a thousand indigent people.
- *Camden County Tutorial Service*—provided tutoring through
suburban and urban volunteers to elementary students in
Camden.
- *Camden Civil Rights Ministerium/Neighborhood Groups Coalition*—filed a sixty-two-page administrative lawsuit with
the Secretary of Housing and Urban Development against
the city of Camden and the Camden Housing Authority,
charging the defendants with an intentional plan of action
aimed at removing African Americans and Puerto Ricans
from the city of Camden.
- *Friends of the Black People's Unity Movement*—a white support group of the Black People's Unity Movement, made up
largely of suburbanites. The group advocated in favor of
concerns and demands for African American economic development, adequate housing and education, and so on.

Similar coalitions address other pressing issues related to
housing, prison reform and assisting recently released prisoners, public education, affirmative action, day care and hunger.

Creating and building coalitions helps the church to advocate with and for the poor and oppressed through direct action. Such coalitions provide a forum for friendships to
develop that go well beyond the barriers of race, sex, religion,
and class. They help the Christian faith to come alive as folks

work together for peace and justice, and they result in victories that can be celebrated.

Living the Faith Through Church-Based Community Organizing

One of the essential structures needed for authentic urban ministry is a church-based community organization. Such a structure is more than a coalition, which can be temporary. Church-based organizing is for the long haul and is by definition living the faith, doing the faith, the church's very reason for existence. It is the manifestation of Emil Brunner's pithy statement that the church "exists by mission as fire exists by burning."[3] In the mid-1960s the CMM brought together representatives of the African American and Hispanic communities to discuss and learn about empowerment through community organizing. The local group agreed in conversation that community organization

- must be, in the fullest sense, democratic and independent; that is, it should allow the people most directly affected to state their own priorities rather than rely on others to state them on their behalf. The organizer would be directly responsible to these people.
- should place a high priority on human values as well as on efficiency, order and technological progress.
- should gather people around issues of the fundamental ills of modern life, particularly the uneven distribution of education, employment, and housing.
- should draw in other organizations to achieve common objectives.
- should seek to be fiscally independent of all outside support, including church support, within two to three years.

Those guidelines were still important to the CMM when in 1982 the Eastern Communities Training Institute (ECTI) was founded to develop and strengthen broad-based community organizations in the Delaware Valley.[4] In early 1984 the board and staff of ECTI decided that the best contribution it could make to the region would be the development of new models of community organizations. Thus, when clergy in Camden asked for the help of ECTI to envision the possibilities for community empowerment, ECTI was interested. Their staff met with interested clergy and laity in Camden and outlined the necessary multiracial and denominational participation required, the financial requirements for at least the first two years, and the city and regional trends upon which such an organization would work to exercise its impact.

A contract was developed between ECTI and seventeen churches, and in the summer of 1985 the Camden Churches Organizing Project (now the Camden Churches Organized for People) was born. The participating congregations celebrated this birth by holding a week of spiritual renewal services. We used the Pentecost story as our scripture and read our covenant each night as part of our liturgy (see appendix). Our worship was centered on the theme, "We Call Camden Back to Life!" Services were held in two Catholic churches (one intentionally urban-suburban white and the other urban Hispanic), an African American Pentecostal church and a Hispanic Methodist church. We ended our celebration with a supper and service at a downtown Episcopal church. The death rattle could be heard in our city, but our spirits were singing! We affirmed together, "The Spirit that God has given us does not make us timid; instead, God's Spirit fills us with power, love and self-control" (see 2 Tim. 1:7).

Now the work of organizing and empowering began. Each church was helped by ECTI staff to develop a church profile: Who are we? What is our geographical distribution? Who are the people in our communities? the businesses? We all conducted a "listening campaign" to learn about one another and develop deeper relationships, because *building relationships is at the heart of church-based community organizing*. We took this listening campaign into our communities and heard the stories of our neighbors: their roots, their aspirations, their frustrations, their anger. We discovered in this process the interests and skills of members and community folk, the issues that concerned them and raised their blood pressure, and insights from each other about institutions and powers that aid and abet the deterioration of our neighborhoods and our city. All our meetings began with prayer, and we centered ourselves on the Word of God, led by laity and clergy. Due to such in-depth listening (both to scripture and to each other), issues surfaced that were the concerns of us all. As a direct result of our analysis of the issues and of powerful institutions and key individuals, we developed strategies and decided where and how to use our power to win some victories. Because of this empowerment through community organizing, we accomplished significant victories at both the neighborhood and citywide levels.

Neighborhood level:
- Vacant and trashed houses boarded up by a certain date.
- Unsafe housing razed according to an agreed-upon time schedule.
- Drug-free zones established around schools and the law enforced.
- Asbestos dumped in a vacant house removed immediately and safely.
- Vacant houses inspected by city code enforcement personnel, and owners notified of violations.
- Neighbors living in apartments without water or electricity given immediate assistance in finding suitable housing.
- A playground for small children, promised to a neighborhood years ago, finally built.

Citywide:
- A mass meeting (more than six hundred people) held with the state-appointed chief of police about the condition of crime and police work in Camden.
- A mass meeting (more than a thousand people) held on our turf so that the state representatives could hear the community's views about law enforcement in our city.
- $2 million in emergency relief awarded by the county to cover unpaid bills of homeowners and renters in Camden for wastewater treatment.
- A commitment received from the governor to prepare and introduce legislation that would match the $2 million from

the county for emergency relief for homeowners, renters, schools, and churches.

- A commitment received from the governor to prepare legislation for a host community benefit for all municipalities hosting a regional wastewater treatment facility.

The Benefits of Church-Based Community Organizing

The Camden Metropolitan Ministry has discovered the many benefits of church-based community organizing: benefits to the city, to our congregations, and to the metropolitan ministry initiative itself. First, laity are encouraged and trained to use and develop their gifts of speaking, chairing meetings, researching issues, negotiating, developing strategies, and evaluating. They are developed spiritually and politicized in such a way that they come to understand community organizing as a powerful and acceptable way of channeling frustration and effecting positive change. Second, those people residing near the churches gain new understandings of the church membership's concern for them. In the course of their involvement with church members, they may experience for the first time prayer and Bible readings that connect with their lives. For the churches, community organization often results in an increase in membership. Ecumenism becomes a reality, and some of the walls of religious prejudice and misunderstanding crumble.

Community organizing identifies the decision-makers in the city and draws attention to the structures through which they operate. For suburban congregants, especially, community organizing provides a way to become involved in issues of justice with their poverty-stricken urban neighbors who are deprived of basic rights. They become conscious of county and state decisions that hurt and exploit the urban poor. Finally, church-based community organizing validates the importance of doing urban ministry and of having the structures to do it.

The road to authentic urban ministry is narrow and hard, but there is the peace of Christ in the pain, the struggle, and the fun of faithfulness. Church-based community organizing makes it clear that the best way to enlighten the powerful is to empower the powerless.

Sam Appel has spent his life as a pastor in urban centers, including Minneapolis, Milwaukee, Brooklyn, Philadelphia, and Camden. He was an urban missioner in Camden for twenty-seven years. He is now retired.

Notes

1. J. Edward Carothers, *The Churches and Cruelty Systems* (New York: Friendship Press, 1970), pp. 32–33.

2. Statistics regularly used by local government officials.

3. Emil Brunner, *The Misunderstanding of the Church*, trans. Harold Knight (London: Lutterworth Press, 1952).

4. ECTI was founded by Kathleen O'Toole, a community organizer and first executive director of the organization.

Appendix

Camden Churches Organizing Project: A Covenant

"God did not give us a spirit of timidity but a spirit of power and love and self-control."

2 Tim. 1:7, RSV

The Camden Churches Organizing Project (CCOP) is a covenant among churches to work together through collective action in addressing the many problems facing families and congregations in the city.

Unemployment, crime, inadequate housing and health care, the un-met needs of our youth and senior citizens are all contrary to the foundations of Judeo-Christian values. Thus, many people in our community are unable to hear Christ's call because they have found religion to be irrelevant and impractical in their everyday lives.

We accept this challenge to take the Bible as a serious guide for involving ourselves in the community in order to promote love and justice and to enhance the dignity of every member of our congregations and community.

The goal of this covenant is to build an organization initially composed of churches that strengthens relationships in each congregation, between congregations and in other parts of the community. By congregations identifying and addressing common concerns through the process of community organization, we can put our values into action—not just on Sunday—but seven days a week!

Theological Education and the Preparation for Public Ministry

• 25 •

TEACHING MINISTRY

IN THE CITY

Glenda Hope and Penny Sarvis

Recentering seminary education on ministry, rather than on seminaries or students, does more than slide the same process into a new location. It uproots it from its old soil and plants it in new ground. It demands, requires, that education be done differently. The dis-integration between academic material and the practice of ministry that is usual, even inevitable, on seminary campuses becomes nigh impossible when classes are taught in the places where ministry is occurring. Refugees clustered around a coffeepot in the next room, men and women shuffling down a food line on the sidewalk, a group of older women meeting for fellowship in a church basement, teenagers taking respite from nights on the street, prostitutes working the corner outside, a youth group dealing with the suicide of one of their own—these are not the usual constituencies of academic corridors, but they define the turf when classes are taught where urban ministry is happening. Education in such a setting can have a tremendous impact in creating effective urban ministers, but these off-campus programs have proven very difficult to sustain. The Network Center for the Study of Christian Ministry (NCSCM) in San Francisco was just such a ministry-centered seminary education program.

The Beginnings

In late 1972, eight people gathered in a San Francisco living room to begin a ministry with unchurched young adults, ages

327

eighteen to thirty-five. One of the eight had just resigned her position as assistant pastor of the Old First Presbyterian Church in order to devote herself full time to developing the San Francisco Network Ministries. She and the other cofounders believed that ministry with most young adults in the city must be developed along lines other than the traditional parish, though they had little idea of what those lines might be. They began by forming a house church, and by the end of the first year, six house churches, scattered throughout the city, met at various times of day and night.

In 1973, Network began outreach and pastoral care work in residence clubs, started women's workplace organizing in several large corporations, and opened the Network Coffeehouse in donated space. From the outset, the coffeehouse drew a lively mix of people: young intellectuals, artists seeking a chance to perform, lonely young adults from nearby single-room-occupancy hotels and residence clubs, street people, addicts, and mentally ill persons from the adjacent Tenderloin district.[1] Volunteer and paid staff made coffee, offered over-the-counter counsel, planned programs, mediated disputes, led Bible studies, washed dishes, discussed philosophy and current events, and took semiconscious addicts to the nearby hospital emergency room. After seven years of operation, the owners of the space became anxious about the clientele and terminated the arrangement. Deprived of their primary place of contact with Tenderloin residents to whom Network felt a deep commitment, the ministry sought other ways to engage with this population. What at first seemed a major ministry loss proved to be the opening for Network's present deep involvement with the poor.

In September 1974—long before the development of the Network Center for the Study of Christian Ministry in 1982—the Network Ministries program itself became a site for intensive field education (30 hours a week for one seminary term) for students enrolled in the Pacific School of Religion in Berkeley, California. This contract continued until fall 1982, when NCSCM was established. During these early years fifty-three students, five to twelve students each year, were educated on site in this urban ministry program. Supervision was done largely in a group setting, and it quickly evolved into discussion of "practics" integrated with biblical and theological studies as they related to the experiences the students were having. Case studies were presented as a means of learning pastoral care on the job. Students received field education credit only.

In early 1978, the Seventh Avenue Presbyterian Church, with an active membership of about twenty people, asked one of the pastors of Network to preach on New Year's Day and then extended the pulpit invitation through Easter. The church was laboring under all the problems experienced by small urban churches, especially declining membership and the advancing age of the congregants. In addition, the presbytery had forbidden them to call a pastor until they had three years' salary in the bank.

A solution seemed obvious. The congregation wanted clergy leadership, and the Network desired a base for ministry with the large young-adult population in that area of downtown San Francisco. So in June 1978, the two ministries entered into a contractual relationship providing Network with space for gatherings (two years later the coffeehouse reopened here), and the church agreed to pay Network Ministries a small monthly fee in exchange for twenty hours a week of pastoral leadership. All four Network Ministries staff members, including a Catholic nun, served as the pastoral team. This relationship continued for eleven years, during which time the church grew to 115 members, the budget increased to 2.5 times its original size, and the average age of the congregation dropped by more than twenty years.[2]

From Network's inception, the program's staff and constituents had been actively involved with movements addressing, for example, racial justice, alternatives to incarceration, disarmament, women's liberation, ecology, and the issues of gay men and lesbian women. It was deemed essential to be working on social justice, not simply informing others and urging them to do so. So it was not surprising that Seventh Avenue Church declared its intention to be fully inclusive of all who came regardless of race, gender, or sexual orientation and to extend to them all rights and responsibilities of membership including election and ordination to the offices of deacon and ruling elder. It was one of the first San Francisco congregations to welcome publicly those diagnosed with AIDS and to provide congregational and pastoral care for them. Seventh Avenue became a sanctuary church for Central American refugees, adopted a refugee family from El Salvador, and participated in the wider Sanctuary movement. Several church members joined Witness for Peace delegations to Central America. The congregation continued and expanded its historic effort to care for the elderly.

Congregants worked with Network in the Tenderloin district, especially through Tenderloin ElderFriends, a program that began when a Catholic nun on Network's staff began visiting frail elderly people in dingy Tenderloin hotels. It quickly became apparent that the magnitude of the need of these people could not be addressed by professional staff alone. Network drew together the Visiting Nurses Association, St. Boniface Catholic Church, and Catholic Charities to develop Tenderloin ElderFriends. Volunteers were recruited from the Tenderloin itself as well as from Seventh Avenue Church and were trained to be resourceful friends for the elderly poor. Volunteers—including students—themselves were supported through monthly meetings.

Some Tenderloin residents came to worship at Seventh Avenue, and a few joined the church. The church supported efforts to open a house in its neighborhood as alternative incarceration for women felons, allowing them to have their children with them. Congregants volunteered in this program, and the women and children participated in worship, education, and fellowship in the church.

Network people also became more heavily involved in political organizing and advocacy in the Tenderloin. They played a major role in displacing a traditional, medical-model mental-health-care program and replacing it with the Tenderloin Self-Help Center, a peer counseling drop-in program open twenty-four hours a day. This effort was consistent with Network's emphasis on facilitating empowerment rather than dependency. Other urban ministry outreach programming, still functioning today, includes:

- an extensive pastoral-care support ministry for people with AIDS in the Tenderloin, most of whom are also drug- or alcohol-addicted and all of whom are poor. Network staff drew together a coalition to develop data and to lobby the city for improved, expanded prevention education and care programs concerning HIV infection for this heavily affected, badly underserved community, resulting after four years of struggle in the Tenderloin AIDS Resource Center;
- Women Emerging, an outreach and support group for prostitutes desiring to extricate themselves from the sex industry. Network staff worked with the group for more than two years until Women Emerging was well established and ready to become an independent organization;
- a program to help low-income people obtain stable and decent housing by offering no-interest loans for last month's rent or for a security deposit, or both. Typically, these amounts are only a few hundred dollars but are, nevertheless, out of reach for poor people, especially single mothers. Network staff conduct thorough interviews and counseling sessions, helping applicants to think through their financial situation, and follow up with additional counsel after the loans are made;
- a strategy that provides programs for the Chinese immigrant tenants of a low-rent hotel, including English-as-a-second-language classes, personal and family counseling, assistance with obtaining citizenship, and a variety of activities for children. This initiative is being considered as a model by other possible joint ventures in low-rent housing elsewhere in the area. Network received funding for a feasibility study leading to a joint venture in permanent housing, including the provision of services, programs, and classes, for low-income families and senior citizens;
- a Tenderloin Community Church, which meets weekly for prayer and Bible study on the Latin American base community model. In hotel rooms, offices and lobbies, on the streets, in the park, Network clergy staff regularly perform memorial services for Tenderloin dead and lead an annual memorial service for homeless people who have died on San Francisco streets during that year;

- a monthly publication, *Network Journal,* which started as an in-house newsletter and became a serious publication including essays on social and theological topics, poetry from the broad spectrum of Network people, political information, and vegetarian recipes. The subscription list expanded and the *Journal* has become a major ministry in itself, amplifying the wisdom and gospel insights of the poor and disenfranchised.

Network Center for the Study of Christian Ministry

Together, members of this small urban parish and the Network staff, in partnership with people pushed to the margins of society, produced the idea for a seminary education that would be ministry-centered rather than classroom- or student-centered. In 1981, conversations were begun with the Pacific School of Religion, and in 1982, the Network Center for the Study of Christian Ministry enrolled ten students in a nine-month program of seminary education designed to integrate active ministry experience, classroom studies, and spiritual direction. In subsequent years, the Pacific School of Religion was joined by San Francisco Theological Seminary (a Presbyterian institution), American Baptist Seminary of the West, and Church Divinity School of the Pacific (which is Episcopal)—all members of the Graduate Theological Union—as sponsoring seminaries.

How the Program Worked

Students in the Network Center program (NCSCM) worked twenty hours a week for two semesters in sites throughout the city; those sites were also the location for twelve hours of classroom work each week. Work sites, or "placements," ranged from affluent white to mostly racial-ethnic constituencies, from massive agencies to storefront operations, and a variety of parishes. All sites functioned in the midst of the whole swirl of urban issues and attempted to deal with at least some of them. The classes, too, dealt with those issues as through the year they rotated among the sites.

Moving courses off campus did not reduce academic rigor. On the contrary, it ensured that rigor operated in two directions: The sites constantly tested the relevance of the material even as the material and the assignments deepened students' engagement with their sites. On a quiet campus, it is possible to remain at a safe and detached level of abstraction. The push and shove of the city affords no place to hide; academics must address the urgent, sweaty issues that are pressing all around. An Old Testament course titled "Strangers and Sojourners" provided a context for students as they ministered with the homeless, with runaways, with castaways. A theology class grappled with how a struggling urban church can decide which of myriad neighborhood needs it will address. Students confronted their own faith in gospel promises as they conducted memorial services in grimy hotel lobbies or on the streets and then brought the impact of those confrontations directly into their New Testament courses. An ethics class wrestled with difficult decisions faced by Christians in high-level government and business positions. A course on church development met in the basement of a church facing a changing neighborhood and trying to decide whether to stay or move, and how to build its membership if it stays. What did the course have to say to that situation? Abstractions alone would not do. In ministry-centered education, there is no place to hide.

The impact of classes taught on site extended beyond the course content itself. Turf also affects power relationships, and changing the turf changes those relationships. When seminary professors came out to do their teaching where students were working, teachers and students were on a more equal footing. In addition, those clergy and laity who taught in the program were really on home ground. Their credibility was heightened because their experience was their most important credential. Thus, the status of all participants tended to be equalized. The effect was usually a high degree of collegiality. Everyone was engaged in the same struggle: to apply the resources of the tradition to the exigencies of the sites. Everyone was in a position to contribute, and everyone had something to learn from the others.

Students became involved in this program by making application to NCSCM itself. They registered and paid fees at their respective seminaries, which, in turn, paid the Network Center on a formula basis. Those who were accepted were asked to interview at two or three of the possible placement sites. Sites and students then mutually chose each other.

A church or agency that agreed to participate in the Network Center program understood itself to be a place of teaching. It made a commitment to provide a broad educational experience for the student, not to regard the student as inexpensive additional staff, and it agreed to provide supervision sessions for the student for an hour each week. Student and supervisor, as a first step, designed a "learning-serving covenant" outlining mutual expectations for the nine months and specific means for achieving those goals. The weekly supervision used the covenant as a reference. The supervisors at the various placements agreed to gather four times during the nine months for continuing-education sessions with field education faculty from the participating seminaries. Additional supervision and support for students were provided by lay committees, which were formed at each site and which met with the student every six weeks or so. Lay members also participated in writing and reviewing the learning-serving covenant.

Theological reflection was a part of all supervisory sessions—even as it was integral to classroom work. This was a primary intention of the whole seminary education program. "Integration" found its focus here. Too often seminary students can write theological papers but do not learn to translate the stuff of their daily experience into a working, conscious, ever-evolving theology. How is God at work here? What is happening to my faith because of what I'm seeing and doing? These are questions to be grappled with regularly, in the midst of the fray.

As still another venue, the Network Center study program offered individual spiritual direction to all students. It was not mandatory, but most students took advantage of it. One of the courses offered each semester is called "The Spiritual Discipline of the Minister." It taught methods of meditation and prayer and linked them to the practice of social justice. This course lent itself especially to theological reflection upon issues that arose in particular placements. Colleagues, students, and teacher discussed, analyzed, argued and prayed, all in an attempt to discover collectively how God is at work.

Current Situation and Future Plans

Funding problems and lack of institutional support within theological education threaten the future of alternative seminary education programs that attempt to relate to urban ministries—ministries that often exist with marginal funding themselves. Despite being enthusiastically received by student and faculty participants over the first eight years, the center finally did not generate enough student applications to enable the program to continue. There seem to have been a variety of reasons, but the two most critical appeared to be the financial needs of students and the "outsider" status of the program vis-à-vis the seminaries.

The burden of debt with which many students graduate has made internship and field education settings that can pay a significant stipend ever more attractive. Participating placements in NCSCM paid into a pool, which was then divided among students. We had been able to generate stipends of $300 a month for each student. That amount was not nearly enough to live on and did not forestall students' going further into debt.

A major task before us as we attempt to bring the study program back to life is to find other sources of funding to supplement what the sites can contribute. This problem has serious implications for all seminary education and ministry in general. Many potential urban (and rural) placements for such a program are themselves financially strapped. The pressure of debt pushes students away from ministry in those locations. Yet ministry—as well as student field education—is desperately needed there.

The fact that NCSCM was an independent entity, located in the city rather than at a seminary, was both a major strength and a major weakness. The program's emergence from the still thriving Network Ministries gave it credibility among other urban placement sites. Many of the churches and agencies that participated, along with the clergy and laypeople who taught some of the classes, had a history of working with Network Ministries and had developed respect for its personnel and programs. In addition, NCSCM itself had generally lived up to their expectations. When we announced that we would be unable to continue for now, a number of city parish clergy and agency staff stated that they would not take seminary students under any other program. When asked why, they said that students engaged in urban ministry need a degree of support and interpretation that only a comprehensive program such as NCSCM could provide. The supervisors by themselves cannot do it; they are already stretched too far. Without the whole context of support created by NCSCM, the student would become a greater burden than the supervisor would be able or willing to take on.

The location of this study program in the heart of the ghetto was definitely an advantage regarding parish and agency placements in field education and for the classes that met there. However, its location detracted from its ability to maintain a relationship with the overall program of the seminaries. The physical distance of NCSCM from the campuses meant that the seminary institutions did not accept ownership of the program. Field education faculty—who compose a good part of the still extant Network Center for the Study of Christian Ministry Board—were, and *are*, enthusiastic about this program. They attempted to recruit students they thought were appropriate. Other professors, however, did not tend to be recruiters for the program. For the most part, the energy to make the program known, to recruit, to make a case for it, came from NCSCM staff, who were frequent visitors to the campuses and who were also immersed in other aspects of Network Ministries. Over and over, students told us that they learned about the program almost by accident and that they had to work to ferret out information. Too often, that information did not get to students early enough in their seminary careers to enable them to plan their course work in a way that would allow them to participate.

Making a case for NCSCM was even more necessary, and

perhaps more difficult, among faculty and administrators. The program was "alternative" and originated outside the school. It challenged normal educational procedure, pulled faculty off campus, and reduced the number of courses a participating professor could offer on campus. Without deep commitment to the educational model of NCSCM, it was hard for the seminaries to justify it, let alone support it enthusiastically, especially at a time when seminaries were also feeling many institutional pressures. The field education faculty have told us that, as much as they support a Network-style program, they have neither the energy nor the resources to create one themselves. If it is to exist again, we will have to be the source of it.

We continue to be committed to the process of seminary education in the urban setting. At present we are researching our experience with the program in an attempt to make it more accessible. We are interviewing former students, faculty, and supervisors about their experience and about their vision for the future not only of NCSCM but of urban ministry and seminary education in general.

Along with this research and formulation of an urban model of education, we want to design better means of faculty development so that what instructors learn about teaching in such on-site study programs will have greater impact on their teaching on campus. We need to discover new sources of funding and better methods of publicizing and recruiting. We need to do a better job of presenting our uniqueness and alternativeness as strengths. A program that is not disruptive to normal scheduling, procedures, and assumptions is attractive to a wide range of people, but the educational outcomes are far less effective for the training of ministers than are those of a challenging program such as NCSCM. We are convinced that radical change is necessary if seminary education is to prepare people for faithful ministry today.

Our principle is simple: Seminary education must occur in the field. We see ourselves as urban ministers and urban educators. The raison d'être for the Network Center study program was to provide an alternative model of seminary education in preparation for the church's ministry in the city. This is a worthy and compelling objective for the future of the church.

Glenda Hope, a Presbyterian minister, is founder and codirector of San Francisco Network Ministries and of the Network Center for the Study of Christian Ministry.

Penny Sarvis, a United Church of Christ minister, is associate director of San Francisco Network Ministries and of the Network Center.

Notes

1. The Tenderloin district is a poverty ghetto in downtown San Francisco.

2. In October 1986, Howard Rice of San Francisco Theological Seminary carried out a study of this unique model, whose staff served as a bridge connecting a ministry with the urban poor and a middle-class Presbyterian parish. He concluded,

Alternative forms of ministry exist in many different locations without the base of a congregation to provide those benefits which the San Francisco Network Ministries derives from its relationship with Seventh Avenue Church. There are also many dying urban congregations which are no longer able to sustain a full-time pastor and yet need the services which an alternative ministry staff can provide and may even experience the renewal and new lease on life which Seventh Avenue Church is presently having. . . . Perhaps the most important single factor which is transferable from this model is the potential for a multiple staff ministry in a small urban parish. One of the greatest debilitating factors which faces most urban congregations is that they are fortunate to be able to afford a single pastor. The pastor is without much intellectual or emotional support and is expected to possess skills and knowledge of resources which no single individual can possibly have. Thus, pastors get drained by the continuing range of demands placed upon them and they, along with their congregations, get caught in a survival mode which only produces further decline. . . . The contract between Seventh Avenue Church and the Network provides a potential model for a way to do urban ministry which should be explored by others.

• 26 •

TRAINING MINISTERS
FOR URBAN MINISTRY
WITH THE CULTURAL RIGHT

Tex Sample

Central to the success of urban ministry is a consideration of how the church can relate more effectively and prophetically to the traditional, local folk on the cultural right who constitute a very large lifestyle group. Cultural-right folks are characterized by a local perspective, a "respectability" orientation, generally fewer years of formal education, and belief in traditional values, conventional morality, and country. Though often stereotyped as rural, these people compose the large majority of congregations everywhere and are a sizable plurality in virtually any urban church, with the possible exception of some large, high-status churches that draw successful professional and managerial people, who usually hold more liberal values, and their families.[1]

In mainline churches, urban ministers typically have educational backgrounds and personal and social tastes quite different from traditional local folk. Such differences are the source of no little "culture shock" for those trained in the university and create dismay for cultural-right folk who find such clergy often unconcerned about and unrelated to the issues seen by them as most important.

University training in general and the seminary experience in particular tend to make people unfit for working with local folk. Higher education tends to make one cosmopolitan in outlook, taste, articulation, values, and norms, while the people who constitute the largest group in city churches are local in their frameworks for dealing with the world and are deeply committed to popular religion and its traditional values, morality, and theology.

It does not take much imagination to see why a formally educated clergy and a locally oriented laity may have difficulty relating. Clergy find that such laity are often uninterested in social justice issues, if not outright hostile to them. Why is this so? Why do feminist clergy, for example, find some of their most vigorous opposition among women who seem to be the very victims of the sexism the pastor is challenging? Why are these congregants so patriotic that they seem unwilling to tolerate criticism of U.S. foreign policy?

A possible answer is that local people in urban churches operate from a radically different logic of meaning than do seminary-trained clergy because their social location is vastly different. The ways in which arguments are marshaled in the university or the seminary are not cogent in the lifeways of local folk, who deal with life in terms of the concrete, lived relationships of their situation. We are not concerned here only with white traditionalists. The numbers of African Americans, Hispanics, and Asians who are local in orientation certainly match in proportion, or even exceed, their white counterparts.

Local Folk in an Urban World

Life in the city has by no means destroyed the attachment to locality that characterizes local folk. In fact, a large body of research supports the persistence of primary-group structure in complex networks of friends and family in formal as well as informal associations. Rooted in the family, these networks continue to provide powerful socialization and support. They are micro-universes "around which experiences may be structured and interpreted in the modern world."[2]

Noted author and theologian Joe Holland has said that "university training tends to create an uprooted, highly individualized ego that finds identity in career."[3] Such a statement would characterize a good many urban clergy. In contrast, local folk are much more likely to find their identity in the neighborhood, in the local church, in their love of country, and, of course, in family and friendship ties. They are more likely in this sense to be oriented toward "life" than career, concerned with making life come out right for their families and friends. They know that they are not going to be successes in the wider culture's terms, although they hope their children or grand-children will be. It is struggle enough just to keep family, home, school, church, and job together. It has been said that most of these folk are more concerned with making life than with making history.[4]

Local folk are territorially rooted. For them, neighborhood is the center of meaning and value for their lives. Issues are en-gaged there. They know about the larger world and under-stand that the neighborhood is not independent of the larger society, but their way of understanding and dealing with is-sues, of arriving at judgments, of knowing what constitutes a moral determination grows out of a close personal engagement with the local community and its people.

Three Lifestyle Groups

In a study titled "The Nine American Lifestyles," conducted by the Stanford Research Institute, Arnold Mitchell reports on three lifestyle groups that can be said to be locally oriented.[5] The first of these groups is the "belongers"; numbering 60 mil-lion, they constitute the largest single lifestyle group in U.S. society. They are joiners, intensely patriotic, and for the most part contented and pleased with their lives. Belongers, how-ever, are not well fixed financially; the median family income is eighteen thousand dollars a year. Of belongers, 68 percent are women.[6]

Mitchell describes another lifestyle group as "survivors," numbering 6 million. These are the poorest of the poor and quite old: the majority is over sixty-five years of age. Women constitute 77 percent of this group, and the income of indi-viduals within the group never exceeds seventy-five hundred dollars a year. A conservative group, they are poorly edu-cated and tend to be despairing, depressed, withdrawn, mis-trustful, and rebellious about their situation. According to

Mitchell, they are the most likely to think things are changing too fast.[7]

A third group with local orientation is the "sustainers." Numbering 11 million, they are the poor and near-poor. Most inhabit the inner cities of the United States and are angry and resentful of the system. Streetwise, they hustle a livelihood in the underground economy of the society. They are 55 percent female; 58 percent are under thirty-five years of age. Unlike survivors, however, sustainers continue to have hope even though (or perhaps because) they are the least satisfied of the groups with their financial situation and the most eager to get ahead economically.[8]

Of these three, the group most likely to be involved in the church is the belongers.[9] Quite often in urban ministry, the effort is to get belongers interested in the issues faced by survivors and sustainers as well as by belongers who are struggling, financially and otherwise. One can see why churchgoing, relatively contented belongers might not want to seek increased contact with despairing, rebellious survivors and angry, resentful sustainers.

Acknowledging that members of the cultural right operate in their own unique logic of meaning, we must arrive at a way of addressing the theological, ethical, and missional concerns of urban ministry, a way that attempts at the same time to understand and respect the concrete social experience of this group.

The Logic of Meaning: Liberation and Transformation

The logic of meaning displayed by the cultural right is a complex interplay of popular religion, traditional values, conventional morality, and folk theology. A full appreciation for this kind of logic involves the capacity to see the psychological, social, and religious needs it meets; the way in which traditional values are rooted in the local relations of the people; the economic, historical, and work patterns that influence conventional morality; and the fact that any theology—and certainly folk theology—grows out of a certain set of cultural conditions.

Popular religion: how it meets psychological, social, and religious needs

In his treatment of popular religion, author Robert Schreiter refers to the religion of the "masses," or the "ordinary" people, and lists a number of its basic characteristics:

1. belief in a highly providential God, a deity intimately involved in the immediate, day-to-day events of 'life—anything that happens can be attributed to God's will;
2. significant trust placed in mediators, who provide access to God for people who believe they cannot approach God directly;
3. a strong communal character, which gives it a strong corporate dimension, especially in celebrations, feast days, anniversaries, rites of passage, and seasonal events;
4. stress on devotion and private favor-seeking from God. Devotional exercises take on an instrumental character, such as seeking protection from illness and tragedy, asking for success, and so on;
5. an associational nature, aligning itself with confraternities, fellowship groups, and pious organizations;
6. a view of the world as highly interconnected and controlled, a dangerous, hostile place from which one needs protection. Divine aid is sought in dealing with immediate needs. Concern is for both life and afterlife;
7. a view of "official" religion as lacking in credibility. While the clergy are sought out for their blessings and are requested to play a role in rites of passage, in celebrations, and in processions, they lack authority in directing most other activities, and their teachings are ignored.[10]

Yet it is crucial to understand that the priority of popular religion is not to develop a rational, coherent view of reality that can withstand the assaults of contemporary intellectual criticism. Rather, popular religion seeks to meet a broad range of needs, especially for power, and subsequently to provide for a providential God who can even the odds in a hostile and dangerous world. Adherents to popular religion seek to have mediators working on their behalf who have access and sway with such a God. Popular religion is centered on survival, need, and life, not on defensible positions in academic discourse.

The Role of Traditional Values

Traditional values grow out of the close personal kinship and friendship ties of local people. When these folk consider an issue, form a judgment, decide on a next step, or involve themselves in a community struggle, the basic framework from which they operate is rooted in traditional values, the most important of which are listed below.

Family.   Some local folk continue to believe in self-denial for the sake of the security and stability of the family. Issues will often be understood in terms of their perceived impact on this key set of relationships.

Community or neighborhood.   The neighborhood, home to family and friends, is the center of meaning and value for local people. The struggle to assure that life stays on the "straight and narrow" occurs primarily with this community in mind.

Faith.   People on the cultural right tend to have higher rates of church attendance and participation than other self-proclaimed religious people in U.S. society.

Flag.   Love of country is deep in the hearts of local folk. Such national devotion grows from a profound sense of gratitude for the country, its people, its symbols, its national experience, and for the loss of loved ones in wars of years past. Most folks on the cultural right know not to idolize the nation, know that in fact the nation falls short in a number of areas, but feel nonetheless that the nation is worthy of gratitude and appreciation.[11]

The reason that most cosmopolitans—including urban ministers—fail to be effective in their attempts to speak to the pressing concerns of the local populace is that they lack awareness of these traditional values and the deep commitment to them on the part of local folk.

One illustration: Locally-oriented women are often opposed to the Equal Rights Amendment (ERA) and to the "choice" side on the abortion debate, yet they believe strongly that women should receive equal pay for equal work.[12] While these two points of view may seem mutually exclusive, they in fact are not. Because these people view the world as a hostile place (the traditional view of religion) they have a deep sense of family, particularly their ties to other women in the kinship structure. These women view the ERA and abortion as threats to the traditional family structure and especially to their crucial ties to other women. When feminism is sensed to be an attack on the traditional family, they see it as an attack on women themselves. Yet many of these women must work outside the home and know that they deserve a fair wage.

My point here is not that we should drop support for an equal rights amendment or for procreative choice but rather that, in working with local folk, a sensitization to and appreciation for the role of traditional values opens up a great range of opportunities for legitimating and supporting such policies in terms of the cultural right's logic of meaning. If it can be communicated that support of the ERA and pro-choice positions would make women less, not more, vulnerable and would increase opportunities for women to be mutually supportive, the position of locally oriented women on such issues might be significantly altered.

Conventional Morality

The third aspect of this logic of meaning, one that follows from the above, is that of conventional morality. Such a moral position rejects virtually everything about the sexual revolution, the women's movement, and the issues raised by gay men and lesbians. There is much in conventional morality that is immoral. Merely to suggest that such conventional morality is shortsighted invites harsh criticism from the cultural right and fails to search for the significance of conventional morality. The responsibility of ministry is to look for liberating and transformative dialogue and actions. The process begins with understanding the sources of conventional morality.

Conventional morality is, in part, economically based. Local folk are not typically well-to-do, and any complications that might disrupt their barely adequate income exercise a suppressive influence on the way they understand personal and moral issues.

The historical antecedents of conventional morality are ambiguous. There is no question that conventional morality is rooted, at least in part, in patriarchy. For that reason, if for no other, it requires critique and change. It also has other sources. For example, proscriptions against alcohol grew out of times in early industrial capitalism when severe alcohol abuse threatened family survival. Part of conventional morality grew from protective efforts of women themselves against male domination.

Conventional morality grows out of the work experience of people who do physical work for a living, work under close supervision, or hold monotonous, routine jobs such as those on assembly lines or in clerk-typist pools. Such work affects people's consciousness when they are not on the job. It tends to encourage either-or thought: "There is a right way to do things, and any other way is wrong."

Folk Theology

Varieties of folk theology abound throughout local communities. In the United States they can be found among groups such as fundamentalists, evangelicals, Pentecostals, and others. Six distinct groups can be described.[13] *Fundamentalists* are "truth"-oriented, a group whose major focus is on adhering to "correct" beliefs. *Evangelicals* are conversion-oriented; being "born again" is critically important. *Devotionalists* center themselves on spirituality and the life of devotion through guides such as *The Upper Room* periodical. *Ethical types* are seen as service-oriented people who express their religious faith in a broad range of activities: working at church, performing community service, and the like. *Pentecostals* are a group for whom baptism in the Spirit is key; this experience is central to their religious life and experience. Finally, *church-going, denominationally identified Americans* make up what is probably the largest of the groups. These folk are deeply committed to sustaining respectability in family, church, and community. They see themselves as denominationally based: Baptist, Methodist, Campbellite, Catholic, and so on, and they are loyal Americans. They are not as explicitly ideological in their theological stance as most of the groups above.

Not all fundamentalists, evangelicals, devotionalists, and so on are located on the cultural right, but many are. Among these groups, one will find folk theology dominant. Folk theology is based in an oral tradition and is usually narrative, making frequent use of story. Folk theology approaches ethics and morality through the teaching of proverbs and the quotation of scriptural texts on specific questions. Preaching is quite popular and a central part of folk theology as well. Testimonials are also important and often characterize oral communication. In cross-cultural perspective, folk theology usually is found in isolated and enclosed societies, but in the United States it can occur among the poor and locally oriented urban people.[14] Finally, while the typical faith expressions of middle-class religion can be characterized as "thinking and doing," those of the lower classes—based in folk theology—tend to be "believing and feeling."[15]

One has only to reflect on the above characteristics to see how distant are the theological education and lifestyles of most mainline white Protestant clergy from folk theology. In fact, except for those who are largely self-trained and who have enough experience to work in its settings, most urban ministers find themselves uncomfortable with, even alienated by, folk theology and its traditional expressions.

Theology in mainline Protestantism and Catholicism seems to aim at a "critical, rational account of faith using the tools of a discipline that can offer the most exact form of knowledge known to the culture."[16] Such a theological approach is clearly necessary, especially in settings where the church faces competing worldviews. Yet one can also see that, if nothing else is added, theological training in "exact knowledge" hardly prepares one for working with local folk! Such a situation needs reevaluation and change. It can begin with a consideration of doing theology and theological education in the framework of the logic of meaning of the cultural right.

In conclusion, the effectiveness of urban ministry with the cultural right will depend upon new ways of approaching and doing theology and theological education. A careful analysis of the relationships of local people, their communities, and their kinship and friendship networks will need to be made. The seminary-educated clergy's success in taking positions on issues, legitimating action on these, and mobilizing support among local people will grow from a liberating and transformative concern about their way of life and how it can become more livable. Urban ministry thus requires at least two subcultural logics and languages, two approaches to analysis, and two to action. Such a ministry begins in the practices of local people themselves and then reflects on the deeper meaning and significance of such practices, the final aim being one of change and transformation.

Tex Sample is professor of church and society at the Saint Paul School of Theology in Kansas City, Missouri. He is the author of Blue Collar Ministry *(Judson Press, 1984) and* U.S. Lifestyles and Mainline Churches *(Westminster/John Knox Press, 1990). He is an ordained elder in the United Methodist Church.*

Notes

1. See Tex Sample, *U.S. Lifestyles and Mainline Churches: A Key to Reaching People in the 90's* (Louisville, Ky.: Westminster/John Knox Press, 1990).

2. Wade Clark Roof, "Traditional Religion in Contemporary Society: A Theory of Local–Cosmopolitan Plausibility," *American Sociological Review* 41 (April 1976): 197.

3. Joe Holland, *Flag, Faith and Family* (Chicago: New Patriot Alliance, 1979), p. 7.

4. Richard Flacks, "Making History vs. Making Life—Dilemma of an American Left," *Working Papers for a New Society* 60 (Summer

1974), quoted in Harry C. Boyte, *The Backyard Revolution: Understanding the New Citizens' Movement* (Philadelphia: Temple University Press, 1980), p. 180.

5. Arnold Mitchell, *The Nine American Lifestyles: Who We Are and Where We're Going* (New York: Warner Books, 1983).

6. Ibid., p. 171, and Arnold Mitchell, "Nine American Lifestyles," *The Futurist* (August 1985): 9.

7. Mitchell, *Lifestyles*, p. 176, and Mitchell, "Nine American Lifestyles," p. 5.

8. Mitchell, "Nine American Lifestyles," pp. 9–10.

9. Ibid.

10. Robert J. Schreiter, *Constructing Local Theologies: Searching for Self-Fulfillment in a World Turned Upside Down* (Maryknoll, N.Y.: Orbis Books, 1985), pp. 124–131.

11. Sample, *U.S. Lifestyles*, pp. 70–82.

12. Jerome L. Himmelstein, "The Social Basis of Anti-Feminism: Religious Networks and Culture," *Journal for the Scientific Study of Religion* 25, no. 1: 1–15.

13. I borrow from Samuel S. Hill in describing the first four groups. See his "Fundamentalism and the New South," *Perspectives in Religious Studies* (Liberty, Mo.: William Jewell College, 1987). The final two groups are developed in my *U.S. Lifestyles and Mainline Churches*, pp. 62–64.

14. Schreiter, *Constructing Local Theologies*, pp. 80–85.

15. For a greater discussion of this distinction not mentioned by Schreiter, see Yoshio Fukuyman, "The Major Dimensions of Church Membership," *Review of Religious Research* 2, no. 4 (Spring 1961): 154–161.

16. Schreiter, *Constructing Local Theologies*, p. 88.

• 27 •

Contextualization
of Theological Education

Lynn Rhodes and Nancy Richardson

> The problem, unstated 'til now, is how
> to live in a damaged body
> in a world where pain is meant to be gagged
> uncured un-grieved-over The problem is
> to connect, without hysteria, the pain
> of any one's body with the pain of the body's world.
> *Adrienne Rich*[1]

In recent years, numerous studies have addressed issues of "alternatives" in theological education. All of these attempt to assess a pervasive dissatisfaction with the enterprise itself as well as with what it purports to accomplish. The problem is variously defined as the context, or the method, or the ministerial competence of the graduates, or the social and political engagement of the church. The sources of the dissatisfaction and the solutions proposed reflect initial assumptions about the meaning and task of theological education.

Our dissatisfaction with seminary education, and the proposals we make here for new educational directions, reflect our assumptions about the starting point for theological education. We claim that theological education must address the problem of how

> to live in a damaged body
> in a world where pain is meant to be gagged
> uncured   un-grieved-over

350

and how to make the connection with the reality that if one member suffers, all suffer together. In order for the gospel to be proclaimed, theological education must make connections with the concrete realities of the world's pain.

A central problem in theological education today is the dualism—between self and world, theory and practice, intellect and spirit, academy and church—that continues to reign. Because of this viewpoint, creative work that could reshape theological education has been marginalized and trivialized or stymied by charges of anti-intellectualism. Many fear that the loss of the traditional worldview will lead to irrationality, chaos, and lack of coherence, thus undermining the "acceptable" boundaries of dialogue within the academy. This debate signals fundamental differences among various scholars about the questions and methodologies appropriate to the theological enterprise.

If a central task of theological education is to bring about an understanding of the relatedness of suffering, we are required to engage in communal dialogue and actions that shape and are shaped by our faith commitments. An educational approach such as this requires that teachers and learners be specific about our social location and think critically about experiences that inform our worldviews. In addition, an openness to diverse world realities and faith perspectives is essential. Several alternative educational programs are or have been informed by this perspective.[2]

Issues that Arise in Alternative Educational Programs

What is the literal and symbolic meaning of the term *alternative?* The word refers to a choice between options. Symbolically, it implies otherness, nonnormativeness. In the face of the power of dominant institutions to define the enterprise of theological education, "alternative" reflects a certain reality— of marginality. In such a situation, alternative programs face tension around questions of accountability: To whom should we be accountable, and whose questions should we take most seriously as the basis for program evaluation? This issue is symptomatic of a broader challenge: Whose language, whose experience, whose questions, whose definitions of reality have value and weight in theological education?

In accordance with the admonition to ground theological education in "that peculiar combination of action and reflection that emerges among people struggling self-consciously for liberation from oppression,"[3] we understand the point of entry for ministry education to be communities struggling for self-understanding and empowerment. Addressing systemic oppression—racism, sexism, class elitism, imperialism, heterosexism—is, then, a primary task. It is here that content issues and the questions for the educational task are grounded.

In such a context, the traditional disciplines of theological education are reformed. How do ongoing struggles for survival and meaning affect our interpretation of biblical material? What do we learn theologically by dealing with people living with AIDS? What does our interaction with battered women say about the content of hope? What ethical questions are raised by the relationship between our own personal needs and resources and the needs and resources of marginalized and exploited people?

As we explore these questions, we begin to learn that *difference* is a critical category for theological reflection. Beginning with recognition of difference and avoiding universal claims about the meaning of human experience opens new approaches to some of the basic questions about Christian identity, mission, and stance in relation to questions of pluralism.

The attempt to linger—as an educational strategy—with the reality of difference and explore it honestly raises the possibility for critical thinking and eventually for communal social transformation. This happens when our stories encounter the stories of others who are differently situated. When we do this, we have to struggle with what is similar, what is different, what is incomprehensible, and whether there is, in fact, any point of contact. Differences, identified and understood, become resources for change. The sharing of stories is, in itself, not adequate. But it sets the stage for truth-telling, and it provides data essential for the learning process.

Theology, then, is not a dogma but a dialogical process, an encounter with the contradictions and insights of life itself.

The study of the tradition can then be an exciting partner in this dialogue as the questions people face in concrete historical situations are viewed and contrasted. At the same time, one's own story, understood as part of a collective reality, becomes the ground on which one stands to confront and challenge the claims of a tradition that carries within it the fact of systemic oppression.

A set of common strategies for theological education grows from questions that arise from those who live at the margins: the poor, the disenfranchised, women, people of color. These strategies include:

- preparing people for collaborative styles of ministry;
- developing a diversity of methodologies to increase flexibility in meeting different contexts;
- focusing intentionally on supervisory processes that help students learn community development and empowerment ministries;
- emphasizing the political nature of ministry in which confrontation and conflict are expected;
- learning how to help faculty teach out of a praxis-based context;
- developing accountability to specific contexts of ministry for what goes on in the classroom;
- encouraging students and faculty to encounter their own "boundary" experiences and to be exposed to diversity;
- exploring the relationships between spiritual development, ritual, worship, and classroom study.

Although these characteristics reflect an adaptation of educational approaches common in schools of social work or adult education, they represent a departure from "normative" theological education.

The Importance of Analyzing Power and Economics

When we start with a focus on communities struggling for self-understanding and empowerment, issues of power and economics are central. Doing theological education from this perspective is especially difficult for the dominant Protestant,

Catholic, and Jewish denominations and congregations in the United States, which often identify subconsciously with dominant political and economic systems. Issues of power and economics are often avoided. This relationship between the church and economic systems is, at its heart, a question of values and of idols, of what and whom we worship.

One alternative program of theological education, The Urban Training Organization in Atlanta, deals with these issues through its focus on community organizing, addressing the relationship between government, church, and economic systems in its analysis of the communities in which it works. Through a combination of direct community organizing and classroom study, students in the program learn to see the relationship between the power and the economic basis out of which organizations operate and the attendant value systems that they uphold. Moreover, they gain insight in understanding the multiplicity of external authorities that affect lives. They learn to name the sources that give rise to personal and community anger, resistance, or resignation in the face of disempowerment.

In raising questions of power and economic relationships, we also begin to look at these relationships in our own theological institutions, among student constituencies, and in local church life. Analyses of these relationships are often most revealing because we are faced with our own complicities, paradoxes, and conflicts. These analyses provide an important context for biblical and historical study and spiritual discernment, formation, and discipline.

Collaborative Teaching and Learning in Context

When the focus of theological education shifts to faith communities, especially communities struggling for empowerment, the power dynamics behind education likewise shift. When the context of learning is the seminary and the academic discipline is the focus, certain kinds of academic criteria are the standards by which all must work and by which faculty contributions and student learnings are measured. However, in the ministry context, the credibility of each group's knowledge is rooted in its capacity to provide resources for ministry at appropriate moments in the learning process.

When the larger community is the context, there is a broader dialogical "testing" of legitimate authorities. A seminary-based faculty member who enters into such dialogue may find that her or his particular training and expertise are being challenged because the assumptions of the context are different from those of the seminary. The dialogue that ensues can provide an opportunity for faculty members to identify new questions with which they must grapple within their teaching field. In this process, the academic discipline and the ministry setting are each challenged and enriched.

At a basic level, changing the turf changes the dynamics of power; a shift in levels of discomfort takes place. It is no longer just the community-based "teacher" who must enter the academic arena and "adjust" to norms and expectations; it is now the seminary-based faculty and students who enter the community and must learn language and symbols that give meaning to life in that place. A biblical expert who really listens to what people have to say in this situation begins to understand how his or her particular training and expertise are resources beyond the seminary context and begins to be a learner as well as a teacher.

As long as theological education is based in the academy, community-based resource people must adjust to the rules of the academy. Their credentials are usually suspect or at best viewed as "practical" (read inferior). Changing the locus changes the rules: The community-based person is still teaching in an academic program, but in one with a focus on community, so both academic and community norms and insights apply. No one person or group owns the power to define the rules, and genuine collaboration is possible, even though comfort levels are often disturbed.

Mutuality and dialogue are hallmarks of collaborative teaching. Pastors and agency-based supervisors, who daily face issues of suffering in people's lives, usually do not have opportunities to reflect on the meaning of what they are learning. Seminary-based faculty do have this opportunity, but they are less often faced with the day-to-day implications of what they are learning. When community-based and seminary-based faculty engage in dialogue about these issues, both groups discover resources that are supportive as well as challenging.

Teaching and learning in different contexts is not easy for most seminary-based faculty and students. Students and seminary faculty come to this situation out of years of traditional schooling. Students are accustomed to being accountable to what the teacher wants and to their own individual interests. Faculty are accustomed to being accountable to a corpus of material and to individual student development. Both groups bring from their past experience presuppositions about learning that are often unexamined and lead to frustration, confusing signals, and chaotic processes. New approaches to learning, to provoking response, to providing information, and to holding each other accountable are required.

One faculty member, convinced that the ways students learn biblical exegesis shapes the way the Bible actually functions in the life of the community, developed a seminary class on the New Testament in an alternative seminary educational setting. While teaching in the San Francisco Network Ministries program, the faculty member engaged with a group of students in their various ministry locations, teaching and learning the Bible together in relation to the daily activities within the local churches.[4] When he tried to implement the same methodology in a traditional seminary environment, the students rebelled. They had paid their money to learn from him and were not interested in learning from each other. His analysis of the situation was that students were accustomed to an individualized, competitive methodology that was teaching students to despise each other's resources and insights and, in turn, to assume the role of the expert in the congregation and despise their parishioners' insights into biblical material. Collaborative teaching/learning and collaborative ministry are integrally related.

To change basic educational assumptions requires experimentation and time in order for a collective and mutually responsible educational process to develop. Everyone has to learn new skills. Students have to learn how to take responsibility for their own education and to be accountable to a larger constituency than themselves. Faculty have to learn how to listen to student and community issues well enough to know how to use the resources of their discipline effectively. Learning to work collaboratively becomes a part of the educational process itself.

In collaborative teaching and learning in a community ministry setting, traditional procedures for accountability and evaluation are minimally effective. For this reason, the development of learning "covenants" is a very important aspect of a collaborative teaching/learning model. With such covenants in place, individual needs, collective responsibilities, accountability structures, and negotiation skills can create a learning environment in which both individual and corporate needs are met.

Student Constituencies

Once a collaborative teaching/learning process is engaged, the significance of the makeup of the student constituency becomes increasingly important, profoundly shaping the questions raised and issues addressed. This is particularly true when the student constituency itself is representative of marginalized groups resisting systemic oppression. Two alternative programs, the Women's Theological Center in Boston and New York Theological Seminary, provide examples.

The Women's Theological Center directs its education toward justice for women. Its constituency includes women who are preparing for church-based ministries as well as women who are totally alienated from the church. Questions arise here that do not arise with the same force in more traditional settings. What is the relationship between theology and violence against women? What do we have to learn from religious traditions that are based in women's experience? How do we deal with our own forms of oppression in an all-women group? What is the relationship between sexuality and spirituality? theology? ethics? This program is providing a deepening of feminist analysis and theology, a task made possible because the significant presence of women from marginalized and oppressed contexts challenges the patriarchal assumptions and expectations of traditional theological education.

The New York Theological Seminary program directs its structure and curriculum toward the needs of the urban church, serving a group of older, already established pastors in a racially mixed context. The reality of oppression is very concrete for these pastors and the people in their congregations. The process and style of education in this program grow out of the needs of urban ministries. Educational assumptions based on traditional middle-class and Anglo culture are constantly challenged. Through its encounter with cultural and theological pluralism, this program is providing theological education with critical resources for working effectively across cultural differences.

Taking Local Churches and Communities Seriously

Most alternative educational programs begin by exploring the contexts in which specific religious communities struggle to find meaning. Consequently, students in these programs discover that there is no single model of ministry. Different local churches require different leadership. Each church offers different possibilities and assumes different responsibilities vis-à-vis social transformation.

This means that educational programs cannot settle for a uniform understanding of ministry. Rather, they must be designed to enable students to learn how to assess a situation, know themselves, deal with conflict, and develop flexibility. Students must learn to work collaboratively with the people. In this process, they can learn the importance of interdependent forms of ministry.

Understandings of what it means to develop leadership for the church undergo subtle changes in such settings. Seminarians learn the skills of community analysis and community-building. They learn how to make connections between themselves, specific communities of faith, and the larger community in order to promote transformation.

Embodied Spirituality

The alternative forms of theological education require students to learn how to become involved in a community as pilgrims rather than tourists, as participants rather than voyeurs. To be pilgrim-participants in communities struggling to find meaning is to encounter the devastating effects of the ways the dominant culture has split the spiritual from the political dimensions of a community's life. Ritual, worship, and meditation take on different meaning when they are integral to our social and political work and are accountable to specific communities. When this is the case, the spiritual dimension becomes an authentic part of the classroom experience, opening participants to the possibility of approaching the educational process with all of who they are: intellectually, emotionally, politically, sexually, spiritually.

To separate social activism from contemplation is to disempower both dimensions of human and community life. To struggle with these issues is a matter of seeking not a "balance" of the two but a new sense of what it means to be self-in-community.

Theological education programs across the country are grappling with the upheaval that has developed around the meaning of spirituality and Christian formation. The process and context of education form and shape how we understand spirituality. The methodology is part of the content we communicate. Connecting the "pain of any one's body with the pain of the body's world" requires taking historical reality seriously in every aspect of theological education. The teaching and practice of biblical exegesis and theology as well as clinical pastoral education (CPE) and preaching must be rooted in concrete historical experience—that is, they must be embodied. Otherwise, they will remain in an abstract world, disconnected from and disempowering to communities struggling for meaning.

Furthermore, embodiment of spirituality means getting in touch with our sexuality. Audre Lorde states that the erotic is a source of power.

In touch with the erotic, I become less willing to accept powerlessness, or those other supplied states of being which are not native to me, such as resignation, despair, self-effacement, depression, self-denial.[5]

That claim is a major challenge for our education concerning spirituality. As yet, we are just beginning to understand what devastation has been wrought by the separation of body, spirit, and mind in our understanding of our faith.

Conclusion

Who owns theological education? Alternative programs of seminary education share the view that an adequate approach to theological education requires a base that extends beyond the seminary walls. The challenges to build this base are many. We must incorporate in significant ways a mix of races, cultures, and sexes that can explore ministry in genuine mutuality—a rare phenomenon in our churches. Programs must deal sufficiently with women's realities and with the realities of people of color. We need to find more adequate ways to provide spaces for distinctive groupings.

In addition, we need to learn how to develop programs for mutual learning with people in congregations, ways to involve laity in the program development and evaluation of candidates for ministry. We need more effective ways of measuring our accountability to the people with whom we work in churches and communities.

Ownership of education is about language. What is necessary for silenced voices to be heard, for oppressed people to become legitimate partners in the theological dialogue? How important is the "theological" language of the academy? What does it reveal, and what does it obscure?

Our priority is to connect the pain of our embodied selves with the world's pain in order to participate in social transformation. It is therefore essential in our approach to theological education that we continue to search for ways to encounter our differences and historic barriers to connection: language, culture, race, gender, economic injustice, and nationalism. Our vision is that we may find ways of *connecting* to all creation rather than of dominating creation. The theological claim that "the earth is God's and all that is in it, the world, and those who live in it" (Psalm 24:1) calls God's people to face honestly the systemic structures that do violence to oppressed communities, that create and sustain the "pain of the body's world," and to stand with tenacity *against* the forces of destruction and *for* transformation.

Nancy Richardson is codirector of the Women's Theological Center, Boston.

Lynn Rhodes is associate professor of ministry and field education at Pacific School of Religion, Berkeley, California.

Notes

1. Adrienne Rich, *Your Native Land, Your Life: Poems* (New York: W. W. Norton & Co., 1986), p. 100.

2. Our work with six alternative theological education programs has reinforced our own analysis and provided field data for this paper. The programs included Urban Academy in Chicago, Urban Training Organization in Atlanta, Women's Theological Center in Boston, Seminary Consortium for Urban Pastoral Education in Chicago, New York Theological Seminary (ISTEM program), and the San Francisco Network Center for the Study of Christian Ministry.

3. Karen Lebacqz, "Getting Our Priorities Straight," in *Theological Education for Social Ministry*, ed. Dieter T. Hessel (New York: Pilgrim Press, 1988).

4. See Hope and Sarvis, "Teaching Ministry in the City," in this volume. The Network Ministries seminary education program no longer exists in this form.

5. Audre Lorde, *Sister Outsider: Essays and Speeches* (Trumansburg, N.Y.: The Crossing Press, 1984), p. 58.

Acknowledgments

Grateful acknowledgment is made for permission to reprint material in the following chapters.

Chapter 2, "The Second Reformation Has Begun," by Jim Wallis, first appeared in *Sojourners* 19, no. 1 (January 1991) and is used by permission of the author.

Chapter 4, "A Home for the Homeless," by James P. Stobaugh, first appeared in *Leadership* 9, no. 3 (Summer 1988) and is used by permission of the author.

Chapter 5, "The New Urban Reality: Hope for a Remnant," by Clinton E. Stockwell, first appeared in *The Christian Ministry* (March/April 1989). Copyright 1989 Christian Century Foundation. Reprinted by permission from the March/April 1989 issue of *The Christian Ministry*.

Chapter 6, "Whatever Happened to the Golden Rule?" by James A. Forbes, Jr., was delivered by the author as a sermon on April 30, 1989, at the Riverside Church in New York City and is used by permission of the author.

Chapter 10, "Church and City: African American Christianity's Ministry," by Robert Michael Franklin, first appeared under the title "Church and City: Black Christianity's Ministry" in *The Christian Ministry* 20, no. 2 (March/April 1989). Copyright 1989 Christian Century Foundation. Reprinted by permission from the March/April 1989 issue of *The Christian Ministry*.

Chapter 11, "The City as Battered Woman," by Letty Russell, first appeared in *The Other Side* 24 (May 1988) and is used by permission of the journal.

Chapter 14, "Looking for God in the City: A Meditation," by Barbara Brown Taylor, first appeared under the titles "Cities 1988: The New Wilderness," in *The Witness* 71, no. 1 (January 1988): 14–17 and "Meditations in the City," in *The Witness* 71, no. 2 (February 1988): 10–11 and is used by permission of *The Witness* and the author.

Chapter 17, "The Feminization of Poverty: Challenge for the Church," by Dennis Hollinger and Joseph Modica, appeared in an earlier form in *Urban Mission* 5, no. 5 (May 1988) and is used by permission of the journal.

Chapter 20, "The Uprooted Poor: Mandate for Mission," by Valerie E. Russell, first appeared in *Prism: A Theological Forum for the United Church of Christ* 4, no. 1 (Spring 1989) and is reprinted by permission of Prism Publishers.

Chapter 23, "An Ecumenical Approach to Urban Ministry," by David C. Bloom, first appeared in *Church & Society* 78, no. 1 (September/October 1987) and is used by permission of the journal.

The lines from *Contradictions: Tracking Poems* from YOUR NATIVE LAND, YOUR LIFE, poems by Adrienne Rich, are used with the permission of the author and the publisher, W. W. Norton & Company, Inc. Copyright © 1986 by Adrienne Rich.